Satchel Paige and Company

ALSO BY LESLIE A. HEAPHY

Black Baseball and Chicago: Essays on the Players, Teams and Games of the Negro Leagues' Most Important City
(McFarland, 2006)

The Negro Leagues, 1869–1960
(McFarland, 2003)

BY LESLIE A. HEAPHY AND MEL ANTHONY MAY

Encyclopedia of Women and Baseball
(McFarland, 2006)

Satchel Paige and Company

Essays on the Kansas City Monarchs, Their Greatest Star and the Negro Leagues

EDITED BY LESLIE A. HEAPHY

McFarland & Company, Inc., Publishers
Jefferson, North Carolina, and London

All photographs courtesy of NoirTech Research.

LIBRARY OF CONGRESS CATALOGUING-IN-PUBLICATION DATA

Satchel Paige and company : essays on the Kansas City Monarchs, their greatest star and the Negro leagues / edited by Leslie A. Heaphy.
    p.   cm.
Includes bibliographical references and index.

ISBN-13: 978-0-7864-3075-8
softcover : 50# alkaline paper ∞

1. Paige, Satchel, 1906–1982. 2. Baseball players — United States — Biography. 3. African American baseball players — Biography. 4. Kansas City Monarchs (Baseball team) — History. I. Heaphy, Leslie A., 1964–
GV865.P3A3 2007
796.357092 — dc22 [B]   2007020808

British Library cataloguing data are available

©2007 Leslie A. Heaphy. All rights reserved

No part of this book may be reproduced or transmitted in any form or by any means, electronic or mechanical, including photocopying or recording, or by any information storage and retrieval system, without permission in writing from the publisher.

On the cover: Publicity shot of Satchel Paige

Manufactured in the United States of America

McFarland & Company, Inc., Publishers
  Box 611, Jefferson, North Carolina 28640
    www.mcfarlandpub.com

Acknowledgments

This book developed out of the Ninth Annual Jerry Malloy Negro League Conference, and so the first debt of gratitude goes to the late Jerry Malloy for his inspiration to other researchers. He loved the game of baseball and he loved researching and sharing whatever he learned with everyone. In an effort to keep that spirit alive, this annual conference was named in his honor and we started a publication to share the work and research of those involved. Thanks, Jerry, for your inspiration.

This book was made possible by the presenters at this year's conference and their hard work in turning their presentations into articles. In addition to the presenters at the conference in Kansas City, special thanks goes to Tim Rives and Larry Lester for their added papers. Some shorter pieces were also provided by Michael Harkness-Roberto and David Marasco. NoirTech Research provided the photographs that accompany the text and Dick Clark came through with great fact checking.

Finally, special thanks are offered to all the players and owners whose stories are told in these pages; their dedication and love of the game of baseball kept them playing even when the odds were stacked against them. And to Satchel Paige, that consummate showman and standout ballplayer, thanks for sharing your passion for America's national pastime with all of us.

Table of Contents

Acknowledgments   v
Introduction (*Leslie A. Heaphy* and *Larry Lester*)   1

Part I: Satchel Paige

1. Leroy "Satchel" Paige: The Mystique and Milestones of da Man (*Larry Lester*)   7
2. Satchel Paige, the Baltimore Black Sox and the Politics of Remembrance (*Daniel A. Nathan*)   13
3. Satchel: Ruse and Reality (*W. Bryan Steverson*)   21
4. The Historical Satchel Paige: True Stories and Tales Truly Told (*Larry Lester, David Marasco* and *Patrick Rock*)   35
5. Cracking a Chink in Jim Crow: Satchel Paige and the Integration of Baseball (*Terrie Aamodt*)   54
6. "They're All Gonna Jump Like That": Paige as Personality (*Rick Kenney* and *Jesse Stringer*)   73
7. Satchel Paige and Hap Dumont: The Dynamic Duo of the National Baseball Congress Tournament (*Travis Larsen*)   89

Part II: The Kansas City Monarchs

8. The Monarchs: A Brief History of the Franchise (*Michael Harkness-Roberto* and *Leslie A. Heaphy*)   99

9. J.L. Wilkinson: "Only the Stars Come Out at Night" (*Larry Lester*) — 110

10. Tom Baird: A Challenge to the Modern Memory of the Kansas City Monarchs (*Tim Rives*) — 144

11. Jackie Robinson and the 1945 Monarchs (*Leslie A. Heaphy*) — 157

PART III: THE NEGRO LEAGUES AND INTEGRATION

12. Popularity and Perceptions of the Negro Leagues (*Stephanie Fleet-Liscio*) — 165

13. Jackie Robinson: The Desegregation of Baseball and the Fight for Civil Rights (*Jared Evan Furcolo Wheeler*) — 179

14. Integration and the Homestead Grays (*Nathan Lovato*) — 190

15. "We Can't Never Lose": *The Bingo Long Traveling All-Stars & Motor Kings* 30 Years Later (*Raymond Doswell*) — 198

Appendix A: A Satchel Paige Chronology (*Larry Lester*) — 207

Appendix B: Milestones, Achievements and Records from Kansas City's Blackball Past (*Larry Lester*) — 218

Appendix C: Rosters of Kansas City's Black Teams (*Leslie A. Heaphy*) — 225

Appendix D: A Biographical Dictionary of Select Kansas City Monarchs (*Leslie A. Heaphy*) — 231

Bibliography: Black Baseball in Kansas City (*Leslie A. Heaphy*) — 259

About the Contributors — 291

Index — 295

Introduction

Leslie A. Heaphy and *Larry Lester*

Baseball is America's national pastime and as such has enjoyed a long and storied history. People have grown up reading about and watching the game and their heroes. Some heroes stand taller than others, their legends having grown with time. Babe Ruth calling his homerun shot, for example, or Satchel Paige sitting down his outfielders and striking out the side. What makes some of these stories endure and grow a life all their own?

The mythology of baseball is as old as the game itself. The pastoral nature of the original game has often been seen as one of the reasons. It tends to evoke memories of happier and simpler times. Legends have been passed down that are both truth and fiction. The nineteenth century poem "Casey at the Bat" is a tale of a mighty hero who fails at the crucial moment, something that happens often enough in baseball that we have no trouble imaging it as truth. The real-life stories of ball players have been no less compelling: the pathos of Lou Gehrig, the power of Babe Ruth, the fortitude of Jackie Robinson, the showmanship of Satchel Paige.

Why are we fascinated with legends? American folklore in particular is filled with them. John Henry, the legendary steel driver, was noted in ballads and tales, a black man whose death was nevertheless a triumph of the will, one that made him a savior of sorts for the working class of the early industrial age. Paul Bunyan, a lumberjack, had similar appeal; a man of fantastic size and strength, he symbolized frontier ruggedness and enterprise. Uncle Remus, before he as Joel Chandler Harris's narrator, was likely a slave legend whose fables were clever subversion. Each of these legends was propelled by historical circumstances that the heroes, as surrogates for the average American, overcome or subvert or celebrate.

Away from the plantation, away from the timber land and away from the railroad yard are the fields of everyone's dreams, the ball yard. The ballyard legends continue to grow. How about the time a gimpy Dodger, Kirk Gibson, blasted the Athletics' Dennis Eckersley's pitch downtown to win the first game of the '88 series? Remember when Reggie Jackson bit the dust, after a steady diet of fastballs from Dodger Bob Welch in the '78 series? Or the walk-off homer by Bill Mazeroski over the left-field wall off Ralph Terry in the 1960 Series? And, nine years earlier, N.Y. Giants announcer Russ Hodges shouts, "The Giants win the pennant! The Giants win the pennant! The Giants win the pennant!" after Bobby Thomson's global shot to beat the Dodgers shook up the world.

Myths are stories that inspire our imaginations. They help to amuse and entertain us, to engage us with the past. We are both fascinated and awed by the accomplishments of historical figures. Our memories over time can exaggerate their stories and give us someone to look up. As Beldon Lane has said, the power of myths and legends to endure "shows us to be incurable storytellers, molded by the power of myth."[1]

This book grew out of the stories surrounding the great pitcher, baseball figure, and folk hero Satchel Paige. Why did newspapers describe him taller than he was? Why did they exaggerate his accomplishments, which needed no embellishment? Paige was a great pitcher and his achievements won him election into the Baseball Hall of Fame. And yet so much of what we hear about Paige may or may not have actually happened. Or it may have happened but for different reasons or maybe the details of several stories ran together in the retelling. And the question still is why? What fascinates us so much about heroes such as Paige and Ruth?

The essays in this book attempt to explore this question and many others about Satchel Paige and the Kansas City Monarchs. Why are certain things remembered about him and not others? What can we believe and why? How much credence should we put into the stories about him sitting down his outfield and striking out the side, or, better yet, sending them in to the dugout and then striking out the side? How did the newspapers of the time talk about Paige and the Negro Leagues? Were there differences from black newspapers to white papers? And if so, why? Is this part of the answer?

Stephanie Fleet-Liscio's article grapples with the question of newspaper coverage by examining the accounts of Negro League games from a variety of different papers. Raymond Doswell takes the question of coverage in a different direction with his examination of the film *Bingo Long and the Travel-*

ing All-Stars. This popular Hollywood movie generated a particular image of the Negro Leagues, raising the questions why and what does this do to the real history? How has this film affected the memories and images people have of the Negro Leagues and their style of play?

How do we separate the reality from the myth when we look at Satchel Paige and the Negro Leagues? Do we absolutely have to make those distinctions? What is gained and lost if we do not identify what is myth and what is reality? These questions and many like them are explored in some of the other essays presented in the pages that follow. The authors explore the history of the Negro Leagues through the primary lens of Satchel Paige and the Kansas City Monarchs since they played such a prominent role in the history of the leagues. W. Bryan Steverson begins this exploration by showing the reader four stories about Paige's career and asking whether they are true or simply mythical. He offers a variety of support and then leaves the readers to decide. Larry Lester, David Marasco and Patrick Rock explore a variety of legends in the Negro Leagues. Did Satch and Josh really square off in a World Series game? Did Rube Foster have his team bunt their way to a victory?

During his long career Satchel Paige played for many teams in many places. Since he traveled the country many of the articles explore the history of the Negro Leagues beyond the confines of Kansas City. Paige pitched on integrated teams in the West and on lesser known teams in the East as well as for powerhouses such as the Homestead Grays. For example, Daniel A. Nathan examines the year Paige spent with the Baltimore Black Sox and why we know so little about that time in Paige's career. Then there is Travis Larsen's discussion of the importance of Paige to the success of the National Baseball Congress Tournament, while Terrie Aamodt examines Paige's role in the *Denver Post* Tournament and early attempts at integration. Nathan Lovato explores the question of integration and why another team did not beat Rickey to the punch.

Still other essays take the Negro League story a step further and examine many of the people Paige encountered in his career, players and owners alike. Tim Rives considers the story of Tom Baird and what the truth may be about his connections to the Ku Klux Klan, while Larry Lester introduces us to the man behind the legend of night baseball, Monarchs owner J.L. Wilkinson. Jared Evan Furcolo Wheeler shows us another side to the legendary story of Jackie Robinson, who played for the Monarchs in his brief Negro League career.

Readers will also find a number of articles introducing you to some of the players of Satchel's career, beginning with a short biography of Paige himself. We meet Jackie Robinson, Byron Johnson, Newt Allen, Hilton Smith, Buck O'Neil and the list goes on. These are the men that saw the real Paige, who knew the real stories and not just the legends and myths. These men had lengthy careers with the Monarchs, getting to see Paige pitch or playing for Hall of Fame owner James Leslie Wilkinson.

Finally, a series of appendices chronicle the main highlights of the Kansas City Monarchs history, the highlights of Paige's career, and the real stars of the Monarchs. The book ends with an extensive bibliography touching on all the topics introduced by the various essays.

The National Baseball Hall of Fame created a traveling exhibit called "Baseball as America." In their description of the exhibit the curators write, "Ballparks—particularly older parks—beckon to us as nostalgic links to a shared history and heritage."[2] We invest players with the same cultural significance, and re-telling their stories is on some level a way of making them ours. The stories about Satchel Paige and all the other Negro Leaguers whose names and feats survive belong to all of us now—and in part because of the circumstances that limited their prospects as professional athletes (and citizens). Unlike the achievements of white big leaguers, which were noted daily in papers nationwide, the great games and feats of Negro Leaguers were spread often by word of mouth, mostly within black communities. They became an important part of the oral history for these communities and eventually for us all.

Notes

1. Belden C. Lane, "The Power of Myth: Lessons from Joseph Campbell," *The Christian Century*, July 5–12, 1989, 652–654.
2. http://www.baseballasamerica.org/exhibition_8.htm.

Part I
Satchel Paige

1

Leroy "Satchel" Paige: The Mystique and Milestones of da Man

Larry Lester

Back in the day, there was this tall, talented, tan, talkative traveler from Mobile, Alabama, known for his athletic achievement, phenomenal longevity and crowd-pleasing persona, which earned him the distinction of being baseball's greatest gate attraction. His name was Leroy Robert "Satchel" Paige.

He was boastful and unpredictable. He was a brilliant pitcher with an infectious personality. Always entertaining, he had impeccable control as he delivered from four different windups. One windup was called the "hesitation" or "hiccup" delivery — which Major League Baseball later banned. Paige claimed someone called his delivery "stepin pitchit." Paige added, "I don't care what name they do give it long as the batter don't Stepin Hitit."

His pitching arsenal included the blooper, the trouble ball, a long Tom (super fastball) and the microscopic be-ball ("it be where I want it to be"). Former St. Louis Cardinal pitcher Dizzy Dean claimed, "I've seen all of them fellows except Matty [Christy Mathewson] and [Walter] Johnson, and I know who's the best pitcher I've seen, and it be old Satchel Paige, that big, lanky colored boy."

Paige was born in 1906, the sixth child of 12 (that included a set of twins) to John Paige, a gardener, and Lula Coleman, a domestic worker, in a four-room house on 754 South Franklin Street in Mobile. "Satchel" acquired his nickname as a seven-year-old by carrying passengers' luggage or satchels on

Cecil Travis and Dizzy Dean listening to the advice and wisdom of Satchel Paige.

long poles across his shoulder at the Mobile train station. At age 12, he was found guilty of shoplifting and truancy from W.C. Council School and was sent to the Industrial School for Negro Children in Mount Meigs, Alabama.

There he developed his pitching skills and later joined the semipro Mobile Tigers in 1924. After two seasons with the Tigers, he signed his first semipro contract with the Chattanooga Black Lookouts of the Negro Southern League. He made his professional debut against the Birmingham Black Barons on May 1, 1926, beating the club 5–4.

His early success against the Black Barons prompted them in 1928 to purchase his Lookouts contract, paying him $275 a month. Paige stayed with the Barons until late into the 1930 season, before joining the Baltimore Black Sox for their final games. The following year, the Nashville Elite Giants purchased the tall, hard-throwing right hander. However, the financially troubled Nashville club moved to Cleveland as the Cubs in mid-season where they eventually dissolved the franchise, forcing Paige to travel east.

The entrepreneurial Gus "Big Red" Greenlee, owner of the Pittsburgh Crawfords, encouraged Paige to join his 1932 ball club. It is here that Paige's professional and private life took on new direction and meaning. In the steel town, he met waitress Janet Howard and married her on October 26, 1934. Famed toe-tapper Bill "Bojangles" Robinson served as his best man.

The newlywed picked up another ring with the talent-laden 1935 Crawfords as they won the Negro National League title. The team had four other future Hall of Fame members in Oscar Charleston, James "Cool Papa" Bell, William "Judy" Johnson, and Josh Gibson. Paige stayed with the Crawfords until 1937, when the Dominican Republican dictator Rafael Trujillo enticed him and other prominent Negro League stars to play on his politically-motivated team. Stripped of the team's nucleus, an angered Gus Greenlee sold Paige's contract to Effa Manley's Newark Eagles. Paige refused to report to the Eagles and headed for Mexico to play, where he quickly developed a sore arm. His future now appeared in limbo.

Soon after, in 1939, Paige is found with the Kansas City Monarchs' B-team, called either the Stars or the Travelers, depending on what part of the country they were playing. He pitched a few innings every week, while playing mostly at first base. After many therapeutic rubdowns by "Jewbaby" Floyd, using a special lotion, his once lame arm was rejuvenated. Monarch owner J.L. Wilkinson immediately called for Paige to rejoin the parent club.

It did not take long for Paige to become the ace of the staff, leading the Monarchs to World Series appearances in 1942 and 1946. In the first series, the Monarchs swept the powerful Homestead Grays in four games. Paige appeared in all four contests, getting credit for three wins. The Monarchs would lose the 1946 series to Manley's vengeful Eagles in a closely contested seven-game series.

Paige remained with the Monarchs until 1948, when owner Bill Veeck of the Cleveland Indians signed him to a major league contract. It just happened to be Satch's 42nd birthday party. He was a rookie playing hooky from the Negro Leagues. Many fans viewed the signing of this middle-aged man as a box office draw. And it was! A record night-game crowd of 78,383 fans watched Paige make his first appearance in Cleveland's Municipal Stadium. Later, in his first starting assignment, he defeated the Washington Senators, 5–3, in front of 72,434 diehards. In his third big league appearance, 51,013 fans jammed into Comiskey Park.

Despite being baseball's oldest rookie, the ageless one in less than three months claimed six victories and one loss, guiding the Indians to an American League pennant. He made his only World Series appearance against the Boston Braves. To capitalize on the media frenzy, writer Hal Lebovitz and Paige collaborated on a semi-autobiographical work called *Pitchin' Man: Satchel Paige's Own Story* (1948).

In 1949, Veeck sold his controlling interest in the Indians, forcing Paige to seek employment back in the Negro Leagues. Two years later, Veeck purchased the lowly St. Louis Browns and promptly signed Satchel Paige again. Incredibly, the next year, at age 46, Paige enjoyed one of his finest major league seasons. He won 12 games with one of baseball's worst teams, and was selected to the American League All-Star team, becoming baseball's oldest major league All-Star.

After the 1953 season, Paige was released. He barnstormed around the countryside until the Miami Marlins signed him in 1956. Once again, under the tutelage of Veeck, now club vice-president, he spent three years with the International League team. In three seasons, the great Satchel walked only 54 batters in 340 innings; quite an achievement for a player now in his fifties.

A change of mind in 1961 found Paige returning to baseball with the Portland Beavers of the Pacific Coast League. At Portland, the ageless wonder, now 55, struck out 19 batters in 25 innings. He wrote his second semi-autobiographical text with David Lipman, appropriately called *Maybe I'll Pitch Forever*. The book was filled with the anecdotal travels of the baseball legend. Meanwhile fans thought this to be the final chapter for the Paige turner.

However, in 1965, Charlie O. Finley, owner of the Kansas City Athletics, signed Paige to a two-month contract for $4,000. On September 25, Paige made his final major league appearance against the Boston Red Sox at Municipal Stadium in Kansas City, Missouri. The 59-year-old youngster pitched three scoreless innings, yielding a stingy hit to future Hall of Famer Carl Yastrzemski. At last, Paige appeared to retire permanently from baseball.

Now in retirement, he served as a deputy sheriff in Kansas City before losing a Democratic primary bid for the state legislature on August 6, 1968. He gathered only 382 votes against 3,870 votes collected by political veteran Leon M. Jordan.

A week later, on August 12, the Atlanta Braves president William Bartholomay announced the signing of Paige as an advisor and part-time pitcher. The Braves assigned Paige his retirement age, 65, as his jersey number. Although Paige never pitched for the Braves, he was able to get the 158 days needed to qualify for his major league pension as a coach.

Fittingly, on August 9, 1971, he became the first player from the Negro Leagues to be elected to the National Baseball Hall of Fame in Cooperstown, New York. With Hall of Fame credentials, Paige's popularity surged with a guest appearance on the then popular Ralph Edwards Show, *This Is Your Life*, on January 26, 1972. Special guest appearances were made by his old catcher Frank Duncan, friends and several family members.

Paige, age 75, suffering from lingering emphysema, made his final public appearance on June 5, 1982. Only three days before his death, speaking from a wheelchair with the aid of a respirator, he graciously acknowledged the dedication of Satchel Paige Memorial Stadium, a $250,000 renovated park in the heart of Kansas City.

Funeral services were held at the Watkins Brothers Memorial Chapel with the Rev. Emanuel Cleaver (later to become mayor of Kansas City) giving the eulogy. A 1938 Packard hearse carried Paige's body to the Forest Hill Memorial Park Cemetery in the city. He was survived by his wife and eight children. Later, in 1989, the original headstone was removed and replaced with a 6' 8" tall, 7,000-pound granite monument, on a remote island along Racine Avenue.

Despite little formal education, Paige was honored on October 9, 1991, with the dedication of a new magnet school in Kansas City, called the Leroy "Satchel" Paige Classical Greek Academy. The academy promoted the Greek philosophy of "body and spirit." Over a span of five decades, the spirited Paige established himself as one of the most physically talented bodies to play the sport of baseball. And his legend lives on through his accomplishments and the stories that continue to reverberate through every baseball discussion in America.

Quotes by Satchel Paige

"Any big-league starter who hits .200 shouldn't be where he is. He ought to be waiting outside the gate to get in the park."

"Don't pray when it rains, if you don't pray when the sun shines."

"I sure get laughs when I see in the papers where some major league pitcher says he gets a sore arm because he overworked, and he pitches every four days. Man, that'd be just a vacation to me."

"Throw high risers at the chin; throw peas at the knees; throw it here when they're lookin' there; throw it there when they're lookin' here."

"I never rush myself. See, they can't start the game without me."

"Age is a question of mind over matter. If you don't mind, it don't matter."

"Just take the ball and throw it where you want to. Home Plate don't move."

"I generally don't like running. I believe in training by rising gently up and down from the bench."

"When the green's floating around, make sure you get your share."

Satch's Famous Rules on How to Stay Young

- Avoid fried meats which angry up the blood.
- If your stomach disputes you then lie down and pacify it with cool thoughts.
- Keep the juices flowing by jangling around gently as you move.
- Go very light on the vices, such as carrying on in society — the social ramble ain't restful.
- Avoid running at all times.
- Don't look back, something might be gaining on you.

Satch's Pitches

4 day rider	Submariner	Alley-oops
Jump ball	Trouble ball	Blooper
Nothin' ball	Looper	Bat dodger
Be-ball	Drop ball	Midnight creeper
Whipsey-dipsey-do	Wobbly ball	Stepin-pitchit

All quotes gathered from *Satchel Sez: The Wit, Wisdom and World of Leroy "Satchel" Paige*, by David Sterry and Arielle Eckstut (Three Rivers Press, 2001).

2

Satchel Paige, the Baltimore Black Sox and the Politics of Remembrance

Daniel A. Nathan

In 1930, early in his peripatetic and incredibly long career, Satchel Paige pitched for the Baltimore Black Sox. Despite being an excellent ballplayer, Paige was not yet the charismatic showman he would become, the man who eventually graced the pages of *Time* and *Sports Illustrated* and was the first Negro leaguer inducted into the Baseball Hall of Fame. At the time, the Baltimore Black Sox was a talented, veteran team owned by a white businessman, restaurateur George Rossiter. The year before, the Black Sox won the American Negro League's first and, as it turned out, only pennant—because the league soon thereafter collapsed.[1]

The Black Sox, however, continued to play ball. And in retrospect, the 1930 team may have been even better than the previous year's pennant-winning squad. However, "without an eastern league and standings and averages, team excellence was mostly a matter of opinion," writes journalist James H. Bready, who nonetheless concludes that "the unaffiliated 1930 Black Sox were a powerhouse."[2]

This was true despite the team's losing its superb third baseman Oliver Marcell, who was involved in a fight the previous winter in Cuba that left him "with a badly lacerated nose."[3] Otherwise, the championship team remained fundamentally intact at the beginning of the season. Indeed, it was considerably strengthened by the addition of outfielder Fats Jenkins (who

The 1929 Baltimore Black Sox won the American Negro League pennant, and then Paige joined the team in 1930. Top row, from left to right: Robert Clarke, Heavy Johnson, Scrip Lee, Oliver Marcell, Jesse Hubbard, Red Ryan, Pete Washington, Bill Force; front row: Rap Dixon, Jay Cooke, Domingo Gomez, Frank Warfield, Jud Wilson, Dick Lundy and Laymon Yokely.

was also a professional basketball player), slugging first baseman Mule Suttles, formerly of the St. Louis Stars, and Paige, a tall, lanky, hard-throwing right-handed pitcher.[4]

Precisely how the twenty-three-year-old Paige joined the Black Sox roster is unclear. One biographer, Mark Ribowsky, suggests that the owner of the Birmingham Black Barons, Paige's team since 1927, "leased him" to the Black Sox.[5] This is certainly possible, as doing so appears to have been a common practice.

What we know with more certainty is that Paige's arrival in Baltimore was hyped; the *Baltimore Afro-American* literally made him into a larger than life figure. Introducing the young Alabaman to its readers, the newspaper reported on March 22: "Black Sox Manager, Frank Warfield, has to look up to his new pitcher who stands seven feet. He will be known to baseball fans this season as 'Slim' Page."[6] Besides the hyperbole — Paige was tall (about 6' 4"), but he was not that tall — the *Afro-American* misspelled the ballplayer's last name, a not-so-subtle indication that the pitcher was not yet the legendary Satchel Paige.

Still, he was an accomplished ballplayer. In his first game for the Black Sox, against a local white team from the Bloomingdale Athletic Club, Paige "revealed promise," wrote *Baltimore Afro-American* columnist Bill Gibson: "In the first game he worked in the outfield, but took the mound for a couple of innings in the nightcap. He showed plenty of speed and a knack of getting the ball over the plate." Gibson also shared an anecdote that suggests something about Paige's confidence. After one particularly "hot" pitch, Black Sox catcher Eggie "Clarke is said to have cautioned him. 'Boy,' Paige is reported as saying, 'you ain't seen no speed yet. Just wait until the weather warms up.'"[7]

The next week, on Easter Sunday, Black Sox veteran Laymon Yokely, who was also a tall, lanky, hard-throwing right-handed pitcher from the South, and Paige, both struck out eight batters from another local white team, the Bugle Coat and Apron Company. Paige pitched the second game of the doubleheader and gave "a masterful display of hurling."[8]

A week later, perhaps having earned the confidence of manager Frank Warfield, Paige pitched and won the first game of a doubleheader against Chacon's Cuban Stars, scattering eleven hits and striking out seven. "In the pinches," the *Afro-American* recounted, "the Alabaman hurler was invincible."[9] It is worth noting that at the top of the same page, the newspaper printed photos of newcomers Paige and Mule Suttles. Still occasionally misspelling Paige's surname, the *Afro-American* explained that the pitcher, "sometimes called Satchell [sic], comes from Birmingham, and has shown more speed than Yokely, and since joining the Sox has won many friends by his performances in the box and on the coaching line."[10] Both Paige and Suttles were described as big, energetic, hard-working ballplayers, "and their addition to the Sox has the fans talking already."

At Maryland Park the following week, in what the *Afro-American* described as "the official opening of the 1930 season," which is odd given that the team was not in a league, Paige yet again pitched well, this time against the Hilldale Daisies, winning the doubleheader's second game, 8–2.[11]

On a roll, "the lanky Sox hurler" won his fourth straight game the next week, this time on the road against the Pennsylvania Red Caps; the score was 15–1 and Paige helped his cause by getting a hit and scoring a run.[12]

Back in Baltimore on June 8, the undefeated Paige again beat Hilldale, this time 14–0. According to the *Afro-American*, "Paige, the Black Sox fast ball artist, was in great form in the first game, allowing only four hits and striking out eight of the Darby batsmen."[13]

The following Sunday, June 15, Paige and the Black Sox lost the first game of a doubleheader to the Lincoln Giants 7–5 in New York. The Lincolns were led by pitcher Bill Holland and centerfielder Norman "Turkey" Stearnes.

It was a difficult day for Paige: playing left field and batting seventh in the second game, he went 0–5 at the plate.[14]

Two weeks later, on June 22 at Maryland Park, once again facing the Bugle Coat and Apron Company team, Paige dominated the opposition, winning 12–2. Perhaps inspired by Grantland Rice, the era's most popular and influential sportswriter, who had a penchant for purple prose, the anonymous writer for the *Afro-American* reported that the "Black Sox moundsman, shot fire and smoke over the pan to make even the heaviest of the invading clouters look like shuffleboard players. Sixteen times the Buglers beat the air with their staves in a vain search for the horsehide-covered pellet."[15] This was the last time Paige pitched for the Black Sox. As was to become his habit, Paige jumped the team, and went back to the Birmingham Black Barons.

In some ways this was unfortunate, as it meant that Paige would not be on the Black Sox roster when the team played a doubleheader against the Lincoln Giants in Yankee Stadium on July 5.[16] The games were a benefit for the Brotherhood of Sleeping Car Porters and marked the first time Negro teams were allowed to play at Yankee Stadium.[17]

Following in Fats Jenkins's and Mule Suttles's footsteps, both of whom also jumped the Black Sox that season, Paige left unannounced. *Afro-American* columnist Bill Gibson wrote: "Neither Paige nor Suttles suffered salary cuts, Mr. Rossiter asserts, and he is still wondering just where the elongated pitcher man can be."[18] For much of the rest of the summer, the *Afro-American* reported, perhaps wishfully, that Paige was on his way back to Baltimore.[19]

Then in mid–October, a ballplayer named "Paige" is listed in the box scores of Black Sox games against local "white league All-Stars."[20] For the rest of the month, this mystery Paige played the outfield and batted lead-off for the Black Sox against the white All-Stars.[21] His first name was never given. Was it Satchel? Unlikely. Was it his future teammate on the Pittsburgh Crawfords, outfielder Ted Page? Perhaps. Was it a ruse concocted by George Rossiter to improve the gate? It is impossible to know.

All these years later, what is clear is that few people are aware of Satchel Paige's brief career with the Baltimore Black Sox. Obviously, this is not a tragedy. The three months Paige played for the Black Sox were not particularly important historically and were but a drop in the bucket of baseball's longest playing career. Furthermore, there are good reasons most people do not know much about this chapter in Paige's biography, even though Paige is probably the most well known and popular Negro leaguer and has been for generations.

To begin with, Paige does not discuss his half season with the Baltimore Black Sox in his autobiographies. Neither *Pitchin' Man*, which was told to journalist Hal Lebovitz and published in 1948, when Paige played for the Cleveland Indians, nor *Maybe I'll Pitch Forever*, which was told to journalist David Lipman and published in 1962, contain accounts of Paige's tenure with Baltimore.

In *Pitchin' Man*, which Cleveland Indians player-manager Lou Boudreau accurately described as a "rollicking chronicle," Paige says of 1930: "I moved up for a spell with the Cleveland Bears [sic], playin' with fellows like Jim Wells, George William Perkins and Sam Streeter. Then over to the Baltimore Black Sox."[22] That's it. He then quickly turns his attention to the Pittsburgh Crawfords, for which he played, off and on, during the early and mid–1930s.

In *Maybe I'll Pitch Forever*, Paige devotes more attention to 1930, but his memories are not consistent with the historical record. According to Mark Ribowsky, Paige's connection to the Black Sox

> was so tenuous that in recalling it he got nearly every fact about his stay there wrong — placing it *after* the '30 season, when he said he was sold to the Black Sox not by the Black Barons but by the Memphis Elite Giants, for whom he would play briefly in 1931. In fact, Satch maintained that he didn't actually play *in* Baltimore at all, or anywhere near it, but rather out on the road on a Black Sox barnstorming gig with a big league all-star team he said was led by Babe Ruth — a team that never existed.[23]

Ribowsky himself makes some mistakes when writing about the Black Sox (e.g., he incorrectly identifies Dick Lundy, rather than Frank Warfield, as the ballplayer who bit off part of Oliver Marcelle's nose in a fight), but he is probably correct when he says that if Paige "had trouble remembering the details of Baltimore, it may have been that he didn't care to remember" because in some ways it was a difficult experience for the young pitcher.[24] Far from home, an outsider on a veteran team, unused to being overshadowed by another pitcher (Laymon Yokely), Paige was probably disgruntled, despite playing well. That he chose not to dwell on this experience in his memoirs is understandable.

If Paige himself gave short shrift to and misremembered his season with the Baltimore Black Sox, and he did, other people can hardly be faulted for doing so as well. Many stories are often written based on what others have to say.

Of course, memories are necessarily selective and incomplete. That is part of the nature of remembrance — and written history. It is a given that memories are always fragmented and partial. Just as obvious, they are often revised: sometimes deliberately and sometimes unconsciously. "In each construction of a memory," argues historian David Thelen, "people reshape, omit, distort, combine, and reorganize details from the past in an active and subjective way. They mix pieces from the present with elements from different periods in the past."[25]

Additionally, memories are frequently contested, fought over, often bitterly. Think of the battles over the memory and meaning of the Civil War. Think of the conflicts over the memory and meaning of Vietnam. Think of the struggles over the memory and meaning of JFK.

There is, in other words, a politics of remembrance, which may seem obvious given that specific memories, whether individual or collective, always depend upon who is doing the remembering. At the same time, if remembrance of the past begins with the remembrance of people, and some argue that it does, then Satchel Paige was and remains extremely important in terms of shaping popular perceptions of black baseball before integration.

So why and how is Satchel Paige remembered? What does he signify? How or to what ends is his memory used?

Paige has been dead for close to a quarter of a century, yet his memory is alive and well. His image continues to grace book covers, artists continue to represent him, and purveyors of replica memorabilia continue to sell his jerseys. He has even made it on to a U.S. postage stamp, the ultimate sign of one's national celebrity and social acceptance.

Certainly nostalgia plays a role in all of this, the desire to connect with what seems like a simpler era and a less pampered generation of professional athletes. But just as certainly different people — his family, his teammates, his fans, black and white — remember Satchel Paige differently.

Still, most would probably agree that the public remembers Paige first and foremost because he was a great ballplayer and a great showman who pitched in thousands of games all over the United States and the Caribbean, and thus was seen by hundreds of thousands if not millions of people. "Given his constant travels and ability to pitch virtually every day," observes historian Rob Ruck, "it is likely that more fans personally witnessed Paige play than any other ballplayer."[26]

Just as significant, Paige was savvy, a shrewd manipulator of his image, a public relations genius. He was, former Kansas City Monarch Buck O'Neil explains, "one of the first ballplayers to realize that sports is show business."[27] And he almost always put on a good show. As Paige himself once put it: "You got to think of the fans if you want to be big in the majors."[28] That he did so was in his self-interest, of course, but was complicated by racial politics.

To advance or sustain their careers, African American athletes (and other cultural performers) during Paige's lifetime had to negotiate ways to appeal to mass (i.e., white, middle-class) audiences without "selling out" or denying their racial identity. Jackie Robinson agreed to endure the inevitable racial taunts and threats of violence he would receive his first few years with the Brooklyn Dodgers. Joe Louis allowed his handlers to craft an image of docility and patriotism to minimize resistance to a black heavyweight champion.

And Satchel Paige often "walked the necessary but impossible tightrope between 'acting black' (by white racist expectations) as the situation demanded (and when dignity did not greatly suffer, or could be redeemed by humor or subtle table-turning) and the explicit courage of directly making demands and taking action."[29]

Not surprisingly, then, as a cultural icon Paige did not and does not mean one thing, he meant and means many. He was a folk hero and an entrepreneur (the ultimate free agent), a trickster always on the move, a showman and a symbol of black pride and artistry, as well as that most American of qualities, rugged individualism. He was witty and comedic, yet at the same time he insisted: "I ain't no clown. I ain't no end man in no Vaudeville show. I'm a baseball pitcher and winning baseball games is serious business."[30] Too many people have chosen to neglect or perhaps willfully forget this side of Paige, preferring instead to emphasize his humor, lightheartedness, and eccentricities— which taken alone is belittling.

Satchel Paige's half season with the Baltimore Black Sox was not momentous, but it was successful, in ways he could not have imagined. Yes, Paige pitched well and won most of his games. Much more important, though, Paige's brief career as a Black Sox player reminds us that, for all the words devoted to him, some parts of his complicated life and lengthy career remain virtually unknown, clouded in memory and all but lost to history; it reminds us that there are chapters in his life which even he left unwritten.

Notes

1. Robert Peterson, *Only the Ball Was White: A History of Legendary Black Players and All-Black Professional Teams* (New York: Oxford University Press, [1970] 1992), 90.
2. James H. Bready, *Baseball in Baltimore: The First 100 Years* (Baltimore: Johns Hopkins University Press, 1998), 167.
3. "Black Sox Player Jailed Following Fight in Cuba," *Baltimore Afro-American*, February 8, 1930, 14.
4. James A. Riley, *The Biographical Encyclopedia of the Negro Baseball Leagues* (New York: Carroll and Graf, [1994] 2002), 423, 753.
5. Mark Ribowsky, *Don't Look Back: Satchel Paige in the Shadows of Baseball* (New York: Simon and Schuster, 1994), 65.
6. *Baltimore Afro-American*, 22 March 1930, 10.
7. Bill Gibson, "Hear Me Talkin' to Ya," *Baltimore Afro-American*, 19 April 1930, 16.
8. "Sox Celebrate Easter by Lambasting Bugle Outfit," *Baltimore Afro-American*, 26 April 1930, 14.
9. "Double Plays, Heavy Blows, Feature Two Sox Victories," *Baltimore Afro-American*, 3 May 1930, 14.
10. "Black Sox Boast a Pair o' Kings," *Baltimore Afro-American*, 3 May 1930, 14.
11. "Daisies Give Sox Pasting, Then Turn Cheeks for One," *Baltimore Afro-American*, 10 May 1930, 14.
12. "Ball Park Jim Crow Denied by Rossiter," *Baltimore Afro-American*, 17 May 1930, 14.
13. "Sox Divvy with Hilldale, Play Lincolns in New York," *Baltimore Afro-American*, 14 June 1930, 15.

14. "Giants Beat and Tie Black Sox," *New York Amsterdam News*, 18 June 1930, 17.
15. "Lincoln Giants Split With Baltimore Team," *New York Times*, 6 July 1930, 117.
16. "Local Nine, Re-vamped, Will Face Test with New Yorkers," *Baltimore Afro-American*, 12 July 1930, 14.
17. Lawrence D. Hogan, "Joe D., the Babe and Pop," *New York Times*, 5 July 1998, 13.
18. Bill Gibson, "Hear Me Talkin' to Ya," *Baltimore Afro-American*, 12 July 1930, 14.
19. Bill Gibson, "Hilldale Will Face Black Sox Sunday," *Baltimore Afro-American*, 2 August 1930, 14; "Hilldale and Sox to Clash Here Sunday," *Baltimore Afro-American*, 6 September 1930, 15.
20. Harry Gilbert, "Sox Bats Spell Doom Again to White Pros," *Baltimore Afro-American*, 11 October 1930, 15.
21. "Big Leaguers' Bow Again to Black Sox," *Baltimore Afro-American*, 18 October 1930, 1; *Baltimore Afro-American*, October 18, 1930, 15; *Baltimore Afro-American*, 25 October 1930, 15; "Champ Battery Turned Back by Sox, 5–3," *Baltimore Afro-American*, 1 November 1930, 17.
22. Leroy Satchel Paige (as told to Hal Lebovitz), *Pitchin' Man: Satchel Paige's Own Story* (Westport, Conn.: Meckler, [1948] 1992), 22, 30.
23. Ribowsky, *Don't Look Back*, 65.
24. "Black Sox Player Jailed Following Fight in Cuba," *Baltimore Afro-American*, 8 February 1930, 14; Ribowsky, *Don't Look Back*, 65.
25. David Thelen, ed., *Memory and American History* (Bloomington: Indiana University Press, 1990), ix–x.
26. Rob Ruck, "Paige, Satchel," American National Biography Online, http://www.anb.org/articles/19/19-00162.html, Feb. 2000.
27. Buck O'Neil, "Unforgettable Satchel Paige," *The Reader's Digest*, April 1984, 90.
28. Paige, *Maybe I'll Pitch Forever*, 249.
29. Stephen Jay Gould, "Good Sports & Bad," *New York Review of Books*, 3 March 1995, 23.
30. Paige, *Pitchin' Man*, 16.

3

Satchel: Ruse and Reality

W. Bryan Steverson

Satchel Paige was an outstanding baseball player. As a member of our National Baseball Hall of Fame, his accomplishments on the diamond are well documented. Satchel, however, was much more than just a baseball player. His wit and showmanship created an inventory of stories which can amaze and amuse anyone. According to sportscaster Bob Costas,

> much of what we know of Satchel Paige comes to us by word of mouth, by tales handed down over the years subject to the perspective and storytelling style of the witness. Much of it is undoubtedly true, some of it is probably apocryphal, all of it contributes to his legend as a ball player and one-of-a-kind personality.[1]

In this article, five such tales are retold. With each tale, background and supporting information are provided. The reader can then decide for themselves, based upon this information, if the stories are truly fiction or fact, myth or reality, apocryphal or true, embellishment or real.

The stories retold in this article are "The Poor Squirrels," "The Pick Off Move," "The Hole in the Wall," "The Throw," and "The Chewing Gum Wrapper." Each tale provides "hot stove" fodder for comparisons of Satchel Paige to past and present greats of our national pastime.

The Poor Squirrels

"Well, all I know is what I read in the papers."[2]
— Will Rogers, U.S. humorist and showman (1879–1935)

Stephen Banker (a Canadian and publisher of Tapes for Readers) tells a story about the time a Negro League scout went to Satchel Paige's home looking for this youngster who was supposedly a top pitching prospect. Paige's mother said her son was in the woods trying to get some dinner. The scout found Paige throwing rocks left-handed at squirrels and hitting them every

Satchel Paige in the dugout before a Monarchs game.

time. "'You're pretty good,' said the scout. 'But I didn't know you were left-handed.' "Said Paige, 'I ain't left-handed, but if I use my right hand there's nothing left to eat.'" In an October 1992 issue of *USA Today*, there appeared a similar story in the sports section under Gary Mihoces's byline.[3] Quite a story. Is it a myth or reality?

In *Satchel Paige: In the Shadows of Baseball* by Mark Ribowsky, Satchel's boyhood friend Willie Hines stated, "We'd go out in the woods and shoot at birds and while I had a BB gun, he only had them rocks. But he'd hit a bird flyin' in the air — bang, right in the head, and it'd fall out of the sky. He threw real straight, on a line. Nobody could throw like that. And because he could, he'd go down to the gravel pit and pick out rocks that fit his hand. He'd put 'em across his shoulder, in a bag, and he'd be like Robin Hood. He'd pick out the right rocks to fight with or hunt with."

Satchel himself said, "That's when I found out I had control. It was a natural gift, one that let me put a baseball just about where

Publicity shot of the great Satchel Paige.

I wanted it about anytime I wanted to. I could hit anything with one of those rocks ... chickens, flying birds. Most people need shotguns to do what I did with rocks."

His friend, Ed Otis, father of future Kansas City Royal All-Star Amos Otis, said, "People think he was lyin,' but I witnessed this myself. Satchel killed butterflies with clamshells. He could throw, always he could throw." [4]

It is an interesting story and quite an accomplishment. Probably many a boy has killed a squirrel with a rock. How many actually hunted with rocks? Of these, how many threw with the opposite hand?

Opposite hand throwing, although rare, has occurred, even in the major leagues. On September 28, 1995, Greg Harris[5] of the Montreal Expos became the most recent ambidextrous major league pitcher. Of the four batters he faced in the ninth inning against the Cincinnati Reds, he pitched to two right-handed and two left-handed.

But did Satchel do it as a youth with rocks? Is it a myth or reality? Interestingly, there is a similar story regarding HOF left-hander Robert Moses "Lefty" Grove. In the SABR-published book *Lefty Grove, American Original*, by Jim Kaplan, a story is told to ballplayer Bill Weber by Philadelphia A's scout and former A's player Ira Thomas.

> As Thomas told it, he found the Grove home in Lonaconing (Maryland) at almost dusk. He knocked on the door and was greeted by Grove's mother, who told him that her son was squirrel hunting but would be coming down the railroad right of way towards home "any time now."
> Thomas elected to stroll up the rail tracks and soon saw the tall angular Grove approaching with squirrels swinging dead, their tails fastened under his belt. Introductions over, Thomas inquired as to the absence of a gun.
> "Don't use no gun," was Lefty's response. "I kill 'em with rocks." Noting the incredulity on Thomas' face, Lefty took from his coat pocket a large smooth stone and, throwing with his right arm busted a glass insulator on a telephone poll some sixty feet distant. Said the thoroughly astounded Thomas, "But I was told you were a lefthander."
> "Am," said Lefty, "but if I throwed at 'em lefthanded I'd tear 'em all up."

The author does say the story "was almost certainly apocryphal."[6]

A similar story exists about the discovery of former Detroit Tiger and Chicago White Sox ace Virgil "Fire" Trucks. In 1952, Virgil Trucks threw two no-hitters as a Detroit Tiger.[7] Along with Johnny Vander Meer of the Cincinnati Reds in 1938, Allie Reynolds of the New York Yankees in 1951 and Nolan Ryan of the California Angels in 1973, he is one of the few ever to throw two no-hitters in a single season.

Trucks also tossed a one-hitter and a two-hitter with the Detroit Tigers and faced Satchel in St. Louis on August 6, where Satchel was pitching for the St. Louis Browns. Satchel pitched 12 innings of 7-hit ball with 9 strikeouts in his 1–0 victory.[8]

I talked to Virgil about his discovery and the similar opposite hand, squirrel hunting story. Virgil, then 89 years old, said, "It was between half right and half wrong." He mentioned walking two miles to school each day. The path he took was along the railroad tracks. Trucks would pick up rocks and throw at animals and other targets, adding, "I must have broken a million insulators." He did hit squirrels and one day he hit one but did not actually kill it. ("The squirrel bit me on the thumb.") Trucks was unaware of the similar story about Satchel or Lefty Grove.[9]

In Virgil Trucks's autobiography, former Memphis Red Sox outfielder, Joe B. Scott rated Virgil Trucks as one of the top two pitchers he ever faced. The other top pitcher was Satchel Paige.[10]

Was Satchel really that accurate with rocks or a baseball?

In Lawrence Hogan's recent book, *Shades of Glory*, the author states, "Control was the very essence of his game. At his first professional tryout, he knocked 14 out of 15 cans off a fence from sixty feet. While touring, one of his favorite tricks was to set a ball on a box at home plate and bet he could hit it at least once in three tries. He usually won. It's been said that he could pitch between two batters, facing each other six inches apart, and knock cigars out of their mouths."[11]

Now is the Satchel story apocryphal, half right and half wrong; a myth or reality?

There are two additional references somewhat related to the squirrel story. In *Satchel Paige*, by Kathryn Long Humphrey, the author states, "Yet the Paiges had barely enough money for food, and none for luxuries such as toys. Satchel often entertained himself by throwing rocks, and he developed a good aim. Whenever his mother sent him to bring a chicken from the coop, he killed it with a rock."[12]

Also, in *Maybe I'll Pitch Forever* Satchel himself says, "I could hit about anything with one of those rocks. Like the day Mom sent me out in the back yard to get us a bird from our chicken coop. Three chickens came prancing along the path toward me. The one in the middle looked the plumpest. I picked up a rock. The chickens were about thirty feet from me. I took aim and threw. There was squawking and feathers flew and two chickens went tearing off. The third one, the one in the middle, was knocked dead on the ground. After that I used to kill me flying birds with rocks, too. Most people need shotguns to do what I did with those rocks."[13]

It is also reported Satchel "attracted the attention of the manager of the Chattanooga Black lookouts, who marveled at the youngster's uncanny ability to hit tin cans with rocks."[14]

The Pickoff Move

According to Frazier Robinson, "The only weakness that Satchel had was that he didn't have such a good move to first base. But since Satchel could throw hard from the stretch, you didn't get that far off first off him either."[15]

In an interview former Negro League pitcher Charlie Davis related the following story regarding Satchel Paige's pickoff move. The Monarchs were playing the Memphis Red Sox team of Charlie Davis and Lonnie Harris. The year was probably 1953 or 1954. Lonnie was a swift outfielder for the Red Sox and patterned his base running after Jackie Robinson. Homer "Goose" Curry was the Memphis manager. Satchel walked Lonnie. Goose had said to Lonnie Harris, "If Satchel picks you off, I'm going to fine you $2.00." Lonnie took a long lead off first base in the style of Jackie. Satchel stepped off the pitching rubber a couple of times and yelled each time to Lonnie, "If you don't get back, I'm going to pick you off." Satchel was always talking to batters and runners and getting into their heads. Lonnie again took his lead again and Satchel threw the ball behind his back to first base and picked Lonnie off "by 4 steps," according to Charlie Davis.[16]

Mr. Davis was there and witnessed the event. Pancho Herrera was the Monarchs first baseman for the game. Pancho Herrera played first base for the Kansas City Monarchs from 1952 to 1954 before playing in the major leagues for the Philadelphia Phillies. Former player Carl Long also remembers hearing the story. Could Satchel throw behind his back that hard and that accurately? According to Davis's recollections Paige could.[17]

It is known Satchel liked to take infield practice, especially at third base, with the other infielders. Ralph Kiner (HOF 1975) remembers playing against Satchel as a young man: "The way he warmed up for ball games, he would take infield at third base and then go out and pitch. No one I ever saw ever did that."[18]

Former Pittsburgh Crawford and Homestead Gray first baseman, Maurice Peatros has stated, "He [Satchel] could throw behind his back from third, faster than most third basemen."[19]

The ability to accurately throw behind the back from third to first base was an exceptional but not necessarily unique talent. In 1951, "the Chicago American Giants added a white clown named Ed Hamman, who was noted as a great pepper player and who was able to do such tricks as throw from third to first behind his back."[20] Hamman later became the owner of the Indianapolis Clowns. Bruce Johnson writes, "Ed Hamman is the only person in history to be able to accurately throw a baseball backhanded the width of the field."[21] With what Maurice Peatros said, maybe Hamman was the second person to do it and Satchel was really the first.

Don Cardwell (later a 14-year major leaguer including an 8–10 record with a 3.01 ERA in 152 innings pitched for the world champion 1969 New York Mets) was a teammate of Satchel's on the 1956 Miami Marlins. Don remembered the first ball game Satchel played as a Marlin. "They flew him in a helicopter to the bullpen. Satchel relieved me in about the 8th or 9th inning. A ball was hit right back to him. Satchel made a perfect throw to our 1st baseman, Ed Bouchee, without even looking. Satchel was looking ahead at home plate the whole time."[22]

Former teammate and catcher Larry LeGrande has said that Satchel would field ground balls at third base and look into the opposite teams' third base dugout. He would throw perfectly to first base, on the money, while still looking into the dugout and never looking at first base. According to LeGrande, too, Satchel could throw behind his back.[23]

A former major leaguer and teammate on the 1956 Miami Marlins, Tom Qualters, told me the following story about Satchel's throwing ability. "It was one of their first games and the Marlins were winning. The opposition had the tying or winning runs on base in the final frame. There were two outs and Satchel had come in relief. The Marlins third baseman came to the mound and told Satchel to be careful of the next hitter, a former major leaguer. Satchel delivers and the batter hits a sharp, one-hopper back to the mound. Satchel fields the ball and turns and walks to the third base dugout. The rest of the Marlins were in amazement since they knew the ball had hit the ground! 'Did Satchel think he had caught the ball on the fly?' Satchel walks off the pitching mound and without looking, throws the ball under his arm to 1st base. He never looked at 1st base. The runner was called out and the game over. Marlins win."[24]

Tom also said that Satchel enjoyed taking infield practice. He would precede each throw to first base with the word, "*Strike!*" Mr. Qualters considered Satchel a very good fielder. Also, in 179 major league games, Satchel never committed a single error.[25] So is the behind-the-back pickoff story a myth or reality? It is another one left for the reader to decide based upon the supporting stories.

The Hole in the Wall

In the book, *White Rat: A Life in Baseball,* Whitey Herzog relates an incident from 1956 when he and Paige played together for the Miami Marlins in the International League.

> We were on the road in Rochester one night, screwing around in the outfield. They had a hole in the outfield fence just barely big enough for a baseball to go through, and the deal was that any player who hit a ball through there on the fly would win $10,000.

I started trying to throw the ball through the hole just to see if I could do it. I bet I tried 150 or 200 times, but I couldn't do it, so I went back to the dugout.

When Satch got to the park I said "Satch, I bet you can't throw the ball through that hole out there."

He looked out at it and said, "*Wild Child* (his nickname for Whitey Herzog), *do the ball fit in the hole.*"

"Yeah, Satch," I said. "But not by much. I'll bet you a fifth of Old Forester that you can't throw it through there."

"*Wild Child,*" he said, "*I'll see you tomorrow night.*"

So the next night Satch showed up for batting practice—first time in his life he'd ever been early. I took a few baseballs, went out to the outfield, and stepped off about 60 feet 6 inches, the distance to the mound from home. Satch ambled out, took the ball, brought it up to his eye like he was aiming it, and let fire.

I couldn't believe it. The ball hit the hole, rattled around, and dropped back out. He'd come that close, but I figured it was his best shot.

Satch took another ball and drilled the hole dead center. The ball went right through, and I haven't seen it since.

"Thank you, Wild Child," Satch said, and then went back into the clubhouse.[26]

The same story appears in *Josh and Satch: The Life and Times of Josh Gibson and Satchel Paige*, by historian John B. Holway, on the MLB.com Web site in an article by Kevin Czerwinski and in Fay Vincent's *The Last Commissioner*, where the details are slightly altered.

There was a hole in a scoreboard somewhere about the size of a big grapefruit. There was a local promotion: Anybody who hit a home run through the hole would win a free suit. No suits, of course, were ever given away. Herzog and some others approached Paige:

"Satchel could you throw a ball through that hole?"

"Oh, for sure."

"From sixty feet, six inches?"

"No problem. But not for free."

"How much you want?"

"A hundred bucks and I'll throw two balls out of three through the hole."

So Herzog and his boys went around and collected the hundred.

They paced off sixty feet, six inches, from the scoreboard and gave Paige three balls. He went into his big windup and hit the wall with the first one.

"That's just to get your attention," he said.

The second ball went through. As did the third.

Satchel said, "You get another hundred, we'll do it all over."

Satchel had all sorts of game.[27]

Did Rochester's park have such a challenge related to a hole in the wall? In my conversation with former Birmingham Black Baron pitcher and later member of the Rochester club in 1956, the Rev. William Greason, the hole was located in right field.[28] Current Rochester Red Wing president and CEO

Gary Larder also confirmed the presence of the hole as a childhood memory.[29] Interestingly, the Rochester Red Wing Stadium, later renamed Silver Stadium, was also the home to the New York Black Yankees in 1948.[30]

Is it true? In separate phone discussions with former major leaguers Ray Semproch and Tom Qualters, they both state they witnessed it. Tom even said of the bet that Satchel had never even seen the hole. He was only told the ball would fit through it. In the wager, there was no mention of the distance to stand from the hole or a limit on the number of tries. Satchel walked off 60 ft. He never warmed up. He just smiled and threw the ball right through the hole.[31]

Could Satchel throw the ball through such a small hole from 60 feet 6 inches? You've heard how accurate he was with rocks and clamshells. Could a man at reportedly 50 years of age throw that accurately and that hard and out-throw future major leaguers? Considering Satchel was 11–4 with a 1.86 ERA in 1956 with the Marlins, and three witnesses say it happened, there may be more reality than myth in the retelling.

The Throw

In *Josh and Satch: The Life and Times of Josh Gibson and Satchel Paige*, a story is told of a bet between Satchel and his friend and catcher on the St. Louis Browns in 1952 and 1953, Clint Courtney. The wager was $50.00 on whether Satchel could throw the ball from the outfield to home plate. The estimated distance was 320 feet.

> Clint says, "I'll give you three throws."
> "I'll tell you what I'll do, Scrappy, I won't even take a step."
> He stood flat-footed and threw the first ball against the screen behind home plate.
> "That's just one warm-up. You said I could have three."
> "Give him the xxxx money," Clint growled; and adds Hunter (shortstop Billy Hunter), "Satch threw the next one into the upper deck behind home plate."[32]

To put Satchel's throw into perspective, the *Guinness Book of World Records* longest throw with a baseball is 445 feet and 10 inches (135.89 meters). This was achieved by Glen Gorbous on August 1, 1957.[33] Gorbous played in the majors as an outfielder for the Philadelphia Phillies from 1955 to 1957. "Babe" Didrikson has the women's record at 296 ft. (90.22 meters). It is reported that when Gorbous set the record, he had a running start and the ball "bounced and bounced and rolled and rolled. After all was said and done the baseball covered a total of 445 feet 10 inches."[34]

Other reports state "that Gorbous threw a baseball 445 feet, 10 inches on the fly to establish a record that still stood at the time of his death. He threw the ball from the right-field corner to the left-field corner at Omaha Stadium and was allowed a six-step running start."[35]

Satchel is said to have thrown the ball from 320 feet. In calculating home run distance for a baseball, one formula[36] used is:

Flight distance = horizontal distance + (elevation × cotangent value)

Using the following assumptions:

a. Wager took place at Sportsman's Park in St. Louis, home of the St. Louis Browns in 1953. The backstop at Sportsman's Park was changed to 67 feet in 1953. It had been 75 feet since 1942. Billy Hunter's only year with the Browns was 1953 when both Satchel (p) and Billy (ss) were American League All-Stars.
b. Distance to home plate was 320 ft. The left field fence was 351 ft. and left center 422 ft.
c. An upper or second deck height estimated at 50 feet. The Green Monster in Fenway Park is 37 ft. tall and below the upper (2nd) deck. Mickey Mantle hit a home run in to the second deck at Yankee Stadium on September 12, 1953, that broke a chair situated 80 ft. above the field.
d. A cotangent value of 0.8 (i.e., not a line drive throw).
e. And no bounce or roll included.[37]

Satchels' throw could have been

$$(320 + 67 + [50 \times 0.8]) = 427 \text{ feet}$$

Did a man over 45 years of age, with little or no warm-up or run-up and without the benefit of a bounce or roll, throw a baseball within 20 feet of the world record?

Whitey Herzog said, "The Marlins [i.e., Miami Marlins, Class AAA International League] once had a distance-throwing contest before a night game. Landrum and I had the best arms of any of the outfielders. We were out by the center-field fence, throwing two-hoppers to the plate. Ol' Satch came out, didn't even warm up, and kind of flipped the ball sidearm. It went 400 feet on a dead line and hit the plate. I wouldn't believe it if I hadn't seen it."[38]

How about a throw by the legendary Honus Wagner? "In a Field Day event held in Pittsburgh between the Louisville and Steel City ballclubs, October 16, 1898 ... Honus Wagner made what was considered a record-breaking throw of 403 ft., 8 in. in his (successful) attempt at gaining the day's top throwing prizes."[39] Did Satchel outdistance Honus Wagner?

Interestingly, the record holder, Glen Gorbous, was a teammate of Satchel's on the 1956 Miami Marlins. Also the record prior to September 7, 1952, was 426 feet, 9 inches established by Larry LeJeune in 1910. LeJeune later played outfield in the National League for Brooklyn in 1911 and again for Pittsburgh in 1915.[40] If this $50.00 wager occurred in 1952 prior to September 7, could it be said Satchel had some claim on a world record?

Although Clint Courtney is deceased, I was able to locate and talk with Billy Hunter. Hunter witnessed the event. His comment to me was, "It's a fact." Billy said Clint had teased Satchel that anybody could throw from the pitcher's mound. As a catcher, Clint had to throw all the way to second base. Billy said the event did take place at Sportsman's Park. He stated they were approximately 20 feet from the fence when Satchel threw the ball, and Satchel threw the baseball into the upper deck flatfooted and without taking a step.[41]

Imagine the talent of this man who could throw so accurately through a hole in the wall and so strongly for distance?

The Chewing Gum Wrapper

Many former players and teammates have related the story of witnessing Satchel warming up over a chewing gum wrapper. In the Negro Leagues Baseball Museum, you can hear former Monarch and Philadelphia Phillies pitcher Hank Mason also confirm the story.

For reference, home plate is 17 inches across. The foil on a chewing gum wrapper is approximately 2⅞" × ⅞" while the paper is about 2¹¹⁄₁₆" in the length dimension. This translates into warming up over less than 17 percent of the available home plate when the gum wrapper is horizontal.

Former Negro League pitcher, Clifford Layton told me that Satchel often carried a small 2" × 2" plate with him in his back pocket. He would warm up over it or a chewing gum wrapper. The 2" × 2" plate represents less than 12 percent of the available lateral surface.[42]

In addition to former Negro Leaguers remembering the chewing gum wrapper episodes, Cleveland Indians catcher Jim Hegan and St. Louis Browns catcher Clint Courtney also confirmed it.[43]

In the recent book *Joe: Rounding Third and Heading Home*, Joe Nuxhall talks of his experiences while with the Red's Birmingham Barons farm team. In 1944, he went to watch Satchel and the Kansas City Monarchs play the Birmingham Black Barons at famous Rickwood Field, America's oldest ballpark.

> Joe bought a ticket that Sunday and took a spot on the worn bleachers and watched as the mighty Monarchs took on the Black Barons. He doesn't remember how many white people were there with him. It didn't seem to matter. He was too taken with the moment and the masterful Paige, who pitched that day for Kansas City.
>
> "I'm sure you have heard the story and you may have doubted it, but I saw him do it," Joe says. "Satchel took a stick of gum, unwrapped it and stuck it in his mouth. Then, he took the wrapping and put it on the ground.

"He turned around and walked sixty paces and started to warm up. He used the gum wrapper as the plate and he didn't miss. Move it over here, move it over there. Pfffft! Right over the wrapper. Call me a liar! I saw it. He did it every time. Damndest thing I've ever seen."[44]

Tom Qualters also remembers Satchel warming up over a chewing gum wrapper. Qualters however said he would fold the foil wrapper so it was just small enough so he could see it from the mound. Satchel would talk to himself and those listening as he warmed up, such as, "Bases drunk. Josh Gibson at the plate. Count 3–2, etc." When he released the ball, he would say "Low and away" as the ball passed over the edge of the folded foil wrapper.[45]

Beyond the chewing gum wrapper or the 2" × 2" plate, in 1948 Satchel had his tryout with the Cleveland Indians. Manager Lou Boudreau said, "I put a handkerchief down on the ground, and Paige went back to throw. He pitched over the corner of that handkerchief nine times in nine tries."[46]

Former Indianapolis Clown Hubert "Daddy" Wooten, Jr., was Satchel's young manager with the Clowns in 1967. Hubert recalls Satchel warming up with him over an unfolded matchbook cover. This happened in Comiskey Park in Chicago and there was a photographer watching and taking pictures. The photographer could not believe Satchel could even see the matchbook cover much less throw a pitch over it. Hubert said he never had to move his glove. Satchel's screwball hit it every time. An unfolded match book cover measures 3¾" in length. This would represent 22 percent of the width of home plate.[47] Satchel would have done this in 1967 at age 61!

Did Satchel warm up over a chewing gum wrapper representing less than 17 percent of home plate? Did he warm up over a folded wrapper? Even folded in half it represents less than 10 percent of the available plate?

Satchel's preferred gum was reportedly Wrigley Spearmint.[48]

Summary

Satchel once said, "Ain't no man can avoid being born average, but there ain't no man got to be common."[49] Satchel's talents were God given. His application of those talents, in setting the stage for important changes to come, was an uncommon fulfillment of those talents.

Widely acclaimed baseball writer Roger Kahn has written, "I think it is reasonable to suggest that without Jackie Robinson, Martin Luther King would have lived out his days delivering eloquent sermons in an obscure Baptist church in Georgia."[50]

John Holway stated, "Without Satchel Paige, there just might not have been a Jackie Robinson in Brooklyn."[51]

Satchel Paige's contribution to our society went above and beyond baseball. He is remembered for his achievements on the ball field as well as the contributions he made to integration. His involvement in this regard is no myth. It is a reality. Whether or not all the stories told about Paige are accurate, there can be no denying, Leroy Robert Paige was special.

Notes

1. David Sterry and Arielle Eckstut, *Satchel Sez: The Wit, Wisdom, and World of Leroy "Satchel" Paige* (New York: Crown/Random House, 2001), 7, 74.
2. *New York Times*, 30 September 1923.
3. Gary Mihoces, *USA Today*, 28 October 1992, 2C.
4. Mark Ribowsky, *Satchel Paige: In the Shadows of Baseball* (Da Capo Press, April 2000).
5. *Baseball Digest* (July 2000), 8.
6. Jim Kaplan, *Lefty Grove, American Original* (Cleveland, Ohio: SABR, 2000), 84–86.
7. Virgil Trucks, interview on *Baseball Almanac* by Harold Friend, January 2006.
8. David Marasco, "The Master Goes Twelve," *Diamond Angle*, http://www.thediamondangle.com/marasco/negleg/12satch.html.
9. W.B. Steverson, phone conversation with Virgil Trucks, 12 January 2006.
10. Virgil O. Trucks, *Throwing Heat: The Life and Times of Virgil Fire Trucks* (Pepperpot Publishing, 2004), 90.
11. Lawrence D. Hogan, *Shades of Glory: The Negro Leagues and the Story of African-American Baseball* (National Geographic, 2006), 272, 366.
12. Kathryn Long Humphrey, *Satchel Paige* (Franklin Watts, 1988), 12.
13. Leroy (Satchel) Paige, as told to David Lipsyte, *Maybe I'll Pitch Forever* (University of Nebraska Press, 1993), 18.
14. Hogan, *Shades of Glory*, 251–52.
15. Frazier "Slow" Robinson, *Catching Dreams: My Life in the Negro Baseball Leagues* (Syracuse University Press, 2000), 33–34.
16. W.B. Steverson, phone conversations with Charlie Davis, 12 January 2006.
17. *Ibid.*; W.B. Steverson conversation with Carl Long, 26 March 2006.
18. Fay Vincent, *The Only Game in Town: Baseball Stars of the 1930s and 1940s Talk about the Game They Loved* (Simon and Schuster, 2006), 210.
19. Nathan Volk, "Negro Leaguer Saw a Different Ballgame," *Lansing State Journal*, 13 August 1994.
20. Hogan, *Shades of Glory*, 363.
21. Bruce Johnson, "The Indianapolis Clowns, Clowns of Baseball," *The Clown in Times: A Hysterical Historical Journal* 6, no. 3 (2000).
22. W.B. Steverson phone conversations with Dan Cardwell, 27 February 2006.
23. W.B. Steverson phone conversations with Larry LeGrande, 12 March 2006.
24. W.B. Steverson phone conversations with Tom Qualters, 7 April 2006.
25. Satchel Paige Web site, http://www.satchelpaige.com/index.html; Qualters conversation.
26. Whitey Herzog and Kevin Horrigan, *White Rat: A Life in Baseball* (Harper Collins, 1987), 54–55.
27. Fay Vincent, *The Last Commissioner: A Baseball Valentine* (Reed Business Information Inc., 2002), 271.
28. W.B. Steverson phone conversation with Rev. Wm Greason, May 2006.
29. W.B. Steverson phone conversation with Gary Larder, 30 May 2006.
30. Wikipedia, Rochester Red Wing Stadium (February 2006).
31. W.B. Steverson phone conversations with Ray Semproch, 7 April 2006; Qualters conversation.
32. John B. Holway, *Josh and Satch: The Life and Times of Josh Gibson and Satchel Paige* (MecklerMedia, 1991), 214, 210.
33. Guinness Book of Baseball World Records Web site.

34. "The World's Longest Baseball Throw," Web page sponsored by AVI Joiner.
35. "The Sporting News," 2 July 1990, 44.
36. "When a baseball player hits a home run, how do they know how far the ball traveled?" http://www.Howstuffworks.com.
37. Sportsman's Park, http://www.ballparks.com; John Thorn, Pete Palmer, Michael Gershman, and David Pietrusza, *Total Baseball*, 6th edition, 967, 1031; "The Stories of Mickey Mantle's Ten Longest Home Runs," http://www.themick.com/10homers (2006).
38. Herzog and Horrigan, *White Rat*.
39. "Evidence in the form of yesteryear's throwing contests," http://www.baseball-fever.com.
40. Thorn, Palmer, and Gershman, *Total Baseball*.
41. W.B. Steverson phone conversation with Billy Hunter, 22 April 2006.
42. W.B. Steverson phone conversation with Clifford Layton, 19 April 2006.
43. William Marshall, *Baseball's Pivotal Era 1945–1951* (University Press of Kentucky, 1999), 224; William Price Fox, *Satchel Paige's America* (Fire Ant Books, 2005), 30.
44. Joe Nuxhall, *Joe, Rounding Third & Heading Home* (Orange Frazer Press, 2004), 121.
45. Qualters conversation.
46. Maury Allen, *Jackie Robinson: A Life Remembered* (Easton Press, 1996), 161.
47. W.B. Steverson phone conversation with Hubert "Daddy" Wooten, Jr., 8 June 2006.
48. Satchel Paige Web site.
49. Satchel Paige Web site.
50. Roger Kahn, *October Men* (Harvest Edition, 2004), 11.
51. Holway, *Josh and Satch*.

4

The Historical Satchel Paige: True Stories and Tales Truly Told

Larry Lester, David Marasco and *Patrick Rock*

Baseball is about legends. In the Negro Leagues there is probably no greater legend than Satchel Paige, the tall, lanky right-handed pitcher who had more deliveries than the local milkman. Baseball is rich in apocryphal stories; it had hundreds of urban legends before we ever called them that. Did the Babe really call his shot in the '32 World Series? Did Josh really hit a fair ball out of Yankee Stadium? Did Satch really walk the bases loaded to get to Josh in the '42 Series? One tall tale has Josh Gibson hitting a ball out of Forbes Field only to be called out when it was caught the next day in Philadelphia. Not surprisingly, Satchel Paige as the Negro Leagues' most famous player also stars in many such stories. One of these is recounted in his autobiography *Maybe I'll Pitch Forever*:

> One day I pitched a no-hitter for the Crawfords against the Homestead Grays. That was on July 4. I remember because somebody kept shooting off firecrackers every time I got another batter out. Those firecrackers still were popping when I ran out of the park, hopped into my car, and drove all night to Chicago. I got there in time to beat Jim Trent and the Chicago American Giants one to nothing in twelve innings.[1]

This seems more than a little unbelievable. A full nine innings followed by an all-night drive to be topped with a twelve-inning shutout? Even if one does believe in Paige's pitching abilities, his memory might not be trusted.

Rube Foster posing with his Chicago American Giants. Foster is best known as the "Father of the Negro Leagues."

Home run hitter Josh Gibson caught looking at a strike.

His autobiography was written in 1962, and while that was only one year removed from his pitching for AAA Portland, it was nearly 30 years after the fact. Also to be considered is that the only Trent that played for the Chicago American Giants was Ted Trent. This calls for a little digging. Fortunately both Chicago and Pittsburgh had active press corps in their African American communities, so many pieces of this puzzle can be found.

The *Pittsburgh Courier* splashed the banner headline "Paige Hurls No-Hit Classic" across the top of their July 7, 1934, weekly edition. So the first part of Paige's story is true. This was a game for all time as Paige struck out 17 batters, and but for a walk and an error would have had a perfect game. Only four balls left the infield, one of them a low line drive by Harry Williams that was snagged on a diving catch by Vic Harris. The Crawfords were a loaded team, and they played like it that day. Cool Papa Bell led off their half of the first with a ball to left that was played into a speed-induced triple. He was plated by Josh Gibson's sacrifice fly. In the fifth Leroy Morney doubled, but when Paige sacrificed him over nobody covered third. Morney took a wide turn and Buck Leonard, playing first, threw high to the man backing up the play. Morney scored on the error. In the seventh the Crawfords chased the Homestead's starter and scored two more runs. All that was left was for Paige to complete the no-hitter. Despite pinch-hitting for the two last batters, the Grays could not stop Paige. To understand his dominance that day, observe his strikeout totals inning by inning: 3, 2, 3; 2, 1, 1; 1, 2, 2. According to the plot Paige was now to drive to Chicago, which becomes the next story to verify.

The "Father of the Negro Leagues," Rube Foster, in uniform for his Chicago American Giants.

The most popular

newspaper of the Chicago African American community was the *Chicago Defender*. However, when the paper is surveyed for Paige's victory over Trent no record can be found. It is well known that records from that era are spotty at best, but a Trent-Paige showdown should have received some press. Ted Trent was having a marvelous year in 1934, and would go on to start in the Negro Leagues' East-West All-Star Game at Comiskey Park. Paige was so well known that many times he appeared simply as "Satchel" in box scores. He would win the East-West game that year. Given their fame, a twelve-inning duel between the two would be quite newsworthy. The only twelve-inning game involving Trent was a match he won on the road at Nashville on the 24th of June. That game was a Herculean effort. As recounted in the *Defender*,

> One of the finest efforts of Trent was his twelve inning win over Nashville last week, played under a blazing southern sun. Trent was suffering from cramps from the first frame to the final, and yet continuing through to win. At the conclusion of the game and with the arrival of victory, Trent collapsed and had to be removed to the club house on the shoulders of his mates.

This does not resolve the mystery of the Trent-Paige showdown, but the next week's edition of the *Defender* reveals some clues. A large picture of Satchel Paige was featured on the sports page with the title "Twirls No Hit Game," and below the picture are details of his July 4 feat against the Grays. Also included is an account of Willie Cornelius's near no hitter. Cornelius and Paige matched up for a pitchers' duel on the 8th of July. The two put up zeros across the board for the first nine, but it was Cornelius who was the more effective. While Paige had allowed 6 runners on 5 hits and a walk, Cornelius had given up no hits, allowing only walks to Bell and Gibson, with Bell reaching a second time via an error. However, in the tenth Cornelius fell apart, giving up five hits and three runs. Paige then shut down the American Giants in the bottom of the tenth to take the victory.

At this point Paige's actions in Pittsburgh on the 4th should be more closely examined. As it turns out, the Grays and the Crawfords actually played a double header that day. After Paige had won the first game, the stadium was cleared and another game was played. With the Crawfords enjoying a 2–1 lead in the seventh, the Grays put two men on base. The Crawfords responded by bringing in from the bullpen Satchel Paige! After striking out the first man he faced, Satchel gave up a double to the pitcher, which plated two runs. Paige could not stop the bleeding and another run scored. While he recorded three more strikeouts for a day's total of 20, he was responsible for a blown save in the second game loss since they were ahead when he came in the game. With Paige pitching twice on Wednesday, what were Trent's activities? After his twelve-inning effort the week before, Trent pitched on Saturday the 31st.

He then came in and pitched three innings of relief on Monday the 2nd. Finally he had a complete game against the Crawfords on the 7th.

So according to Paige, after he pitched his no-hitter he drove all night to Chicago and then beat Trent in a twelve-inning game. The reported facts support Trent pitching a twelve-inning game the week before in Nashville, and then Paige beating Cornelius in ten innings four days after his no-hitter. For Paige's version to be true, Trent must have achieved the following tasks: Sunday the week previous he had to pitch a twelve-inning game where he was carried from the field. The following Saturday he started in a game against the Cleveland Red Sox, and then came in as relief on Monday night. According to Paige, on Thursday he was to have competed in yet another twelve-inning game, and then started yet again on Saturday. All but the twelve-inning game against Paige have been documented. In addition to Trent's efforts, Paige must have pitched a nine-inning no-hitter, a part of the second game in the double header, a twelve-inning shutout and a ten-inning shutout over the span of five days. All of this and yet no reporting of the Trent-Paige twelve-inning affair.

The historical truth is that after pitching his famed no-hitter Paige blew another game the same day. Four days later he would beat Cornelius, and after almost thirty years he would confuse not only the chronology of the events, but Cornelius with the far better Trent.

Another nail in the coffin comes from a comment in the July 14 edition of the *Chicago Defender*. It mentions the fact that Paige's victory over Cornelius was his third shutout over the Chicago American Giants that year. A quick search of that year's *Defender* reveals the other two. On their opening weekend, Satchel and the Crawfords visited the American Giants and defeated Trent 7–0. A month later Paige would return to Chicago and this time weave a one-hitter to once again triumph 7–0. With the three shutouts verified, it appears unlikely Satchel could have posted a 1–0 victory over Trent and the Giants on the 5th of July, but we may never know for sure. Perhaps the newspapers missed the shutout.

If Paige did not pitch against Trent, then what were his activities between his no-hitter and his start against Chicago? These facts are revealed in the November 17 edition of the *Pittsburgh Courier*. According to an article that reviewed Satchel's season, after pitching on the fourth Satchel left with Crawfords owner Gus Greenlee and arrived in Marion, North Carolina, on the night of the fifth. Leaving North Carolina on the night of the sixth, Greenlee and Paige drove 1000 miles to Chicago, arriving on the eighth just forty-five minutes before the start of Satchel's game. So as it turns out, this legend is seemingly false. While this is to be regretted, it does not detract from the fact that in a little over two weeks Ted Trent had a 12-inning victory, Paige pitched a no-hitter and Cornelius and Paige faced each other for ten innings with a near no hitter. While Satchel may not have had all the facts straight, the greatness of these men and their feats is by no means exaggerated.

Bases Loaded and No Outs

Legend also has it that Satchel Paige often loaded the bases intentionally, called in his outfield, sat his infielders down, and then struck out the side. However, did he ever accomplish this feat in a documented league game?

On July 2, 1944, at Ebbets Field against the New York Cubans, the legend attempted the fabled feat, with some refinement. Before approximately 14,000 fans, Paige matched wits with West Indian ace Victor Greenidge. Pitching on a moment's notice, Paige normally would pitch only three innings. In this case he was scheduled to pitch again two days later (on July 4) against the Brooklyn Bushwicks, a strong semipro team, in Dexter Park.

Instead of the usual three innings the fans received the royal treatment and were witnesses to 11 innings of superb pitching from the legend. Paige struck out 15 Cubans, and in the ninth inning he filled the bases deliberately, with no outs. The Cubans had only scored an unearned run in the fifth, on a fielding error, two stolen bases, and a passed ball by catcher Sammie Haynes. The Monarchs opened the ninth inning leading 2 to 1, when Hector Rodriguez slapped a single to center. Next Showboat Thomas hit a fly to center that was muffed by outfielder Hilton Smith, normally a pitcher, which allowed the speedy Rodriguez to score. With the score tied, 2–2, next to bat was Louis Louden, followed by the always dangerous dynamic duo of Pancho Coimbre and Tetelo Vargas. All three men were perennial all-stars at Comiskey Park. Coimbre and Vargas would later be elected to the Puerto Rican Baseball Hall of Fame.

Paige intentionally walked Louden and Coimbre to load the bases and the drama was on. To the fans' delight he struck out Vargas. With one out, another all-star performer, Rogelio Linares, came to bat. Linares hit a hard grounder to Herb Souell at third, who fired to Frank Duncan (who had replaced Haynes as catcher) for the second out of the inning, keeping the score evenly deadlocked. Rabbit Martinez, who appeared in 10 all-star games, flied out to end the threat. The Monarchs captured the victory with a run in the eleventh inning, triumphing 3–2.

The great Paige did not bring in his outfield, or sit his infielders down, but he did load the bases, strike out a batter and get out of the jam with no further damage. The great Satchel Paige showed his incredible cool and control to finish off the New York Cubans in stellar fashion.[2]

Another reporting of this incredible display of showmanship was written by Bob Ray for the *Los Angeles Times* on September 11, 1935. Ray reports of a game Paige pitched for the North Dakota team that offered him a Benjamin for each game hurled. Ray writes, "Anyhow in a recent contest Satchel had blanked the enemy until the ninth inning and had the game in the bag. So the lean, ebony hurler decided to give the fans a little something different. Satchel waived his outfielders and infielders all off the field and sent them over to the dugout as he prepared to hurl the final round. Paige struck out the first two batters, but the third hit a pop fly that fell just out of Satchel's reach on the third base line. But that failed to disturb Paige, who whipped three fireballs past the next batter to fan him and then strut off the field amid cheers."

Bunts 'R Us

Some of these legends are an amalgam of different but similar events. Some are part fact, part fiction, and part mystery. Such is the legend that Rube Foster, finding his team behind by a large margin to the ABCs on a muddy field in 1921, ordered his men to bunt many, many times, and by that effort and a propitious grand slam or two, eked out an 18–18 tie for his efforts. Rube Foster's story is told with a variety of twists.

Myths are important in sports, but the truth should have an equal place at the table. While the storyteller is much more interesting than the historian is, a good storyteller will rarely let the truth get in the way of a good punch line. Negro League research has moved far past the days when it dealt solely with anecdotes and tall tales, and must now deal in hard evidence.

One version of Rube's story is told by John Holway in his *Complete Book of Baseball's Negro Leagues* in his section on the 1921 season: "In one game against the ABCs, Chicago was losing 18–0 after seven innings, and Rube ordered his 'race horses' to lay down 18 bunts in a row. Cristobal Torriente, the only slugger on the team, blasted a grand slam, and George Dixon another. The Giants scored nine runs in the eighth and nine more in the ninth to end in a tie."

In Paul DeBono's book *The Indianapolis ABCs*, a somewhat more accurate picture emerges: "In a much talked-about game on June 26, 1921 ... the ABCs were ahead of the American Giants 10–0 to start the eighth inning. The Giants chalked up nine runs in the top of the eighth, making the score 10–9. The ABCs responded confidently by putting eight runs on the board themselves in the bottom of the eighth, making the score 18–9 to start the ninth. In a move said to be 'demonstrative' of Rube Foster's coaching style and genius, in the eighth and ninth innings he ordered 11 batters in a row to bunt, executed six squeeze plays and allowed slugger Cristobal Torriente to knock a grand slam, and somehow the Giants knotted the score at 18-all in the ninth. The bizarre game was called on account of darkness with the score tied at 18."

Both Holway and DeBono drew their references from news stories appearing in the *Chicago Defender* and *Chicago Daily Tribune*, whose sources for their reports were probably Rube Foster or one of his employees, as the game was played in Indianapolis. While these newspapers are contemporary references, their accuracy is in question on several points.

SABR researcher Gary Ashwill reports that three Indianapolis daily newspapers (the *Star*, *News*, and *Times*) reported the game quite differently. They agreed that the game had finished in an 18–18 darkness-shortened tie and that the two teams had combined for 17 runs in the eighth inning, but differed sharply from the Chicago reports otherwise. None of the three Indianapolis papers made any mention of the American Giants bunting, concentrating instead on the accomplishments of their local players and emphasizing the offensive side of the game.

Even more interesting, the Indianapolis newspapers reported the scoring by innings much differently, agreeing that the Giants scored nine and the ABCs eight in the eighth inning, but showing a much more seesaw game with Chicago taking a 15–10 lead into the bottom of the eighth and scoring only three runs to tie in the ninth. Both published accounts speak of 11 or more consecutive bunts, while the actual game story in the *Defender* stated that there were a total of 11 bunts in the two innings, without any detail other than the mention of six "perfect" squeeze plays.

What is the truth of the matter? Unknown. It is known that the American Giants and ABCs played a nine-inning, 18–18 tie game on June 28, 1921, but the details are too sketchy to confirm whether the story is true or not.

The scoring as reported in Chicago:

```
Chicago        0 0 0 0 0 0 0 9 9 — 18
Indianapolis   6 0 4 0 0 0 0 8 0 — 18
```

The scoring as reported in Indianapolis:

```
Chicago        0 0 0 0 4 0 2 9 3 — 18
Indianapolis   1 0 0 6 0 2 1 8 0 — 18
```

While examining this game, another game that involved bunting from behind was uncovered. A game played on August 22, 1923, in Birmingham's Rickwood Field matches many aspects of the story as well. News accounts in the *Birmingham News* and *Age-Herald* reported that Rickwood was already muddy when the game began, and a 10-minute rain stopped play in the fourth, but umpires still felt the field playable, and by the end of six, the American Giants were down by a 3–2 count.

Noting those exceptionally muddy conditions (newspapers reported ankle-deep mud in places on the infield), Foster ordered his men to bunt for hits in the seventh, and they tallied three to make it 5–3 Chicago. It got so bad for Birmingham third baseman "Ruby" Miller that he just let them roll to a stop before picking them up, forcing manager Joe Rush to swap him and second baseman Connie Wesley, to no avail. However, the Black Barons managed to gain a tie in the bottom of the inning when their young left fielder, identified in news accounts only as "Sellers," hit a rare home run out of the cavernous ballpark. This was Mule Suttles' first home run against top-level competition.

Foster pushed his advantage and ordered his men to continue to bunt for hits. With his lineup of skilled bunters and fast runners, the team manufactured two more runs in the eighth and another three in the ninth to win 11–5, with only a double by John Beckwith, who was not a good bunter, to break the monotony. Dave Malarcher was the Giants' third baseman and was skilled at handling bunts, even in the mud, though it did not really matter. The Black Barons were no match for the Giants' bunting skill any more than they could match Malarcher's ability at third.

The accounts in the two daily newspapers make clear that the field was extremely muddy on that August day in 1923, and that Rube's men bunted almost exclusively. While it did not have the element of a fictitious 18-run deficit, the game was well covered by two newspapers, and the strategy (and its success) are documented.

Did Rube Foster ever employ the strategy of almost exclusively bunting to take advantage of extreme field conditions? Absolutely. Did he do so to come back from an 18-run deficit? Almost assuredly not.

No box score has as of yet been found for the 1921 game, but here is one from August 22, 1923:

American Giants	AB	R	H	RBI	Black Barons	AB	R	H	RBI
Gardner, rf	4	1	1	0	Wesley, 2b-3b	5	2	3	0
DeMoss, 2b	4	3	3	1	McAllister, 1b	5	0	1	0
Torriente, cf	4	0	1	2	Meredith, ss	4	0	1	1
Malarcher, 2b	5	2	0	0	Suttles, lf	4	2	2	2
Beckwith, 1b	5	2	5	3	Kemp, cf	3	1	1	0
Kenyon, lf	5	1	1	1	Miller, 3b-2b	4	0	0	0
R. Williams, ss	4	0	2	2	Mitchell, rf	4	0	2	2
J. Brown, c	5	2	2	2	Means, c	4	0	1	0
L. Johnson, p	3	0	1	0	J. Juran, p	3	0	0	0
Owens, p	2	0	1	0	Salmon, p	1	0	0	0
Totals	41	11	17	11	Totals	37	5	11	5

Chicago   1 0 0 0 0 1 3 2 3 — 11
Birmingham   1 0 0 0 0 2 2 0 0 — 5

E—Malarcher, Wesley, Meredith, Suttles, Miller, Salmon.
2B—Beckwith 2, Kenyon.
HR—Suttles.
SB—Wesley.
SH—Torriente, R. Williams, Meredith.
LOB—Chicago 7, Birmingham 7

	IP	H	R	ER	BB	SO
L. Johnson	6	7	3	3	1	2
Owens (W)	3	4	2	2	0	2
J. Juran	6.1	8	2	2	2	2
Salmon (L)	2.2	3	9	8	0	2

Umpires: Whitehead and Swacina
Time: 2:05
Attendance: unknown

And the stories just continue, as one considers the great showdown between Josh and Satch. As does Rube's bunt-from-behind tale, the legend of Satch versus Josh has in it a grain of truth. How many grains of truth it has is an open question.

Josh vs. Satch

There were two legends of baseball fame who engaged in a battle of wits, a battle of brag, and a battle of power. In the 1942 Negro League World Series, a gentle giant named Josh Gibson went head-to-head against a slender, talkative traveler named Satchel Paige. It was the high drama of a home run hitter against a fastball pitcher. Power against power. Legend against legend.

Josh Gibson and Leroy "Satchel" Paige. Now Josh was not your typical power hitter. The big burly catcher's stroke never resembled the sweeping strikeout prone swing of Babe Ruth, the over-striding swing of Frank Howard or the pretzel-flexing swipe of Reggie Jackson. Instead Gibson employed a moderate stride, coupled with a compact swing and engaging violent wrist action. This ability allowed Gibson to be fooled by a pitch, instantly adjust his hitch, and drive any pitch out of the park. At times, his home runs defied description. Void of the typical steroid wattage of a power hitter, Gibson seldom struck out, and often hit for high averages.

Meanwhile, Paige was unlike most successful pitchers; for he didn't have a speedball like Nolan Ryan, a curveball like Bert Blyleven or Camilio Pascual, or the darting slider of Bob Gibson. Instead the wiry right-hander had something called a long Tom (a super fastball), a microscopic be-ball, a bat dodger and of course a little Tom (a "slow" fastball). You couple all these pitches with impeccable control and a hiccup windup that some fans called the "hesitation," and you get the great Satchel Paige.

Now Josh was a jovial, kind, fun-loving man, with a quiet persona. Satch was boastful, sometimes unpredictable, with an infectious personality. While their public images differed vastly, their legends, their stories were equally mythical.

Back in 1991, in Chicago, Jimmie Crutchfield, a former Crawfords teammate of Gibson, tells this story:

> One night in Canton, Ohio, we were playing the Nashville Elite Giants. The Boston Braves had a farm team down there and it was all advertised everywhere about Josh Gibson. Boy, the park was crowded. The Boston Braves' farm club had all come out in their team jackets to see the great Josh Gibson.
>
> Andy Porter was then pitching for the Elite Giants. And Candy Jim Taylor, the manager, said he finally got a man who could get Josh out. Porter was a sidewinder, tall and lanky like Satchel. Anyway, [Manager Oscar] Charleston gave me the bunt signal and I squared off and took the pitch. On the next pitch, I singled to centerfield. Cool Papa [Bell] scored and I went to second on the throw to the plate. Josh then came up. Porter threw Josh something. Boy, did he hit it.
>
> I just stopped between second and third. I looked out to centerfield and the lights were shining through the trees. The ball just took off and then it looked like it just stopped! But it was still going, but it stopped and waved at us and took off again. Incredible!![3]

With a couple of eye winks and a sly smile, Colonel Crutchfield got the awe shucks response he wanted.

Concerning a tall tale about Paige, Bill Veeck, owner of the St. Louis Browns had this revelation about Satchel from a 1951 game:

> Satchel had been called on for a ninth inning relief job against the Washington Senators. I told Satch to make it quick because the team had to leave by train in less than an hour.
>
> Paige then proceeded to strike out three Senators with only ten pitches. Afterwards, Satchel apologized to me. When they were boarding the train, Satch said, "Sorry about that extra tenth pitch. But the umpire missed one!"[4]

Chet Brewer, a former Monarch pitcher, recalls another Gibson story: Once a young boy asked Josh if he could have one his broken bats. "Son," replied the gentle giant, "I don't break bats, I wear them out. But I think I can find you one."[5]

Whitey Herzog, in his book *White Rat*, recalls this Paige story during their time together with the Miami Marlins:

> The Marlins once had a distance-throwing contest before a night game. [Don] Landrum and I had the best arms of any of the outfielders. We were out by the centerfield fence, throwing two-hoppers to the plate. Ol' Satch came out, didn't even warm up, and kind of flipped the ball sidearm. It went 400 feet on a dead line and hit the plate. I wouldn't believe it if I hadn't seen it.

Herzog also recounts the story of Paige's throws from approximately 60 feet, through a grapefruit-size hole in the outfield wall at Rochester. [For a full discussion of the story, as told by Herzog and others, see W. Bryan Steverson's essay in this book.]

No pitcher had better control than Satchel Paige, and no one could control the power of Josh Gibson. (Sam Hairston, once a scout for the Chicago White Sox, chimes in with a story about the mighty Josh after Jimmie Crutchfield's taffy puller. He played against him in 1944 and nearly got killed when he tried to play in thinking he would bunt. Josh sent a screaming line drive right past his chest and he had backed up on to the grass after his manager ordered him back.) Never have two men been promoted as much as these two legendary heroes. They were the total marketing package, a combination of versatility and invincibility. They were real-life comic book superheroes with indescribable adjectives and superlatives. You will decide if this next story is real or imaginary.

The living legends began their big showdown at the first game of the '42 World Series in Washington, DC. It was the Kansas City Monarchs versus the Homestead Grays. In the opener, Paige pitched five shutout innings, giving up two hits and striking out five, before Jack Matchett threw goose eggs over the final four innings for an 8–0 victory. Third baseman Newt Allen led the attack with three of the 13 hits off Grays pitcher Roy Welmaker.

In the second game in Pittsburgh, Paige relieved the great Hilton Smith after six innings, with a 2–0 lead. The Monarchs went ahead 5 to 0 before Paige gave up four runs in the bottom of the eighth frame. The Monarchs cushioned their one-run lead with three more runs in the top of the ninth. Before a crowd of 5,219 fans and with the score 8–4, the stage was set for one of baseball's greatest duels.

There have been many versions reported of the celebrated duel between Joshua and Leroy. Was the quintessential combat between these dudes a lark? Paige teammate John "Buck" O'Neil gave his eye-witness account of the story.

Buck O'Neil was a hard-hitting right-handed first baseman for the Monarchs that day who later became the first black coach in the majors scouted for the Kansas City Royals, and now serves as chairman of the Negro Leagues Baseball Museum. "Buck" recalls the high drama of that day:

> This friendly feud started when Satchel and Josh were playing on the powerhouse Pittsburgh Crawfords. With five future Hall of Famers, they may have been one of the best ball clubs ever assembled. Well, this was before the Pennsylvania Turnpike was built and we would have to go over the mountains to get out of Pittsburgh. When you got half way up through the mountains, they had places were you could pull off the road, so you could put water in your car or bus. The

guys would pass the time by throwing rocks and stones down the mountain side, while the chauffeur was filling the radiator.

Well, Josh and Satchel started chatting. Satch said to Josh, "You know, Josh, we're on the same team ... you may never have a chance to hit against me or me pitch against you. But one of these days, we gonna be on different ball clubs and we gonna see what you can do against me and I against you."

Well, that day had finally arrived. We [the Monarchs] were not even thinking about Satchel's boast. This was the second game of the World Series. Now, we had won the first game over there in Washington, D.C. We are leading the ball game in the ninth inning with two outs. We had scored three insurance runs in the top of the ninth for an 8 to 4 lead. After pitching the first game of the series, Satchel was weakening. He had given up four runs in the eighth inning.

So in the ninth inning, their lead-off hitter, Jerry Benjamin hits the ball down the third base line for a triple. Now, Satchel calls (he called me Nancy), he said, "Hey, Nancy come here. You know what I fixin' to do?" I said, "What Satch?" Now, we already got two outs. "I gonna put Howard Easterling on base." Now I know the next batter is Buck Leonard, a pretty good hitter. Satch adds, "And next I gonna put Leonard on. I wanna pitch to Josh with the bases jammed, I got something to prove." I said, "Aw, Man! You GOT to be facetious." Satch said, "I don't know what you want to call it, but that's what I'm gonna to do." I cried, TIME!

So Frank Duncan, who was managing the ball club, trots out to the mound. I said, "Frank! Skipper, listen here. I want you to talk to Satchel. Then I said ..."wait, I'll let Satchel tell you." So Satch tells Frank, "We gonna put Easterling on, then Leonard on and I gonna pitch to Josh." Frank turns to me and says, "I tell you what Buck, you see all these people here? They came out here to see Satchel pitch and so whatever Satchel wants to do, then let him do it." So Satchel walks Easterling. As he is throwing four balls to Leonard, he hollers to Josh in the on-deck circle. "Hey Josh, do you remember the time when we were going over those mountains and we were playing on the same team and I told you what was going to happen someday?"

Josh yelled back, "Yeah, Satchel, I know what you said." Satch then said, "Well Josh, this is the day to see who is the best! Let's see who's gonna win." Then Satch hollered, "TIME!" Floyd ..."Jewbaby" Floyd was our trainer and he traveled all over the country with Satch. Wherever Satch would go, Jewbaby would follow. Jewbaby was like our team doctor. So after Satchel walked those guys, Jewbaby in his white doctor's coat and his black medicine bag marched out to the mound. Satchel had always had trouble with his stomach. Jewbaby opened his bag and mixed up some concoction, I imagine Alka Seltzer or something, in a cup and shook it up. Now mind you, this was happening right there on the mound. Now everybody in the stands KNOWS what's happening. Satchel had walked these two men and now the people are all standing, some 40,000 people. He took the cup from Jewbaby and drunk it down, right there on the mound, and gives the cup back to Jewbaby. He stretches out there and gives out a loud belch, that echoes through out the ball park. So Jewbaby goes off the mound and now he ready to pitch to Josh.[6]

Paige bent over slightly, letting both arms hang freely and wiggles his shoulders, to loosen up. He straighten ups and steps to the back of the mound and picks up the rosin bag. He drops the bag to the ground and fingers the seams on the horsehide, looking straight at Josh and then slams the ball into his glove.

Satch said to Josh, "I gonna throw you some fastballs. Nothing but fastballs." Josh replies, "Come on and throw 'em." Satch counters, "I'm not gonna trick you. I gonna throw you some fastballs right at your knees."

Satch wounded up and tethered on one leg and fired.... Josh didn't move his bat. Strike One! Satch bragged, "Now I gonna throw you another one, but this one is gonna be just a little faster than that one, Josh." And BOOM, Josh froze, strike two! "Now Josh, you know in this situation, when I got two strikes and no balls on you, I supposed to knock you down. Back you off the plate." But he said don't worry. "I not gonna knock you down now. I not gonna throw this smoke at your yoke, but a pea at your knee." The crowd grew very quiet, as Gibson steeled himself for the big pitch. Satch revved up, double pumped and threw Josh another Long Tom, right here [Buck motions, knee level], BOOM! And Josh still didn't move his bat. Struck him out! Satchel looked like he got two inches taller, he straightened out, pulled his shoulders back and strutted off that mound. When he walked by me, he whispered, "Nancy, nobody, but nobody, hits Satch's fastball."

Trainer Jew Baby Floyd never traveled without his tools of the trade. He used these tools to help keep Paige's arm limber and ready to go nearly every day.

Yes, nobody hit Satch's fastball. After his heroic conquest of Joltin' Josh, the Monarchs and Grays drew 30,000 fans at their next stop in New York City. The third game saw Paige pitch a seven-hitter, striking out three and winning 9–3. On a Sunday afternoon in Kansas City, the four game sweep was completed when Paige beat Johnny Wright, 9–5. Satchel Paige would record three victories in the four game conquest over the once mighty Grays.

You know — there is no joy back in the old homestead in Pittsburgh, for mighty Josh struck out. According to one historian, in the July 18, 1981, issue of the *Sporting News* says this game was never played. The article was titled, "Satch vs. Josh — Classic Duel Was a Lark."

How do we know this colorful story isn't just a black version of the classic "Casey at the Bat" poem? Fortunately, unlike fictional Mudville, Pittsburgh does exist and their local newspapers covered the game in great detail. To follow are revelations from super sleuth SABRite Patrick Rock.

The local press boasted, "Highlighted by Satchel Paige's dramatic feat of striking out Josh Gibson with the bases loaded, the Kansas City Monarchs scored an 8-to-4 victory over the Homestead Grays last night at Forbes Field in the second game of the Negro World Series."

Reports of game two were carried in three Pittsburgh dailies (the *Post-Gazette*, the *Press*, and the *Sun-Telegraph*) as well as the *Pittsburgh Courier*, *Chicago Defender*, *Kansas City Call*, and *Baltimore Afro-American*, though the *Call* and *Press* did not print a box score. The *Afro-American* and all three Pittsburgh dailies reported that Paige struck out Gibson with the bases loaded and two out in the seventh inning, though making no mention of any showboating on Paige's part.

A review of the box score in a number of newspapers show that not one agreed completely with any other. However, a few facts emerge clearly from the reports: the two men who batted in front of Josh Gibson drew zero walks between them; Jerry Benjamin did not hit a triple in this contest; and Satchel Paige did not walk a single man in the game.

Here is what we know from the actual game accounts:

Paige entered in the sixth inning of game two in relief of Hilton Smith, protecting a 2–0 lead. According to the *Pittsburgh Press*, he struck out the first two men he faced, Buck Leonard and Sam Bankhead, and then ended the inning by corralling Ray Brown's weak pop-up.

The Grays loaded the bases in the seventh against Paige on singles by Roy Partlow, Vic Harris, and Howard Easterling. Facing Gibson with two out and the bases loaded, Paige struck him out on three pitches. Gibson fouled off the first two and then swung and missed on the third.

The Monarchs scored three runs in the top half of the eighth to open up a 5–0 lead, but Paige quickly let his guard down and got in trouble, and surrendered four runs in the bottom of the eighth. He allowed singles by Leonard and Bankhead, and was burned when Willie Simms dropped Ray Brown's fly ball for an error, allowing Leonard to score. Jud Wilson's pinch-hit double plated Bankhead and Brown, and Wilson scored on a ground out by Benjamin. Gibson did not bat during that half-inning. The Monarchs added three more runs in the top of the ninth, and Paige retired Easterling, Gibson, and Leonard in order to end it 8–4.

The first known appearance of the legendary part of the story is in Paige's 1962 autobiography *Maybe I'll Pitch Forever*, written 20 years after that game, and 15 years after Josh Gibson's death. All other stories about the alleged event follow afterward.

Contemporary reference says that Paige gave up no walks that day. Several reports confirm that he struck Gibson out with the bases loaded, but while the *Afro* described it as a "storybook" duel, and the *Post-Gazette* and *Sun-Telegraph* described it as "the most dramatic moment" of the game, no report made of that game made any reference to Paige taunting Gibson as he pitched.

However, from Paige's 1948 semi-autobiography with Hal Lebovitz, "Pitchin' Man," he claims: "Now you're too smart to fool, so I'm goin' to tell you what's comin.' I'm going to throw you two sidearms fast balls down around the knees. The umpire was John Craig, I remember clearly."

> Well, the first two were strikes! "Now," I said, "Josh, you're too good for me to waste any pitches so I'm going to throw you a sidearm curve. That's your weakness." I threw it and Josh stepped back. It broke over and he swung a slow motion strike three.
>
> Josh come out to the box and shook my hand. They had to halt play for about an hour to clear the field of straw hats."

Paige was a consummate showman, but the game was on the line, and he was in danger of allowing the game to turn. Logic says that Paige would not have been clowning at a moment like this, or trying to show up Gibson; he would have been a complete professional.

Here is the correct "composite" box score, from the *Pittsburgh Post-Gazette*, *Pittsburgh Sun Telegraph* and *Pittsburgh Press*:

Monarchs	AB	R	H	RBI	*Grays*	AB	R	H	RBI
Simms, lf	5	1	1	0	Benjamin, cf	5	0	3	1
Allen, 3b	4	0	0	0	Harris, lf	5	0	1	0
Cyrus, 3b	0	0	0	0	Easterling, 2b-3b	5	0	1	0
Strong, rf	5	2	2	0	Gibson, c	4	0	0	0
W. Brown, cf	4	2	1	0	Leonard, 1b	4	1	1	0
Greene, c	5	3	3	1	Bankhead, ss	3	1	1	0
O'Neil, 1b	4	0	1	2	R. Brown, rf	3	1	1	0
Serrell, 2b	4	0	3	3	C. Williams, ss	3	0	1	0
J. Williams, ss	4	0	2	0	(a) Wilson, ph-3b	1	1	1	2

Monarchs	AB	R	H	RBI	Grays	AB	R	H	RBI
H. Smith, p	2	0	0	0	Partlow, p	3	0	2	0
Paige, p	2	0	0	0	Wright, p	0	0	0	0
					(b) Whatley, ph	1	0	0	0
					Welmaker, p	0	0	0	0
					Carter, p	0	0	0	0
Totals	39	8	13	6	Totals	37	4	13	3

(a) Wilson batted for C. Williams in the 8th
(b) Whatley batted for Wright in 8th

Kansas City   1 0 0 1 0 0 0 3 3 — 8 13 1
Homestead   0 0 0 0 0 0 4 0 0 — 4 12 4

Errors— Benjamin, Simms, V. Harris, Bankhead 2.
2B — J. Williams 2, Strong, Green, Wilson
3B — Serrell, Benjamin
SB — Green, J. Williams, O'Neil, W. Brown
SH — Bankhead, Cyrus
LOB — Kansas City 8, Homestead 10

Monarchs	IP	H	R	ER	BB	SO
H. Smith (W)	5	5	0	0	2	2
Paige (Sv)	4	8	4	2	0	3

Grays	IP	H	R	ER	BB	SO
Partlow (L)	7.2	9	5	5	0	3
Wright	0.1	0	0	0	1	0
Welmaker	0.2	3	3	2	0	1
Carter	0.1	1	0	0	2	0

HBP — by H. Smith (Leonard)
Umpires— John Craig, M. Harris, W. Harris
Attendance — 5,219

However, there is one further twist in this story. In the fourth and final game of the 1942 Series, Paige completely dominated the Grays. Relieving Jack Matchett with two out in the fourth inning, Paige retired 15 of the next 16 men, allowing only one man to reach on a fielding error. However, with two out in the ninth inning and the Monarchs ahead by four, Paige proceeded to walk Vic Harris and Howard Easterling before disposing of the cleanup batter for the final out. Did Paige deliberately walk the two men to face Gibson for the final out? We cannot say whether he did so deliberately, as available news reports are silent on that issue, but Paige had to that point walked only one batter in his 16 innings in the Series, and his sudden lapse of control merits suspicion. However, there is one final fact to consider: Paige did not face Gibson for the final out. Gibson had left the fourth game after two innings and his sub, Bob Gaston, stood in for that final at-bat.

Satchel Paige, besides being one of the greatest pitchers ever, was an unabashed self-promoter, and it is entirely possible that he created his story out of whole cloth. There are enough clues to make one wonder if it simply was not a matter of two or more events combining themselves in the mind's eye.

Did Rube Foster really order his team to bunt time after time in a game, noting a muddy field and using the strategy to come from behind in a game? While not in a hopelessly lost game, he did use such a strategy in 1923. Did he do so in that game of June 28, 1921? There is evidence that he relied heavily on his team's bunting skills, but not in such a dramatic fashion as legend would have it.

Did Satchel Paige strike out Josh Gibson with the bases loaded in game two of the 1942 World Series? Absolutely yes. Did Satch set up the confrontation by walking two men to fill the bags? Absolutely not. Did Satch taunt Josh as he threw pitches past him? Probably not. Are the events of game four close enough to decide that the event was an amalgam of the two? Possibly. Case closed? Never. Where would the fun be in that?

As we all know, our memories fade with time. Indeed, the event actually happened, regardless of the misstatements. Whether you believe Satchel's version or Buck's version or the newspapers, after more than 60 years, that Buckaroo can still spin a yarn. And we continue to be fascinated by these tales.

Sources

Ashwill, Gary. Agate Type. http://agatetype.typepad.com/.
Baltimore Afro-American, September 19, 1942, 31.
Birmingham Age-Herald, August 23, 1923, 18.
Birmingham News, August 23, 1923, 11.
Chicago Defender, July 2, 1921, 10.
Chicago Defender, September 19, 1942, 23.
Chicago Tribune, June 29, 1921, 19.
Clark, Dick, and John B. Holway. "Charleston No. 1 Star in 1921 Negro League," *Baseball Research Journal* 14 (1985): 63–70.
Holway, John. *The Complete Book of Baseball's Negro Leagues: The Other Half of Baseball History* (Fern Park, 2001), 398–399.
Lester, Larry, and Buck O'Neil. "Satch vs. Josh," *The National Pastime* 13 (1993): 30–33.
Philadelphia Inquirer, September 30, 1942, 38.
Pittsburgh Courier, September 19, 1942, 17.
Pittsburgh Post-Gazette, September 11, 1942, 18.
Pittsburgh Press, September 11, 1942, 38.
Pittsburgh Sun-Telegraph, September 11, 1942, 28.

Notes

1. Satchel Paige, *Maybe I'll Pitch Forever*, 81.
2. *New York Amsterdam News*, July 5, 1944.
3. Interview with Larry Lester, 25 November 1991.
4. *Kansas City Call*, October 19, 1951
5. Telephone interview with Larry Lester.
6. Interview with Larry Lester, 13 September 1990.

5

Cracking a Chink in Jim Crow: Satchel Paige and the Integration of Baseball

Terrie Aamodt

In his 1962 autobiography *Maybe I'll Pitch Forever*, Satchel Paige included a 1945 quote from the *Detroit Free Press*: "Paige ... is the Negro counterpart of the greatest names in big league baseball. As a drawing card he has been the magnet that has jammed baseball fans–Negro and white–into parks all over the country for the last twenty-one years."[1] In post–World War II America, large media markets were just beginning to notice what small town sports editors and the black press had known for decades: African American athletes, led by Satchel Paige, had taken integrated and interracial baseball into the furthest corners of the country, particularly in the Midwest and West. Although their large, enthusiastic crowds may not have realized they were on the cutting edge of social change, they did understand the excellence of top-flight athletes, alive and in the flesh and more real than the newspaper sports page photographs of major leaguers.

Baseball is a game of numbers, and it supplies endless inducements to compare performances. How closely does a player compare to the very best? Many athletes never had the opportunity to answer that question directly: Babe Didrikson, who wondered if her splendid athletic gifts could translate into meaningful baseball league play; talented semipro players whose life choices kept them off a track to the major leagues; African Americans whose skills, no matter how great, would never be recognized in direct, head-to-

The Denver White Elephants played for the second straight year in the *Denver Post* tournament in 1935, after receiving an invitation in 1934. Top row, from left to right: Bill Carey, Lefty Banks, Robert Clay, Pete Albright, Ed Stewart, Reginald Cooper, Fleming Von Dickersohn; middle row, A.H.W. Ross, Red Threets, Boogie Woogie Pardue, Logan Harper, Little Johnny, George Walker; front row, Ike Bell, Willard Stevenson, bat boy, Joe Tucker, Theodore Johnson.

head league competition with the best white players. When 1940s talking heads fussed over the effects impending integration would have on baseball, they overlooked something. It had already been done — not in the elegant superstructure of the major leagues, but in the foundational spaces of the house of baseball. Experiments in interracial and integrated play took place during and after World War I, especially in the context of 1920s social changes, but in the 1930s Satchel Paige made them an art form. Paige's interracial and integrated play in the 1930s, although practically unnoticed by national media, changed America. It elevated competition and performance in the towns where his teams played, whether against crack barnstormers, local semipros, minor league teams at every level, or in national tournaments. Paige's play also eroded society's walls of segregation, or, as Paige said, it "cracked another little chink in Jim Crow."[2]

Satchel Paige's play with and against white teams was particularly notable during the years when the Negro Leagues had their most serious struggles. The onset of the Great Depression, the death of Negro National League

Winners of the 1937 *Denver Post* tournament, the 1937 All-Star squad defeated the Texas Oilers to take the prize. Top row, from left to right: Josh Gibson, Harry Williams, Tony Castano, Rodolfo Fernandez, Robert Griffith, Perucho Cepeda, Bill Perkins; middle row, Lazaro Salazar, Dr. Joe E. Aybar, Satchel Paige; bottom row, Enrique Lantigua, Leroy Matlock, Jose Vargas, Cool Papa Bell, Sam Bankhead, Silvio Garcia and Francisco Correa.

president Rube Foster in 1930, and the collapse of that league in 1931 led to several years of instability, particularly for teams in the Midwest and South. The Kansas City Monarchs owner, J.L. Wilkinson, withdrew his team from the crumbling league in 1931, knowing that because they were equipped with their own portable electric light system, they could barnstorm though Iowa, Dakota, Nebraska, Kansas and the West and make money.[3] At about the same time, according to Paige, Gus Greenlee gave him a contract with the Pittsburgh Crawfords for the 1931 season, along with battery-mate Josh Gibson. League play was sparse, and both the owner and his star pitcher looked for additional games. Greenlee began booking Paige to pitch freelance when his team was not playing. Paige made up to $500 per game and discovered the lure of extra-league play and enhanced income. The best opportunities tended to be in the Midwest and West, and they often involved white players and white teams.

At the end of the summer of 1933, the *Chicago Defender* passed along a story that Paige might leave the Crawfords to pitch for a South Dakota semi-pro team. The team Paige actually became involved with was in Bismarck, North Dakota, where an enterprising car dealer, Neil Churchill, was in his second year of building a strong semipro team. Churchill sought not only to triumph over rivals in nearby Jamestown but also to capture the state semipro championship and win the national semipro tournament. In September 1933 he managed to persuade Paige to join the team for a local tournament. Paige recalled in his memoir that "It wasn't until after I signed up with Mr. Churchill that I found out I was going to be playing with some white boys. For the first time since I'd started throwing, I was going to have some of them on my side. It seemed real funny. It seemed like they couldn't hold out against me all the way after all."[4] Jamestown countered by signing Willie Foster, the left-handed ace of the Chicago American Giants. Paige ultimately defeated Foster 3–2 in the tournament's final game, batting in all of his team's runs.[5]

Paige played for the Crawfords again in 1934, but he continued to fit in freelance assignments that led toward tournament action. In 1934, the popular *Denver Post* semipro tournament decided to admit black teams for the first time, and accordingly a well-known local team, the White Elephants, signed up. The Kansas City Monarchs, knowing they had an excellent chance to win the tournament, entered as well and enlisted the Chicago American Giants players Willie Foster and Turkey Stearnes to bolster their roster. The ever-watchful Ray Doan, a white baseball entrepreneur who at the time was the booking agent for the House of David traveling team, detected an opportunity. The House of David team, whose core players were members of a religious commune in Benton Harbor, Michigan, had played against black teams for years, and they had spent several weeks barnstorming with the Monarchs throughout the Northwest and Canada. For this occasion, however, they would make a black player one of their own. Doan went straight to the top and lined up Satchel Paige.[6] The *Kansas City Call*, although still confident that the Monarchs would win the tournament, noted this detail as the competition neared:

> The Monarchs have given the white players some knowledge of the game which the white boys expect to use against the Kansas City team in the tournament. Nor are the white boys a bit prejudiced. They have sent east and Satchel Page [sic] of the once famous Birmingham club but now of the Pittsburgh Crawfords of Negro National league, will hurl for the House of David team.[7]

Top black athletes occupied Denver's playing fields. The city had never seen anything like it. The Monarchs, who had lost 10 of 125 games played in 1933, quickly became tournament favorites. After they defeated the Greeley Advertisers 12 to 1 in the opening round, with Chester Brewer fanning 19, Leonard Cahn of the *Post* proclaimed them the team to beat. The House of David team, based on tournament appearances in earlier years, however, were "still the people's choice," the *Post* noted.[8] In another first round game, 3,500 spectators cheered the bearded team and their regular ace, Spike Hunter, to a 16–0 romp over Italian Bakery of Denver. Hunter surrendered 6 hits and struck out 14. "More colorful and stronger than ever," the *Post* reported, "House of David fired a broadside of base hits to signalize its return to Cool Colorado." Then, after 8 strong innings, Hunter gave way to Satchel Paige, who played the role of closer and also antidote to what had been a monotonous game. The fans found their voices "when Satchel shuffled to the mound":

> Imagine their surprise when the outfielders jogged in and stationed themselves just beyond the grass back of the infield. Hadn't they read about such Rube Waddell goings-on in story books? And here it was presented to them in the flesh.
> Red Luchette led off with a single, but that was only a teaser. Satchel, as limber as that good old fishing rod, started whipping his fast one thru there with the speed of a bullet, the ball smacking with a loud thud into the big mitt of Cy Perkins, his colored battery mate.[9]

Already, within hours of the beginning of the 1934 tournament, the Kansas City Monarchs and the House of David team, two highly skilled, highly entertaining squads, were vying for spectator and press attention. The scenario could have been a scriptwriter's dream. It also boosted the tournament's income.

The papers focused on Satchel Paige as the House of David team readied for its second contest, against the Eason Oilers of Enid, Oklahoma. Kansas City Monarchs players verified that Satchel was the best of the Negro League pitchers, and Grover Cleveland Alexander, the manager and occasional relief pitcher for the House of David team, said Paige's fastball was "one of the best." While Kansas City squeaked through its second game 4–3 on Sunday afternoon, the House of David, with Paige, posted a decisive 6–1 victory over the Eason Oilers before a crowd of 4,034. Paige, described as "gangling and loose-jointed, with a magic fireball, which claimed fourteen strikeout victims, a hesitation delivery and a bagful of mound shenanigans, was cast in the leading role and played the part to the king's taste," and inspired the Davids to "the finest game they have ever played in Denver." Because he had been a bit wild in the game, he was slated to pitch the next game as well, since he was reputed to thrive on frequent mound appearances.[10]

In the fourth round, the Monarchs squeaked past the Schneider Jewelers team from Kansas in 10 innings on Tuesday, while Paige, earning the moniker the "Chocolate Whizbang," whose "mercurial shoots [mowed] down strikeout victims row on row," led his team to a sparkling 4–0 victory over the Humble Oilers of Overton, Texas. "A crowd of 6,314 looked on in wonder," noted a sportswriter, "as Satchel meted out a dose of his famous black magic to the hitherto undefeated Texans." In his second start in three nights, Paige struck out 17 and stretched his streak of scoreless innings to 16.[11] It was clear who had emerged as the focus of spectator interest, and Paige continued to dominate the sports pages for the rest of the tournament.

A scriptwriter's dream unfolded when, just over halfway through the tournament, the Monarchs and the House of David met in a Friday night game. It would be "the game of games! ... the House of David, most colorful club in the independent field, and Kansas City Monarchs, Negro champions of the world" were the only unbeaten teams remaining in the tournament. "The greatest Negro pitcher in the world pitching against the greatest Negro club!" the paper proclaimed. The predictions lived up to reality. The paid attendance of 11,120 was "record-breaking," said the *Post*, and thousands more were turned away. Satchel Paige, starting for the third time in five days, pitched the House of David to a 2–1 victory over Chet Brewer and the Monarchs. As predicted, this was the "game of games."[12]

Although Paige was expected to start against the Humble Oilers of Overton, Texas, which would have been his fourth start in 7 days, manager Alexander astutely chose to start another pitcher, Warren Weirman, perhaps to remind the team that they could indeed win without Paige. Weirman scored a couple of runs himself and pitched an eight-hit, 8–2 complete game victory, aided by Overton's "four atrocious errors" and the resulting six unearned runs. Alexander had Paige warm up just in case Weirman faltered, and once the fans saw him, they clamored unsuccessfully for their favorite player to enter the game. The sports editor, C.L. Poss Parsons, chuckled, "I got a kick out of Paige warming up sitting down–that is a new one!"[13]

On Monday, August 13, the two top teams met for the championship: the House of David, still undefeated, and the Kansas City Monarchs, whose slender 2–1 defeat against the Bearded Beauties was their only loss. They would play an evening game, and if the Monarchs won, a second game that night would be required to determine the champion. Like most observers, the *Post* writers expected Paige to start the first game. They anticipated a sportswriter's dream: a dramatic meeting between two well-matched, exciting teams. Because the antagonists were "two of the greatest teams ever to play in THE POST tournament," the sports page read, "another tremendous throng was assured."

Approximately $1000 was on the line, the article said–the difference between first and second place. If Paige pitched that first game, and if the House of David won, most of the first place differential would go to Paige, who got paid by the victory. Perhaps keeping this in mind, manager Alexander elected to hold Paige in reserve for a possible second game, disappointing the 8200 ticket holders who jammed into Merchants Park to see him pitch the championship game. As it turned out, the second game was not necessary. House of David scratched out two runs with timely hits, and Spike Hunter, the club's regular ace, shut out Kansas City. As Walter Judge observed, "the Monarchs lacked the fire" they had in the first game between the two teams. "Evidently the Beards took something out of them on that occasion they never recovered." The House of David, the "people's choice," ran its record to 7–0 and became the first team to go through the tournament undefeated since 1922. Furthermore, noted Walter Judge, the team won the final game with "virtually its own lineup, too. Every man ... with the exception of Cy Perkins, colored catcher, wore a beard."[14] The victors claimed the $5,458.75 check, and the Monarchs received $4,844.05.

During those weeks late in the 1934 season Paige's non-baseball life was nearly as complicated as his freelance pitching schedule. He got married in October and soon thereafter tried to renegotiate his contract with Greenlee. The Crawfords' owner refused, having already threatened to ban Paige from the Negro Leagues for excessive freelancing. Paige abandoned his contract with Greenlee and signed on with Neil Churchill's Bismarck semipro team for the 1935 season. Churchill, about to embark on his fourth season, had the biggest prize in the nation, but he also spent much of the 1935 season assembling a "dream team" to run at the national semipro tournament.

Meanwhile, the archrival Jamestown Red Sox took another path. The team had hired several black players in 1934, including Barney "Lefty" Brown, but in 1935 Jamestown decided to go with an all-white team, leaving Brown and his other black Jamestown teammates free to sign with another rival, the Valley City Hi-Liners. The story of the North Dakota 1935 semipro season is largely a story of the fates of the two leading teams, all-white Jamestown and the increasingly darker-hued Bismarck team. In early May the Bismarck paper introduced Paige as the "nationally-known speedball artist" who had recently won 17 straight in West Coast winter league play and would pitch the opening game. At the beginning of the season he and Irving "Lefty" Vincent, the ace of the 1934 Bismarck staff and an erstwhile Pittsburgh Crawfords player, were the team's only black players. Churchill planned to acquire in early June the Negro Leagues catcher Quincy Trouppe, who had been the Kansas City Monarchs' backup catcher during the spring, according to the *Bismarck Tribune*.[15] Most of the players who began the season in Bismarck had minor league experience. Meanwhile, Jamestown picked up a pitcher from the House of David, Ed Brady, to anchor their staff.

On the first day of the season, May 5, Bismarck and Paige lost to Brady 2–1. The winning run scored on a passed ball. A week later Paige returned the favor, shutting out Jamestown and Brady 4–0, striking out 15. Over the next few weeks Paige became a team enforcer as well as an outfielder and a relief pitcher. In the early weeks of the 1935 season Lefty Vincent struggled with a sore arm. On May 24 Vincent started a game against the Valley City

Hi-Liners, and the team erupted for 4 runs in the first before Churchill brought in Paige with the bases loaded to face the Valley City pitcher, Lefty Gaines, in the number-9 spot. Paige plunked Gaines squarely on the throwing arm with a fastball and forced him out of the game before he ever threw a pitch.[16] That move forced in the fifth run of the inning, but it also forced Valley City to come up with a new pitcher, and if the game had not been called in the seventh inning because of darkness, Bismarck might have overtaken them. On May 28 Paige one-hit the Devils Lake Lakers team, the rookie club of the Cleveland Indians. Two days later he won both ends of a doubleheader from the House of David. Paige pitched the final inning of the first game, which was tied 7–7 when he entered in the top of the ninth. He dispatched the visitors, and in the home half of the inning Quincy Trouppe, who had just joined the team earlier in the day, stole home to win the game.[17]

During the month of May, Paige was 7–1 with one save. In 70 innings he struck out 86, walked 7, and achieved a 1.04 ERA. He was involved in 10 of the 11 games the team played that month. Not even Satchel Paige could maintain that pace for an entire season, and Churchill continued to juggle his staff, trying to find an adequate supporting cast for Paige. The team lost more games than they won for a couple of weeks while they regrouped.[18] In mid–June Bismarck and Paige met the Kansas City Monarchs in Winnipeg. In their first encounter the two teams fought to a scoreless tie when darkness ended the contest after nine innings. It was "the finest mound duel ever unfolded in Winnipeg," according to a Kansas City journalist.[19] A few days later the two teams split a doubleheader in Bismarck, with Paige defeating Chet Brewer in the second game 2–0. By the end of July, the team had a solid rotation, and they were all Negro Leaguers: Paige, Barney Morris, Lefty Vincent, and Ted "Double Duty" Radcliffe, "four of the greatest colored hurlers ever assembled on one team," according to a Bismarck sports writer.[20] The team's "murderer's row" of Joe Desiderato, Red Haley, Quincy Trouppe and Moose Johnson were tearing up opposition pitching, and the Bismarck Capital City team mowed down its opponents, both other nearby semipro teams and national barnstormers.[21] In late June they encountered the Colored House of David team, which had won its last 33 games and 43 of 48 overall. Bismarck handed them 3 straight defeats.

When the Israelite House of David had passed through a few days earlier, the Bismarck players received some advice from John Tucker of the Davids' famed pepper team. The champion Mexican team, the La Junta Charros, were touring the U. S., headed for Bismarck. According to Tucker, "They have the greatest ball team on the road, bar none. Every player on the squad is a sensational fielder, they have worlds of hitting power and that pitching staff–well, there are few that compare to it." Tucker was right. The team was

46 and 2 in their last 48 games, and they won the first game in Bismarck, 3–0. The teams were tied in the second game when it was halted by rain. Eventually, Bismarck won that game and a subsequent game as well. When the Minnesota semipro champion team, the St. Cloud squad, visited North Dakota in August, the Bismarks swept them in three games.[22]

The rivalry with the all-white Jamestown team continued to sharpen. Paige won his 17th game of the season against them on July 7 (he had also lost 2 and tied 2), and the two teams met later in the month for an epic four-game series. On Saturday, July 20, the two teams met in Winnipeg, Manitoba, and Bismarck won 12–8. On Sunday they moved to Jamestown, where Paige started against the Jamestown ace, Ray Starr, formerly of the minor league Minneapolis Millers. Bismarck led 3–2 when the starters gave way in the fourth inning to Barney Morris and Ed Brady, and Bismarck eventually won the game 11–4. Jamestown had just installed floodlights in their park, so a Monday game was played at night, and the Jamestown pitcher Phil Schmidt won 9–6. Ray Starr, knowing that Paige would be starting the Tuesday game in Bismarck, asked to start for Jamestown. Paige told his team to score him one run and he would take care of the rest. Red Haley opened the fourth with a home run for Bismarck, and Paige won the 1–0 contest with a 3-hit shutout, striking out 15. The following week Bismarck shut out Jamestown twice. In the end, Bismarck won the seasonal series between the two teams 9 games to 3.[23]

The Bismarck squad, which had undergone many pitching changes and several key injuries to key players, came together as a team in the latter part of the season. Shutouts proliferated and winning margins increased. In five late-season tournaments Bismarck achieved a 16–1 record. The team peaked just as it prepared to travel to Wichita, which for the first time was serving as the host of the national semipro tournament. "Bismarck's recognized strength is no idle gossip this season," noted the hometown paper. "Manager Neil Churchill has gathered together the strongest lineup ever to represent the Capital City.... It is generally conceded that the team that defeats Bismarck will undoubtedly win the national title."[24] The team had come a long way from the blustery, cold days of May when one pitcher had to do almost everything. The Bismarcks won every team series it played that summer. The feat was "all the more remarkable," according to the local paper, "when it is remembered that during the first part of the season the team performed with practically a one-man mound staff. Satchel Paige carried a major share of the pitching duties until the middle of the season."[25]

The mighty Bismarck team closed out the regular season on August 11 by crushing the Twin City Colored Giants 21–6 in a high, blustery wind. It was the last time the home folks saw Satchel Paige pitch in the home uniform. In Bismarck's last at-bat the team batted from the opposite side of the plate, and when the Twin City team batted in the ninth Satchel Paige and his battery-mate, Barney Morris, took the field while all the other players except the first baseman remained in the dugout. The stunt cost two runs, but as the team ended its season with Satchel Paige on the mound, nearly alone, it was not too different from the way the season had begun. Bismarck won its last 12 games and 66 during the season, against 14 losses and four ties. Paige was responsible for nearly half of the victories.

The season was strong enough to make Bismarck one of the favorites in the Wichita tournament, which had accepted 32 teams from the 300 that had applied. Twenty state champions were represented. To ensure a solid performance in the series, Bismarck acquired a fifth Negro League pitcher, Chet Brewer of the Kansas City Monarchs, who had been Paige's chief antagonist in the *Denver Post* tournament the previous summer. The two had also met earlier in the 1935 season, battling to a scoreless 9-inning tie on June 8 and and a 2–0 Bismarck win on July 16. While Paige had relished the opportunity to play on the same side as white players when he began playing for Bismarck, by the time his team arrived at the 1935 national tournament it had begun to look like a Negro Leagues reunion. Several of its five Negro Leagues pitchers doubled as position players, and during the tournament there were always 4 or 5 black players on the field. Paige pitched in the first round of the tournament, striking out 16 as the team defeated the Monroe (Louisiana) Monarchs, a Negro traveling team, 6–4. In the second round they drew the local favorites, the Wichita Water team, state champions of Kansas. In the intense heat, Chet Brewer gave out during the seventh inning, and Paige finished the game. According to the Associated Press, "a great club of negro and white players from Bismarck trounced the Wichita Watermen, Kansas state champions, 8–4 here Sunday.... The great Paige fanned seven opposing batsmen during the two and two-thirds innings he was on the mound."[26] Quincy Trouppe belted a home run and two doubles in the first two games, leading Bismarck hitters. One newspaper reported that Paige was ill on the first day he pitched. "If Paige was sick when he struck out 16, I'd like to see him when he was in A-1 condition," the sportswriter commented.[27]

In the third round Bismarck faced the winner of the 1935 *Denver Post* tournament, the United Fuel of Denver team. Paige led his team to a 4–1 victory, and they became the team favored to win the tournament. Over 7000 fans jammed the ballpark to overflowing for each of Bismarck's games, insuring a generous purse to the eventual winners. After defeating Shelby, North Carolina, in the fourth round, the Bismarcks faced the Duncan, Oklahoma, team, the other undefeated club in the double elimination tournament. The front page of the *Bismarck Tribune* reported the result of this fifth round game: "Marching straight toward a national championship, a swashbuckling band of ball players from North Dakota's Capital City, Friday night put the dimmers on the last remaining title threat. Conquering the previously undefeated Duncan, Okla., club, the Bismarck crew chalked up its fifth straight tournament victory as ebony Satchel Paige turned in a masterful five-hit hurling feat and scored his third triumph."[28] His teammates got nine hits against the Duncan team, the Halliburton Cementers. Up to this point Paige had struck out 52 batters in 29⅔ innings.

In the sixth round Bismarck encountered the Omaha team, host of the 1934 national tournament. Although the Bismarck pitcher's name was not recorded, his team trounced Omaha 15–6, setting up the final round game between the two top teams, Bismarck and the once-defeated Halliburton Cementers. If Halliburton won, a subsequent playoff would be required; if Bismarck won, the tournament was over. Satchel Paige had rested for four days and sought his fourth tournament victory. Ten thousand fans packed into the stadium to watch the seventh-round game on Tuesday night, August 27. The Cementers started their ace, Augie Johns, who had pitched for the Detroit Tigers in 1926 and 1927. Halliburton scored one run in the first inning, but Johns held Bismarck scoreless until the seventh. With one run in and the bases loaded, Johns was sent to the showers, and Paige himself hit a two-run single off the relief pitcher. Bismarck scored two more in the eighth and won the game 5–2. Paige struck out 14, totaling 66 for the tournament.

The 1935 season was an interesting odyssey for Paige and his Bismarck teammates. There was some discussion about just how much credit Paige should receive for the remarkable season and the tournament that culminated it. Jack Copeland, the sports columnist for the *Wichita Beacon*, pointed out the contributions the entire team had made during the tournament: "There could be no denying that 'Satchel' had the stuff and was great on the mound, but he needed help and got plenty of it from his mates," observed Copeland. "Bismarck deserved to win the championship. They have a hustling ball club that refuses to give up and this despite a series of injuries and bad breaks which would have caused most clubs to give up the ship." He described the praise major league scouts had heaped on the tournament and predicted that the tournament's most promising young players would be signed to professional contracts.[29] What Copeland left unsaid was that the high drama of the tournament was generated by the play of Negro League players who would have already been starring in the major leagues if they had been white.

Copeland, writing from Wichita, could not have known the extent of the contribution Satchel Paige had made to get the Bismarck team to the tournament. His crucial role had been acknowledged by Bismarck sportswriters before the regular season ended. Interestingly, the Bismarck paper did not cite

Paige, perhaps the most quotable figure in the history of sport, even once during the season. The only Paige picture they published was taken a year earlier, and he wore a Crawfords uniform.[30] Of all the players on the team, black and white, however, the paper singled out Paige for frequent physical descriptions. Paige was frequently "dusky," "lanky," or "ebony." He was also a "dusky speedball sensation," a "dusky, raw-boned ace," an "ebony stalwart," and a "dusky wonderboy."

The generally sober sports page almost never referred to the humorous things Paige typically did on the ball field. The only extended description came in an account of the May 20 game when he relieved young Ben Anderson for four innings in a game Bismarck eventually won 14–5: "The dusky ace in his usual colorful style toyed with the Williston stickers, shooting an underhand ball and taking things easy."[31] The article did not note that their star pitcher had appeared in every game the team played up to that point, and the ever-astute Paige knew that with his comfortable lead he could save his arm. The paper also did not report the less than ideal playing conditions Paige endured in a climate of high winds and temperatures so cold they sometimes forced the cancellation of games in progress.

The Bismarck team never returned home after the Wichita tournament. They won three of four from the House of David in a Colorado exhibition and disbanded in Kansas City after playing there against the Monarchs.[32] The next time Paige would play a regular season with a white team was when he was signed by the Cleveland Indians 13 years later. The Capital Citians owner-manager, Neil Churchill, did return home with the three players who lived there. While the team had prospered, his car dealership had suffered from neglect, so Churchill decided to end his four-year managing career at the very best place–the top. The *Bismarck Tribune* understandably lavished praise on its favorite son, who, the paper said, "in four seasons brought baseball at the Capital City from an exceedingly low ebb to the pinnacle of the national semi-professional game.... A major share of the laurels [for the state championship] belong to the master mind behind the baseball enterprise–Neil O. Churchill." The returning Churchill embodied the triumph of the absent team members. In addition to his astute managerial skills on the field and his willingness to pull pitchers when they floundered, Churchill worked the phones and the telegraph endlessly to pull together a remarkable collection of athletic talent. He pursued Double Duty Radcliffe for nearly two months as the Negro League player attempted to extricate himself from his Brooklyn Eagles contract.

The *Bismarck Tribune*'s tribute to Churchill also included praise for team members. The article noted that shortstop Axel Leary and third baseman Joe Desiderato were likely to be signed by American Association teams. It noted that Satchel Paige, the "'Dizzy' Dean of the Negro pitching world," would join Chet Brewer and the rest of the Kansas City Monarchs for a winter tour of the south. "There is no doubt," the paper noted further, "but that Paige, who got his nickname while toting baggage at the depot in Chattanooga, had he been of a lighter hue, would have been grabbed up by the major league scouts long before the national tournament. As it was the dusky hurler received the unanimous choice of the tournament committee for the outstanding pitching award." Neil Churchill noted that a Texas team, the Centennials, which Bismarck had "humbled" 5–0, had defeated the Israelite House of David to win a major semipro tournament at Council Bluffs, Iowa: "This and the fact that several of the teams were backed by millionaire manufacturers with players on the payrolls who would ordinarily command high salaries in organized baseball, illustrated the brand of baseball that was played at Wichita, Churchill said."[33]

Satchel Paige returned to the Crawfords for the 1936 season, but he set his eyes on the *Denver Post* tournament once again. This time the team was put together by Gus Greenlee and his sometime ally Ray Doan. As a Denver sportswriter noted, Paige's team this time was "a club of his own race."[34] The Negro All-Stars, the account continued, were one of the finest teams ever assembled outside the major leagues, and it included his Pittsburgh Crawfords teammate Josh Gibson as well as Cool Papa Bell and a host of other players from four different Negro National League teams. The other tournament teams knew they had an opportunity to match their skills with top athletes, and Denver spectators knew they had never seen such a talented collection of ballplayers in any game. Fans attending the first game, noted *Denver Post* sports editor C.L. Parsons, "marveled at the speed of the Negro National All-Stars. A majority of the players are streamline, tall and rangy. It's undoubtedly the fastest team ever to appear in the tournament." After they defeated their first opponent 11–0, sportswriter Leonard Cahn enthused,

> It's true what they say about this All-Star team from the Negro National league. They have everything! These Brown Bombers from the big wheel of colored baseball ... are the cream in your coffee, the icing on your cake, the champagne in your cocktail. They're CLASS! They have pitching and plenty of it. They can hit that old apple. They hotfoot it around those bases like nobody's business and field their positions in tailor-made fashion. And what's more they have spirit. It's no misnomer when you call this team an all-star aggregation.[35]

Paige pitched the second-round game against the top Denver team, M. and O. Cigars. Since this game would be the first Paige had ever pitched in a Denver tournament in the daylight, the Cigarmen were confident they would have a better chance, because "all pitchers are faster at night."[36] The game drew the largest daytime crowd ever, 8600, but M. And O. lost 7–2. Although Paige was indeed less sharp than usual, giving up 8 hits and walking 3, he had developed a curveball unseen before in Denver. It baffled hitters who looked for his usual fastballs.

The tournament lacked the high drama of the 1934 duels between Paige and Chet Brewer, and attendance at the final game was only half the size of the crowds who had witnessed those battles two years earlier. Still, they cheered enthusiastically as Paige blanked the Enid, Oklahoma, Oilers 7–0 on two hits, striking out 18. Paige toyed with his opponents in the second inning:

> Capably coached by Josh Gibson, star catcher of the Crawfords, the elongated shuffling carefree hurler loaded the bases and no one would have given him one cent for his chances of getting the side out without several runs with the three heaviest hitters on the Oklahoma team coming to bat. Paige pulled a Chief Bender stunt. He looked towards the outfield and grinned. He pulled at his belt. He stretched and let go the ball across the plate. Not an Enid man saw home plate. The three heavy hitters, bemoaning either their bad luck or Paige's pitching, walked back to the bench — each a victim of Paige's fast ball and each having struck out.[37]

According to Walter Judge of the *Denver Post*, Paige was the "hero of the hour." In spite of extended fan discussion of which All-Star pitcher (Paige, Ray Brown, or Robert Griffith) was the best, the answer was simple for Judge: "There's only one Dizzy Dean and there's only one Satchel Paige, the Negro counterpart of Diz in many ways."[38] Paige was now 6–0 in *Denver Post* tournament play. In spite of the modest attendance at the final game, overall gate receipts were second only to 1934, and the first-place All-Stars divided nearly $5100 in prize money.

The 1936 tournament proved that the typical tournament participants could not compete with the best of the Negro Leagues, but some tournament promoters thought retired major leaguers could spin the ballpark's turnstiles and excite the crowds. Accordingly, Grover Cleveland Alexander showed up in 1937 for his third tournament, this time with the McVittie-Alexander club of Springfield, Illinois, and Rogers Hornsby, "the biggest name of the tournament," appeared with his Denver Bay Refiners team. Hornsby, 41, had just played his last major league game, with the St. Louis Browns, on July 20. Local stars on both teams were the big early news of the tournament, but the Negro All-Stars were back, this time with little fanfare at the beginning.

The team included infielders Pat Patterson, Sam Bankhead, Chester Williams, and "Showboat" Thomas; outfielders Cool Papa Bell, Clyde Spearman, and Red Parnell; and Cy Perkins was the regular catcher. The pitchers noted at the beginning of the tournament included LeRoy Matlock, Bob Griffith, and Chet Brewer. The team was known as the Trujillo All-Stars and named for its sponsor, the dictatorial leader of the Dominican Republic, who had lured Satchel Paige to leave the Crawfords again, this time for a very short, very lucrative, and utterly miserable season of tropical baseball. When their season finished in June the Negro Leagues barred the Trujillo players from league play, so the group was available for the Denver tournament. The team received little attention from the Denver press until it met Hornsby's Bay Refiners in the third round. Ten thousand fans jammed the park to see the local favorites lose 12–0. Robert Griffith, just 23 years old, fanned Hornsby three times. The All-Stars recorded four runs in the first inning before the first out, and "it almost required the services of the fire department to extinguish the Stars in subsequent innings," Leonard Cahn reported in the *Denver Post*.[39] It was Grover Cleveland Alexander's turn in the fifth round, when his McVittie team lost 12–1.

The tournament did not really catch fire until the sixth round, when Paige finally showed up. After a mysterious 12-day absence, he flew in from Chicago on Sunday morning with a tale about recovering lost wages from Trujillo and forgetting his baseball uniform. Clearly Paige was intending to pitch the seventh-round championship game on Monday evening, collect the $1000 share due the winning pitcher, and be on his way again. What Paige wanted was also what the tournament organizers also wanted, because a Paige start in the seventh game would sell tickets. In the Sunday afternoon sixth-round game the newly-arrived Paige watched his teammates defeat the Pampa, Texas, Oilers 10–1 behind the three-hit pitching of Bob Griffith. Paige was introduced to the 7000 fans before the game to prove he was really there and, of course, to promote attendance for the seventh-round game the next day.

After the game began, however, the long love affair between Paige's teams and the Denver fans evaporated. Although all the All-Star victories had been blowouts, the players continued to play with intensity and perhaps even cranked it up a notch as the tournament proceeded. In the first five games they had allowed a total of 2 runs and had struck out 59 in 45 innings. The Oilers pitcher, Soldier Sam Dailey, held the All-Stars scoreless in the first inning, and the crowd anticipated the first interesting battle of the tournament. Instead, the Oilers fell apart when the All-Stars batted in the second. Pat Patterson, the Trujillo third baseman, led off the inning with a single, and Chester Williams, his teammate, bounced a ball to the bag at second. Dewey Bondurant, the Oilers second baseman, arrived at the ball just as Patterson slid hard into the base, and the ball went flying. The Oilers gathered around second base, protesting interference, but Umpire Darnell called Patterson safe, and the Oiler manager, Fred Brickell, resumed the game under protest. The fans, too, according to the *Post*, were in a "belligerent mood." A ground-out and a sacrifice fly scored Patterson, but the Trujillos produced back-to-back singles with two out. Cool Papa Bell brought the two base runners home with an extra-base hit that he stretched into a triple by flying into third with spikes high, dislodging the ball from the glove of Sammy Hale, the Oilers third baseman, and launching what the *Post* called "the most serious incident in twenty-two years of tournament competition."

Hale came up furious, bleeding from cuts on his hands, and the two players started punching. His teammates congregated from the field and the nearby third base dugout while the Ciudad Trujillos "rolled out of their first-base dugout like oranges." The *Post* account continued, "Players on both squads grabbed bats and started swinging. Police and the umpires, Darnell, Everett Shelton and Bruce Lott, plunged into the embroglio and succeeded in separating the embattled players before serious injury could befall anyone. Quick barring of the entrances into the playing field by the police prevented spectators from rushing onto the diamond. The mixed crowd, while excited, was orderly." Hale and his teammate, the relief pitcher Mills, were taken off to have spike wounds treated, and the police ejected four Trujillos: first baseman Showboat Thomas, right fielder Spearman, manager George Scales, and Satchel Paige, who had waded into the melee swinging a bat. Bell stayed in the game, batting 2 for 5, but near the end he was injured so severely in another base path collision that he was unable to play for the rest of the tournament.[40]

The championship game seemed over before it started. After all, Paige was pitching. Yet the seventh game turned into the most exciting game of the tournament. Paige was overpowering for the first four innings, striking out 11 batters. But catcher Robert Palm (Cy Perkins was playing left field) committed three passed balls, apparently unable to keep track of the fastballs blurring past, and a fourth inning walk plus the Cementers' first hit scored the first run of the game. The Trujillos tied it up in the fifth and took a 4–3 lead into the eighth inning, but the Oilers rallied to score two, sending the fans into a frenzy, "yelling like Comanches and leaving their seats and up and down the aisles so excited they didn't care if the teams continued to play ball until daybreak or not." The Cementers tacked on one more in the ninth (Paige had been lifted for a pinch hitter), and the Trujillos' 6–4 defeat, after they had been listed as an 8-run favorite to win, was noted "as one of the epochal feats of Post tournament history." The *Post* published a large photo of ecstatic fans celebrating the Cementers' eighth-inning rally. Paige allowed just five hits and struck out 14, but he uncharacteristically struggled with his control, walking three, and the near-perfect Trujillo fielders made four errors.

The tournament was not over, however. Each team had lost one game, and one needed to lose two, even if it took the rest of the night. The Cementers seemed dazed by their unexpected victory, but the Trujillos reverted to form. Cy Perkins went back behind the plate, and the team's lefthanded ace, LeRoy Matlock, won his third game of the tournament, 11–1. As a gesture of mercy to the faithful fans, officials halted the game after 7 innings. No one protested. It was 1 A.M. The next day the Trujillos collected their nearly $5200 prize check, and Matlock, not Paige, received its $1000 slice reserved for the championship pitcher. After it was all over, the suggestion arose that the outcome of game seven was orchestrated, that the All-Stars preferred Matlock to receive the winning pitcher's bonus since he won three games to Paige's one.[41] Other factors were involved as well. Cool Papa Bell's replacement, Roy Parnell, let two balls go through his legs for extra bases. And the fracas the day before had not been forgotten.

The uneasy end of the 1937 tournament provides a closing parenthesis to this phase of Satchel Paige's interracial baseball life. Clearly, Paige's three appearances at the Denver tournament transformed the event and raised issues many people had never faced before. The superb athletic excellence of the Negro League players made a shambles of retired major leaguers' dreams of one more shot of glory, and it reminded both the spectators and the major league scouts that if these players' skin had been a different color, they would have been playing in Yankee Stadium in the real World Series instead of in Merchants Park in the Little World Series. A solid semipro team entering the *Denver Post* tournament in 1934, 1936, or 1937 was participating in the Depression-era equivalent of a baseball fantasy camp. Ordinary players had a chance to measure themselves against the very best.

What was the result of Satchel Paige's integrated and interracial play in the 1930s? In hundreds of individual communities and on the major stages of semipro tournaments, Americans in the Midwestern and Western United States were compelled to acknowledge that the best black players performed at the major league level. These events were significant for American society as well as for baseball. When the integration of baseball began beneath the major league level, it involved players, management, and fans from all races and all stations of life. The change of institutions, whether social or sporting ones, is as dependent on incremental, everyday achievements as it is on path breaking, watershed moments. We cannot explain how the eventual integration of major league baseball would have been different without the earlier experiences of Paige and others, but it would likely have begun even more slowly and have taken longer to accomplish.[42]

Although Paige was just one of countless athletes who played integrated baseball, his involvement was crucial. Because he was a highly skilled player eager to match himself against the most talented white opponents he could find, because he had a flair for the dramatic and the quotable phrase, and because his play with and against white athletes was more visible than anyone else's, Paige achieved a level of excellence that was impossible for even the most confirmed bigot to ignore. The inclusion he achieved may have been less than complete, but it was significant. Satchel Paige was the ultimate impact player, but the impact fell mostly on players younger than himself.

Although Paige played a significant role in making the integration of baseball an inescapable reality, the glacial rate of institutional change ate up the prime of his long career. Still, as he looked back on those years as he prepared *Maybe I'll Pitch Forever* for publication, he grasped their larger significance. Understanding that he was part of the process that eventually removed the color line from the major leagues, Paige commented as he described his play with the Bismarck team in the 1930s, "I'd cracked another little chink in Jim Crow." American sport and American society would never be the same.[43]

Notes

1. *Detroit Free Press*, Sept. 6, 1945, quoted in Paige, *Maybe I'll Pitch Forever: A Great Baseball Player Tells the Hilarious Story Behind the Legend* (Lincoln: University of Nebraska Press, 1993, reprint edition), 69.
2. Paige, 88. Paige made this comment while describing the first time he played for a white semipro team in Bismarck, N.D.
3. *Kansas City Call*, Apr. 17, 1931, 2-B. The article also laments, "Has the death of Rube Foster ended all possibilities of a successful western league? Our answer is that it looks very much that way."
4. Paige, 86, 88. See Mark Ribowsky, *Don't Look Back: Satchel Paige in the Shadows of Baseball* (Da Capo Press, 2000), 113–117, for a description of interracial play in North Dakota. Paige entered a complex situation where black players were shuffled in and out of several teams; Ribowsky points to gambling income as a powerful incentive for these moves. Whatever the motive, "a quiet integration was fomenting throughout the Dakotas," Ribowsky notes (113). The public and clandestine reasons for pursuing this practice benefited individual players from the Negro leagues because teams in the Dakotas were willing to pay up to double what they could earn on their original teams.
5. *Chicago Defender*, Aug. 19, 1933, 8; Sept. 9, 1933, 11.
6. Another House of David team, sponsored by the rival City of David colony in Benton Harbor, competed in the 1933 tournament, without guest players, and tied for fifth place.
7. *Kansas City Call*, Aug. 3, 1934, 6. Perhaps a bit nervously, the paper also reported that the House of David team might also import "another Negro hurler by the name of Jones from the famous Hilldale club of Darby, Pa.," but Paige was the only black pitcher employed by the House of David for the tournament.
8. *Denver Post*, Aug. 2, 1934, 21; Aug. 3, 1934, 27.
9. *Denver Post*, Aug. 4, 1934, 13.
10. *Denver Post*, Aug. 6, 1934, 16; Aug. 7, 1934, 21.
11. *Denver Post*, Aug. 9, 1934, 23.
12. *Denver Post*, Aug. 10, 1934, 33; Aug. 11, 1934, 13. The difference in the game was walks: Brewer issued four and Paige none.
13. *Denver Post*, Aug. 13, 1934, 16.
14. *Denver Post*, Aug. 14, 1934, 19. A few days later (August 23), the House of David, without Paige and Perkins, defeated the Monarchs in a 2–1 thriller in Colorado Springs. When the two teams met again in May 1935, the *Kansas City Call* reported that "The Monarchs have never forgiven the Bearded boys for putting one over on them and knocking them out of some real coin [at the 1934 Denver tournament]" (*Kansas City Call* Aug. 24, 1934, 6; May 3, 1935, 17).
15. *Kansas City Call*, June 21, 1935, 12.
16. Gaines was about to embark on a long career (1937–1951) on several Negro league teams; see Dick Clark and Larry Lester, eds., *The Negro Leagues Book* (Cleveland, Ohio: Society for American Baseball Research, 1994), 188.

17. *Bismarck Tribune*, May 6, 1935, 8; May 13, 1935, 8; May 29, 1935, 6; May 31, 1935, 8.
18. In Paige's early experiences with the team there were some tense moments caused by racial issues. In his memoir, Page describes a disagreement with his outfielders. When he scolded them for their ineptness they made racial slurs in response and refused to go back on the field the following inning. He struck out the side and then apologized to his outfielders. He had no further racial problems on the Bismarck team (Paige, 89). In his biography of Paige Mark Ribowsky identifies the event as the first game Paige pitched with the team in the fall of 1934 (115).
19. *Kansas City Call*, 21 June 1935, 12.
20. *Bismarck Tribune*, July 29, 1935, 6.
21. In June the top Bismarck hitters were batting .469 (Johnson), .392 (Trouppe), .333 (Haley), and .328 (Desiderato). Haley, along with Trouppe, was from the Negro leagues, Desiderato was a white player who had played for the All-Nations team, and Moose Johnson came from the Sioux City Cowboys of the Western League. The only thing that stood between Johnson and a major league career was his drinking habit. See Kyle McNary, "North Dakota Whips Big Leagues," Pitch Black Baseball (2001), www.pitchblackbaseball.com/northdakotabaseball.html, accessed July 5, 2006.
22. *Bismarck Tribune*, July 2, 1935, 8; July 13, 1935, 6; Aug. 5, 1935, 6.
23. *Bismarck Tribune*, Aug. 1, 1935, 8.
24. *Bismarck Tribune*, Aug. 6, 1935, 6.
25. *Bismarck Tribune*, Aug. 7, 1935, 8.
26. AP article published in the *Bismarck Tribune*, Aug. 19, 1935, 6.
27. Unnamed newspaper, quoted in the *Bismarck Tribune*, Aug. 20, 1935, 6.
28. *Bismarck Tribune*, Aug. 24, 1935, 1.
29. Quoted in *Bismarck Tribune*, Sept. 4, 1935, 6.
30. Shortly after the Wichita tournament, the *Kansas City Call*, which had reported extensively on Paige's career, published a large photograph of Paige in his Bismarck uniform to announce a game between the Monarchs and the Bismarck team on September 5 (*Kansas City Call*, Aug. 30, 1935, 6).
31. *Bismarck Tribune*, May 20 1935, 8.
32. According to the *Kansas City Call*, Monarchs fans had looked forward to watching the great Paige pitch in person. They were not disappointed. "Paige showed Wednesday night just why he is considered one of the world's best pitchers" as he struck out 15 Monarchs on the way to an 8–4 Bismarck victory over Chet Brewer and the Monarchs. When the game (and thus Paige's responsibility to the Bismarck team) was over, Paige immediately joined the Monarchs for a winter tour. Paige lost to a major league all-star team and its star pitchers, Dizzy and Paul Dean, 1–0. The all-stars' run was unearned. Later Paige and the Monarchs defeated Schoolboy Rowe, Charley Gehringer, and other major league stars 8–2 in Omaha (*KC Call*, Sept. 6, 1935, 12; Oct. 11, 1935, 6; Oct. 25, 1935, 11).
33. *Bismarck Tribune*, Sept. 11, 1935, 6.
34. *Denver Post*, July 30, 1936, 21. The paper noted that "Paige and virtually ever other member of the club would be in the big leagues if they were white."
35. *Denver Post*, July 31, 1936, 26; July 31, 1936, 27.
36. *Denver Post*, Aug. 2, 1936, 5:1. The article noted that in the daytime doubleheader Paige had played against the Israelite House of David the previous September, he had had more trouble than in the night games he pitched in the 1934 Denver tournament.
37. *Kansas City Call*, Aug. 14, 1936, 12.
38. *Denver Post*, Aug. 12, 1936, 19.
39. *Denver Post*, Aug. 5, 1937, 25.
40. *Denver Post*, Aug. 9, 1937, 18, 19.
41. In *Black Baseball's National Showcase: The East-West All-Star Game* (Lincoln: University of Nebraska Press, 2002), 99, Larry Lester documents these events and also notes that the tournament's organizers urged the Trujillos to pitch Paige in game seven in order to ensure a large crowd.
42. Jules Tygiel documents Paige's continued interracial play in the early 1940s, when he focused on putting together teams of black all-stars to play against major league all-stars. According to Tygiel, "In the 1940s the example of Satchel Paige, whose legend had spread

into the white community, offered the most compelling argument for the desegregation of the national pastime." See "Black Ball: The Jim Crow Years," in *Extra Bases: Reflections on Jackie Robinson, Race and Baseball History* (Lincoln: University of Nebraska Press, 2002), 67; originally published in *Total Baseball: Official Encyclopedia of Major League Baseball*, ed. John Thorn, Pete Palmer, and Michael Gershman, 7th ed. (Kingston, N.Y.: Total Sports Publishing, 2001).

43. Paige, 88. Paige's personal response to the difficult integration struggle that he participated in appears within and between the lines of his well-known comment about the decision by Will Harridge, the president of the American League, to ban Paige's hesitation pitch when he was a 42-year-old rookie on the Cleveland Indians. Paige's scorn and condescension sear the page as he describes the struggles of young, pampered white players to connect with his trick pitch: "It was pretty tough on those boys having to play against somebody like me. They hadn't had to get by like I'd had to. They'd had expensive coaches and guys like that to teach them how to throw. They didn't have to figure things out for themselves.

"They had those trainers to rub them down all the time. And they'd gotten plenty of rest between games. They hadn't had to come up with those trick pitches just to rest their arms and work out the tiredness. They never had to pitch every day for a month at a time or play the whole year round....

"So even if it wasn't in the rule book, he called my hesitation illegal. He didn't want to cause none of them kids who came up against me [had] any hardships" (Paige, 202).

6

"They're All Gonna Jump Like That": Paige as Personality

Rick Kenney and *Jesse Stringer*

Because Leroy Robert "Satchel" Paige played much of his career in Negro league baseball, in barnstorming games, and elsewhere, his record appears destined to remain forever incomplete. Black newspapers of the day were no better able to provide ongoing, full, and balanced coverage of Negro baseball than their white counterparts were able to for major league baseball. Some books assert that Paige won more than 30 games in a single season, whereas others report a more modest victory total of eight or 13 or so. By one report, he started 29 games in a single month, and Paige himself, in his 1993 autobiography *Maybe I'll Pitch Forever*, incorrectly recalled pitching a no-hitter and a shutout in different cities on the same day. But reliable accounts indicate that Paige did peak as a player in the 1930s, when he pitched for the Pittsburgh Crawfords, playing in the East-West All-Star Game twice, in 1934 and 1936.

Besides providing some narrative and statistical coverage of baseball, the black press, along with Negro league histories and biographies, have painted Paige as a personality of Ruthian proportions: every bit as colorful and quotable as the Babe, and no less proficient at baseball, albeit in separate but equal leagues. Today, Paige, who finally was allowed into major league baseball in his 40s, is often remembered as much for his advice on life and longevity, such as his admonitions "Don't look back; something might be gaining on you" and "Age is a question of mind over matter; if you don't mind, it don't matter."

In fact, an exposition of the remarks he uttered — or sometimes screamed — in the heat of battle, though lesser known, can help flesh out our understanding of the human near-deity that is Satchel Paige. Among his notable expressions was the pronouncement once when an umpire removed a baseball Paige was alleged to have scuffed, which caused its baffling movement: "You may as well throw 'em all out, 'cause they're all gonna jump like that." Such bravado, as well as bench jockeying, has long been part of baseball, of the interaction among players. With his sharpest barbs included in press accounts and other histories, however, Paige left a substantial legacy of what today is often described as *trash talking*. Although trash talking was common in sports long before the term was coined, considered in retrospect, Paige appears to have been one of its progenitors and the top trash-talker of his time.

Through a close reading of the archives of the *Pittsburgh Courier*, the hometown black newspaper of the Crawfords, supplemented by biographies and histories that included retellings of the legends of Satchel Paige, this chapter examines how local sportswriters constructed Paige not just as a pitcher without peer, but also as a powerful personality given to colorful boasting and nonverbal intimidation.

Method

This study is based on research of both primary and secondary sources: archived newspaper accounts; retellings of those accounts by Paige and by others about him in popular books; citations of those accounts in scholarly works, such as dissertations; and Paige's own recollections in his "as-told-to" autobiography. In addition, the primary sources represent newspaper articles found in a search of the archives of the *Pittsburgh Courier* during Paige's prime as a Crawfords pitcher, 1933–36. The *Courier,* a black newspaper that was established in 1907 and which peaked during World War II at a national circulation of more than 200,000, with 14 regional editions, according to Patrick Washburn's article on the black press's influence, was the "hometown" newspaper for the Pittsburgh Crawfords and the Homestead Grays of the Negro league. Accounts of Paige's exploits as a Negro League baseball star would likely also have peaked during this period.[1]

Sports writing in the *Courier* was not much different from — and certainly no worse than — that found in the more widely circulated mainstream press. Logical design and use of photography or informational graphics— including baseball box scores— let alone any methodical planning or "packaging" of the news— was yet a half-century in the future. Still, as Mark Ribowsky noted in his 1994 book *Don't Look Back: Satchel Paige in the Shadows*

Monarchs ace Satchel Paige getting ready for a game at Yankee Stadium.

of Baseball, to read the "wonderfully stilted period prose was like vespers to blacks who depended on [the *Courier*] for news of the black culture not available anywhere else. Young black men could read ... and dream." Furthermore, the newsroom was peopled by "young black journalists ... some of them open activists and some among them who believed that Negro ball could and should go its own way." The result: the *Courier* was "a marvelously chaotic bulletin board of diverse, even contentious black opinion."[2]

For numerous other reasons—among them production deadlines, limited resources, travel constraints, and problems securing lodging in other cities—*Courier* sports writers might have covered home games at Forbes Field in Pittsburgh but would not have had the financial support to follow the team on the road and file timely accounts of each game. Even at home games, however, sports writers of the day were relegated to distant press boxes and would not have been within earshot of the on-field verbal jousting that occurred during games. As exemplified by the purple prose of mainstream writers such as Grantland Rice, Westbrook Pegler, and Damon Runyon, beginning in the 1920s, sports journalism was more entertainment than information. Their hyperbole painted portraits of athletes larger than life. Mark Inabinett's (1994) *Grantland Rice and His Heroes: The Sportswriter as Mythmaker* describes how in the 1920s Rice created national heroes out of athletes such as Babe Ruth (baseball), Red Grange (football), and Jack Dempsey (boxing). Before the advent of televised sports events in the 1950s, audiences were unable to see these athletes and their heroics firsthand and were left to rely on the exaggerated accounts of games, matches, and bouts.

Further, sports writing in any American newspaper had not yet reached the level of sophistication that exists today. That is to say, writers of any color in the 1930s were not in the practice of traipsing into what passed for baseball clubhouses immediately after games and interviewing players to obtain telling quotes, as they routinely do today. Therefore, research expectations were low that any single *Courier* article would include the colorful quotations or anecdotes of the in-game banter for which Paige became known. Yet, about a quarter of the articles discovered did include such material. The body of *Courier* articles overall from 1933 to 1936 that reference Paige, though, is sufficient enough such that the researcher and even the casual reader can infer a great deal about Paige's personality.

Findings

A close reading of stories about Satchel Paige resulted in two main findings: one, that the black press of the day constructed Paige as a mythological, even religious, figure through literary devices of hyperbole, simile, and metaphor; and two, that although Paige is widely and well-remembered for his folksy advice about life and living, he was also skilled at spontaneous verbal sparring and repartee — early forms of trash talking — which may have served to intimidate opponents, motivate teammates, and entertain fans within earshot. This section cites both primary and secondary sources that render Paige as a colorfully discursive personality, both by description (the Larger-Than-Life Action Figure) and by quotation (the Trash Talker).

The Larger-Than-Life Action Figure

It is difficult to pinpoint when Paige's exploits first began to be reported in consistent patterns of hyperbole or when writers began to describe him metaphorically. Ribowsky (1994) noted that Leroy Page followed his brother John Jr. in changing the spelling of his last name as a way of differentiating themselves from their father. The timing of this is unclear; Ribowsky gives both the early 1930s and 1928–29 as the time when "per Satch's orders ... the name of 'Satchel Paige' began to creep" into the pages of the *Pittsburgh Courier*. Anyone reading those papers would see that other forms turned up for a number of years afterwards. But as Ribowsky noted, it is clear from Paige's pitching record and from press accounts that by the end of the 1929 season, he was a star.[3] He had made headlines for the first time anonymously in the *Chicago Defender* two years earlier after a June 27 game in which Paige, pitching for the Birmingham Black Barons, beaned three straight batters from the St. Louis Stars and was ejected. The headline read, "Near Riot at St. Louis When Donaldson Removes Pitcher." Paige appeared in the game account and box score only as "Satchell [sic]." His stature grew, however, and by summer's end he was the no. 3 starter and also the stopper. He finished with an 8–3 record, with 80 strikeouts and only 19 walks. Over the next two seasons, Paige was 23–15, and led the league in 1929 with 184 strikeouts in 196 innings.[4]

By June 1932, the front page of a *Courier* sports section was touting Paige as a "born showman" who "presided on the mound like a learned jurister on the bench." The entertainer image stuck. On July 1, 1933, the *Courier* again described Paige as an "elongated and consummate showman"; the metaphor and simile flowed from there: "whose whipcorded right arm rifles a ball plateward with the speed of a bullet, has as fast a ball as any ever uncorked in big league baseball." And in October that year, the *Courier*'s William G. Nunn called Paige "Satchell [sic] the mighty."[5]

The *Courier* reprinted an out-of-town newspaper article that capsulated the rare air of the altitude, both literally and figuratively, at which the *Denver Post* tournament was played in mid–August 1934. Within that one brief article, "the invincible" Paige's 2–1 victory for the House of David team over the Kansas City Monarchs was described as "the game of games, a standout of standouts" and "a titanic struggle": "And what a ballgame it was!" wrote Leonard Cahn of the *Post* in the article reprinted in the *Courier*. Paige "the colored Whizbang did not disappoint."[6]

The *Courier*'s own William G. Nunn topped that hyperbole in his article with these first three paragraphs about the East-West All-Star Game at Comiskey Park in Chicago.

> We saw a baseball epic unfold itself on this historic field.
> No diamond masterpiece was this game! No baseball classic! Those words are relegated into the limbo of forgotten things in describing the titanic struggle for supremacy....
> And Satchell [*sic*] Paige, pitching sensation of the Pittsburgh Crawfords, "stole the show."[7]

Having provided only the score up to this point, Nunn's story went on for another two paragraphs of purple prose that managed, finally, to eke out Paige's pitching line.

> [Paige] went on to give one of the greatest mound exhibitions modern baseball has ever seen as he twirled three more scoreless innings to enable the East to chalk up their first victory.
> Today's game was more than a classic! It was really and truly a diamond epic!
> The facts of the game will be covered by others. This article is a paean of praise to "the man who stole the show...."[8]

Dave Hawkins of the *Courier* called Paige the "Black Matthewson," referring to the great New York Giants pitcher Christy Matthewson. That comparison was made not only by the black press, however.[9] Dan Burley of the *Courier* had lifted a long passage written by Marvin McCarthy in the *Chicago Daily Times* about that East-West classic that included references to Paige as "Black Matty," "Black Matthewson," and "Black Magic"; "an African giant"; and "a master who knows he is a master." McCarthy, the Chicago writer, had described Paige's movements on the mound this way:

> He mounts the bag, faces third—turns a sorrowful, but burning eye toward the plate, nods a nod that Hitler would give his eye for—turns his gaze back to the runner on second—raises two bony arms high toward heaven, lets them sink slowly to his chest....
> Suddenly that long right arm shoots back and forward like a piston on a Century engine doing 90. All you can see is something like a thin line of pipe smoke. There's an explosion like a gun shot in the catcher's glove. "Strike wun," howls the dusky umpire.[10]

A postseason story that same year suggested that Paige could pitch a shutout virtually in his sleep. An article that appeared in the *Courier* without a byline asserted that after leaving Marion, N.C., the night of July 6, 1934, and driving 1,000 miles to Chicago for a game at 2 P.M., July 8, Paige pitched "the only game ... he ever won without remembering how it was done." Priding himself on being able to "review a game, re-tell how every batter was served, how many hits, how many runs he gave up — and when and where," Paige recalled after the game only "nodding in the dugout between innings."[11]

Such exploits and the colorful reporting of them in the black press helped serve the purpose of promoting black players such as Paige to level the playing field in hope of integrating baseball. Comparisons to white baseball players were part of the campaign rhetoric. The *Courier*'s Chester Washington likened Paige to the major leagues' greatest player of the era: "What Babe Ruth has meant to the Yankees and the American League, Leroy 'Satchel' Paige has meant to the Pittsburgh Crawfords and the National Association of Negro Baseball clubs." Implicit was Paige's draw at the gate, his entertainment value as "baseball's most nonchalant showman."[12]

There is evidence, however, that the *Courier* sought to balance Paige as personality against the magnitude of the game itself. Two brief articles in April that year were designed to both pressure and praise Paige. The first, a three-paragraph article, outlined the consequences should Paige not "decide to behave" and instead boycott the Crawfords' spring training. The brief noted that "the Craws, the league, and the press helped make Paige what he is today."[13] Still, Paige stayed away and spent the summer playing in Bismarck, N.D. Once he rejoined the team the next season, he was restored to status, described in the *Courier* the next year as "one of the greatest speedball pitchers in the game" and "the highest-salaried colored baseball player in the country."[14] The *Courier* refers to Paige as "a prime 'gate' attraction" when the Crawfords set to travel to Cleveland to play a doubleheader against the Newark club.[15] William G. Nunn of the *Courier* described Paige as "the magnet which has drawn thousands and thousands of people through the turnstiles."[16]

Other *Courier* stories about Paige in 1936 included biblical references and elevated him to a messiah of sorts. Having returned to the Pittsburgh Crawfords, he is called in one lead paragraph "long, lean Leroy 'Satchel' Paige, prodigal son of the clan" by writer Chester Washington on August 22, 1936. His celestial origins were metaphorically implied in the passage "Paige is another one of those stars that fell on Alabama." By now, it was as if Paige had been elevated to black baseball's savior. One game preview merited a large headline that refers to the "*coming of* Satchell [sic] Paige" (italics added for emphasis), who was expected to draw a record crowd at an out-of-town game.[17]

In all, the (mostly black) press accounts of the day helped construct Paige as a player of almost mythic performance and proportion, and subsequent histories, biographies and two autobiographies have reinforced and expanded that notion, painting him as larger than life. No doubt, Paige's pitching merited such description since hyperbole and promotion were the coin of the realm in sports writing then. Equally entertaining to consider is how Paige has been constructed as a trash talker.

The Trash Talker

Conceiving of Paige as a trash-talking athlete is not a new notion. Sportswriters of the time and subsequent biographers and researchers—and Paige himself in full candor—have long noted his penchant for jawing at other players and sometimes even his own. Paige as "the Trash Talker" is a construct that emerges from analysis of his speech quoted in the black press; his speech recalled by other players; his own recollection of incidents; and in anecdotes cited by scholars and other writers. Although the terms *trash talk*, *trash talking* and *trash talkers* had yet to be coined in the 1930s, the *Courier*'s coverage acknowledged Paige's powerful personality as well as the discursive Paige, which it had helped construct and promote. He towered over black baseball physically and perhaps psychically, as Nunn of the *Courier* wrote: "Long, tall, dark, and with that 'color' which sets him apart from the mob."[18]

The phrase *trash talk* came into popular use in the mid–1980s, according to David G. LoConto and Tori J. Roth in their 2005 article "Mead and the Art of Trash Talking: I Got Your Gesture Right Here." A few writers and scholars referred to Paige as one of its earliest practitioners. Sportswriter Gregory Clay asserted in his article, "Robinson was the politically correct choice to break baseball's color line," that Paige was not only a pitcher of renown but also "50 years ahead of his time in another arena—trash-talking": "Paige, the ever-clever philosopher, talked trash on the field, lots of it to intimidate batters, much like today's NBA players. 'Hey, you can't hit Satchel's "troubleball" today,' he would boast about one of his patented pitches."[19] In the article, "East-West game was jewel of Negro Leagues," sportswriter Marcus Hayes explained why "whites mingled among African-Americans" at Negro leagues games: not only "to worship some of the best to ever play the game" but also because they "would hear of how Paige would talk a little trash, then back it up with his wicked pitches."[20] Robert Story noted in the *Pittsburgh Post-Gazette* that "Paige ... was pure theater. A pioneer of 'trash talk' who sauntered up to the mound (often after arriving late), the Kansas City Monarchs' leading hurler badgered his foils with words and jest as unanswerable as his nicknamed pitches, the 'hesitation' and the 'bat-dodger,' to name a few."[21]

In his as-told-to autobiography, *Maybe I'll Pitch Forever* (1993), Paige did not reveal himself to be much of a trash-talker until reaching his peak in the mid–1930s. He appears to have mellowed by the time he reached the major leagues. Writing in Chapter 1 about his rookie season there in 1948, Paige described a memorable game against the Chicago White Sox in which he pitched his first shutout. Despite his euphoria over the accomplishment, he was restrained as he walked off the field: "I felt like yelling, 'When I throw, nobody hits.' But I didn't. I just laughed and pushed my way toward the locker room." Instead, he seemed content to let the others do the talking. Recalling his famous relief stint in the 1934 East-West All-Star Game, he recounted fan reaction to his arrival on the field: "I headed for the mound.... That's when I heard this guy in the stands. 'It's Paige. Good-bye ball game.' He didn't know how right he was." Of course, Paige retired nine of the 10 batters he faced in the final three innings and earned the win.[22]

Paige's own first admission of "riding" other players came when he described his experience playing for the first time with white ballplayers in 1934, after he had left the Pittsburgh Crawfords to play for a Bismarck, North Dakota, team owned by a car dealer named Neil Churchill. Resenting his treatment there under Jim Crow laws that left him and his wife living in an old railroad freight car that had been converted into a bunkhouse for work gangs, Paige admitted, "it ate at me," he said in *Maybe I'll Pitch Forever*. Paige wanted everyone to know he was upset with his situation and so he made sure his teammates were aware that he did not appreciate the way they played for him.

> I even got to riding some of my own ballplayers and those white boys didn't take too good to that.... I really lit into three of them. They were my outfielders and the inning before they'd let so many fly balls drop around them that the club we were playing scored a run....
> "If you did that in the league I play in you'd get booted fast," I yelled at them. They just walked away, but one of them muttered "dirty nigger" or something that sounded like that.
> "I'm sure clean enough to be playing with your kind," I said. "Where would you high and mighty boys be without me?"[23]

Paige subsequently took the mound in the next half-inning only to find that the three outfielders stayed in the dugout and refused to take their positions on the field. When no one was able to persuade them to play ball, Paige decided he had something to prove and the motivation to do it. So he struck out the side, just to show them who was boss. In retelling that story, Holway added this admission from Paige: "'from then on, I decided I'd be the quiet guy, like I'd always been before.'"[24]

During an exhibition in the winter of 1934–35, having heard Dizzy Dean on a pregame radio show disrespect his curveball, Paige launched a verbal volley as Dean came to bat.

> "Hear say you goin' around tellin' people I ain't got a curve?" I yelled at him. Diz just grinned. "Well, then, you tell me what this is."

> I threw him a curve. He swung and missed.... I threw him two more curves and he missed both of them, too, striking out.
> "How's that for a guy who ain't got a curve ball?" I asked.[25]

Paige appeared to have enjoyed the verbal sparring — or what he called "high old times." After hearing repeatedly what a tough out Pepper Martin was, Paige became interested in testing that idea. He wanted to know who Martin was so he could show him who was tougher. When Martin came up to hit against Satchel he challenged him with his best stuff.

> "They tell me you can hit," I said. He just grinned. "Then hit this." I threw my bee ball.
> I only fired that bee ball three times when Mr. Martin struck out and went back to the dugout.[26]

Reporting in the *Courier*, Washington provided this firsthand account of the trash-talking Paige:

> As if to prove that one of the over-anxious Duck batters was "all wet" about his idea that he could get a hit, Satchel yelled to Catcher Josh Gibson: "What one'll you have now, Baby?"
> Gibson dropped two fingers below his mitt.
> "Well, there you are," Satch called as he shot it across the pan.
> The bewildered batter reached in vain, like a man reaching for the moon, and the ball whizzed by.
> "How'd you like that one, Sweets?" Satch smiled.
> Again the crowd roared ... and of course, the Crawfords won.[27]

In his autobiography, Paige elaborated on that incident as he faced the number four hitter for the Ducks. The player boasted to all who would listen to him that Satchel could not throw a ball past him.

> "That tall, skinny guy ain't got enough meat to blow a fast ball by me," he saying. "You just watch it. I'll send it clear out of the country...."
> "Pump it in here, buddy, and watch it go," he yelled at me, still playing the big man.
> I just laughed and called down to Josh Gibson, "What one'll you have now, Baby?"
> "Fast ball, low and on the outside corner," Josh called back.
> That's just where I put it, but bigmouth still swing and missed for strike one.[28]

Paige continued to fire two more strikes right down the middle as Gibson asked for, and on three straight pitches he had his strikeout.

Another incident in 1936, during a game against Philadelphia, illustrated how Paige's excitability could get the best of him and still be manifest in his triumphant cockiness. Leading by four runs, Paige finally lost his shutout in the eighth on his own fielding error. After a bunt loaded the bases with none out, Judy Johnson decided to try to mess with Paige's concentration.

The Stars, Judy told him, "were hoping you'd get in this spot — them people in Philly been sayin' you nothing but a big pop off." Now Satch got serious. He exploded third-strike fastballs by Roy Parnell and Dewey Creacy. But his old nemesis, Boojum Wilson, drove in two runs with a single. Now holding a one-run lead, Satch faced the dreaded Turkey Stearns [sic] in the game's climactic moment. Satch kicked high, reared back, and scorched one Trouble Ball after another. Turkey never had a chance; he went down on three swings.

"Now go back to Philadelphia and tell 'em about that!" a BB-eyed Satch screamed into the Philly dugout as he walked from the hill.[29]

Not all of Paige's trash talking was actual speech. One example of an attempt to intimidate opponents through nonverbal communication was the act of calling all of his fielders to come and sit in the infield, sending a message that he intended to strike out the side. Apparently this was repeated often enough to merit its own signal between Paige and his fielders, which once proved comical. In his 1991 book John B. Holway wrote:

> The signal was to turn to them and wipe his forehead. One hot day he took off his cap and absentmindedly wiped the sweat, then turned to face the batter, who hit a soft fly to short right field. Paige turned to see his fielders all sitting down laughing uproariously while the batter legged it around the bases for a homer.[30]

One particular anecdote that illustrates the trash-talking Paige perhaps best reveals his playfulness as well his talent. In what was arguably Paige's greatest performance — his July 4, 1934, no-hitter — Buck Leonard, a Negro leagues rookie who would become a baseball Hall of Famer, had come to bat and, astonished at how the ball moved at an alarming velocity, asked the umpire to remove it from the game on the grounds it was defective. The umpire declined, and Leonard struck out. After two more batters repeated the plea, the umpire finally tossed the ball out. Then Paige uttered his ultimate boast, which must have deflated all hopes that day: "'You may as well throw 'em all out,' he bellowed, 'cause they're all gonna jump like that.'"[31]

Any or all of these trash-talking speech events may well be apocryphal. Or they all might be true. The truth possibly lies somewhere between those extremes. Whatever the case, the retelling of some of these incidents has served to complement the character construct of Satchel Paige that has emerged over the past 75 years.

Discussion

By all accounts, Satchel Paige was a great baseball pitcher and a proficient trash talker. How might we conceive that those two aspects of his persona interacted or were intertwined? What significance does trash talking hold in the context of athletic achievement of a star of Paige's magnitude? In short, what ends could Paige have hoped to achieve through trash talk, and did he achieve them?

Sociology of Trash Talking

The origins of trash talking in the athletic arena are difficult to trace, partly because sports journalism was in its infancy when organized professional sport began in the mid–1800s. It would be almost a century before sportswriters moved beyond mere armchair quarterbacking and began covering the games and their participants closely enough to have noticed the social dynamic that in the mid–1980s would flourish and come to be known as "trash talking, talking smack, woofin', crackin' or jackin'."[32]

One sociological study of trash talking from a Meadian perspective — that is to say, a look at how the self is structured — determined from interviews with athletes that the successful trash talker becomes so by first becoming adept at taking on the attitudes of many individuals (a generalized other) toward himself or herself and governs himself or herself accordingly. "By learning to speak, gesture, and play in 'appropriate' ways, the individual is brought into line with the accepted symbolized roles and rules of the social process."[33] The self of the athlete develops through trash talking as he or she takes and understands the role and perceptions of the other and takes the necessary action to gain the desired effect; in the vernacular of sports, the trash talker gets into an opponent's head. As Paul Taylor noted in a seminal *Sports Illustrated* article in 1992, "when you get right down to it, intimidation is the ultimate goal of almost every smack talker."[34]

Herbert D. Simons in a 2003 article argued that the institutionalized penalties in sports for behaviors such as trash talking seemed out of proportion to their importance since they provide little competitive advantage. Further, he argued, the undue attention given these behaviors is racially motivated, as they reflect African-American cultural norms in conflict with white mainstream norms. This conflict arises in part, Simons contended, because whites fail to recognize the strong performance motivation that African-Americans bring to sports.[35] Trash talking is an extension of African-American verbal aggressiveness, which for African-American athletes serves, among other functions, not as a prelude to violence, but as a substitute for fighting.

Sociology of Black Baseball

Neil Lanctot, in his unpublished 2002 doctoral dissertation, *Helping the Race Morally and Financially: Black Professional Baseball and the Philadelphia Stars, 1933–1952*, noted that since Negro league baseball games functioned simultaneously as a social and athletic event, they attracted a broad cross-section of the population — presenting the ballpark on game days as a microcosm of the black community. Class divisions were reflected in the black bourgeoisie's growing concern that fan misconduct would thwart racial progress. The *Chicago Defender*, a black newspaper, rebuked "unruly fans" and accused "players of inciting them with bush league histrionics."[36] Regardless, there seems to be no anecdotal evidence that trash talking catalyzed unruly fans or players. In fact, the most notable account of a brawl, actually characterized as a riot, occurred after a disputed call led a player to assault an umpire, which set off fighting on the field involving most players and 500 fans.[37]

No doubt, Paige had his detractors among fans and players, but they had to give him his due because of his immense talent. Many of the criticisms of his on-field persona, in fact, seemed to derive from what Judy Johnson referred to as his popping off at the mouth. It is difficult to imagine that Paige needed to psych himself up by talking trash. His particular brand of trash talk, as we now know it, was rather mild, featuring assertions and admonitions meant to spread the news of his superior talent, which by the mid–1930s was already well-established and well-publicized. The possible intended effects, then, need to be viewed in hindsight as perhaps having simply been twofold: to get into his opponents' heads and to entertain fans. Paige, the *Courier*'s Washington noted, "thrives on the roar of the crowd, rises to the greatest heights under the most 'pressure' and stars when the stands are banked with the masses of cheering humanity."[38] The entertainment value of Paige's trash talk helped bring African-Americans back to games while enticing as many white fans as possible — thus increasing the chances that he and other Negro league players might be discovered, appreciated, and allowed into the major leagues. Clay, however, suggested that Paige's discursive strategy worked against him. Paige's talking trash, "plus his deeply rooted black cultural roots, hurt his chances of being the Jackie Robinson of major league baseball." Clay asserted, "Robinson was the politically correct choice to break baseball's color line."[39] It is certainly worth noting that by the time he did reach the majors in 1948 as the first African-American pitcher in the American League, he had mellowed considerably; as noted earlier, when he first realized he had achieved success on the full national stage with his first major-league shutout, he refrained from shouting it from the mountaintop.

Conclusion

Limitations of the Study

This study — and all scholarship of athletes in antiquity — might be enhanced by better attention to period documentation: the close reading of the record represented in historical accounts of newspapers and radio and television broadcasts. Given the interest in the sociological phenomenon of trash talking in sports, it may serve future scholars to go back deep into all archives of sports journalism to discover the roots of such discursive practices and how they were conveyed.

In no way does this study demean or detract from the fuller, richer story of Satchel Paige — or from the efforts of sportswriters and scholars who have sought to capture Paige's essence. Read with the perspective of time and the march of professionalism in journalism since the 1930s, the *Courier*'s coverage still rings as both entertaining and informative. Its hyperbolic prose is little different from that of Grantland Rice and other notable writers of the era from the sports sections of mainstream papers. And these stories were not without their own sophisticated analysis. The *Courier*'s Nunn concluded his classic description of the 1934 East-West Game by quoting John Henry "Pop" Lloyd's aphorism, "Remember what I told you last year. You can't beat unbeatable pitching."[40] More than a clever turn of phrase, Lloyd's — and by extension, Nunn's — assessment reflected an emergent trend toward informative, objective journalism, even in the sports pages.

Silent Satch?

Satchel Paige may well have been all things to all baseball fans of his era — at least those who bothered to follow his career and maybe even go to watch him pitch: pitching great and showman nonpareil. Even the incomplete records of the Negro leagues are bursting with proof of his achievements, and his longevity in reaching the major leagues remains a miracle unmatched half a century later. Had he remained reticent all his career, a sphinx on the mound, a silent enigma to batters, sportswriters, and fans, he likely would have been no less a ballplayer. Standing on his accomplishments alone, he remains the Larger-Than-Life Action Figure. Whether he would have become the personality, the celebrity he is remembered as today, without having been cocky and outspoken, will have to remain a matter of debate. There is no doubt, however, that Paige the Trash Talker constitutes a colorful character worthy of our attention and study in the context of contemporary competitive athletics, in which woofin', crackin', and smackin' are increasingly a part of the games people play.

Notes

1. Patrick Washburn, "The Black Press: Homefront Clout Hits a Peak in World War II," *American Journalism* 12: 359–66.
2. Mark Ribowsky, *Don't Look Back: Satchel Paige in the Shadows of Baseball* (New York: Da Capo Press, 1994), 58, 69, 88.

3. Ribowsky, 27, 57.
4. Ribowsky, 57.
5. Ribowsky, 92, 96, 97.
6. Leonard Cahn, "Satch Wins 3 in Five Days in Big Denver Tourney," *Pittsburgh Courier*, 18 August 1934, 4.
7. William G. Nunn, "'Satch' Stops 'Big Bad Men' of West Team," *Pittsburgh Courier*, 1 September 1934, 4.
8. *Ibid.*
9. Dave Hawkins, "Satchell to Oppose Jones in Stadium," *Pittsburgh Courier*, 29 September 1934, 5.
10. Dan Burley, "Looking Back at the East-West Classic in Chi.," *Pittsburgh Courier*, 8 September 1934, 4.
11. "1934 Was Satchell's Biggest Year," *Pittsburgh Courier*, 17 November 1934, 4.
12. Chester Washington, "Satchell Has Been 'Babe' to Colored Baseball," *Pittsburgh Courier*, 12 January 1935, 5.
13. "Satchell Must Join Camp or Be Ousted," *Pittsburgh Courier*, 13 April 1935, 5.
14. "Paige to Aid Craws Pennant Chances," *Pittsburgh Courier*, 25 April 1936, 4.
15. "Cleveland All Excited over Coming of Satchell Paige and the Craws," *Pittsburgh Courier*, 13 June 1936, 4.
16. William G. Nunn, ""Satchel Is Magnet at E-W Game," *Pittsburgh Courier*, 29 August 1936, 6.
17. "Cleveland All Excited."
18. Nunn, 1936.
19. Gregory Clay, "Robinson Was the Politically Correct Choice to Break Baseball's Color Line," *Knight Ridder/Tribune News Service*, 12 April 1997.
20. Marcus Hayes, "East-West Game Was Jewel of Negro Leagues," *Philadelphia Daily News*, 7 July 1996.
21. Robert Story, "A Museum of Their Own," *Pittsburgh Post-Gazette*, 10 July 1997.
22. Leroy Paige and David Lipman, *Maybe I'll Pitch Forever* (Lincoln: University of Nebraska Press, 1993), 11, 82.
23. *Ibid.*, 89.
24. John B. Holway, *Josh and Satch: The Life and Times of Josh Gibson and Satchel Paige* (Westport, Conn.: Meckler, 1999), 77.
25. Paige and Lipman, 91–92.
26. *Ibid.*, 93.
27. Chester L. Washington, "Satchel's Back in Town," *Pittsburgh Courier*, 9 May 1936, 4.
28. Paige and Lipman, 111–112.
29. Ribowsky, 143.
30. Holway, 77.
31. Ribowsky, 100.
32. David G. LoConto and Tori J. Roth, "Mead and the Art of Trash Talking: I Got Your Gesture Right Here," *Sociological Spectrum* 25 (March-April 2005): 215–230.
33. *Ibid.*, 218–219.
34. Paul Taylor, "Crackin', Jackin', Woofin' and Smackin'," *Sports Illustrated* 77: 82–86.
35. Herbert D. Simon, "Race and Penalized Sports Behaviors," *International Review for the Sociology of Sport* 38 (1): 5–22.
36. Ribowsky, 69.
37. Holway.
38. Washington, "Satchell has been 'Babe,'" 5.
39. Clay, 1.
40. Nunn, 1934, 4.

7

Satchel Paige and Hap Dumont: The Dynamic Duo of the National Baseball Congress Tournament

Travis Larsen

Within the vast history of baseball, there are times when the stars align and perfect relationships and teams are born out of circumstances. Such is the case with the relationship between Leroy "Satchel" Paige and Raymond "Hap" Dumont, arguably two of the greatest showmen ever to participate in or promote the game of baseball. Had an inadvertent match not caused the fire that destroyed Island Park on Ackerman Island in Wichita, Kansas, after the 1934 season, leaving the Kansas State semi-professional baseball tournament without a home, the tournament's promoter, Dumont, would never have conceived the idea to establish a national semipro baseball tournament in Wichita. By formulating a plan to promote a national semipro tournament, Dumont hoped to convince the Wichita city council to fund a new ballpark. Dumont's argument prevailed, and with the help of the Works Progress Administration (WPA), the city of Wichita constructed Lawrence Stadium (now Lawrence-Dumont Stadium) near Payne's Pasture by the Arkansas River. The new ballpark was completed and ready to go for the 1934 National Baseball Congress's Kansas State semiprofessional baseball tournament.

Bismarck, North Dakota, team wins the National Baseball Congress tournament. Top row, from left to right: Hilton Smith, Red Haley, Barney Morris, Satchel Paige, Moose Johnson, Quincy Trouppe, and Double Duty Radcliffe; front row: Joe Desiderato, ? Leary, owner Neil Churchill, ? Oberholzer, ? Hendee.

With construction well underway, Dumont planned for the first, but hopefully not the last, National Semipro Baseball Congress (NBC) national tournament in 1935. Dumont's plan for establishing a successful tournament revolved around enticing a big name star to come to Wichita and participate in the inaugural tournament. With all of the major league baseball players still playing in middle to late August, Dumont turned his attention to the biggest name not competing in the American or National Leagues, Leroy "Satchel" Paige. Paige left the Negro National league's Pittsburgh Crawfords in mid-season and the lanky hurler headed west to play with the Bismarck, North Dakota, Corwin-Churchill semipro baseball team, just as he did in 1933 and 1934.

To entice Paige and the rest of his teammates to Wichita, Dumont needed a dynamic proposal. The most common story told about Dumont's proposal was that the enigmatic NBC honcho offered Paige $1,000 dollars to bring the Bismarck team to Wichita to play. However, in Mark Ribowsky's Satchel Paige biography, *Don't Look Back: Satchel Paige in the Shadows of Baseball*, the author states that the entire team was guaranteed $1,000 dollars per victory.[1] The truth about the guaranteed money probably lies somewhere in between. It was well known in many baseball circles that Paige commanded a $250 appearance fee, and Dumont probably figured that the pitcher would appear four times in the tournament, thus establishing the $1,000 dollar benchmark for his appearance.[2] The $7,000 dollars that Ribowsky mentions was not guaranteed money, but rather the winner's purse for capturing the national title. This winner's purse was split equally among Paige's teammates. As for Satchel Paige's compensation, the "official" history, as used on the National Baseball Congress's Web site, is that Dumont offered Paige $1,000 to bring the team to Wichita to play in the tournament.

Dumont did not stop with Paige and his integrated Bismarck team. The imaginative promoter invited a Native American team from Wewoka, Oklahoma, and a Japanese-American team from Stockton, California, not to mention four other teams that consisted entirely of African American baseball players. These teams were the Texas Centennials of Dallas, Texas, the Ft. Scott Blackhawks of Kansas, the Memphis Red Sox of the Negro National League and the Monroe (Louisiana) Monarchs.[3] For the first NBC national tournament Dumont came up with an eclectic assortment of 32 teams from 24 states. Dumont even had a team that was comprised of nine brothers (the Stanzal Brothers), who came in from Waukegan, Illinois, to participate in the tournament.

An air of excitement filled the coffee shops and diners of downtown Wichita in anticipation of the first national tournament held in the United States.[4] *Wichita Eagle* sportswriter Pete Lightner wrote:

> By Sunday, teams will be arriving for the national semi-pro tourney. Some of the teams have booked games en route to help absorb the expense. It takes plenty of money to get those teams here. The tournament headquarters estimate that each team will spend at least a thousand and in some cases considerably more to get here and live while here.[5]

The Bismarck team piled into two cars, a Chrysler Airflow and a Plymouth Sedan, supplied by team owner Neil Churchill, who owned an automobile dealership in Bismarck. The team then headed south. Along the way, the team "barnstormed" through the Midwest, picking up games to pay for their expenses. One of these games occurred 60 miles from Wichita, in McPherson, Kansas. *The McPherson Daily Republic* reported:

> Satchel hadn't been used and the fans were yelling for him to take the mound. In the final inning he accommodated the spectators. He walked to the mound after waving his outfielders to the bench. He struck out the first two batters, and then sent his infielders to the bench. The final out came when Britt rapped one down the center of the field, Paige snagged the ball and chased down Britt before he reached first. Bismarck defeated the Dickey Oilers 14–0.[6]

The showmanship of Paige and the notoriety of his playing ability, not to mention the press coverage, delighted Dumont. Pete Lightner wrote in the *Wichita Eagle*:

The tournament has been planned to give everyone a fair chance and to satisfy the visitors that Wichita is a good place to come back to. The tournament may be a permanent fixture here if it's successful from a financial standpoint. Frankly, it will have the highest expenses of any sports event put on here in many a season. All the national sporting goods houses and magazines are supporting the event. It would mean a vast amount of publicity for Wichita to have it here each year. That's what the plans are right now.[7]

Paige echoed many of Lightner's sentiments when his Bismarck team arrived in Wichita. Paige commented years later to author David Lipman, "You never saw anything like Wichita. That whole town was baseball crazy, and lots of them were crazy about Ol' Satch. They'd heard of him, and you better believe it."[8]

When the Bismarck team finally showed up in Wichita, they carried with them a twelve game winning streak and a season-long record of sixty-six wins, fourteen losses, and four ties. However, when Neil Churchill went to secure the team's reservations at a local hotel, he found the desk clerk and the manager less than star-struck. The hotel refused to give rooms to the six African American ballplayers on Bismarck's squad. Satchel and Ted "Double-Duty" Radcliffe had been through Wichita before and knew where to look for lodging for the six black players left without accommodations. Even though Churchill was greatly embarrassed, Radcliffe laughed about it later and said, "Churchill thought we were mad. He didn't know we preferred to stay there. There were roomin' houses all over the country where we stayed. That was our family. Since you couldn't bring white girls into them hotels, you had to have a room, man. We stayed in this place for three dollars a night and got two home-cooked meals. We didn't need no hotel."[9]

The overt racism did not end with the team's living accommodations. When many of the opposing managers realized that Paige and Radcliffe were among the players for the Bismarck squad, they tried to have them barred from the tournament. Satchel commented,

> They wanted me out because I was too good. A real big fight got going, with the fans wanting me to play and lots of the managers saying I was really a major leaguer and they couldn't match me with any of their white boys. They figured keeping me out would even the games up. It might even up those games, but it sure would hurt the gate. And semi-pro or not, that gate was a mighty big thing. Anyway, the fans wouldn't have it. So I stayed for the tournament.[10]

If the fans would not allow the opposition's managers to expel Paige, then Dumont certainly would not allow his star attraction to be run out of town. Dumont's naiveté, coupled with a lack of pure baseball experience, may have led the inimitable promoter to overlook the social and competitive issues that surrounded the inclusion of Paige and Radcliffe. While Dumont should have known the social ramifications that would have followed allowing any African American baseball players to compete in the tournament, it is less likely he knew of the complications that would have followed the duo's participation in the tournament. Regardless, Dumont was not going to be detoured from making a profit, even at the expense of the teams who were complaining about Paige and Radcliffe, who were the main attractions.

While Dumont counted on Paige to draw in huge numbers of people, he did not necessarily favor Paige's team. Rather, the promoter made the Chicago Sheridans the favorites, by sheer guessing many observers later commented. Perhaps another theory could be that Dumont knew that by seeding Paige's team lower it would leave the impression that the field was stronger than it really was. Another possible scenario could be that Dumont and his baseball advisers did not want to make the road to the championship easy for the Corwin-Churchills, instead thinking that by making the games a little more competitive because of the lower seeding, more fans would turn out for the tournament. No one could really testify to Dumont's thought process in those days, except for the fact that the wily promoter wanted to give the fans a show and make a profit at the same time. However, *Wichita Eagle* sports columnist Lightner and many others were unapologetic in their support for Paige and Bismarck. Lightner wrote, "They say that Paige will bring victory to any club he pitches for. He's the greatest colored pitcher in the country and perhaps the greatest regardless of race. He can't pitch every day, but he's no bush leaguer."[11]

Paige took the mound for Bismarck on August 14 against the Stanzal Brothers. Many of the Bismarck fans crowded into that city's Prince Hotel to get game updates via telegraph. However, Paige struggled early and the team allowed two unearned runs on third basemen Joe Desiderato's uncharacteristic throwing error. Paige then fell into his normal groove, but by the seventh inning Bismarck trailed 3–2. Then the team rallied for four runs and came away with a 6–4 victory. Julius Stanzal of the Stanzal Brothers remarked, "Paige was incredible. All I can remember is the catcher, Radcliffe, having to put a piece of steak in his glove so Paige wouldn't take his whole hand off."[12]

In the second game of the tournament, Chet Brewer, whom Bismarck picked up in Kansas City before the tournament, started on the mound. In the sixth inning, and only leading by one run, Brewer walked the bases loaded. Paige came on in relief and struck out the side to end the threat. Bismarck cruised to an 8–4 victory.[13]

The Wichita Watermen were Bismarck's next opponents. Satchel drove in two runs in what ended up being a 4–1 win. Game four came against a team from Shelby, North Carolina. Bismarck, behind Brewer's two-hitter, defeated the North Carolinians 7–1. The next game however would be the team's greatest challenge as they faced the Duncan, Oklahoma, Cementers.[14]

Up to this point in the tournament the Cementers were the best offensive squad; they averaged 13 runs a game. To play it safe, Churchill sent Paige to the hill for the start. Paige, in customary form, shut down the hard-hitting Oklahomans. When the Kansas dust had settled, Paige ended up with sixteen strikeouts, and a 3–1 victory. To make the championship game, Bismarck needed to defeat the Omaha V-8's, which they did by a final score of 15–6.[15]

The championship game was scheduled for two days after the Omaha game, giving Paige three days of rest between his last start and the title game. Due to the double elimination rules of the tournament, Bismarck faced off against the Duncan Cementers once again. A well-rested Paige shut the Cementers down, giving up only two runs and striking out fourteen batters. He also helped his own cause by driving two runs in for the 5–2 victory and the first NBC national championship.[16]

The individual honors also came Paige's way for his tremendous performance during the two-and-a-half week tournament. For his record-breaking sixty strikeouts and four wins the twenty-nine year old pitcher was named tournament most valuable player, and its outstanding pitcher. Paige's sixty strikeouts for a tournament is still a record he holds as of 2006. Through the years Satchel claimed that the Bismarck Corwin-Churchills were perhaps the greatest team ever. He may have been right, as many other people involved with baseball at the time thought so. For example, after the tournament concluded Dumont approached Quincy Trouppe, the African American outfielder of Bismarck, and told him, "Boys, I was talking to a couple of scouts yesterday at the ballpark. What do you suppose one of them said to me? This one scout said he would recommend paying each of you boys $100,000 to play ball if you were white." Of course, all were banned from competing in major league baseball because of their color of skin, but their talent was unmistakable.[17]

The tournament finished with over 50,000 fans attending over a two-and-a-half week span. Hap Dumont declared it a rousing financial success, making money even after paying Satchel Paige his $1,000 appearance fee and all of the shares to the other teams in the tournament. The NBC national tournament was scheduled for 1936, but outside influences prevented Dumont from inviting any integrated or African American teams. The 1936 tournament saw Honus Wagner named as high commissioner of semipro baseball (he had served in a similar capacity the year before). Wagner and tournament advisers George Sisler, native Kansan Fred Clarke, Ty Cobb, and Tris Speaker declared that integrated teams would be excluded from that year's tournament.[18] Wagner, Cobb, and Speaker, men who were not known for their tolerance of African Americans, certainly did not want to promote "black" baseball, hence their exclusion. The aforementioned men advised Dumont on baseball matters, as the promoter admittedly knew little about the intricacies of the game. Clarke, Wagner, Sisler, Speaker, and Cobb also lent an air of credibility to the tournament, and Dumont felt that they would help sell tickets if the games were a bust. All-black teams would be accepted in future years, but that would be up to individual member states that were part of the National Baseball Congress to decide. From 1936 on, the winners of the state or regional tournaments were granted entry into the national tournament, with Hap Dumont and his associates picking and choosing teams to round out the field.[19]

In subsequent years, Dumont would entice Paige back to Wichita to make celebrity appearances at the NBC tournament. In 1960, Satchel actually joined the Wichita Weller Indians baseball club for the NBC tournament to pitch once again. On the 25th anniversary of his appearance for Bismarck, North Dakota, in the 1935 tournament, Paige pitched well enough to get the win for the Wichita Weller Indians. While Paige did not dominate the hitters as he did in the 1935 tournament, he certainly gave the fans a show by breaking out his legendary arsenal of pitches such as the bat dodger and the hesitation pitch, just as Dumont and likely Paige himself hoped he would. Paige proved to be no mere sideshow, as his performance proved.[20]

Many things happened in the professional lives of both Dumont and Paige after their glorious run together in the 1935 tournament, up until Paige made his last appearance at Lawrence Stadium. Paige would eventually make it to the major leagues and pitch for the Cleveland Indians, St. Louis Browns, and the Kansas City A's. Dumont turned the NBC semipro baseball tournament into the greatest show on earth not held under a big top, running every August and continuing to this day.

Dumont's promotions became notorious in baseball circles such as his attempt to stage a baseball game without any lights and the introduction of the fluorescent orange ball that he sold through his National Baseball Congress organization. Dumont did not stop at playing baseball in the dark; the promoter also tried to change the rules of baseball by allowing the batter to run to either first or third base in an exhibition game. Needless to say this created mass confusion and the idea was scrapped after its initial run. Dumont's schemes also had some enduring impact on the game of baseball, as he introduced the designated hitter rule into the tournament in the early 1940s. Dumont also brought in a female umpire and used a deaf-mute umpire to officiate the tournament in its initial years. Paige was likely amused by Dumont's ideas, and even admired the Wichitan's showmanship. Both men were often imitated, but never duplicated, and Dumont and Paige truly were characters of a game gone by.

Without Paige and his celebrity status, it is arguable whether the inaugural NBC tournament would have been as successful as it was. When Dumont biographer Bob Broeg asked Paige about Wichita and Hap Dumont in 1980, the elderly pitcher replied, "The mostest man." Both men were the "mostest" indeed.

Notes

1. Mark Ribowsky, *Don't Look Back: Satchel Paige in the Shadows of Baseball* (New York: Simon and Schuster, 1994), 131.
2. Bob Broeg, *Baseball's Barnum: Ray "Hap" Dumont and the National Baseball Congress* (Wichita, Kansas: The Center for Entrepreneurship at Wichita State University, 1989), 43.
3. Broeg, 43.
4. A national semipro tournament had been bandied about in the past by promoters in New York City, Chicago, and San Francisco to no avail.
5. Broeg, 43.
6. Kyle McNary, "Satchel Stages a Show," North Dakota Baseball History/Pitch Black Negro League site, 2000–01, http://www.pitchblackbaseball.com/northdakotabaseball.html (accessed October 19, 2005).
7. Broeg, 43.
8. David Lipman and Leroy (Satchel) Paige, *Maybe I'll Pitch Forever* (New York: Grove Press, Inc., 1963), 84.
9. Ribowsky, 129–130.
10. Lipman and Paige, 84–85.
11. Broeg, 43.
12. McNary.
13. *Ibid*.
14. *Ibid*.
15. *Ibid*.
16. *Ibid*.
17. *Ibid*.
18. Associated Press, "Tris Speaker Is Named Chairman of Semi-Pro Body," *Chicago Daily Tribune*, December 26, 1937, B2.
19. Associated Press, "Negro Semi-Pro Teams Eligible in U.S. Tourney," *Chicago Daily Tribune*, January 6, 1937, B5.
20. Bob Overaker, "Just Thinking It Over," *Wichita Eagle*, August 24, 1960, 2B.

Part II

The Kansas City Monarchs

8

The Monarchs: A Brief History of the Franchise

Michael Harkness-Roberto and *Leslie A. Heaphy*

To understand the significance of the Kansas City Monarchs requires one to go back to one man in particular, J. Leslie Wilkinson. In 1912, Wilkinson along with J.E. Gaul organized the All Nations team, which was an amalgamation of players from all racial and ethnic backgrounds, including a woman, whom he promoted as "Carrie Nation," to play second base.[1] The All Nations team undoubtedly had the most complete racial mix of any team in baseball history.[2] This newly formed team traveled all over the Midwest in a Pullman coach in which the team could eat and sleep. The scene resembled a traveling circus, as the team traveled with a wrestling squad and an orchestra. At each destination, the group would play a baseball game, give a dance and hold a wrestling match. Wilkinson even managed to bring portable seating and canvas fences. To add to the oddity that was the All Nations, the players were also members of the band. This traveling extravaganza attracted large crowds, but it was soon apparent that the group also had some extremely talented ball players.[3] The team defeated Rube Foster's Chicago American Giants in 1915 and 1917, and won two consecutive games and three out of four from the 1916 black world champion Indianapolis ABCs.[4]

The start of World War I brought the gradual end of the All Nations, which was a common occurrence of many independent ball clubs with players leaving by means of war conscription. With one third of the team off to the battlefront, the team disbanded in 1918 despite finishing 34–1. Many of the players joined the American Giants or left to join other semipro teams.

Wilkinson reorganized the team in 1919 for a short season and then moved the team from Des Moines, Iowa, to Kansas City. Kansas City was known for its tradition of vivacious black baseball dating back to the semipro Kansas City Maroons in 1890 and to Wall's Laundry Grays in 1897, sponsored by Chinese laundryman Quong Fong. However, this team was more known for brawling than for their play on the ball field.[5] J.W. Jenkins of Jenkins Music Company also organized a team in 1897. In line with this heritage Wilkinson reorganized his team again in 1920, opening the door for their illustrious tenure in the Negro National League.

When Rube Foster organized the NNL, he initially attempted to do so with the input of Wilkinson. Communication did not go well, given the racial tensions of the time, despite Wilkinson later being viewed as a powerful and respected ally to black baseball. Foster instead chose Dr. Howard Smith, superintendent of Kansas City's black hospital, to form a team. However, Smith had no baseball experience and lacked the financial clout to support a league entry. Most importantly, he lacked a lease to play baseball in a suitable stadium, whereas Wilkinson possessed a lease to American Association Park. With such financial power, Foster was forced to work with Wilkinson, which in retrospect turned out to be a brilliant alliance.[6]

Wilkinson enjoyed a long tenure in the black leagues, earning the respect and admiration of those who worked with him. Wilkinson was also well liked by the African American community because he treated them with respect and dealt with them fairly.[7] Being that Wilkinson was the only white owner in the NNL, he was able to create financial deals with white businessmen for leasing stadiums and booking exhibitions that might not have been possible had he been black. The Monarchs often paid public tribute to Wilkinson during his ownership.[8]

With the new league forthcoming the owners quickly adopted a constitution for the newly created National Association of Colored Professional Base Ball Clubs and the Negro National League, which was followed by trading players to create parity in the league. Foster's dream of creating a league forced him to trade future Hall of Famer Oscar Charleston from the American Giants to the Indianapolis ABCs, which drew the ire of fans. Foster also sent pitcher Richard Whitworth to the Detroit Stars, while Kansas City received Jose Mendez, a former great pitcher who played shortstop in 1920, and the great John Donaldson from Detroit. Outfielder Jimmie Lyons was shipped from the St. Louis Giants to Detroit.[9] With players being traded from team to team, fans disliked the frenzied state of player movement because it made it hard to follow their favorites. However, Foster answered these complaints with an altruistic retort: "only in uniform strength is permanent success."[10]

The birth of the league also drew the indignation of the players because it eliminated the opportunity to make more money by jumping from team to team. This common practice of jumping eliminated any form of trust between players and managers, so the league was a practical way of eliminating a denigrating factor in professional baseball. Organization and solidity would bring revenue into the stadiums, consequently producing elevated player earnings and giving players the incentive to develop their skills knowing that there would be a future in the game.[11]

The first Kansas City team was an amalgamation of core players from Wilkinson's All Nations team, and players recruited at the recommendations of John McGraw and Casey Stengel, owner of the New York Giants and manager of the New York Yankees, respectively. The two major-leaguers told Wilkinson of a former army team at Fort Huachuca, Arizona, from the 25th Infantry Unit which included future Hall of Famer Wilber "Bullet Joe" Rogan.[12] Upon the organization of the team, players wanted the team to be called the Kansas City Browns. However, star pitcher John Donaldson suggested the Kansas City Monarchs, exemplified by the later *Kansas City Call* headline naming the club "Monarchs of All They Survey."[13]

The team would enjoy success from the start of the league. In their first season under manager Jose Mendez the Monarchs finished in a tie for second place with a record of 41–29. Under Mendez's leadership in 1921 the Monarchs again finished in second place with a 50–31 record. After Sam Crawford took over as manager in 1922 the

Posing for the cameras is one of the anchors of the Monarchs staff, Bullet Joe Rogan.

Kansas City players could still finish no better than second place at 46–33. The Monarchs' fortunes improved in 1923 when they captured the first of three Negro League pennants from 1923 to 1925. Jose Mendez came back to lead the Monarchs in winning the initial Negro World Series against future Hall-of-Famer Judy Johnson's Hilldale team of the Eastern Colored League, 5 games to 4, in 1924. In a losing effort, Johnson led both teams in hitting with a .341 average with seven extra-base hits. The teams met once again in 1925, after the Monarchs defeated the St. Louis Stars 4–3.[14] This time the Monarchs were not as fortunate, as they lost to the Hilldale Giants 5–1 in the series.

The Monarchs came in to Philadelphia for the first game of the 1924 Series hoping to play better on the road than they had during the season. While going 34–7 at home, the Monarchs were only 21–15 on the road. As a club they hit .313 to top all teams in the Negro Leagues and beat the Chicago American Giants by four games to take the crown and earn a trip to play Hilldale. Bullet Rogan led a dominating pitching staff with 16 wins while William Bell finished at 10–2.[15]

In 1925 the Monarchs again returned to the World Series only to lose this time to the Hilldale club. Part of the trouble for the Monarchs rested on the fact that they were without the services of Bullet Rogan and Dink Mothell for the series. Mothell was the club's leading hitter coming in to the end of the season.[16]

The Monarchs finished first in 1926 under manager Rogan but lost in the playoffs to the American Giants. The Monarchs played well in 1927, finishing second to the Chicago American Giants. They finished second in 1928 as well, this time falling short to the St. Louis Stars. Rogan led the Monarchs to their final pennant in the 1920s with a first place finish in 1929, though no World Series was played that year with the leagues in decline and Foster no longer there to provide leadership. The Monarchs beat out the Cuban Stars in the final games of the season, winning a double header 4–3 and 4–0 before capturing the final contest 14–10 in a hitter's game. After winning the NNL the Monarchs played a three game series with the Mexican champion San Luis Potosis. They won the first game 9–3, the second 6–0, and the final game was an 11–0 romp. William Bell got the victory in the first while Army Cooper shut them out in the second and Chet Brewer tossed a 4-hit shutout in the final contest. In 1930 the Monarchs came in third in their final league season for a while. They finished behind both Detroit and St. Louis.[17]

From 1931 to 1937, the Monarchs were not a member of any league, and instead played independent ball. This departure can be attributed to Wilkinson's losing large amounts of money during the Great Depression, as a result withdrawing the team from league play in the summer of 1930.[18] The team could earn more barnstorming without the expenses of belonging to a league. In 1932, with the large drawing power of the Monarchs no longer a constant revenue producer, the Negro National League would exist in name only. Wilkinson and the Monarchs had little to lose, as they were able to play 100+ games against white teams. Wilkinson had one other advantage when he added a portable lighting system for his club, enabling the playing of night games; he was heralded as the "father of night baseball." Thomas Edison is historically credited with such an invention in 1880, as two teams from Boston department stores played in Hull, Massachusetts. Nevertheless, the event was really an exhibition of electricity, not baseball.[19]

In the course of their run as an independent club, the Monarchs enjoyed success in eighteen states and two foreign countries (Canada and Mexico). They also played in front of large crowds, with an even mix of white and black fans. Racial tensions seemingly lessened during the 1930s, as the Great Depression did not discriminate as to whom it affected. In 1934, the Monarchs, "one of the best baseball clubs in America, regardless of race," were invited to play in the *Denver Post* tournament, dubbed as the "little World Series of the West."[20] The eighteen-team tournament culminated with the title game pitting the Monarchs against the Satchel Paige–led House of David, with Paige winning 2–1 in front of a raucous crowd of eleven thousand. The victory for the House of David also captured the club a prize of $7,500, the reward for winning the tournament.[21] Paige, who was "loaned" to David promoter Ray Doan, was voted most popular player by winning a tournament record three games in five days, striking out 44 in 28 innings, which included 23 consecutive scoreless innings.[22]

From 1932 to 1937 Thomas Y. Baird, partner to J.L. Wilkinson, served as the booking manager for both the Monarchs and the House of David. Benjamin Franklin Purnell established the Israelite House of David, a religious community, in Benton Harbor, Michigan, in 1903. The purpose of this colony was to gather the twelve lost tribes of Israel for the "Ingathering," to await the Millennium and be counted among the lucky few that would inherit the earth. As part of their pious identity, members did not shave their beards or cut their hair. Members also followed a healthy lifestyle that included a strict vegetarian diet and rigorous physical exercise, with baseball viewed as an effective means to satisfy one of these demands. The House of David baseball team began in 1912 after a group of the colony boys had played some local Benton Harbor teams and had won. The team soon began working out with the Benton Harbor Speed Boys, a semipro team, and was soon beating local factory-sponsored teams in western Michigan. The team later branched out to play Rube Foster's Chicago American Giants and to tour the east coast.[23]

With Baird serving both clubs the House of David leased the Monarchs' lighting plant for at least the first half of each summer. Wilkinson's brother Lee and his nephew Dwight traveled with the House of David as mechanics for the lighting system. Once Wilkinson and Baird had saved enough money from renting the lighting system to the team, they would start the Monarchs' season.[24]

Often the Monarchs and the House of David traveled together over the last two months of summer. The Monarchs would play through an area first, defeating all the local teams that they met. A few days later, the House of David would play the same teams and again defeat the local talent. The Monarchs and the House of David would then return to these small towns together and would play each other in a well-attended championship game, including the aforementioned summer in which Alexander pitched against Paige.[25]

Looking for a large revenue-producing crowd, the Monarchs began a forty-day tour of Canada and Mexico, teaming up with the House of David. A local sportswriter in Winnipeg, Canada, reported on a game won by the Monarchs, stating, "The exhibition of baseball the House of David and the Kansas City Monarchs dished up may never be equaled again. You don't see many games that go eleven innings with errorless ball, and a pitcher knocking at baseball's hall of fame."[26]

In addition to their Canadian tour the Monarchs went to Mexico in late October 1932 for twenty scheduled games against the best teams that country had to offer. Bullet Joe Rogan came back from pitching for semipro clubs to join his teammates on the trip. Wilkinson also added Turkey Stearnes to the lineup to bolster the offensive power of the Monarchs. In the first eleven games local papers reported the Monarchs won 9 and lost only two, one to the Aztecas and one to the Gallos.[27]

In 1933 the Monarchs continued their barnstorming even though the other owners pressed Wilkinson to rejoin the league. They played all over the Western states and into Canada as they successfully operated in the black while the NNL teams could not seem to get out of the red.

During the 1936 season the Monarchs played in Canada and out West during the middle of the summer. They played a series of games in Wyoming and Montana against teams such as the Caspers, East Helena, Missoula and the Kelloggs before going on to Spokane and taking two from the local nine. With Harry Else doing all the catching the Monarch pitchers got good run support and fine fielding from the whole team. Fans came out in large numbers to see the famous Monarchs come in to town.[28]

After the team barnstormed for the next couple of years, owners in the Western states banded together in 1937 to form the Negro American League. Wilkinson followed their lead and served as either vice-president or treasurer, as the Monarchs began their first year as a league member in nearly six years.[29] However, further bickering over player contracts and jumping created the same problems that had doomed preceding leagues.

The Monarchs won the first-half pennant, followed by a victorious playoff series against Chicago in 1937 under the steady hand of Andy Cooper. No World Series was played, but the Homestead Grays, champions of the NNL, played a postseason series with a team composed of Kansas City and Chicago players. The Monarchs won the NAL pennant in 1938 and 1939, defeating the St. Louis Stars 3 games to 2 in the postseason series in 1939. The series was originally supposed to be seven games but parks could not be secured for the final two games and the teams agreed to a five game championship. The first two games were played in Oklahoma and the last three in St. Louis.[30]

They continued their success with pennant victories in 1940–42, defeating the Homestead Grays in four straight games in the 1942 Negro World Series. Andy Cooper led the Monarchs to five first place finishes while he managed from 1937 through 1941. In 1940 the local papers claimed the Monarchs had a 112–39 record. In 1942 former catcher Frank Duncan led them to another first place finish and then to World Series victory. Satchel Paige was credited as the winning pitcher in three of the four games.[31] This series was the first played since 1927, due in part to the new financial stability from rising attendance at games. Wilkinson brilliantly used patriotism as a viable excuse for fans to attend games while many of the major leaguers were away at war. Throughout the war, the Monarchs drew larger gates than any other team in the league, including routinely outdrawing the white Kansas City Blues, the farm team of the ever-dominant New York Yankees.[32]

After three unsuccessful years due in part to many players' leaving for the battlefront, the postwar Monarchs again returned to prominence in 1946, winning the NAL pennant but losing the World Series to the Newark Eagles 4 games to 3. In 1947 Duncan managed his final year with the Monarchs and led them to a second place finish. In 1948, the Monarchs finished with the second-half best record, but were defeated by the Birmingham Black Barons 4 games to 3 in a playoff for the pennant. The Monarchs lost the first contest 5–4 in 11 innings and the second 6–5 in 10 innings. The teams came in to the playoff series fairly evenly matched though the Monarchs appeared to hold a slight edge in power and speed.[33]

From 1949 through 1951 the Monarchs under the tutelage of Buck O'Neil finished first, though no World Series was played any of those years.[34] The color line had been broken in major league baseball three years earlier, causing many Negro Leaguers to leave for larger contracts and the opportunity to play in the big leagues. For example, in 1949 the Monarchs lost the heavy hitting of Bob Thurman and the defensive skills of Earl Taborn to the Minors.

The years 1952 and 1954 saw the Monarchs finish with losing records though they did finish first in 1953. O'Neil continued to be at the helm for

the Monarchs through 1955, when he relinquished the reins to Jelly Taylor and the team was sold to Ted Rasberry. Rasberry also owned a basketball team called the New York Satellites. The Monarchs continued their success in 1955 by winning the first-half pennant. Taylor had a rebuilding job in 1956 after Tom Baird sold a number of players away before relinquishing control of the team. When the Monarchs finally closed their doors following the 1960 season they had won seventeen pennants and two World Series while providing fans all over America, Canada and even Mexico with quality baseball.

The Monarchs enjoyed a long tenure during the years when baseball in America was segregated. Their success can be chalked up no only to their owners, Tom Baird and J. Leslie Wilkinson, but also to the many stars who dotted the roster of the Monarchs. No star served the Monarchs better than the great Satchel Paige, who brought in the crowds every time he stepped on to the diamond; but Paige was not alone in leading the Monarchs. Fellow pitcher and Hall of Famer Hilton Smith often came on to pitch, finishing the games Paige started when he left to go pitch for another club. Smith pitched for the Monarchs from 1936 to 1948, and during those twelve years he won twenty or more games each season. He was voted by the fans to six consecutive East-West games from 1937 to 1942 and played for seven pennant winning teams in Kansas City.

Kansas City was blessed over the years with twenty Hall of Fame players and 131 players who played in the East-West games between 1934 and 1960. Twenty-one Monarchs also played in the major leagues and an even

Hall of Famer Hilton Smith getting ready to face the opposition. Smith often came in to games after Paige had pitched the opening innings.

Opposite: Kansas City first baseman Buck O'Neil shows off his skills in the field.

greater number in the white minor leagues after Jackie Robinson integrated the modern game in 1947.

For thirty-five years, the Monarchs served as a key communal institution for African Americans in Kansas City. As was written in the *Kansas City Call*, "There is nothing in Kansas City that brings the two races closer together than the Monarch ball games."[35] A collective buzz was created among all followers of the team, regardless of the time of year. The well-traveled Monarchs also created frenzy outside of Kansas City, being recognized by many sportswriters as one of the best teams in the country. Owners welcomed the team with open arms, respecting their great ability to draw large crowds and the ensuing revenue that followed. A comment made by a Kansas City sportswriter summed up the contribution of the team outside of just playing a game and producing revenue by writing, "From a sociological point of view, the Monarchs have done more than any other single agent to break the damnable outrage of prejudice that exists in this city. White fans, the thinking class at least, can not have watched the orderly crowds at Association Park and not concede that we are humans at least, and worthy of consideration as such."[36]

Notes

1. Bill Drake, *Kansas City Call*, 27 July 1928.
2. Robert Peterson, *Only the Ball Was White* (New York: Oxford University Press, 1970), 70–72.
3. Janet Bruce, *The Kansas City Monarchs: Champions of Black Baseball* (Lawrence: University Press of Kansas, 1985), 15.
4. *The Chicago Defender*, 17 September 1917.
5. *Kansas City Call*, 15 December 1922.
6. Janet Bruce, 18.
7. John B. Holway, *Black Ball Stars, Negro League Pioneers* (Westport, Conn.: Meckler, 1988), 20.
8. The *Kansas City Call*, 7 September 1928.
9. Robert Peterson, 84.
10. *The Chicago Defender*, 27 December 1919.
11. Janet Bruce, 20–21.
12. *Kansas City Star*, 11 October 1920.
13. Janet Bruce, 21.
14. Robert Peterson, 237, 257–62; statistics from NoirTech Research Inc.
15. Larry Lester, *Baseball's First Colored World Series* (Jefferson, N.C.: McFarland, 2006), 35, 39, 42–43.
16. Frank A. Young, "1925 World Series Was Won by Hilldale Club," *Chicago Defender*, 12 September 1942 (reprint of story from 1925).
17. "Kansas City Nears League Title," *Chicago Defender*, 9 July 1927, 9; "Kansas City Holds League Lead," *Chicago Defender*, 24 August 1929, 8; "K C Monarchs Downs Cuban-Mexican Team," *Chicago Defender*, 12 October 1929, 8; Dick Clark and Larry Lester, *The Negro Leagues Book* (Cleveland: SABR, 1994), 160.
18. *Kansas City Call*, 17 April 1931.
19. "K. C. Monarchs Team Reorganized," *Chicago Defender*, 4 July 1931, 8; Janet Bruce, 68–69.
20. *Pittsburgh Courier*, 21 April 1934.

21. *Pittsburgh Courier*, 18 August 1934; *Pittsburgh Courier*, 18 August 1934.
22. Joel Hawkins and Terry Bertolino, *Images of America: The House of David Baseball Team* (Chicago: Arcadia Publishing, 2000), 46.
23. Robert S. Fogarty, *The Righteous Remnant: The House of David* (Kent, Ohio: Kent State University Press, 1981), 121.
24. Janet Bruce, *The Kansas City Monarchs: Champions of Black Baseball* (Lawrence: University of Kansas Press, 1985), 73.
25. The *Pittsburgh Courier*, 18 April 1936.
26. Janet Bruce, 77.
27. *Chicago Defender,* 27 August, 29 October and 19 November 1932.
28. "K. C. Monarchs Shine on Tour of Canada and West," *Chicago Defender*, 11 July 1936, 14.
29. Janet Bruce, 91.
30. "Too Much Pitching and Heavy Hitting," *Chicago Defender*, 9 September 1939, 8.
31. "Reno Larks Play Kansas City Monarchs 3 Games," *Reno Evening Gazette*, 25 July 1941, 15; Robert Peterson, 272–77.
32. Janet Bruce, 100–104; *Chicago Defender*, 19 September 1942, 23.
33. "Playoff Series Moves to Kansas City Sept. 19, 20," *Chicago Defender*, 18 September 1948, 11.
34. Robert Peterson, 282–88.
35. *Kansas City Call*, 3 June 1922.
36. Janet Bruce, 130; *Kansas City Call*, 27 October 1922.

9

J.L. Wilkinson: "Only the Stars Come Out at Night"

Larry Lester

Accomplishments have no color.

— Leontyne Price

> Star light, star bright,
> I wish to see a game tonite.
> I wish I may, I wish I might.
> But only Wilkie has the light!
> Star light, star bright,
> Black players overcome their forbidden plight.
> They wish they may, They wish they might.
> That Only the Stars Come Out at Night.

Before 1930, few working baseball fans envisioned their favorite stars showcasing their talents under the darkness of a summer moon. The first known lighting experiment was exposed on August 27, 1910, when inventor George F. Cahill brought his patented system to Chicago's new White Sox Park. Unsuccessful at first, he convinced a doubting Charlie Comiskey to showcase his twenty 137,000-candlepower lights for a game between the local Logan Square and Rogers Park teams.[1] The game drew over 20,000 fans but failed to appeal to the conservative major league owners, who apparently believed with poet Paul Laurence Dunbar that

> Night is for Sorrow and Dawn is for Joy
> Chasing the Trouble that Fret and Annoy.

An advertisement announcing the lighting system bought by Monarchs owner J.L. Wilkinson.

Showing off all the equipment necessary to carry the new lighting system of the Kansas City Monarchs.

The first Negro League night game in Comiskey Park occurred on Thursday, September 2, 1943, with the Chicago American Giants hosting the Memphis Red Sox.[2] Notably, the first Negro League night game played in St. Louis's Sportsman's Park, also on a Thursday, August 30th, showcased the Kansas City Monarchs and the Birmingham Black Barons.[3] Sportsman's nocturnal baptism for major league teams happened on May 24, 1940, the same night as the Polo Ground allowed the artificial sunlight.[4] The city of Cleveland was ahead of the visionaries, when they hosted their first night game under Wilkinson's floodlights on Wednesday, July 9, at Hooper Field, with entertainment provided by the Monarchs against the Homestead Grays.[5]

In 1930, James Leslie Wilkinson initiated the dawning of a new era in baseball with the first portable lighting system. He made it possible for sports enthusiasts to see a constellation of ebony stars perform in the illuminated shadows of the night.

Major league fans had to wait five more spring times, until May 24, 1935, to witness the installation of stadium lights. On this historic day, from his oval office, President Franklin D. Roosevelt flipped a switch that generated close to one million watts of electrical power from 632 fifteen-hundred-watt flood lamps in Cincinnati's Crosley Field. Chicago Cubs fans would have to wait a half a century before nighttime baseball arrived at their Wrigley Field.

The innovator of night baseball was born on May 14, 1878, in the small town of Perry (Southwest of Ames), Iowa, to John Joseph and Myrtie Harper Wilkinson. His father, known as J.J., served as president of the Northern Iowa

Normal School in Algona (near Des Moines). It was a teacher's college existing in the Kosulth County seat from 1886 through 1897. Daddy Wilk served six years as county superintendent of schools prior to being named president of the college by a committee including Gardner Cowles, who later made a name for himself with the Des Moines *Register*. After the turn of the century, he became a building contractor. He applied his trade as far west as Omaha, Nebraska, and eastward to Detroit, Michigan. Meanwhile, young J.L. Wilkinson was attending Highland Park College in Des Moines, Iowa, where he began his brief pitching career with the Hopkins Brothers, the local sporting goods store.[6]

Wilkinson's semipro career was interrupted when a broken wrist halted his pitching career and led him into the management field. His management experience with the Hopkins Brothers gave him the idea for one of baseball's most unique and interesting teams, the All Nations club.[7]

Respected businessman and owner of the Kansas City Monarchs, James Leslie Wilkinson, who brought night baseball and lots of championships to Kansas City.

In 1911, along with local businessman J.E. Gaul, Wilkinson formed an alliance of many nationalities, advertising: "Direct from their native countries, Hawaiians, Japanese, Cubans, Filipinos, Indians and Chinese." The All Nations simply ignored Jim Crow sanctions and barnstormed the Chautauqua loops from Wisconsin to Missouri to Nebraska by Pullman coach. They boasted of travel in their own "Private Hotel Car," a specially built Pullman coach, equipped with full sleeping and cooking facilities. "The All-Nations team traveled in a special private car in those days," said Wilkinson. "We all ate, slept and played together. There was never any trouble. We were a happy family."[8]

At times, their pitching staff included Jose Mendez, who had beaten white major league all-star teams in Cuba; the notorious beanballer "Plunk"

Drake; and strikeout artist John Donaldson. Left-hander Donaldson routinely averaged twenty K's a game against semipro and local opponents. Wilkinson's daughter Gladys recalled, "My dad said if he had been in the major leagues, he would have topped all the men that ever pitched." Wilkinson's son Richard added, "He had a great curve ball, I heard dad say he was one of the best."[9]

The All Nations also bragged about their husky Hawaiian, Frank Blukoi, billed as "the best 2nd baseman outside of Organized Baseball." Blukoi later played with Wilkinson's Kansas City Monarchs. They boasted of a Tokyo player nicknamed Jap Jacobs or Jap Mikado (translated Japanese "Emperor"), a student at Knox College (Galesburg, Il.) registered under the name of Garo Mikarmi.[10]

The All Nations squad also included Sam Crow, an American Indian and "Pops" Steno Gatto, an Italian. Virgil Barnes (later with the N.Y. Giants), Art Dunbar (Chicago White Sox), Art Smith (K.C. Blues), and Rollo Yendez were the white players. Rounding out the team were black players Frank Blattner and Clarence Coleman. Wilkinson's multiracial mix of players demonstrated they could build harmonious interpersonal relationships off the field, as well as play superior ball.

All Nations Team

Carrie Nation (May Arbaugh) (woman)
Couteau (French)
Pedros (Filipino)
Joe Graves (Native American)
Ricardo "Chico" Hernandez (Cuban)
Jess "Cannonball" Jackson (African American)
Schaumberg (German)
Figarolo (Cuban)
Rasmussen (Scandinavian)[11]

The All Nations team was sponsored by the Goldsmith Hardware Store and Hopkins Brothers sporting goods. They played the majority of their games in the Upper Midwest, traveling to Missouri, Kansas, Nebraska, Minnesota, North and South Dakota, and Wilkie's home state of Iowa. With the addition of various circus acts and a small band composed mostly of baseball players, the All Nations team was usually a welcomed attraction for the entertainment-starved farm towns concentrated throughout the Midwest.

Wilkinson found the proverbial melting pot of gold with his rainbow of nationalities. Despite being labeled as a "recreation" team by other baseball nines, the All Nations had some of the finest players in the game. Along with Mendez, Drake and Donaldson, the great Cuban player Cristobal Torrienti later graced the roster. In 1915, they beat a tough Rube Foster team, the Chicago American Giants, two out of three games. The following year they swept a doubleheader, 9–5 and 5–2, and later tied a game (5–5) against C.I. Taylor's Indianapolis ABCs—considered by some sportswriters the country's most dominant black club before the First World War—before losing to them 5–1.

After many successful seasons the military draft caused several teams to short-circuit. Wilkinson recalled, "Well, we were playing out in Casper, Wyoming, and the first draft of the war caught five of our fourteen All-Nation players. This only left us with nine players. But we still had a 35-game schedule before us. We played every one of these games, and won everyone save one. That we lost by a score of one to nothing."[12]

While the United States fought in Europe, a Kansas Citian named Casey "Dutch" Stengel, then playing with the Pittsburgh Pirates, formed an all-star team of major and minor league players. The Dutchman's team traveled to Nogales, Arizona, to play the 25th Infantry Wreckers team at Camp Stephen D. Little. They lost the first game 5–4, although they scored four runs in the first inning. Dobie Moore won the ball game with a tremendous home run. The *Nogales Daily Herald* reported that Moore's homer was "one of the longest hits seen on the local lot."

After losing the series to the army team, Stengel nicknamed the soldiers "the Wreckers." He informed Wilkinson of his new discovery and encouraged him to sign these electrifying black players. Without hesitation, Wilkie signed Bullet Rogan, Lem Hawkins, Oscar "Heavy" Johnson and Moore to play for his new team. This constellation of stars evolved into one of the most successful franchises in Kansas City sports history—the Kansas City Monarchs.

The Monarch moniker was bestowed by John Donaldson, who hailed from Glasgow, Missouri. Wilkinson recalled: "Donaldson suggested the name 'Monarchs' one day when we were feeling around for a name to give to a reorganization of the All-Nations team" Wilkinson added, "Right away the name sounded good and we adopted it."[13]

Shortly after Donaldson had pitched with the newly christened Monarchs, the club lost his pitching services. "The loss was sustained in this way," replied Wilkinson. "One day, a game in which Donaldson won was terminated in the late innings by rain. The teams hurried to get back to the hotel. With the car already crowded with teammates, Donaldson jumped on the running board for the ride back to town. He hung on the side of the car and his pitching arm got wet. In a day or two he complained about soreness in his shoulder, and a few days later found he could not pitch. He never regained the effective use of his arm. That was the end of the greatest pitcher that ever threw a baseball."[14]

Coming Home

When the Armistice was signed in November 1918 ending the war, many former players returned to their respective cities to engage in the national pastime. Unfortunately, that following summer, major race riots broke out across the nation, as black and white GIs competed for limited job opportunities. Violence erupted at a Chicago beach when a black youth swam across an imaginary segregation line and was stoned by whites, eventually drowning. Thirteen days of Chicago rioting followed, causing the death of 15 whites and 23 blacks, with 537 reportedly injured and about 1,000 people left homeless. By late July, the Giants' ball park was occupied by soldiers, forcing teams to travel to the East and to the Midwest for playing. With more than twenty-six riots reported nationally, the bloody aftermath of this world war would be called by activist James Weldon Johnson the "Red Summer of 1919."

The racial climate in most cities, particularly in Chicago, made interracial baseball contests practically impossible to stage. Parks, playgrounds and beaches were the center of constant racial conflict. Recreational facilities were unofficially segregated with full support of the city police. White gangs often victimized blacks, especially at Washington Park — a large recreational area that separated the black belt from Hyde Park and Woodlawn. The most infamous white gang was Rogan's Colt, endorsed by an alderman.

Remembering the successful series in 1915 with Rube Foster's Chicago American Giants, and the current tense climate of the Windy City, the ingenuity of Wilkinson would shine again. Wilkinson contacted his friend Casey Stengel, who had just been traded to the Philadelphia Phillies from the Pittsburgh Pirates. Future Yankee skipper Stengel had lettered in baseball, football and basketball at Kansas City's Central High School before enrolling for three years at Western Dental College.

Despite the racial tension of the nation, Wilkinson suggested to Stengel and Foster a three-game series between Foster's all-black Giants and an all-star team composed of white major leaguers. Stengel, home for the winter, recruited Cotton Tierney and pitcher Roy Sanders from his old Pirates team and got Zack and Mike Wheat from the Brooklyn Dodgers. Zack had led the league in batting the previous season with a .335 average, and was the team's only legitimate star. Alongside an aging Dutch Zwilling — Stengel, a fine player, had hit a respectable .293 that season.

The first game of the 1919 series was won by Stengel's All-Stars, when

Tierney tripled in two runners for a 4–1 victory. Monarch pitcher Donaldson was scheduled to pitch in the second game, but was scratched because of an injury. Instead, Texan Dick Whitworth got the assignment. The Giants lost the second game 8–3, as Roy Sanders struck out thirteen men, giving up seven hits. The Giants salvaged the final game of the series when a pint-size, speedster named Jimmy Lyons (a Ty Cobb prototype) smacked a grand slammer in the third inning. Overall pitchers John Donaldson, Stringbean Williams and Dave Brown combined for the 9–6 victory, before 5,500 fans in Association Park.

A New Era

In 1920, J.L. Wilkinson was elected by team owners as secretary of the new Negro National League. J.L., or "Wilkie," as he was affectionately known by his players, was the only white owner in a league as dark as a country night. He would retain this notoriety throughout the life of the league until its breakup in 1931. When the Negro American League organized in 1937, Wilkinson was elected treasurer. He was with the Monarchs 28 years (1920–1947); for six of those years (1931–1936) his teams barnstormed across the nation's breadbasket, harvesting their popularity.

For 28 years, his Monarchs were often considered the white major leagues' equivalent to the New York Yankees — the winning team that everyone wanted to beat. During Wilkinson's tenure, the Monarchs won 11 league championships, a feat surpassed only by the perennial champion Yankees. During the same period, the Yankees won 15 championships under the managerial directions of Miller Huggins (1918–29) and Joe McCarthy (1931–1946). While the Bronx Bombers played in the World Series each year they captured the league championship, the league champion Monarchs were not so fortunate — appearing in only four World Series: 1924, 1925, 1942 and 1946. The Monarchs could have appeared in more series if it had not been discontinued from 1927 to 1941. During the twenties, thirties and forties, baseball America recognized the Monarchs as one of the dominant teams of Negro League baseball.

While many of the New York pinstripers can be identified by a single name — from the Babe to Lou, from the Clipper to Mick to Maris, Yogi, Dickey, Lefty, Red and Whitey — only a few dedicated fans of the game can recognize their Monarch counterparts. Slowly emerging from the shadows of anonymity are box office stars Donaldson, Mendez, Bullet, Newt, Dobie, Brewer, Torrienti, Duncan, Foster, Turkey, Wells, Buck, Willard, Hilton, Jesse, Mr. Cub, Elston, Connie, Satch, Cool Papa, and, of course Jackie.

New Horizons

In 1921, Wilkie challenged the Kansas City Blues of the American Association League to a postseason exhibition series at Association Park. The small park was a single-level wooden structure with a short right field fence with a thirty-foot-high screen. Association Park, owned by George Tebeau, restricted blacks in attendance to the top fourteen rows of seats—even when two black teams were competing on the field.

For the series, the Monarchs brought in Frank Warfield, third baseman from the Detroit Stars, and John Henry "Pop" Lloyd, the fabulous shortstop from the rejuvenated Columbus Buckeyes. They also added the Buckeyes' pitcher Ed Rile, who had beat Foster's American Giants three times, shutting them out twice.

In the first game, both Baumgartner and Rile were knocked out of the box early; Baumgartner in the second and Rile in the fifth inning. The Monarchs won the premier affair, 7–5. The Blues took the second, 3–2, beating a tough Bullet Rogan, who gave up only four hits, but two wild pitches in the decisive sixth inning led to his defeat. With the series tied at three games apiece, the Blues started Red Ames and the Monarchs designated Ed Rile again. Busloads of fans for the deciding Sunday finale came from across the state from St. Louis, and nearby towns Sedalia and Lexington, Missouri. Also delegations from Omaha, Nebraska, and Topeka, Lawrence, and Atchison, Kansas, were found in the packed grandstands. Not much better this time around, Rile failed to survive the first inning. Slugger Bunny Brief had connected for a triple with two on. Dutch Zwilling followed with a single, scoring Brief. Frustrated, manager Sam Crawford placed himself on the pitcher's rubber. The Blues bumped Crawford for four more over the next four innings, building an 8–0 margin, after five. With the game slipping out of reach, the Monarchs called Hurley McNair infrom the outfield to pitch the final four frames. McNair gave up only one run, while Rogan, Warfield and Pop Lloyd staged a rally, scoring four runs over the next two innings. Wee Wee McNair capped off the final inning with a blast over the right field fence for the fifth and final Monarch tally. The pitching-poor Monarchs lost 9–5, and the Blues were crowned city champions.

The next year the fifth-place Blues met the Monarchs for a rematch. The Blues led the American Association in team batting with a .313 average and had finished second in the home run derby with 112 homers. Eleven Blues had batted over .300 that season, with Bunny Brief leading the league in home runs (42), doubles (51), and walks (117). During this year's postseason series, the Monarchs' pitching staff of Plunk Drake, Rube Currie, Bullet Rogan and Willie Gisentaner successfully met the challenge. They hurled six complete games, and held the Blues to a .278 batting average. The slugging Oscar "Heavy" Johnson of the Monarchs hit three homers in the series, batting .368, with a slugging percentage of .842. The Monarchs beat the Blues in five of six games.

This was to be the last interracial match-up between the Kansas City teams. The *Kansas City Star*, the city's white newspaper, spoke proudly of the Monarchs' triumph:

> The series has done more to boost Negro-organized baseball in this town with the white fans than anything else could have done. While they have always attended in large numbers, still the games they saw were regular league games and they have generally believed that it was an inferior grade of ball. But their eyes are open now to the fact that it isn't lack of ability that keeps the Negro ball players off the big time — it's color.

The Star crowned the Monarchs "The New City Champions." This extravagant headline, considering the social attitudes of the period, appeared not to be in the best interest of "America's Game." The provocative statement prompted Thomas J. Hickey, president of the American Association, to ban interleague, rather interracial, play between the two teams.[15]

The following year, on July 28, the Monarchs moved to Muehlebach Field — the future home of the American League's Kansas City Athletics. The field, named after brew master George Muehlebach, became Ruppert Field in 1937, when Jacob Ruppert purchased the park for his N.Y. Yankee minor league franchise. Normally seating for the Blues games was segregated; however, Wilkinson removed the twisted divider ropes and the crooked segregation signs when the Monarchs played. Fans, regardless of skin color, were allowed to sit wherever they liked at Monarchs games, without fanfare.

Wilkinson's move to desegregate the stands was a significant cultural statement for that period. At the time, the city's public golf course at Swope Park banned tax-paying black citizens from playing the links. Furthermore, Circuit Court Judge Brown Harris rejected a petition by black residents asking permission to play golf at the park. Judge Harris affirmed, "The course at Swope Park was for the exclusive use of whites, the same law regulating that as regulating the teaching of colored and white pupils in separate schools."[16] The hidden "black tax" was too steep a price for minorities to pay for golfing privileges. The ban at the Swope Park links was eventually lifted in 1932.

Prior to the desegregation of Muehlebach Field, black ballplayers had to dress at home or at the local YMCA before entering the ballpark. Despite prevailing social attitudes of the period, the Monarchs were allowed to use the all-white clubhouse facilities, demonstrating Wilkinson's impact on the national game at the local level. The Monarchs celebrated opening day by riding through the urban city in a 300-motorcade parade. Renowned actor and composer J. Rosamond Johnson threw out the traditional first ball. Johnson and his older brother James Weldon once played for the Morehouse University team. Weldon became the first African American to pass the Florida bar in 1897 and later served as secretary to the NAACP. Together they composed, "Lift Ev'ry Voice & Sing"—sung today as the "Negro National Anthem."

Their arrival at the new steel and concrete stadium, seating over 18,000 fans with an electric scoreboard, propelled the Monarchs to their first league championship of the new decade. That year they won 57 games and lost 33.

Depression Blues

Although always a popular team, Wilkinson's Monarchs competed for the entertainment dollar against the more established major league baseball teams. It was always a struggle to pay salaries and traveling expenses. In 1929, the midnight hour struck with the Great Depression. The league's meteoric rise to credibility came to a crashing halt. This forced Wilkinson to frantically search for innovative ideas to keep his team intact and survive the country's financial crisis, invariably causing one of black baseball's darkest moments. Perhaps nighttime baseball was the solution?

Many entrepreneurs had unsuccessfully tried, as early as the 1880s, to play baseball under artificial sunlight. A determined Wilkinson sought out the Giant Manufacturing Company of Omaha, Nebraska, to make his vision a reality. His only competitor for night baseball was his hometown friend, E. Lee Keyser, owner of the Des Moines Demons of the Western League. Keyser wanted to install a permanent lighting system, but Wilkinson saw the commercial value of a portable lighting system for touring the Midwest.

To finance this dream, Wilkinson and Tom Y. Baird, owner of a bowling alley and billiard parlor, put up collateral to secure a $50,000 loan. The loan enabled them to purchase a Sterling Marine 100 kilowatt generator with a 250 horsepower, six-cylinder, triple-carburetor, gasoline-driven engine. The new power plant consumed more than fifteen gallons of gasoline an hour, and required twelve men to install 44 giant non-glare floodlights on telescopic steel poles, mounted on the beds of Ford trucks. The innovative power plant had an estimated illumination power of 198,000 watts.[17]

T.Y. (Tom) Baird spoke proudly of the new lighting system:

> The Kansas City Monarchs invented and built the first and only successful portable baseball lighting plant. This plant was built in 1929 and was first used by the Monarchs in 1930. No other portable light plant could compete in good semi-pro parks. The Kansas City Monarch light plant lit major league ball parks year after year.

We lighted Forbes Field, Braves Field, Crosley Field, Navin (Briggs) field and Ebbets Field and lit most of the double A and triple A ball parks throughout the land. The light plant was built and carried on six trucks. Poles were attached to the trucks. The lights were then assembled on telescopic poles and raised by winches. The trucks were stationed outside the foul lines and were always stationed according to the blueprint plans. The power plant and truck together weighted over sixteen tons and was stationed in deep centerfield.

These trucks would parade into a ball park and in less than one hour the crew would erect poles, assemble projectors and equipment, and have the lights on. We have had the lights on in thirty minutes after entering the ball park. After the ball game the light crew would have the lights down, loaded and ready to go to the next town in 30 to 40 minutes.

This crew of twelve uniformed men were often referred to as a fire department or a circus crew or as a combination of both. Playing night baseball was a sensation in the early thirties, and at some of our first showing in several towns we had to call the police department to keep the curious out of the way so, we could erect the lights and save them from injury. We lit ball parks from Canada to Mexico and from the Middle West to Portland, Maine.[18]

One of the crew men, Floyd Ogle wrote of his experience,

My truck, 1929 Model "A" Ford Truck covered the 3rd base area. Sides were removed — 5 big reflectors were assembled at front where pole shows — 7,500 watts of light on this one truck. Poles were winched straight up and tied off with guide ropes. Power was from a bus chassis with big motor and generator in and cable strung to each trunk.

Team played exhibition games from Eagle Pass, Texas, on Mexican border to North Dakota and eastern Wisconsin. Played small town fields, college fields and big league parks. Crowds were always large — people did not believe you could play baseball at night and had to come and see.

I was 18 years old at time of the above pictures and had two exciting seasons with the team.[19]

It was customary for the Monarchs to tour Oklahoma and Texas during April and May in preparation for the upcoming season. However, the 1930 spring training tour would be different, with the introduction of their portable lighting system.

The Oklahoma tour started on April 23 in a small town about 60 miles southwest of Tulsa called Crescent. Coach Carl Hewitt and his Crescent Stars received an 18–0 trouncing. The Monarch battery of Andy Cooper and Frank Duncan gave up only one hit to the Crescent catcher Roy Waller. Meanwhile the Monarchs slammed 10 home runs. But because of threatening thunderstorms they were not able to assemble their patented lighting system.[20]

The next day, the Monarchs traveled 75 miles northeast to Tonkawa to play the Tonkawa Independents. Anticipating a historic event, Tonkawa's coach John Franke claimed, "They're the best drawing card in baseball. We should draw the largest crowd that ever watched a ball game in this vicinity." William Bell and T.J. Young of the Monarchs combined for a 4–0 victory. But once again, inclement weather delayed the birth of night baseball.[21]

Again, loading up the trucks and cars they traveled 45 miles north across the state line to Arkansas City, Kansas. The game scheduled for April 26 was postponed due to rain. There was no time for rest as the Monarchs were scheduled to play the next day in Okmulgee, Oklahoma, about 185 miles southeast and 45 miles from Tulsa. Okmulgee, the Indian town known as "Babbling Waters,"[22] had a rather large black population (about 20 percent) and expected a sell-out crowd.

The Okmulgee Merchants were the previous year's O-H-O Tri-Country League champions and had won several semipro tournaments. During the previous year the Merchants handed the Monarchs one of their rare exhibition losses. This time the Merchants expected to give the Monarchs their toughest battle of the spring tour. Nevertheless, the Monarchs displayed little respect for their Oklahoma opponents.

With threatening weather, approximately 800 early-arriving fans jammed into Petrolia Park to witness the Monarchs perform their shadow ball warm-up routine. The infield squad performed their drills in rapid-fire fashion, but without the baseball. The show was lead by second baseman Newt Allen, who entertained the fans with his throws to first base, while looking at third. Sometimes Allen would catch infield pop-ups flat on his back, or turn Ozzie Smith–type somersaults before catching high pop flies.

During the game, Chet Brewer intentionally walked three batters before striking out the side. After getting a formidable lead on the Okmulgee team, the Monarchs rotated their fielding positions after each Merchant out. The Monarchs shut down the Merchants by an 11–1 score.[23]

The Monarchs then traveled 155 miles northwest to Enid, Oklahoma (90 miles north of Oklahoma City), to play Phillips University. The sky had finally stopped crying. On April 28, 1930, on an overcast Monday, the Monarchs made baseball history. Before approximately 3,000 enlightened fans, baseball's first nightshift played the Phillips University Haymakers at Alton Stadium.[24]

The Monarchs curveball specialist, William Bell, and catcher, T.J. Young, became the first black battery to generate nighttime excitement. The Monarchs had constructed a canvas fence in short center field to allow illumination of the entire field. Any balls hit over the canvas fence were ruled a two-bagger. Although no home runs were allowed, much excitement was expressed by the ten errors from the amateurish Phillips team. Coach Greene, playing second base, accounted for four of the errors.

The university team jumped on top early with two runs in the first inning and another run in the third. The Haymaker shortstop Eash got to Bell for a double and a single, in his first two at-bats. The veteran Bell reached back for a little "extra" and struck Eash out on the next two plate appearances. Meanwhile, Phillips's first baseman, Leonard, smacked a long fly over the center field fence that would have been a triple in most ball parks, but the ground rules only allowed a double. Player-coach Tobe Greene also reached the center field fence for a ground rule double.

The Haymakers' young pitcher Mullican could not hold the lead. He gave up two runs in the fourth inning and another three in the fifth before collapsing. The seventh inning stretch proved unlucky for Mullican. The Monarchs batted around, showering the Haymakers with power, scoring seven runs, winning 12–4.

A sudden downpour caused this parade into baseball history to be called after eight innings. The *Enid Morning News* on April 29, 1930, gave this detailed box score of the first night game by a professional team:

Monarchs	AB	R	H	E	Phillips	AB	R	H	E
Harding, ss	4	1	1	1	Daugherty, 3b	4	2	0	1
Mothell, 1b	4	1	2	0	Highfill, cf	4	0	1	1
Allen, 2b	3	1	1	1	Leonard, 1b	4	1	2	1
Rogan, cf	4	2	2	0	Eash, ss	4	1	2	1
Taylor, rf	5	2	2	0	Bodine, c	4	0	0	1
Livingston, lf	5	1	1	0	Greene, 2b	4	0	1	4
Joseph, 3b	4	2	2	0	Jess, lf	3	0	1	0
Young, c	4	1	1	0	Killion, rf-p	4	0	1	1
Bell, p	4	1	0	0	Mullican, p	2	0	0	0
					Hildinger, rf	0	0	0	0
Totals	37	12	12	2		33	4	8	10

```
By innings              R  H  E
Monarchs     000 203 70x—12 12  2
Phillips     201 000 10x— 4  8 10
```

Batteries—Monarchs, Bell and Young; Phillips, Mullican, Killion and Bodine.
Summary—Doubles; Mothell 2, Allen, Joseph, Young, Rogan, Leonard 2, Eash, Greene. Bases on Balls off—Bell 2, Mullican 7; Struck Out by—Bell 7, Mullican 3, Killion 1.
Umpires—Watt White, behind plate, Casey Mills on the bases.
Game Time—2 hours, 10 minutes.

The Monarchs completed their nightly trek across Oklahoma by traveling 75 miles northeast to meet the Empire Oilers of Ponca City (April 29) at Conoco Park[25] and finally 150 miles south to Chickasha (April 30), before driving (May 2) to San Antonio, Texas, 475 miles away, and northward, 180 miles, days later to Waco, Texas. The 12-day tour of Oklahoma and Texas, in their struggle buggies, covered more than 1,380 miles over unpaved, often narrow roads, in rain and soaring heat with no air conditioning, averaging 35 to 40 miles per hour and with only a few days of rest.[26] Baseball by daylight, driving by moonlight, and carrying sunlight, the Monarchs lived by the creed expressed in the poem "Heritage" by black novelist Countee Cullen.[27]

Soon minor league teams discovered that the lighting system helped ease the financial burden caused by the Great Depression. The fog of resistance had been lifted. In one of the darkest moments in baseball history, Wilkinson became a tower of power. Club owners found that baseball under the artificial sun often doubled or tripled attendance figures. The *Kansas City Call* hailed the event by stating:

> Night baseball will be a lifesaver; it will revolutionize the old game, restoring small town baseball on a paying basis. It gives recreation for the business and working man who can't afford day games. The Monarchs will probably do to baseball this year, what the talkies have done to the movies.[28]

Former Monarch pitcher Chet Brewer recalled playing in the eye-opening experiment:

> I thought it was great! But it made double work for us. We would play a ballgame during the day and another at night. We played so many games a day, that when we played one game we considered that a day off. But the fans just loved it. In Enid, they came from everywhere. Most of them came out of curiosity. They just couldn't visualize baseball being played at night. They came from miles around and they enjoyed every bit of it.

Brewer added:

> That Wilkinson had a great crew. He took the big bus we used to travel in and put an electric dynamo in there and then he had trucks to carry the other material. We put up our own outfield fence using heavy equipment. They would roll those trucks down there and jack those lights up and run that line over to the bus with the dynamo and turned that juice on — and oh my, it would be as light as day.[29]

Despite Brewer's enthusiasm, the Monarchs' venture into night baseball was not without hardships and setbacks. Their luxurious Pullman coach had to be converted to house the generator. Without their bus available, players had to travel in their cars or "struggle-buggies," as called by the players. Newt Joseph, Monarch third baseman and owner of the Paseo Cab Company (later the Monarch Cab Company), leased four cars to Wilkinson. Four players rode in each car, taking turns driving to the various towns and cities.

Night baseball provided many highlights in baseball history. Less than a month later — on May 6, in Waco, Texas— John Markham, a promising lefthander from Shreveport, Louisiana, billed to replace ace Andy Cooper, pitched the first nighttime no-hitter. He faced only 28 batters in the errorless defeat of the Waco Cardinals from the Texas League, 8–0.[30] Roughly 3,000 fans witnessed the event under 20 mighty portable lights.[31] Markham finished his career in 1947, teaming with Satchel Paige and Cool Papa Bell to form the

Detroit Senators. This short-lived team was managed by W.S. Welch (a former Birmingham Black Baron executive) and financed by Abe Saperstein (owner of the Harlem Globetrotters basketball and baseball teams).[32]

Later in the season — on August 2, 1930, at Muehlebach Field — fans saw two pitching legends, Chet Brewer and Smokey Joe Williams, throw laser beams past frustrated batters. Brewer of the Monarchs struck out 19 batters, ten in a row, including Oscar Charleston, Judy Johnson and rookie Josh Gibson a total of six times. Despite Brewer's brilliant performance, Joe Williams of the Homestead Grays won the 12-inning affair, 1–0, striking out 27 batters. Critics claimed poor lighting conceived this historic event. It is interesting to note that baseball historians accept — without reservations — Johnny Vander Meer's second no-hitter against the Brooklyn Dodgers on June 15, 1938, in the first night game played in Ebbets Field.

Nocturnally Natural

Night baseball was here to stay. Newt Allen, a twenty-three year veteran of the Negro Leagues, told sportswriter John Holway: "We were the first ball club that ever played under the lights, and Wilkinson was one of the finest men I've ever known. He was one white man who was a prince of a fellow. He loved baseball, and he loved his ball players. He traveled right along with us every day. Stayed at the same hotels we stayed at."[33]

Chet Brewer also spoke affectionately of the club owner: "That J.L. Wilkinson was one of best white men I was ever in contact with. He wanted his ball players to look nice. We dress, boy did we dress nice."[34]

Wilkinson's son Richard recalled:

> I never knew a ball player or person that didn't like my dad. He was very calm, a quiet type of person. He never showed much emotion. Always the professional! Never saw him without a suit and tie and hat on. Never drank, never smoked. Just a fine person and he helped a lot of players, financially.
>
> A great baseball man, he helped organize the league. He held that league together. I remember as a kid that Foster and the two Martin brothers from Memphis would call my father for advice. They were extremely close friends. My dad was responsible for scheduling all the games. He was head of the scheduling committee. Dad was just a good business man. He loved baseball.[35]

On June 12, 1930, Thomas Hickey, president of the American Association, who had earlier banned exhibition games between the Kansas City Blues and the Monarchs, spoke notably of Wilkinson's pioneer efforts: "It looks like a life-saver for the game in many cities. I saw my second night game at Indianapolis, Tuesday, and became more impressed than ever by its possibilities. I regard baseball under the lights as an unusual success."[36]

Not all of baseball's gate keepers shared Hickey's observation. Instead of eagerly embracing the technology of the future, major league executives, wedded to daytime play, were reluctant to change their old-fashioned ways. Nevertheless, night baseball spread to the eastern seaboard. Later in 1930, Alex Pompez, owner of the Cuban Stars, installed lights at Dyckman Oval in New York. Located near the Harlem Ship Canal in Upper Manhattan, Dyckman Oval became the first ballpark in New York equipped with stadium lights.

On Opening Day, May 6, 1933, Greenlee Field debuted stadium lights for a game played between the Homestead Grays and the Nashville Elite Giants.[37]

Harlem was considered the cultural center of Negro society or, as the *New York Age* stipulated, "The Crucible of Dark Manhattan." The Harlem baseball club was known for its entertainment-rich audience, routinely featuring Louis Armstrong, Eubie Blake, Count Basie, Lionel Hampton, Lena Horne, Cab Calloway and the sentimental Mills Brothers. Occasionally dancer "Bojangles" Robinson would lightly tap a buck-and-wing routine on the visitors' dugout roof.

That same season, the Chicago American Giants' new owner William Trimble hurriedly installed lights for the Fourth of July weekend series with the Birmingham Black Barons. And Wilkinson's friend, Lee Keyser from Des Moines, Iowa, sold the St. Louis Stars a lighting system for installation in late July.[38]

Former Monarch first baseman George Giles remembered:

> I was with the St. Louis Stars when Wilkie started night baseball. They [the Monarchs] had those portable lights. We had stationary lights on the roof of the Stars' ballpark, there on Compton and Market Street. Playing under the lights didn't make me much difference, as long as I got paid. Shoot, that was during the Depression. Those lights saved baseball. People couldn't go to the baseball games in the daytime — they were working.[39]

Night baseball became a struggling owner's salvation. There was no rain check given here. It enabled teams to combat the economic effects of the Great Depression, despite skepticism from baseball purists. The bright lights allowed baseball to maintain its reputation as a working-class diversion, as fans with as little as four- bits could enjoy seeing their idols perform in the spotlight.

The consequences of the Great Depression had caused the collapse of the Negro National League in 1931. This crisis forced Wilkinson's Monarchs to barnstorm around the country promoting baseball with their new technology. The Monarchs capped a fine season with victories over two white all-star teams. They stomped Grover Alexander and the House of David, 11–2. The next weekend, behind the pitching of Willie Foster, the Monarchs beat the Waner All-Stars, 4–3. The All-Stars included "Little and Big Poison," Lloyd (.314) and Paul Waner (.322); Heinie Meine (19–13) from the Pittsburgh Pirates; Glenn Wright (.284) and Babe Herman (.313) from the Brooklyn Dodgers; Joe Kuhel (.269) from the Washington Senators; and several Kansas City Blues members.

In Wichita, Kansas, the Monarchs repeated their victory over the Waner All-Star team. Chet Brewer shut down the major leaguers, 6 to 2, striking out 14 batters, while shortstop Willie Wells belted a two-run homer. The Waner bunch could not compete with the talented Monarchs.

As the team benefited financially in postseason play, and with the 1932 season approaching, Wilkinson decided not to enter the league. Former player George Giles recalled,

> Wilkie said he wasn't going to start up in '32 ... the Monarchs weren't going to come out. So we all went to the Homestead Grays or the Detroit Wolves [of the new East-West League]. While we were there in Pittsburgh, along about the first part of July, Wilkie contacted all of his ball players and told us to meet him in Chicago to start a new team.[40]

Knowing of Wilkinson's reputation as a solid promoter of the game, his faithful players rushed to the windy city. The reorganized Monarchs, along with Brewer and Wells, added premier performers like Giles, Cool Papa Bell, Dink Mothell, Frank Duncan, Newt Allen and Quincy Trouppe to the team. Given the green light, they won an incredible 42 consecutive games before Willie Foster of the Chicago American Giants stopped them, 2–1, on a five-hitter. They lost only five games that season.

As baseball evolved from the dark ages to a brighter era, Wilkinson's Monarchs achieved other baseball firsts. In 1934, they became the first black team to be invited to the heralded *Denver Post* tournament. The tournament, representing the best minor-league and semipro talent in the Midwest, had previously been restricted, by invitation only, to white teams. Players, baseball executives and fans of the Negro Leagues saw this invitation as an excellent opportunity to demonstrate the quality of baseball played by black athletes. Led by their ace Chet Brewer to reach the finals, the disappointed Monarchs failed to win the $7,500 first place prize. Before a record-breaking crowd of 11,120 they lost the championship game to the bearded House of David team from Benton Arbor, Michigan, 2–1. Ironically, the House of David team had recruited a black battery for the Denver tournament. As catcher they had the cagey Bill Perkins and the lanky Satchel Paige was on the mound.

The Monarchs closed out the '34 season by beating members of the champion St. Louis Gashouse Gang in three of four games. The Dizzy Dean All-Stars, as the St. Louis bunch was called, were trampled, 7–0 and 9–0 in two of the games played. The barnstorming Monarchs could compete against the finest major league pitchers—"Schoolboy" Rowe, "Dizzy" and Paul Dean, Henry "Heine" Meine, Mort Cooper, Grover Alexander, Bob Feller, Mace Brown and many others—and beat them.

Wilkinson's Monarchs joined the reorganized Negro American League (NAL) in 1937, winning their sixth league championship. The playoff victims this time were the Chicago American Giants. They beat the Giants, winning four games to one, and played an extra game, a thrilling 17-inning tie.

After winning the first game of the series 5–4, the Monarchs and Giants met in Chicago. It was Monarch manager Andy Cooper against the Giants' ace Willie Foster. Cooper had seen his best years with the Detroit Stars in the twenties. In 1924, Cum Posey picked him along with Bullet Rogan and Joe Williams of the Grays for his all-star team. Now, years later, the 39-year-old pitched the game of his career.

After giving up two runs in the first innings, Cooper settled down. The Monarchs knocked Foster out of the box in the seventh inning with two runs, and he was relieved by Sug Cornelius. Overall, Cooper pitched 17 innings, giving up 10 hits, including a double and triple, and holding the Giants blankless until nightfall. The inspirational effort by the old man sparked his teammates to sweep the next four games for the NAL championship.

To cap off a great season, the Monarchs met the All-Leaguers, a team composed of white minor and major league players, led by Bob Feller. The Bob Feller all-star team met a one-man assassin in Willard Brown. Brown bombed them for two two-run homers in the first game and blasted four homers in the second game. After losing the first two games, the all-stars salvaged respect with a 1–0 victory behind the four-hit pitching of Bob Feller (9–7), Lon Warneke (18–11) and Mace Brown (7–2). The Monarch attack was led by Bullet Rogan's three hits. For reasons unknown, "Home Run" Brown did not play.

The Monarchs continued their winning ways, with league championships in 1939, 1940, and 1941. In 1942, they met the heavily favored Homestead Grays in the Negro World Series. The Grays, featuring sluggers Josh Gibson, Buck Leonard, Jerry Benjamin and Howard Easterling, were to match up against the pitching prowess of Satchel Paige, Connie Johnson, Lefty LaMarque, Hilton Smith and Jack Matchett.

Team leader Buck O'Neil remembers the drama:

> The Kansas City Monarchs against the Homestead Grays. The Grays must have won a dozen or so championships out East. We were just a young bunch of guys, and nobody thought we could beat this ball club. They had some guys like Josh Gibson and Buck Leonard who could really hit that ball. They could do it all. They didn't think we had a chance. But I knew we had a chance. Hey, we had Joe Green and Frank Duncan doing the catching. Newt Allen at third base, Jesse

Williams at shortstop and Bonnie Serrell at second and I played first. And in the outfield we got Willard "Home Run" Brown, Willie Sims and Ted Strong. Hey, they really didn't know what hit them. Say, we had Satchel Paige, Hilton Smith, Booker McDaniel, a Jack Matchett, and a Connie Johnson. We had guys who could really throw that ball. An outstanding team, we beat them four straight ball games.[41]

The Monarchs swept the Grays, holding the mighty Josh to a paltry .125 batting average.

In 1946, the Monarchs made their final World Series appearance against the Newark Eagles, owned by baseball's queen, the hazel-eyed, silky haired Effa Manley. The Eagles pitching staff was anchored with aces Leon Day and Max Manning. Manning had won the league's Pitcher of the Year award with a 15–1 record. He had lost his first game before rolling off 15 wins in a row. Their infield starred big stick Lennie Pearson at first base, along with a keystone combination of Larry Doby (2b) and Monte Irvin (ss), while the always dangerous slugging, big Johnny "Cherokee" Davis roamed the outfield.

The Monarchs were favorites to win the series. Led by manager Frank Duncan, they had Buck O'Neil (.350) and Willard Brown (.348), the number one and two league leading hitters. With future New York Giant Hank Thompson and Ted Strong, the former Harlem Globetrotter, they featured baseball's black version of Murderers' Row.

Despite first baseman Buck O'Neil hitting .333 and adding two home runs — one a grand slammer — the Monarchs went down to defeat, four games to three. The deciding seventh game was not without controversy, however. Ted Strong and Satchel Paige failed to show up for the championship game. They were reported to be traveling south for winter baseball. Other rumors mentioned payroll dissatisfaction.

During the series, Johnny Davis and Max Manning had made quite an impression on Wilkinson. After losing the title, Wilkie signed Davis and Manning to play with the Monarchs in a series of exhibitions against the Bob Feller All-Stars. In one game, Davis came up to bat against Yankee pitcher Spud Chandler, with one man on base. Davis took a called ball and then took a terrific cut at a waist high fast one. Over in the Monarchs dugout, "Dizzy" Dismukes commented, "Lord, if he throws Cherokee another one like that, they'll never find the ball."[42] On the next Chandler pitch, Big John slammed a two-run homer for a 3–2 win. Wilkinson always displayed a keen eye for talent.

Lights Out!

In mid–July of 1947, while in Chicago, Wilkinson and some of his players were involved in a tragic car accident. As a result of the accident, he ruptured a retina in his right eye. Lacking the science of laser surgery he retained only 25 percent of his vision, according to his son, Richard. Later, Wilkie underwent cataract surgery at the Kansas University Medical Center. Complications occurred, resulting in the complete loss of sight in his left eye, while he still suffered impaired vision in his right eye. Wilkinson was blind about the last 10 years of his life, and he decided to sell the team. His son Richard recalled: "My dad saw the handwriting on the wall. With Jackie going to the Majors, he knew the great days of the Monarchs were over. He knew he had to sell the team."[43]

The following winter, on February 5, 1948, Wilkinson sold his fifty percent ownership of the mighty Monarchs to co-owner and close friend Tom Baird. The contract called for the exclusive rights by Baird to market the name "The Kansas City Monarchs Baseball Club" and a sale price of $27,000. The Wilkinson family, J.L. and his son, Richard Leslie, were allowed to operate another team under the name "Kansas City Monarchs Travelling Club" with restrictions against tampering with any player currently under contract with the original club, except for one player — Leroy "Satchel" Paige.[44] Because of his popularity, Paige was available for pitching duty with either club. He was eventually sold to the Cleveland Indians for $5,000.

According to the contract terms, the new Wilkinson team was restricted from playing in the states of Denver, Colorado, Kansas, Iowa and Nebraska. They hired retired speedster James "Cool Papa" Bell as team manager in 1947. In a 1971 interview with historian Dr. Arthur Shaffer, 68-year-old Bell recalled his last days with Satchel:

> When Wilkinson's eyes went bad, he sold his franchise to his co-owner Tom Baird and give his team to his son, that was Wilkinson, Jr., and that was a farm of the team. They were training ball pitchers developing them to sell to the major leagues who were taking them. So I managed the farm team, and Satchel Paige was with me and he stayed with me a month and nine days and then he went on to Cleveland. But the league team got credit for him, see, they was a league team. See, the public didn't know that. We would play in the territory with this farm team, in the territory of the Monarchs we was the Kansas City Stars with Satchel Paige, and then we'd play out of the territory, we'd say Kansas City Monarchs with Satchel Paige. And a lot of scouts were scouting my team, thinking it was a league team. We sold about 38 players and about twenty of the ball players that I had scouted started and developed were sold to the major leagues. All of them didn't make the majors then, but they were in the farm system. Some of them got too old to be in the majors.

Soon after, officers of the Negro American League met for their annual meeting. Two major decisions came out the meeting. First, they voted (by a slim margin) not to lift the five-year ban imposed on players who had jumped to the Mexican League. But more importantly, by a unanimous vote, they made J.L. Wilkinson a lifetime member of the league.[45]

Two years later Wilkinson severed his remaining ties with one of baseball's greatest franchises. On March 3, 1950, he sold his remaining rights to the Monarch trademark, the "Kansas City Monarchs Travelling Club," to Baird. Wilkie also sold the team's Pullman Dodge bus complete with sleeping facilities for $7,500. In addition he sold the contracts of eighteen Monarchs along with three complete uniform sets for a blue-light special price of $1,500. Baird paid less than $100 bucks per uniformed player. Baird paid an additional one thousand dollar bonus to cover any incidental expenses.[46]

Richard Wilkinson recalled: "We kept that team for two years. We then sold the team to Tom [Baird], along with the sleeper bus. I had that bus specially built. It slept 15 men. I had the bus stripped and made into Pullman booths, converting seats into beds. It was custom built."[47]

Richard added: "Cool Papa Bell was a great manager, one of the finest men I have ever known. He was a lot like my father, never drank or smoked. I never even heard him swear. A fine man. A fine ball player too. He reminded me of the guy who played centerfield for the New York Yankees. Uh, his name was Mick [the Quick] Rivers. He ran just like him, even draped his glove like him. A spitting image of Mickey. He had that funny way of running; you know where he dragged that foot. But, boy he could flat out scat."[48]

Baird was able to recoup most of his investment that season. The Monarchs' profit and loss statement from the 1950 season showed a profit of $20,150.57.[49]

As rumors circulated in the baseball world about more black players entering the major leagues, a special clause was inserted in the contract stating in part:

> ... and shall further pay to first party (J.L. Wilkinson or Richard L. Wilkinson) one-half of the sum or sums received for the sale or assignment of any player on the Kansas City Monarch Baseball Club listed on the 1947 roster over and above the sale or contract price of Five Hundred and no/100ths ($500.00) Dollars, and one-half of any money received for the assignment and transfer of the player, Jackie Robinson.[50]

The color barrier had been as solid as the Great Wall of China. So solid, that during the war years, the majors signed a one-armed player before dipping into the talent pool of the Negro Leagues. Finally, on a Tuesday afternoon, on October 23, 1945, Robinson signed a contract to play for the Montreal Royals. Wilkinson never received any compensation for Robinson. The Brooklyn Dodgers' Branch Rickey claimed Jackie did not have a signed contract with the Monarchs. While Wilkinson and Baird threatened to sue the Brooklyn Club, Robinson responded to the controversy on February 11, 1946, in the *Atlanta Daily World*, stating: "I wasn't signed to a contract because they didn't know whether or not I would make good, so they didn't want to have trouble getting rid of me."

The Monarchs management countered to the *Sporting News*, claiming:

> Any ball player knows that he can be given his release at any time. Robinson was signed by the Monarchs by letter and telegrams. According to the rules and regulation of the Negro Leagues, any player accepting terms by letter or telegram or playing with a club becomes the property of that club. Until the "raid" by Rickey, our only fear of contract jumping was the offers of Jorge Pasquel. We have always held Jackie in highest regard, both as a player and as a gentleman. It is a shame that Branch Rickey had to "spirit" Robinson away, instead of dealing honorably with us.

Wilkinson's son James added, "Dad never got paid for Jackie. Rickey never paid anybody for anything. Nothing could be done about it in those days. If you'd raised a voice about the money, they'd have said, 'Oh, you're trying to hold a man back.' And Dad wasn't like that anyway."[51]

When Wilkinson and Baird were unable to produce a signed contract for the reported salary of $400 a month, they decided not to file a grievance with the new commissioner Happy Chandler, stating:

> Although I feel the Brooklyn [Dodgers] or the Montreal [Royals] clubs owes us some kind of consideration for Robinson, we will not protest to Commissioner Chandler. I am very glad to see Jackie get this chance, and I'm sure he'll make good. He's a wonderful ballplayer. If and when he gets into the major leagues he will have a wonderful career.[52]

Not everyone thought Robinson would have a wonderful career. Rogers Hornsby, who had resigned as manager of Vera Cruz in Mexico because the owner refused to release future Hall of Fame shortstop Willie Wells, did want black players on his team. The two-time Triple Crown winner and seven-time batting king said:

> The Negro Leagues are doing all right and Negro players should be developed and then remain as stars in their own right. A mixed ball team differs from other sports, because ball players on the road live much closer together. ... The way things are, it will be tough for a Negro player to become a part of a closely knit group such as an organized ball club. I think Branch Rickey was wrong in signing Jackie Robinson to play with Montreal and it just won't work out.[53]

Hornsby had long been noted for his stand against integration as far back as 1927. As interim manager for the New York Giants, he blamed the team's black trainer, John "Doc" Jamieson, for the team's poor performance on the field. Subsequently, he fired Jamieson as the Giants finished in third place. Despite having a 22–10 won-lost record, the turmoil caused by his racial policy eventually led to his short tenure with the John McGraw team.

Another critic of Robinson was Bob Feller. Just returning from the war games, Rapid Robert Feller, who pitched three no-hitters and 12 one-hitters in his career, had faced Jackie three times in a '45 postseason game. Robinson had been a member of Chet Brewer's Kansas City Royals, a winter league team based in Southern California. They competed against other Negro League and major league all-star teams. As a member of Brewer's Royals, Jackie greeted the Indians' pitching ace with two doubles. Unconvincingly, a shell-shocked Feller labeled Jackie: "Good field — no hit," and added, "a sucker for an inside pitch. He didn't seem to me to be a big league prospect. He couldn't pull the ball when at bat, probably due to his football days. Most football players get heavy around the shoulders and have the same trouble."[54] But manager Brewer disagreed: "Oh, Jackie was major league talent all the way. He had some of the quickest reflexes I ever saw in a player."[55]

Others agreed. Robinson's last roommate in the Negro Leagues was Gene Benson, an outfielder from the Philadelphia Stars. Benson and Robinson had traveled to Caracas, Venezuela, that winter before Jackie was scheduled to report north to Montreal. Baker tells his thoughts about the barrier breaker:

> You know I was Jackie's last roommate before he went to the major leagues. He had signed with Branch Rickey when we took a team to South American that year. Felton Snow, who was managing the Baltimore Elites at the time, was our all-star manager. He came to me and said Benson, I going to give Jackie to you as a roommate. Because you can help him. You have played against everyone, including the major leaguers, you know what they can do and not do. Jackie needs confidence. You know, Jackie was not the best player in our league. A lot of people could play better than Jackie. But you know he was pick on his educational background. It was my job to try to help him make the adjustments.
>
> I told him, "Jackie, where you're going is easier than where you're came from." He sit straight up in bed when I told him that. He said, "Ben, do you really mean that?" I said, "I certainly do. I could hit those major leagues pitchers better than the pitchers in our league. You see one thing in our league, nothing was outlawed. You know it's a big difference when people are throwing at you. We had to learn how to hit all kinds of pitches. They threw spitballs, sailed the ball, cut it, all kind of stuff. And you know Satchel had that hesitation pitch." I told Jackie if you can hit all these kinds of pitches with no law to it at all, don't you think you can hit something legitimate, better? He responded, "You [may] have something there, Ben."
>
> After he made it, he came back and told me, that I had told him the truth. "Yes, Ben they were a lot easier to hit."[56]

Upon hearing the news of Jackie's signing, Fred "Dixie" Walker, perhaps Brooklyn's most popular player and future managerial material, was very upset. Fred, a high school dropout from Birmingham, Alabama, shared his Southern hospitality, and crowed: "As long as he ain't with the Dodgers, I ain't worried."[57]

Days later Feller adds, "Jackie will be a tough spot. I'm not prejudiced against him, either. I hope he makes good, but, frankly, I don't think he will."

Despite the doomsayers and doubters, Robinson won the Rookie of the Year Award (now called the Jackie Robinson Award). The successful entrance of Jackie Robinson into the major leagues ultimately led to the demise of the once prominent Negro Leagues, something Bob Feller thought would never happen. In a 1949 interview with *Ebony* magazine, Feller once again voiced his belief that few if any black players would shine in the majors:

> There will be no avalanche of Negroes into the big leagues mainly because there are few Negro ball players today who can make the grade...
>
> Baseball today has no politics in playing. There is no discrimination against foreign-born or Negro [players]. Either you have it or you don't...
>
> The hardest hitter for me to pitch to last season was Henry Thompson, who played for a while for the St. Louis Browns. He didn't swing hard, but he had a good eye. Our scout Jos Vosmik reports that Minnie Minoso with our Dayton, Ohio, farm team has the makings of a big league star. There are other Negroes who have been taken from Negro baseball who now are performing in minor leagues, but not many.[58]

Garage Sale

The Monarchs were the heart and soul of the Negro Leagues. The avalanche of ballplayers into the major leagues was patented during Wilkinson's monarchy. The Monarchs won more professional championships than any sports franchise — black- or white-owned — in Kansas City history. Paige, one of their brightest, was not the only star for the Monarchs. Evidence of their great strength is they sent three dozen players to major and minor league ball clubs, more than any other Negro League team. The list reads like a who's who of an all-star roster:

Major League Teams

George Altman — 1b — Chicago Cubs
Gene Baker — 2b — Chicago Cubs
Ernie Banks — ss — Chicago Cubs
Frank Barnes — p — St. Louis Cardinals
Willard "Home Run" Brown — of — St. Louis Browns
J.C. Hartman — ss — Houston Colt .45s
Francisco "Pancho" Herrera — 1b — Philadelphia Phillies
Elston Howard — c, of — New York Yankees
Connie Johnson — p — Chicago White Sox & Baltimore Orioles
Lou Johnson — of — Los Angeles Dodgers

Henry "Pistol" Mason — p — Philadelphia Phillies
Leroy "Satchel" Paige — p — Cleveland Indians.
Curtis Roberts— 2b — Pittsburgh Pirates
Jackie Robinson — inf.— Brooklyn Dodgers
Hank Thompson — inf.— St. Louis Browns
Bob Thurman — of — Cincinnati Reds

Minor League Affiliates

Juan Armenteros, c
Henry Baylis, 3b
Sherwood Brewer, 2b
Gene Collins, p, of
Doc Connors, ss
Bill Dickey, p
Melvin Duncan, p
Duke Henderson, of
Bill Hill, of
Ike "Stonewall" Jackson, c
John Jackson, p
Ernie Johnson, p, of
Jim "Lefty" LaMarque, p

Eddie Locke, p
Enrique "Ricky" Maroto, p
Booker T. McDaniel, p
Nat Peeples, of
Gene Richardson, p
Bill Rowan, of
Bonnie "Barney" Serrell, ss
Ford Smith, pc
Mickey Stubblefield, p
Earl Taborn, c
Don Vaughn, p
Jeff Williams, of
Jesse Williams, ss

A total of 42 talented tan men from the ranks of the Monarchs. In fact, 13 of the 17 roster players from the 1949 team went into organized ball. Buck O'Neil, manager of the club, recalls: "The best club I ever managed was the 1949 team. We had Bob Thurman, Elston Howard, Curtis Roberts, Connie Johnson, Gene Baker, Willard Brown, Frank Barnes, oh man!, Booker McDaniel, Bonnie Serrell, Gene Richardson, Herb Souell, oh yeah! This was a team. All the guys, these Monarchs, prided themselves. We were an institution."[59]

Not on the team was Satchel Paige, baseball's original globetrotter, who played for several teams in the states, in Cuba, Mexico, Panama, Puerto Rico and the Dominican Republic; he summarized the essence of being a Monarch. When notified of his selection to the Hall of Fame, he paid the ultimate compliment to Wilkinson and the Monarchs, by saying, "I'll go into the Hall in a Monarch uniform. And I want it that way."

Another accolade came from one of Jackie Robinson's tutors, Monarch infielder Jesse Williams:

> The Monarchs were like a milestone here. Just like every white boy wanted to join the Yankees, it was every black boy's ambition to join the Monarchs. Shoot, the Monarchs were as popular as the Yankees back in our day. Man, the Monarchs were *the* team! And *every* black kid knew it.[60]

A New Day

In 1955, Kansas City baseball underwent a major change. Blues Stadium was purchased by the city and became Municipal Stadium. The minor league Blues were replaced by the hapless Philadelphia Athletics of the American League. As the Monarchs played their last home game, they entered the era of burlesque baseball in the remaining years. The Monarchs, once the brightest-burning comet of all, were now falling to earth.

Fans both black and white flocked to see the big league A's, who had not won a pennant since 1931, setting an attendance record of 1,393,054. The ripple effect caused the Monarchs a loss of over 10,000 dollars. The once magnificent Kansas City Monarchs were sold to Ted Rasberry of Grand Rapids, Michigan. The profit and loss statement from R.R. Slagel, public accountant, for the 1954 season revealed:

Total Cash Receipts	$ 62,907.80
Operating Expenses:	
Player's Salaries	28,773.62
Officer's Salaries	7,500.00
Lodging for Players	5,894.08
Business Promotional Expenses	3,951.85
Transportation of Players	3,617.45
Loss by Fire	3,091.33
Bus Maintenance & Repair	2,915.27
Player's Meals	2,723.75
Baseball Supplies	2,518.10
Gasoline & Oil for Bus	2,372.60
Telephone & Telegraph	1,250.08
Travel Expense — Management	1,000.03
Miscellaneous Expenses	915.61
Depreciation	810.00
Scouting Expenses	744.76
Stadium Rental	640.99
Bonuses—1955 Players	600.00
Employment Tax Expenses	570.35
Accounting	411.25
Lease Improvements	363.56
Contributions	340.00
Other Taxes	306.76
Laundry	254.91
League Membership Fees	250.00
Medical Expenses on Players	227.55

Operating Expenses (continued):

Postage	173.81
Taxes and Licenses	142.95
Booking Fees	130.45
Legal Expense	100.00
Office Supplies	81.52
Water and Lights	81.21
Bus Storage	75.00
Insurance	71.51
Dues and Subscriptions	19.95
Freight paid on Supplies	11.98
Total Expenses	**72,931.88**
Net Operating Loss for 1954 Season	**($10,024.08)**[61]

Under the Rasberry management, the Monarchs never regained the masterful level of play that once dominated the black diamond of the twenties, thirties and forties. The local black newspaper, the *Kansas City Call*, in respect to Wilkinson's Monarchs, observed: "From a sociological point of view the Monarchs have done more than any other single agent in Kansas City to break the damnable outrage of prejudice that exist in this city."[62]

Wilkinson's remaining years were spent at the University Nursing Home in Kansas City, Kansas.[63] He had brought baseball out of the aberrant light into the spotlight. He had given sight to nighttime baseball, only to lose his own vision late in life. On August 21, 1964, at the age of eighty-six, the "Father of Night Baseball"[64] died.

A public tribute from the *Kansas City Call* on September 7, 1928, summed up this great:

> The Best club owner in the world to work for—
> who is familiar with the game as it is today
> who knows how to plan for the future
> who believes in us at all times
> who stands for a fair and square deal to all
> who gives the best and expects the best in return
> who loves and is loved by his players
> who believes that charity begins at home
> who knows and appreciates real ability
> who instills the fighting spirit in his club
> who practices what he preaches
> who never turned on a friend.

One of Wilkie's favorite players, Buck O'Neil, recalls his friendship with the main man behind the Monarchs:

One of the finest men I have ever known was Wilkinson. J.L. Wilkinson was one of the few men in my life, that was without prejudice. He was a thinking man innovative, he was always thinking of ways to improve or better baseball. He was the type fellow, that it was nothing he had that was actually too good for you. A lot of ballplayers I know, came to Kansas City when the season was over and Wilkie let them have money all year. Wilkie was that kind of man.

A soft man, if he talked to you, you had to listen. You know! I never heard him raise his voice. No matter how excited he may be about a project, he never raised his voice. Always had a nice smile. He wanted to have the best ball club in the world.

You see, before we got there, our reservations were already made. You see, this was all cut and dry. We knew what restaurant we were going to eat in. You took care of business before we got there. We would get here in the spring and I would tell Ora where I was going to be the last day of the season. He was a good organizer. And as far traveling in the South, we knew where to stop. Good hotels, good restaurant owned by black folks. What happened is this, we knew, city to city, where to stop. Stop here, don't stop here. To stop at a filling station, we may have to stop two or three blocks off the main drag, but it would be a black filling station. If you *had* to go to white filling station, the players (from the home town) would tell us which one to stop at.

Racial tension! We had none! Wilkie knew how to avoid the trouble spots. We knew where to go and not to go.[65]

Connie Johnson, former Monarch, Chicago White Sox and Baltimore Orioles pitcher, shared O'Neil's high opinion of Wilkinson.

You know J.L. Wilkinson was one of the greatest guys to ever live. He was just a natural. He wasn't prejudiced, just a natural, down-to-earth human being. Lots of times, he gave money to people on the streets. And you never had to worry about your money. As a matter of fact, he kept a lot of teams going. If he found out a team in the league couldn't make payroll, Wilkinson would let them have some money. Him and Rube kept that league alive. But we, the Monarchs, never had to worry about our salaries. I remember one time I borrowed $25 dollars from him and never paid him back. He never ask for it. J.L. was a nice guy. He helped a lot of people out. He was the type of guy, if you needed money you could go to him. Hey, he was a fantastic man. Yes he was! You could go to him and tell him you were having a financial problem. All he wanted to know was how much you needed and hey, he never asked any questions ... He was one of the finest men I ever knew. That's for sure. You don't find many people like J.L. in this world. He had no conception of discrimination. Everyone was the same to him. All the players liked him. He was for real. No doubt about that. A fine fellow.[66]

Allen "Lefty" Bryant added,

Wilkie even traveled with the ball club. He made sure we eat whatever we wanted. If we couldn't get served. He got the food and brought it too us. Sometimes there were places on the road, where a black man could not get off the bus and go in and eat. He would go in and get the food and bring it out to us. He always saw that we had plenty of food. That J.L. was one of the finest persons I ever knew.[67]

George Giles, former Monarch first basemen, had this to say:

> The best man to ever live. Him and Rube Foster were the ones to start the league back in 1920. You know I tell those guys, that all the time I played ball, I never missed a paycheck with Wilkie in charge. Some of the guys didn't get all their money, but Wilkie always paid off.[68]

Like all great men, Wilkinson was not without imitators. After the Cleveland Buckeyes of the Negro American League won the Negro World Series in 1945, another Cleveland team — the Indians — were put up for sale. In June of 1946, a 32-year-old ex–Marine Bill Veeck purchased Cleveland's all-white team for $1.5 million. Veeck, in a move reminiscent of Wilkinson's master showmanship, advertised that he was "giving the Indians back to the fans." He attracted customers with a 42-inch-tall, 65-pound rookie, brilliant firework displays, and free orchids — all the way from Hawaii, in a nursery located under the stands for the mothers — and free nylon stockings for the ladies. The following year, Veeck provided fans with the utmost enticement, signing the first black player in the American League, a 22-year-old rookie second sacker named Larry Doby. The next year, 1948, while his pennant-driving Indians were setting a turnstile record of 2,260,627 fans, he signed the major leagues' oldest rookie, Leroy "Satchel" Paige, on his forty-second birthday, for a last hurrah.

The Wilkinson and Veeck act was repeated in the sixties when Charlie O. Finley, a former semipro pitcher, arrived in Kansas City with a "genuine" Missouri mule donated by state governor Warren Hearnes. Finley's handsome mule, Charlie O., lived in an air-conditioned trailer equipped with piped-in "mule music." Fans and non-fans alike screamed, for dissimilar reasons, when he imported four British players named John, Paul, George and Ringo to perform "A Hard Day's Night." The fans continued their screaming when Finley dressed his Follies in wedding gown white, Finley gold and Kelly green uniforms and shoed his players with white spikes from the pelts of rare Australian albino kangaroos — as they batted orange baseballs with gold and green painted bats.

Rival club owners cringed when Finley stocked a zoo behind the left-field bleachers with a German short-haired pointer, two peafowls, six capuchin monkeys, six China golden pheasants and six German checker rabbits with litters. He added a couple of grazing sheep, dressed in green and gold blankets, to the hilly terrain beyond the right field wall. For two exhibition games in April 1965, Finley built the short-lived 4½-foot-high wooden

"Pennant Porch" to mimic the short 296-foot right field line of Yankee Stadium. Commissioner Ford Frick declared the bleacher ballyhoo illegal, citing no new fences could be built within 325 feet of the plate.

Later, the never bashful Finley repeated Veeck's exploits and signed now 59-year-old Satchel Paige to pitch three innings. Paige's two-month contract for $4,000 from good-hearted Charlie O. left Paige 186 days short of qualifying for his major league pension.

Like Wilkinson, Finley was light years ahead of his time — proposing that the World Series be played at night. Unlike Wilkinson, in thirteen years, Finley's fanatical efforts failed to produce a single club able to win half its games. The latter day Kansas City team averaged 35 games behind the first-place finishers and an overall .404 winning percentage.

Long before Finley follies and the days of Harvey the mechanical home-plate rabbit (who now resides in a barn in La Porte, Indiana) and promotions like "Farmers' Night" and "Hot Pants Night," Wilkinson was baseball's original drum major. In the mid-'20s, he had introduced "Kids' Day" or "Knothole Day" (kids 15 and under, free) and "Ladies Day" or "Fannettes Day" (all ladies, free) at the ballpark. Earlier, in 1922, Wilkinson hired attractive lady ushers as an added attraction and an incentive for men to use less profanity. In 1939, he initiated one of his most popular promotions with the Monarchs' annual bathing beauty contest.

Mary Jo Weaver, who won the contest of bronze beauties the next year, recalled: "Churches would let out early to promote the Monarch parade. On opening day, some churches would even close. All the stores in town would have a cut on clothes and other goods — because the Monarchs were in town."

One year he offered two free season tickets to anyone who could guess the attendance of the home opener. He also offered prizes, such as free admission to the next game, if fans could guess the final score of today's game or that day's line-up.

During the war years, Wilkinson gave free admission to soldiers in uniform. He declared, "We know that baseball is essential, and we're going to play for the war workers, both day and night games and on Sundays and weekdays." He even adjusted game times to accommodate defense plant workers working the swing-shifts.[69]

Knowing the influence that black ministers played in the inner-city community, he customarily gave them free passes and occasionally played benefit exhibition games for the local churches. Ministers cooperated by dismissing their congregations in time to see a Monarchs game.

He organized a group of prominent black citizens to promote Monarchs baseball. His Monarchs Booster Association became the primary reason for their grand attendance. The Monarch Boosters were able to produce a wide geographical area of fan appeal despite the relatively small Midwestern market. Eventually, the conception behind the Booster Association became the antecedent to the Kansas City Royals' booster organization, the Lancers.

James Leslie Wilkinson was an innovator, a promoter, a beneficiary and personal confidant to his players. He presented our national pastime with a formula for racial harmony and a quality product. Though not given the honor, Wilkinson—not Branch Rickey—was the forerunner of interracial baseball. He produced champions of black teams who lived outside the glow of the national pastime, away from the brightest of white lights.

He also presented a new science to the game, long before televised baseball games, radar guns, laptop computers, pronto replays, plastic grass, faxed scouting reports, caged stadiums and carnival scorecards—and maybe even before aluminum bats and Teflon baseballs.

Future Hall of Fame sportswriter Wendell Smith of the *Pittsburgh Courier* wrote on June 9, 1945, one of the greatest tributes to Wilkinson and his Monarchs:

> One of those who has made a definite contribution to black baseball is J.L. Wilkinson, the silver-thatched, soft-spoken owner of the fabulous Kansas City Monarchs. Wilkinson has been in Negro baseball for more than twenty years, and during that time he has not only invested his money, but his very heart and soul. He has stayed in the game through storm and strife because he has loved it, not because he had to. There is no owner in the country—white or Negro—who has operated more honestly, sincerely or painstakingly. His baseball history is an epic as thrilling and fascinating as any sports story ever written.

Notes

1. *Atlanta Daily World*, 31 August 1938.
2. *Chicago Defender*, 28 August 1943.
3. *Chicago Defender*, 25 August 1945.
4. David Pietrusza, "Night Baseball Comes to St. Louis," *SABR 22 Conference Publication*, 36.
5. *Cleveland Plain Dealer*, 13 July 1930.
6. *Kansas City Call*, 27 July 1928.
7. John B. Holway, "K.C.'s Mighty Monarchs," *Missouri Life*, March–June 1975, 83-89.
8. Janet Bruce, *The Kansas City Monarchs: Champions of Black Baseball* (Lawrence: University of Kansas Press, 1985), 15.
9. *Ibid.*
10. Mark Schreiber, "Long Before Nomo," *The Journal*, July 1997.
11. William H. Young and Nathan B. Young, Jr., *Your Kansas City and Mine* (Kansas City: Midwest Afro-American Genealogy Interest Coalition, 1950), 69.
12. *Ibid.*
13. *Kansas City Call*, 28 May 1948, John L. Johnson's "Sport Light."
14. *Ibid.*
15. *Kansas City Star*, 20 October 1922.
16. *Kansas City American*, 16 August 1928.

17. *Kansas City Star*, 12 June 1930, Kansas Collections, University of Kansas.
18. Tom Baird undated press release, Harriett Baird Wickstrom, Kansas Collection, University of Kansas.
19. Undated letter to the author, circa 1990.
20. *Logan County News*, 17 and 24 April 1930.
21. *Blackwell Morning Tribune*, 25 April 1930, and *Tonkawa News*, 21 and 28 April 1930.
22. *Kansas City Call*, 12 September 1952.
23. *Okmulgee Daily Times*, 27 and 29 April 1930, 7.
24. *Enid Morning News*, 25 April 1930; *Kansas City Call*, 2 and 9 May 1930.
25. *The Daily Oklahoma*, 26 April 1930, 9 and *Ponca City News*, 28 April 1930, 7.
26. This documented travel of the K.C. Monarchs through Oklahoma, Kansas and Texas was done by Michael T. Thompson, of Norman, Oklahoma, in January of 1990, when he was a freshman at Oklahoma University. His father Steve described him as "a good student, a pretty good ballplayer, great fielding right fielder, fine arm, fairly good contact hitter, no power." Besides major Oklahoma newspapers, he also examined the *Newkirk Herald*, the *Blackwell Herald*, the *Oklahoma City Black Dispatch*, *Oklahoma City Eagle*, the *Tulsa Sun*, the *Tulsa Oklahoma Eagle* and the *Enid Daily Eagle*.
27. Gerald Early, *My Soul's High Song: The Collected Writing of Countee Cullen, Voice of the Harlem Renaissance* (New York: Doubleday, 1991) 116.
28. *Kansas City Call*, 38 March 1930.
29. Chet Brewer, interview with author, 22 October 1989.
30. John B. Holway, *Missouri Life*, March–June 1975.
31. *Kansas City Call*, 9 May 1930.
32. Holway, "KC's Mighty Monarchs."
33. *Ibid*.
34. Chet Brewer, interview with author, 22 October 1989.
35. Richard Wilkinson, interview with author, 30 December 1990.
36. *Kansas City Star*, 12 June 1930, Kansas Collections, University of Kansas.
37. Larry Lester, *Black Baseball's National Showcase: East-West All-Star Game* (Lincoln: University of Nebraska Press, 2002) 10.
38. Holway, "K.C.'s Mighty Monarchs."
39. George Giles, interview with author, 25 February 1991.
40. *Ibid*.
41. Buck O'Neil, interview with author, 13 September 1990.
42. Young and Nathan B. Young, Jr., 71.
43. Richard Wilkinson, interview with author, 30 December 1990.
44. Sales contract addendum, dated 5 February 1948, Kansas Collections, University of Kansas.
45. *Kansas City Call*, 27 February 1948.
46. Sales contract, dated 5 February 1948, Kansas Collections, University of Kansas.
47. Richard Wilkinson, interview with author, 30 December 1990.
48. *Ibid*.
49. Harriett Baird Wickstrom File, Kansas Collections, University of Kansas.
50. *Ibid*.
51. *Des Moines Sunday Register*, 20 May 1073, 4-B.
52. *Chicago Defender*, "Chandler Doesn't Believe in Barring Negro Players," 12 May 1945, 8.
53. *Kansas City Call*, "Texas Hornsby Says Negroes Will Fall," 2 November 1945.
54. *Ebony*, May 1949, 40.
55. Chet Brewer, interview with author, 24 November 1984.
56. Gene Benson, interview with author, 6 November 1990.
57. *Chicago Defender*, "End of Baseball's Jim Crow Seen with Signing of Jackie Robinson," 3 November 1945, 9.
58. *Ebony*, May, 1949, 40.
59. Buck O'Neil, interview with author, 13 September 1990.
60. Jesse Williams, interview with author, 25 February 1991.
61. Harriett Baird Wickstrom File, Kansas Collections, University of Kansas.

62. *Kansas City Call*, 27 October 1922.
63. *Kansas City Star*, 21 August 1964.
64. *Ibid.*
65. Buck O'Neil, interview with author, 13 September 1990. Originally published in *Unions to Royals: The Story of Professional Baseball in Kansas City* (SABR, 1996) and SABR 26 commemorative publication.
66. Connie Johnson, interview with author, 25 February 1991.
67. Lefty Bryant, interview with author, 25 February 1991.
68. George Giles, interview with author, 25 February 1991.
69. *Kansas City Call*, 28 May 1948, John L. Johnson's "Sport Light."

10

Tom Baird: A Challenge to the Modern Memory of the Kansas City Monarchs

Tim Rives

No Negro League team won more pennants, sent more players to the major leagues, or has more members enshrined in the National Baseball Hall of Fame than the Kansas City Monarchs. But buried in this glorious history lies a secret as big as the team's storied achievements, and so profound that it will challenge the way the great franchise is remembered and celebrated. The Monarchs' secret is that the man who was associated with the club longer than any other player, manager, owner, or executive was also a member of the Ku Klux Klan. His name is Tom Baird.

Arguably the least known member of Negro League baseball's best-known franchise, Thomas Y. Baird was born 27 January 1885 in Madison County, Arkansas. Baird moved to Kansas City* with his parents sometime after the turn of the century, going to work in the city's industrial district near the confluence of the Kansas and Missouri rivers. A good semipro baseball player, Baird was forced to quit playing the game following two leg fractures suffered while working as a train brakeman. Baird left the railroad to open the first of several pool halls and bowling alleys, but remained active in baseball as a manager and promoter. He started the Monarchs in December 1919 with J.L. Wilkinson, beginning a partnership that lasted nearly thirty years.[1]

---

*Unless otherwise noted, "Kansas City" refers to Kansas City, Kansas.

Tom Baird, Chester Franklin and J.L. Wilkinson gather to look over newspaper ads concerning the future of the Negro Leagues.

Baird and Wilkinson ran the Monarchs according to their abilities. The empathetic "Wilkie," as general manager, spent his time with the players, building remarkably close personal bonds, and becoming perhaps the most admired white man in black America. Tall, lean Tom Baird, whose austere mien did not suggest easy intimacy, covered the business end of the operation, booking games and making deals. Baird spent so much time behind the scenes that some early Monarchs players never knew he owned part of the club.

Baird bought Wilkinson's interest in the team in 1948 to become the Monarchs' sole owner. By the time he retired from Negro League operations in 1955, Tom Baird was the longest-serving owner in black baseball history, and almost certainly the only one who had ever worn a Klan robe.[2]

The evidence tying Baird to the Klan is found on a membership roster in the papers of Kansas governor Henry J. Allen at the Library of Congress. The 1922 ten-page Ku Klux Klan roster names individuals belonging to Klan

The long-time partner of J.L. Wilkinson, Tom Baird. Baird not only worked with Wilkinson to make the Monarchs a success but was involved in the local community as well.

chapters across the state of Kansas. "T. Baird" appears on page three, column four, one of 1,053 Kansas City members.[3]

The Ku Klux Klan (KKK) that counted Baird as a member was the second coming of the Invisible Empire. The first KKK had appeared shortly after the Civil War, when six ex–Confederate officers formed the organization as a social club. Impressed with the effect the club's white hoods and night riding antics had on African American freedmen, other white Southerners appropriated the order as a means to control former slaves and resist postwar Reconstruction. The Klan's influence and violence soon spread across the South, its power and lawlessness alarming federal authorities. The first KKK flourished until 1872, when the weight of mass arrests and convictions finally brought it down.[4]

The Klan remained in the memory of former slaves as an attempt to return them to bondage, and in the memory of white Southerners as a champion of law and racial order. It might have remained merely an object of memory had filmmaker D.W. Griffith not brought it back to life in his film *The Birth of a Nation*. Based on Thomas Dixon's novel *The Clansman*, the 1915 *Birth of a Nation* rehabilitated the image of the Klan in the white mind as a hero of imperiled civilization, striking contemporary resonance with whites concerned by the immigration of southern and eastern Europeans to American shores, and the migration of African Americans to northern cities.[5]

Coinciding with the appearance of *The Birth of a Nation* and capitalizing on its publicity, "Colonel" William Joseph Simmons, a former Methodist preacher, resurrected the Ku Klux Klan on Thanksgiving evening 1915. That night Simmons led fifteen recruits to the top of Stone Mountain, Georgia, where they burned a cross and, in his words, "dedicated themselves to those principles of Americanism embodied in the Constitution of the United States, consecrated themselves, as Protestants, to the tenets of the Christian religion, and pledged themselves, as white men, to the eternal maintenance of white supremacy." Simmons's Klan received a corporate charter from the state of Georgia in July 1916.

At first confined largely to the South, the new Klan might have expired from lack of interest had not two enterprising Georgians sensed its potential as a national fraternal organization and convinced Simmons to hire them. The marketing duo embarked on an aggressive nationwide recruiting campaign. Attracting hundreds of thousands of white, native-born, middle class Protestants, the Ku Klux Klan grew quickly, and by 1922 claimed somewhere between two and four million members. The revived KKK would thrive throughout the twenties. It was particularly strong in the Midwest.[6]

The Klan arrived in Kansas in early 1921. While some politicians endorsed or even joined the Invisible Empire, other elected officials saw it as a threat to public order. The Klan got off to a bad start in Kansas when it interfered in a railroad strike, intimidating African American replacement workers and earning the hostility of Governor Henry J. Allen. The governor suspected that the Klan, technically a Georgia corporation, was operating illegally in the state, and ordered an investigation. Allen also dispatched undercover agents to collect the names of Klan members.[7] He was not alone in this effort. Federal agents from the Bureau of Investigation were also peeking behind the mask of the Klan to see who was filling its sheets, and by November 1922 Governor Allen had the names of thousands of Kansas Klansmen, including the name of the Kansas City businessman who owned an interest in the Monarchs.[8]

There can be little doubt that the "T. Baird" who appears on the governor's Klan list is Tom Baird of the Monarchs. His personal papers are full of corroborating evidence. The newspaper clippings and other items deposited in his personal archive at the University of Kansas's Spencer Research Library document a web of relationships entangling nearly every aspect of his personal, social, business, and political life with other Klan members. Baird's papers show, for example, how he and his family socialized with the families of other men on the Klan list at neighborhood, church, and family (his cousin's husband was a member) events over the years.[9]

The records reveal that Baird not only broke bread with other Klansmen, he literally breathed the same air. His home at 1818 Grandview Boulevard, purchased from Klansman Homer D. McCallum in 1921, sat on the same block as the homes of Klansmen George Scherer, Dr. Cresse P. Rhoads, and Albert L. McCallum. The Boyn Building in the 1700 block of Central Avenue, where Baird ran a pool hall and kept a business office, also housed the local headquarters of the Knights of the Ku Klux Klan and its women's auxiliary. Dr. Rhoads, a dentist, had his practice there, as did the Baird family physician,

Dr. J.W. Sparks, whose name also appears on the Klan list. Another Klansman haunting the premises was William W. Maze, a longtime Baird associate and employee who managed one of Baird's bowling enterprises.[10]

Baird's Klan world would spread east past the state line into the heart of Kansas City's (Missouri) historic African American district with his purchase of 1822 and 1824 Vine Street. He insured his new holdings through agent Harold O. Tinklepaugh, whose name is also on the Klan roster. A parking lot now occupies the property. It sits diagonally from the Negro Leagues Baseball Museum. Tom Baird not only owned the Kansas City Monarchs, he owned part of their neighborhood, the world-famous Eighteenth and Vine.[11]

Klan membership rules and Kansas City population records provide further confirmation of Baird's secret allegiance. Klan chapters were divided by city boundaries. According to the rules, if a man wanted to join Wyandotte Klan No. 5 (the official name of the Kansas City chapter), he had to live in Kansas City, Kansas.[12] The Klan did this because it wanted members with strong local ties, men with roots in a city's past, and a stake in its future. Baird had the ties. He had lived in Kansas City since at least 1903, and would until he died in 1962. According to the city directory, he was the only adult male "T. Baird" residing in Kansas City from 1909 to 1954. The 1920 and 1930 federal censuses confirm him as the lone adult male "T. Baird" in Kansas City. Other similar names—names that might reasonably be confused with Baird's, such as "T. Bird," T. Bair," or "T. Bard"—fail to turn up in the city directories or in the 1920 or 1930 federal censuses of Kansas City. Only "T. Baird." Only Tom Baird.[13]

Baird's signature also supports the charge that he is the "T. Baird" on the Klan list. Baird used "T.Y. Baird" as his professional name, but his signature blurs the Y to the point where it looks like a mere line linking the T with Baird, and making it read "T. Baird." (If you were a Bureau of Investigation agent transcribing a list of signatures for your report on the Klan, you would transcribe it as "T. Baird," too.) The missing middle initial provides a fascinating insight into Baird family history. The Y is for Younger, as in Cole Younger: Quantrill Raider, James-Younger gang member, and great-uncle of Thomas Younger Baird.[14]

Finally, the social profile that emerges from the many associations documented in Tom Baird's papers completes the evidence identifying him as the "T. Baird" of the Klan list. A demographic study of Wyandotte Klan No. 5 found the average member to have been a middle-aged small business owner who voted Republican, frequented lodge meetings, and attended a mainline Protestant church. The middle-aged Baird owned small businesses, supported Republicans, belonged to the Masonic lodge (among others), and attended a Disciples of Christ congregation. Tom Baird, in other words, fit the Klan social profile to a "T."[15]

The evidence documenting Baird's Klan ties is strong, perhaps irrefutable. But it leaves the befuddling question, Why? As co-owner, and later sole owner, of the Kansas City Monarchs, Baird needed a large and prosperous African American community to make a living. White fan attendance at Monarchs games had declined sharply during the peak Klan years of the second KKK, dropping from fifty percent in 1922 to ten percent in 1926.[16] Baird needed black dollars. So why would he risk alienating his team's natural fan base by joining the Ku Klux Klan?

The Klan could have conceivably appealed to Baird for a variety of reasons, but the evidence suggests four: (1) he supported white supremacy; (2) he looked for solutions to social and political problems in mass movements; (3) he thought he could realize his professional ambitions by associating with other Klan members; and (4) he feared his pool halls would be shut down by powerful local regulatory officials who were Klan members.

The most sensitive, and possibly the most damaging reason for the memory of the Monarch franchise, is the first; that Tom Baird joined the Klan because he supported white supremacy. Once again, Baird's personal papers, along with an examination of Klan actions in Kansas City, suggest the answer.

Most modern scholars of the 1920s-era Ku Klux Klan see the order as having been more concerned with the power of Roman Catholics than with the presence of African Americans. The Kansas City Klan experience confirms this observation, but only to a point. Kansas City Klansmen—led in this instance by Baird's neighbor Cresse P. Rhoads—attacked the Roman Church rhetorically and politically, but when it came to African Americans, they took more direct action.[17] Some members advocated measures so extreme that they split the Klan chapter almost in two.

The split occurred after a fight over "methods and operations." Namely, how would the Klan reassert white, native-born Protestant control over Kansas City political and social institutions? Two views battled for the direction of Number Five. One, which might be described as the civic reform faction, favored legal political organizing and moral suasion. The other, perhaps best described as the old school vigilante faction, championed more traditional methods of intimidation such as the horsewhip, the tar bucket, and the hooded robe. The issue came to a head in June 1922 when a secret committee of Number Five Klansmen known as the "Kluxers" proposed a midnight raid on the home of the local school superintendent. The superintendent's crime was his plan to integrate African American children into the city's annual spring school pageant, an untenable proposition to Kansas City Klansmen. The Kluxers plotted to administer what one member euphemistically described as "corrective measures." (Another observer described the plan more explicitly as to "robe and inflict punishment.") Number Five's "Exalted

Cyclops" (president) and "Klabee" (treasurer) volunteered to lead the attack. The Klan officers had recently returned from training with the parent Georgia Klan, where they allegedly learned "how to disguise themselves so they would not be recognized ... by stuffing cotton in their mouths or jaws." The men also learned the finer points of how not to "permanently maim a person or kill them, but just [let] them know they had been dealt with by the Klan." A Klan attorney warned them that their plan constituted a conspiracy to violate federal law. He convinced them to visit the superintendent unmasked and in the light of day, which was done, and the pageant was cancelled. Still, the Kluxers' original plans for the superintendent troubled the Klan attorney and other more conscionable members, and on his advice, 450 men deserted Wyandotte Klan No. 5 at the next meeting.[18]

Number Five's anti–African American actions did not stop with its campaign to keep the school pageant white, however. Black and white newspapers documented cases where Number Five members tried to drive African American residents from their homes. The press also reported efforts by the Klan to restrict a park to whites only.[19] Despite the efforts of some historians to play down the 1920s' Ku Klux Klan's persecution and intimidation of African Americans, the Kansas City chapter apparently took the hooded order's commitment to the "eternal maintenance of white supremacy" seriously, and to heart.

Where were African Americans in Tom Baird's heart? Perhaps more important, what specific actions in his unique role as a Negro League baseball executive did he take — or fail to take — on their behalf?

Baird's personal opinion of African Americans is evident in a letter he wrote to Chicago Cubs farm club director Jack Sheehan in 1949. Former Monarch "Yellow Horse" Morris had applied for a job with the Cubs and given Baird as a reference. In his reply, Baird told Sheehan he did not know Morris well but remembered him as being "above the average in intelligence for a Negro."[20] These sentiments, while distasteful, fell well within the mainstream of white thinking at the time. But that doesn't excuse Baird's belittling prejudice, nor diminish its consequences. For Tom Baird probably had as much power as anyone in Negro League baseball to make or break careers. And he had this power during the most critical time in the history of the reintegration of African American players into the white minor and major leagues. According to his personal papers, he used this power to advance his interests ahead of his players.

Less than two years after former Monarch Jackie Robinson's 1947 major league debut, for example, some white executives already believed they had too many black players. Boston Braves minor league director Harry Jenkins confided to Baird that adding a fourth African American to his Milwaukee roster would make the team "top heavy" with "colored boys."[21] Baird, who was increasingly making his living off the proceeds of player sales to the white leagues, told Jenkins and other prospective buyers not to worry. His players might be black, but they didn't look like it. "Lefty LaMarque," Baird assured Jenkins, "is an intelligent looking Negro, in fact he might even pass for an Indian."[22] "Bill Breda," he told another executive, "looks like a white man from the stands."[23] "Both [Earl] Taborn and ... [Lefty] Bryant are very light in color and could pass for white men."[24] "You can't tell from the stands," he raved of pitcher Gene Richardson in no less than five letters, "whether Gene is white or colored."[25]

It could be argued in Baird's defense that he was trying to help his players by playing to the racist logic of the early post-apartheid market. After all, it would be to their advantage to play in the white major leagues. But that argument is a rationalization at best. The fact is, between 1949 and 1953, Baird had the perfect opportunity to expand the boundaries of organized baseball by insisting that white team owners accept his players on athletic merit alone, but didn't, or wouldn't. Baird apparently held too many bigoted opinions of his own to challenge on anything other than racist grounds the reluctance of the white baseball establishment to integrate its teams more quickly. He was forced to play his only card — the race card — promoting his players by skin tone (the lighter, the better) instead of by baseball ability.

So where were African Americans in Tom Baird's heart? Perhaps his personal feelings are most evident when the adjectives and similes he used to praise them are removed. And if the men he favored were by and large all "intelligent for their race" or "looked like white men from the stands," what would he have said about the rest of them?

Baird's ideological disposition to join mass movements offers another explanation for his Klan membership. Baird was a Townsendite, a supporter of Dr. Francis Everett Townsend's Old Age Revolving Pension plan. The 1933 Townsend Plan proposed to give $200.00 a month to every citizen age sixty and older on the agreeable condition that they spend it. A utopian panacea, the Townsend Plan would, supporters claimed, eliminate poverty among the elderly, stimulate the economy, and end the Great Depression. Townsend's idea proved so popular that Congress quickly passed a water-downed version of it in political self-defense. We know it as the Social Security Act.[26]

Dr. Townsend promoted less savory causes in 1936, supporting Union Party presidential candidate William Lemke. The problem wasn't so much the agrarian radical Lemke as the Union Party's de facto leaders, Father Charles Coughlin and the Reverend Gerald L.K. Smith, both of whom were degenerating rapidly to political positions charitably described as extremist. The Union Party fared badly that November, winning less than two percent of the popular vote and no electoral votes.[27]

Townsend survived both the passage of the Social Security Act and his misadventures with anti–Semites to continue the fight for more federal assistance to the elderly. With the economic uncertainty of old age coming at the self-employed fifty-eight year old Baird like a Satchel Paige fastball, this fight was probably what led him to join Kansas City's Townsend Club No. 11 in 1943. Upon joining, Baird was required to swear fealty "to its principles, to its founder ... to its leaders, and to all loyal co-workers," even apparently, the more notorious co-workers of the Smith and Coughlin variety. Baird's Townsend Club affiliation is important because it confirms his tendency to look beyond traditional governmental structures for solutions to political and social problems. It also shows that the more questionable associations of the movement's leaders and members did not trouble him.[28]

Baird's personal ambition provides another possible answer to the "why" question. From his blue-collar beginnings in Kansas City's industrial bottoms to his years promoting the Monarchs, Tom Baird aspired to be a man of consequence, a civic leader. Ambition led Baird to join numerous business, fraternal, and political associations, all of which paralleled and then merged with the path being blazed to power by the vanguard of middle class men who composed the 1920s' Ku Klux Klan.

Baird fell in line. He joined the Klan sometime in 1921 for the same reason men joined the Masons at other times in American history: for a brief and strange moment in the annals of the white middle class, the Ku Klux Klan was where you went to solemnize business and social relationships in bonds beyond the profane. It was how you became an insider. Klan organizing strategy and the peculiar contours of Kansas City history help explain this curious situation.

The Klan's organizing strategy was to find out what was bothering a community and offer the hooded order as a solution. What troubled potential Kansas City Klan recruits was, in a word, politics. The political trouble began in 1886 when business leaders trying to compete with state-line rival Kansas City, Missouri, created "Kansas City, Kansas" by consolidating the smaller towns of Armourdale, Armstrong, Kansas City, Riverview, and Wyandotte, Kansas. But consolidation failed to unite the new city commercially or politically.[29] More than thirty years later, Armourdale residents—Tom Baird's boyhood neighbors—still complained about the unpopular agglomeration. The adoption of city commission government in 1909 eliminated the last vestiges of the pre-consolidation political units, but again failed to unify the city. In fact, it made matters worse. Displaced community leaders, the old ward heelers, criticized commission government as antidemocratic. These men made the overthrow of the Kansas City commercial and political elites who had foisted the unwanted political changes on them their lifework. Klan organizers played to their discontent. The KKK, organizers promised them, will carry you secretly to power, like a Trojan horse in white sheet.[30]

And it did. United as never before by the infusion of Klan political energy, the old ward heelers took over the local Republican Party machine and rode it back into power. Beginning in 1922, they won more than 100 local political races, for everything from county commission seats to the board of education.[31] The Klan Republicans took City Hall in 1927. Their political success would touch even the Monarchs in 1928 when Mayor Don C. McCombs, whose name also appears on the Klan list, threw out the first pitch of the season.[32] Baird got in the political game in 1929 when he joined thirteen fellow Klan-tied candidates to make up nearly one-third of the field running for seats on the new Board of Public Utilities.[33] Baird failed in his attempt at elected office, but it didn't matter by then. His side of political outliers was now embedded deep inside Kansas City's power structure, a position they would hold for nearly thirty years, even if their formal Klan affiliation would wane in the early 1930s. Klansman Mayor McCombs remained in office for twenty of those years. Tom Baird finally found some measure of political power when he was appointed to the City Planning Board in 1954.[34] The appointment came from Mayor Clark Tucker, himself handpicked to succeed Mayor McCombs by a council led by a man who had appeared on the 1922 Klan list.[35] Thanks to the Klan—or at least to his fellow former Klan brothers—Tom Baird's arc of ambition was complete.

Finally, economic or official pressures may also have led Baird to join the Klan, or the Klan to seek Baird. The city welfare officer made more than 2,600 pool hall inspections in 1920, an extraordinarily high number given the relatively low number (fifty) of pool halls actually in Kansas City at the time. The welfare officer's own membership in the Klan may have forced the pool hall–owning Baird into joining in order to keep his license. This isn't as far-fetched as it may sound. The Klan was obsessed with crime. Klan leaders encouraged members to visit taverns and pool halls, eavesdrop on conversations, and report what they heard to police. Pool hall owners were in the unique position to act as the Klan's eyes and ears on the city's sporting class. This fact made Baird a prime target for heavy-handed Klan recruitment.[36]

Additional evidence may someday reveal whether it was racism, ideological disposition, ambition, coercion, or something else that led or lured Tom Baird into the Klan's embrace. Determining what led him out of the Klan clutch is just as difficult. Kansas City Klansmen had membership tenures ranging from one incriminating meeting to ten or more activist years. Baird's tenure is unknown. What is known, and what complicates the question, is that Baird lived, worked, recreated, and campaigned with other men on the Klan list his entire life — before, during, and after the Klan was in town. This was the genius of the second Ku Klux Klan, if that's right word for it. It recruited existing social networks and enrolled them in its ranks en masse. We now know this enrollment included the social network of the longest-serving team owner in Negro League history, Tom Baird.

Acknowledging Baird's secret Klan past is important for the proper memory and celebration of black baseball history because the Negro Leagues is the one Jim Crow institution celebrated without embarrassment. It was an institution born out of racism, yet it grew to become a symbol of African American achievement, a source of pride. Modern day Kansas City shares in this pride. Strengthened by the presence of the Negro Leagues Baseball Museum and aided by magnanimous former players who stress the team's athletic accomplishments over the city's (and baseball's) racist past, the Monarchs continue to win fans. Thousand of white Kansas Citians now wear the hat and uniform of a team that existed only because their ancestors denied black players the opportunity to play in the major leagues. Such is the irony of history and the strange cunning of nostalgia.

But nostalgia, it has been said, is history with the pain taken out. And before the costs of apartheid baseball in Kansas City and elsewhere — the stolen opportunities, wages, recognition, and pensions — are lost in the mists of sentimental and uncritical celebration, it is important to remember the forces and personalities that contributed to the stubborn segregation of American life and sport. The Tom Baird Klan revelation tempers the modern memory and commemoration of the Kansas City Monarchs with pain, with history.

Notes

1. Clippings, personal Items, and Scrapbook, Thomas Baird Collection, Kansas Collection, Spencer Research Library, University of Kansas, Lawrence (cited hereafter as Baird Papers).

2. James A. Riley, *The Biographical Encyclopedia of the Negro Baseball Leagues* (New York: Carroll and Graf, 1994), 45, 842–843; Janet Bruce, *The Kansas City Monarchs: Champions of Black Baseball* (Lawrence: University Press of Kansas, 1985), 19, 117.

3. Ku Klux Klan Membership Roster, 13 November 1922, Henry J. Allen Papers, Manuscript Division, Library of Congress, Washington, D.C. (cited hereafter as Allen Papers).

4. Shawn Lay, ed., *The Invisible Empire in the West: Toward a New Historical Appraisal of the Ku Klux Klan of the 1920s* (Urbana: University of Illinois Press, 1991), 1-2.

5. Thomas Dixon, *The Clansman: An Historical Romance of the Ku Klux Klan* (New York: Doubleday, Page, 1905); Lay, 4–5.

6. *Ibid.*, 6–8; Robert L. Duffus, "The Ku Klux Klan in the Middle West," *World's Work* 46 (August 1923): 363–372; William J. Simmons, "How I Put Over the Klan," *Colliers*, 14 July 1928, 32.

7. Charles W. Sloan, Jr., "Kansas Battles the Invisible Empire: The Legal Ouster of the KKK in Kansas, 1922-1927," *Kansas Historical Quarterly* 40 (Autumn 1974): 393-394.

8. Allen acknowledged receipt of the list in Henry J. Allen to Marshall Eberstein, 25 November 1922, Allen Papers.

9. Passim, Baird Papers. Baird's cousin was married to Roy L. Thomas, who appears on page three, column four of the list, Allen Papers.

10. Scrapbook, Baird Papers; Homer D. McCallum, page one, column one; George Scherer, page three, column two; Cresse P. Rhoads, page one, column four; Albert L. McCallum, page one, column four; J.W. Sparks, page two, column three; William W. Maze, page two, column three, Allen Papers; 1920 *Gate City Kansas City, Kansas, City Directory* (Kansas City: Gate City, 1921), 43, 344. (Cited hereafter as City Directory.); 1922-1923 City Directory, 69, 95; 1924-1925 City Directory, 90, 235; 1925 City Directory, 110; 1927 City Directory, 636; 1929 City Directory, 196.

11. "Correspondence About Insurance," 1947-1953, Baird Papers. The agent's name is Harold O. Tinklepaugh, page two, column four, Allen Papers.

12. *Constitution and Laws of the Knights of the Ku Klux Klan, Inc.* (Atlanta: Knights of the Ku Klux Klan, Inc., 1926), 9.

13. Passim, City Directory; *Fourteenth Census of the United States: 1920*; Records of the Bureau of the Census, Record Group 29; National Archives and Records Administration; *Fifteenth Census of the United States: 1930*, idem.

14. See numerous examples in Baird Papers; "Quantrill Raiders Reunion" clipping, *Kansas City Post*, 27 August 1926, no page, Clippings, ibid. Cole Younger's full name was Thomas Coleman Younger.

15. Timothy D. Rives, "The Ku Klux Klan in Kansas City, Kansas, 1921-1930" (M.A. thesis, Emporia State University, Kansas, 1995), 56-68.

16. Bruce, 44-45.

17. Shawn Lay, *Hooded Knights on the Niagara: The Ku Klux Klan in Buffalo, New York* (New York: New York University Press, 1995), 76-77. Baird's neighbor wrote the governor, "The Catholic are not entitled to an appointment from you, as none of them helped to elect you" (C.P. Rhoads to Ben S. Paulen, 30 January 1925, Governors Papers, Kansas State Historical Society, Topeka, Kansas). Paulen was widely believed to have been the Klan's preferred gubernatorial candidate in 1924.

18. Kansas, State v. Knights of the Ku Klux Klan, *Plaintiff's Abstract of the Record* (Topeka: n.d.), 41-47; 52-53. "Kluxers Broke Klan's Grip in K.C., Testimony," *Kansas City Kansan*, 1 May 1923, 1-2.

19. "Colored Man Gets Threat of Violence," *Kansas City Kansan*, 13 June 1922, 1; "Don't Fear the Coward," *Kansas City Kansan*, 7 April 1923, 2; "Klan Warns K.C. Colored," *Kansas City Weekly Press*, 5 April 1923, 1; "Shall We Have a Jim Crow Park in Kansas City?" *Kansas City Advocate*, 13 October 1922, 1.

20. Tom Baird to Jack Sheehan, 29 April 1949, Baird Papers.

21. Tom Baird to Lee MacPhail, 12 February 1949, Baird Papers; Harry Jenkins to Tom Baird, 9 March 1951, Baird Papers.

22. Tom Baird to Harry Jenkins, 19 February 1951, Baird Papers.

23. Tom Baird to John W. Mullen, 28 February 1952, Baird Papers.

24. Tom Baird to Jack Sheehan, 3 March 1949, Baird Papers.

25. Tom Baird to Jack Sheehan, 18 March 1949; Tom Baird to R. P. Brown, 23 December 1951; Tom Baird to R. P. Brown, 19 November 1952; Tom Baird to Robert C. Osland, 14 February 1953; Tom Baird to Robert C. Osland, 19 February 1953, Baird Papers.

26. Francis E. Townsend, *New Horizons* (Chicago: J.L. Stewart Publishing Company, 1943), 137-140; Alan Brinkley, *Voices of Protest: Huey Long, Father Coughlin and the Great Depression* (New York: Vintage Books, 1982), 222-226.

27. Duncan Aikman, "Lemke's New Party and Three Key Men," *New York Times Magazine*, 24 July 1936, 6-7, 18.

28. Baird's financial concerns are evident in Tom Baird to J.B. Martin, 1 November 1955, Baird Papers; Townsend Club No. 11 Membership Card, Baird Papers.

29. Leon Fink, *Workingmen's Democracy: The Knights of Labor and American Politics* (Urbana: University of Illinois Press, 1983), 113.

30. Rives, 8-15.

31. *Ibid.*, 72-85.

32. "Monarchs Home to Open the 1928 Season," *Kansas City Call*, 11 May 1928, 1.

33. Primary Ballot, Baird Papers. The other Klan-tied candidates were L.J. Canfield (Allen Papers, page three, column one); E.J. Coleman (page one, column four); B.R. Collins (page one, column three); David Gerber (page one, column three); Theodore L. Grindel

(page two, column three); William G. Morse (page one, column four); J.C. Murray (page one, column one); A.L. McCallum (page one, column four); B.A. Spake (page two, column one); Henry E. Stone (page one, column two); Harry M. Swartz (page one, column three); J. Earl Thomas (page two, column two). Lawrence E. Wilson was the Exalted Cyclops of Rosedale Klan No. 17. Rosedale became Kansas City's eighth ward in 1922.

34. Personal Items, Baird Papers.

35. "KCK's Mayors," *Kansas City Kansan*, 24 February 1985, 2A; J. Earl Thomas, page two, column two, Allen Papers.

36. "K.C. Man Tells of Being High Klan Official," *Kansas City Kansan*, 30 April 1923, 1–2. "Speed Up Welfare Work in Kansas City," *Kansas City Kansan,* 1 February 1921, 2. The city welfare officer in question was N.V. Reichenecker (page two, column one, Allen Papers).

11

Jackie Robinson and the 1945 Monarchs

Leslie A. Heaphy

Jackie Robinson broke the color barrier in major league baseball in 1947, becoming the first African American to play at that level since Moses Fleetwood Walker had played in Toledo in 1884. Robinson played a variety of sports in high school, college, and the Negro Leagues before joining the Montreal Royals in 1946 at the invitation of Brooklyn Dodgers owner Branch Rickey. In fact, Robinson's past prompted Rickey's interest in him. Robinson was born in Cairo, Georgia, one of five children to Jerry and Mallie Robinson. Robinson's family joined the many families migrating out of the South when they moved to Pasadena, California, where he grew up. That move brought him in touch with a different world than he had seen in Georgia. It opened up opportunities and gave him chances he never would have gotten had his mother not decided the family should move.

Jackie Robinson came in to this world on January 31, 1919, in Cairo, Georgia. He grew up on a farm with his five siblings and his parents, Jerry and Mallie. Jackie never got to know his father, who left when he was only months old. His mother moved the family to Pasadena, California, to give her children a better chance in life. Robinson got a chance to play sports as early as the fourth grade, playing soccer against his older classmates. Robinson went on to win varsity letters in football, baseball, basketball and track at Muir Technical High School. He continued to excel at Pasadena Junior College until he left in 1939 to attend UCLA. Robinson enjoyed great success in college and built quite a reputation for himself. Unfortunately, he had to leave school before he graduated to go to work, and then in 1942 he was drafted. While in the military Jackie served under white officers and even had the experience of being ordered to move on a bus by a white officer.

Rickey knew all this about Robinson and much more. He knew that Robinson excelled while playing alongside his white teammates, and had been a standout athlete at the University of California at Los Angeles. He was quite popular with his teammates because of his talent. In addition, Robinson had served in the army for three years under white officers and played shortstop for the Kansas City Monarchs in 1945, hitting .387 in forty-seven games, and playing in the All-Star Game. This all made Robinson an ideal candidate for Mr. Rickey.

Before he became famous for wearing Dodgers blue, however, Jackie Robinson wore the logo of the Monarchs. For one season Jackie roamed the infield for the reigning Monarchs, learning the game and honing his skills. He learned from the best, taking those lessons with him to Montreal and then to Brooklyn.

During his one year with the Monarchs Jackie Robinson played shortstop and earned himself a spot on the roster for the All-Star Game at Comiskey park. Winfield Welch named him the starting shortstop along with teammate Jesse Williams at second. Robinson went 0–5 in the game but played errorless ball in the field, and the West won 9–6.[1] Robinson also found himself selected by manager Quincy Trouppe to play in the 7th North-South Classic in September.

The regular season for the Monarchs opened with its usual fanfare in 1945. The Booster Club led off the parade followed by the Lincoln High and R.T. Coles High School bands. The American Legion Drum and Bugle Corps marked time for the soldiers from Fort Leavenworth and Fort Riley. After all the music died down the season got underway with two games against the famed Chicago American Giants. Manager Frank Duncan believed he had all the pieces for a championship team. The missing link had been their new shortstop, who joined them from the Pacific Coast League. Duncan said, "with Jackie Robinson, the crack Pacific Coast athlete, now playing short, that he has a championship team."[2] Duncan had acquired Robinson after his service and college commitments ended and Robinson approached Hilton Smith to try to get a job with the Monarchs.

After being invited to spring training Robinson won the starting shortstop job. He roomed with veteran pitcher Hilton Smith when the team traveled and would have had the chance to learn not only from him but other veterans on the club. The 1945 roster of the Monarchs shows names such as Manager Frank Duncan, future Hall of Famer Satchel Paige, Double Duty Radcliffe, Hank Thompson and Bonnie Serrell; Robinson would have had many opportunities to grow as a student of the game.

Shortly after the season got underway Robinson went to Boston with Sam Jethroe and Marvin Williams for a tryout with the Red Sox. Manager Joe Cronin watched some of the tryout, and though he acted impressed with Robinson no follow-up ever happened. This allowed Robinson to complete his only season in the Negro Leagues with the Monarchs.

At the plate Robinson often came through in the clutch to help the Monarchs win some big games. Early in the season the Monarchs split a series with the Birmingham Black Barons. Robinson contributed to a 7–0 victory with a line drive base hit that drove in the first two runs. Not

Jackie Robinson playing with the Monarchs in 1945 before signing with the Brooklyn organization and breaking the color line in 1947.

long after that series Robinson again helped his club beat the Cincinnati Clowns with an inside-the-park home run. Robinson took advantage of a little lackadaisical fielding, and his run was all that Hilton Smith and Booker McDaniels needed to shut out the Clowns. The Monarchs beat the Black Yankees in August behind the stellar pitching of Satchel Paige, 4–1, with the final run coming on a Robinson double in the seventh inning. In a series against the Homestead Grays Robinson tied a Griffith Stadium record with seven straight hits in the two games.[3]

Robinson helped his team not only with his hitting but his steady fielding and his base running, which created havoc at times. Robinson loved to make the pitcher have to think about him when he got on base. He tested catchers' arms and took the extra base whenever he saw an opening. Robinson and Jesse Williams developed into a strong double-play combination for manager Duncan throughout the season. At the start of the season there had been some concern as to whether Robinson would be able to make the throw from shortstop, but after Williams hurt his throwing arm Robinson stepped in and won the job.

By the end of the season owner Tom Baird reported Jackie hitting .345 for his ball club. His contract paid him $400 a month and Baird wanted to keep him but lost out to Branch Rickey and his minor league contract. When Robinson signed with Rickey and the Dodger organization many thought a veteran player with more than one year of experience in the Negro Leagues should have been chosen first. Robinson went on to prove that his excellent year with the Monarchs was not a fluke and that he had the skills to make it in the majors. He learned from his teammates and took those lessons with him to Montreal and then to Brooklyn.

While Rickey's scouts searched for possible candidates he got involved in the creation of the United States League (USL) by supporting the Brooklyn Brown Dodgers. Some of the other owners questioned his motives, but Rickey saw this as a way to scout Negro League ballplayers. While the USL folded rather quickly Rickey moved forward in his effort to desegregate major league baseball.

Rickey ordered his scouts to look for a ballplayer with skills as well as no skeletons in the closet, because he did not want any surprises. Rickey wanted just the right player to break the color line in the majors. If he chose the wrong player then it could be many years before the time would be right to try again, if ever. Rickey needed a ballplayer who could take all the insults, the threats and the jeers and keep right on playing. He believed that Robinson would be that player.

Jackie Robinson's signing in 1945 marked a major turning point for major league baseball and America. He became the first black to play at that level in the modern era. His contract altered the face of the game forever, and helped set in motion other changes throughout the United States. After all, America's national pastime changed its look for good. Other sports soon followed baseball's example.

Robinson's first season with the Dodgers organization found him playing for the minor league Montreal Royals. Rickey thought Robinson would have an easier time playing in Canada, facing less outright discrimination than in the United States. *The Sporting News* covered Robinson's year in Montreal extensively and quoted one of the French papers from that city calling Montreal a paradise for minorities.[4]

After getting married to Rachel Isum on February 10, 1946, Robinson and his new family joined the Royals for what would turn out to be an excellent year for Jackie and his new ball club. Robinson debuted for Montreal on April 18 at Roosevelt Stadium in Jersey City and helped the Royals to a 14–1 route. In his first game Robinson silenced a lot of voices with a 4–5 night at the plate, including a three-run homer, four RBIs, four runs scored and two stolen bases. His base running also forced two balk calls against the opposing pitching.

Robinson continued his torrid hitting throughout the season, staying near .370 for much of the season. In fact, the *Sporting News* reported Robinson batting .371 as late as August 14. He went 5–6 in a game against Syracuse on August 6 with four runs scored. On August 15 Robinson went 3–3 with four RBIs and four runs scored to help the Royals defeat the Newark Bears 21–6. By season's end Robinson not only led the International League in batting but he helped the Royals win the Little World Series.

After a successful season in Montreal, Robinson joined the Brooklyn Club in 1947, officially ending the color line and opening the door for others such as Monte Irvin and Larry Doby to follow him. Robinson's first full season with the Dodgers did not pass without trouble, however. Problems ranged from players threatening to strike to hate mail and death threats from fans, to constant badgering and insults on and off the field. Through it all, Robinson remained calm and kept his attention focused on the game.

Eventually, Robinson proved Rickey right in his selection by capturing Rookie of the Year honors in 1947. He followed that achievement by earning the Most Valuable Player Award in 1949, and made six straight All-Star appearances (1949–1954). The honors continued to accrue as Robinson won the National League batting crown and led the league in stolen bases in 1949, as well as participating in six National League Pennant races and one World Series in his ten seasons. In 1962, Robinson received the ultimate honor with his election to the National Baseball Hall of Fame after a ten year major league career in which he hit .311 in 1382 games.

Fans showed Robinson their esteem in a multitude of ways. For example, a 1947 national poll selected Robinson as the second most popular American behind singer Bing Crosby. He later became the first baseball player to appear on a United States postage stamp. In 1961, writer Maury Allen listed Robinson as the eleventh best player of all-time in baseball's top 100, and baseball researcher Bill James ranked Robinson as the eighth best second baseman to ever play the game.

Players who followed Robinson into the major leagues said that Robinson paved the way for them. Don Newcombe stated that Robinson, Larry Doby, Monte Irvin and the other early integrators took the worst abuse.

Satchel Paige later said, "I really believe they got the right man to break the color barrier. I don't know if I could have taken what Jackie did."[5]

Playing honors aside, Robinson's courage as the first African American to walk onto a modern major league field with his white teammates secured his place in American history. Robinson and Rickey helped end the color line and changed the face of America's national pastime forever. Now it could more rightly claim that title.

Kansas City Monarchs Roster (1945)

Abernathy, James — cf
Berry, John Paul — 1b
Carlyle, Sylvester "Junius" — inf
Davis, Lee — p
Duncan, Frank — c/mgr
Gray, Chester — c
Harper, Dave — of
Haynes, Sammy — c
Hood, Dozier — p
LaMarque, James "Jim" — p
Locke, Eddie — p
Long, Emory "Bang" — of
Mack, John — p
Massingale, Garcia "Mack" — of
Matchett, Jack — p
McDaniels, Booker — p
McMullin, Clarence — of
Moody, Lee — 1b/3b
Moreland, Nate — p
Paige, Leroy "Satchel" — p
Radcliffe, Theodore "Ted," "Double Duty" — c
Ray, John — of
Renfroe, Othello "Chico" — inf/of
Robinson, Jackie — ss
Scott, John — of
Serrell, William "Bonnie" — 1b
Smith, Hilton — p
Smith, Theolic — p
Souell, Herb — 3b/inf
Thomas, Walter — of/p
Thompson, Henry "Hank" — 2b
Walker, George — p
Washington, Lafayette "Fay" — p
Williams, Jessie H. — 2b/ss
Williams, Eli — of
Wylie, Enloe — p
Young, Leandy — of

Notes

1. "West Takes All-Star Classic 9 to 6," *Chicago Defender*, 4 August 1945, 7.
2. "Chicago Opens League Race in Kansas City," *Chicago Defender*, 5 May 1945, 7.
3. "Kansas City Divides with Black Barons," *Chicago Defender*, 14 April 1945, 7; "Kansas City Wins 4 to 0 from Cincinnati Clowns," *Chicago Defender*, 28 April 1945, 7; "Paige Defeats Black Yankees," *Chicago Defender*, 18 August 1945, 7; "Grays Defeat Kansas City," *Chicago Defender*, 30 June 1945, 7.
4. Al Parsley, "'Guess I'm Just a Guinea Pig,' Says Robinson," *Sporting News*, 1 November 1945.
5. Dwight Chapin, "The Bad Old Days...," *Los Angeles Times*, 13 January 1977, D4.

PART III

The Negro Leagues and Integration

12

Popularity and Perceptions of the Negro Leagues

Stephanie Fleet-Liscio

Prior to the integration of major league baseball in 1947, Negro League baseball was an institution that drew many fans, both white and black. Even though the Negro Leagues lasted after the integration of the major leagues, they were never the force in popularity and success that they were in earlier years, especially the way they were in the late 1930s and early 1940s. An examination of the two major Negro leagues, the Negro American League and the Negro National League shows how the leagues struggled and also how they were able to succeed and flourish. One can also see how the leagues were perceived by the public, including both white and black fans. The leagues were forced to struggle with two conflicting popular images: the image of hardworking and talented ballplayers and the image of men who clowned and joked on the field more than they played serious ball. Negro League players were often perceived as second-class citizens, or not as talented as white major league players. Even Bob Williams, sports editor for the *Call and Post*, Cleveland's African American weekly newspaper, once said, "The people are tired of paying first class money for second class baseball. They are tired of this foolish ban on the Negro in this one sport when he has added color and excellence to every other sport in which he has participated."[1] Even though it seems as if Williams thought black players were capable and talented enough to play in the major leagues, he thought the Negro Leagues in general were second-class. To attract fans, some teams portrayed the image of clowns and jokers in order to set them apart from the perception that they were part of a second tier baseball league.

One of the great team of the Negro Leagues were the Homestead Grays run by Cum Posey. Top row, from left to right: Charlie Walker, Jr., Mo Harris, William Ross, Buck Ewing, Smokey Joe Williams, George Scales, Judy Johnson and Cum Posey; front row, Vic Harris, Jake Stephens, Oscar Owens, Lefty Williams, George Britt, Bennie Charleston, and Oscar Charleston.

Author Janet Bruce said the Negro Leagues began their success during the Depression, since there was a lessening of racial tensions during that time period, "as both races grappled with the Great Depression, and certainly, black baseball benefited from this." Her example to support this argument is that many semipro clubs in the South were forced to disband for financial reasons and would then need to play black teams in order to fill their schedule. This example doesn't necessarily point to a lessening of racial tensions, but it does point to an improvement of the racial situation based on economic reasons. Bruce does not provide greater details on how exactly racial tensions decreased during the Depression, but because of the financial struggles of certain teams, it did open some doors to Negro teams that might not have otherwise been opened.[2]

Another development that Bruce cites is the increase in night baseball games in the Negro Leagues during the Great Depression. While she notes that there were night games long before the Depression-era Negro Leagues, it was J. Leslie Wilkinson, the white owner of the Kansas City Monarchs Negro League team, who put it into regular practice. In fact, Bruce says that Wilkinson was often referred to as the "father of night baseball." The insightful owner had a portable lighting system, which, Bruce said, "saved the team during the Depression." Initiated around 1930, the lighting system enabled night baseball games, which meant that more people could attend after work in the evenings. Also, it allowed for a greater time frame to be considered when making the game schedule, easing the rescheduling of rainouts. Wilkinson did not escape criticism from the white major leagues, with some critics referring to the lighted games as "outdoor vaudeville." This would not be the last time that someone would refer to a Negro League player or a Negro League team as something that was strictly entertainment and with no tangible value as a sport. Often the African American players were portrayed as something not to be taken seriously, or at least not as seriously as the white major leagues were taken. Other critics said the lights "profaned a great game God meant to go with sunlight." This quote seems to want to paint the Negro Leagues as something almost unholy by playing at night, something the white leagues would never consider doing. It only took white teams about five years to realize the money available in playing at night, though, as the major leagues played their first game under lights in 1935.[3]

Also during the 1930s, the city of Pittsburgh was able to support two Negro League teams, the Pittsburgh Crawfords and the Homestead Grays. In fact, Gus Greenlee, the owner of the Crawfords, helped to build the team their own stadium. Most teams simply rented white major league stadiums to play in, but that posed several problems such as scheduling conflicts and disputes over how much the Negro League teams would pay in rent. During the first game at the Crawfords' stadium on April 30, 1932, against the New York Black Yankees, 5,000 fans attended including the mayor, city council and county commissioners of Pittsburgh and Allegheny County.[4] These dignitaries were probably there more in support of the white owner Greenlee than they were to support the institution of Negro League baseball. It still serves as a great example of how popular Negro baseball must have been in Pittsburgh to support not only two teams, but an independent stadium as well.

One of the most popular competitions within the Negro Leagues was the East-West All Star Game, which took place every year in late July or August. It was started during the Depression by Greenlee in 1933 and was often called the "event of the season."[5] Sports writer Nat Trammell referred to the game in 1934 as "the greatest event that could be put over by anyone for the benefit of promoting interested in Colored baseball." He also said that any fans that would happen to witness the East-West game would be "convinced that Colored baseball players rank on a par with any major leaguer."[6] It was much more popular than the Negro League World Series, which was often played as a "barnstorming" tour through about four or five cities and not just in the cities of the two champion teams like in the white major leagues. Barnstorming is the term used to refer to teams that would travel from city to city playing for a new set of fans each day. Average attendance for a Sunday Negro League game would be around 10,000 while the East-West game never attracted less than 20,000. The game was always played at Comiskey Park in Chicago, until 1946 when due to popularity and the ability to attract fans, they added in a second game at Griffith Stadium in Washington, D.C. There was enough popularity for multiple games in 1947 and 1948 as well when Chicago and New York City both hosted the East-West game. In 1947 the games were held in Comiskey Park in Chicago and the Polo Grounds in New York, while in 1948 the games were held at Comiskey Park and Yankee Stadium.[7] The East-West game was important for several different reasons. This was the one time each year that black talent was showcased and white reporters would take notice. This was also the first chance teams would have to turn a sizeable profit for the season, often pulling themselves out of the red through their share of the profits from the game. These profits would allow teams to pay for their players' salaries and also hold some of the money in order to have a bit to start the next season with.[8] Later, the game held importance as something that scouts from the white major leagues could attend in the hopes of finding new players. A *New York Times* article from 1947 states that at least one major league scout from the Chicago Cubs was in attendance at that year's East-West game. Other than this fact, and a mention a game attendance of 38,402, the article was mainly focused on the statistics of the game and included box scores from each team at the end of the story.[9] A 1948 *Times* article on that year's game also mentions the possible attendance of scouts at the game, and names the players who were "graduates" of the Negro League circuits who were now playing in the white major leagues such as Satchel Paige, Larry Doby, Jackie Robinson and Roy Campanella.[10] The selected players were voted on by fans, with ballots placed in most of the African American newspapers that fans could fill out and send in. Because of the fact that Chicago and Pittsburgh had two of the largest African American publications, the *Pittsburgh Courier* and the *Chicago Defender*, these two cities also had the largest representation in the All-Star Game.[11] Players like Josh Gibson, often billed as the black Babe Ruth, and Satchel Paige, the tall, lanky pitcher, were drawing cards for most fans.

No single player could be considered more of a draw to fans than Leroy "Satchel" Paige. Just as the home run race between Sammy Sosa and Mark McGuire in 1998 is often credited with bringing fans disenfranchised by the 1994 players' strike back to baseball and strengthening attendance wherever the two men played, Paige, an Alabama native, was a draw wherever he traveled. Author Robert Peterson said that "Paige's drawing power was the difference between red and black ink on the ledgers of marginal Negro clubs."

Bill Veeck, the owner of the Cleveland Indians who signed Paige to his first Major League Baseball contract in 1948, once referred to him as a "skinny Paul Bunyan, born to be everybody's most memorable character."[12] Author Neal Lanctot said that the rise of Paige "reflected black baseball's new vitality," as Paige became a national celebrity, crossing the boundaries of both white and black newspapers. Lanctot credits his popularity to his "outstanding pitching, various eccentricities and uncertain age"[13] (a reference to the fact that many were uncertain of the great pitcher's age, as he was often rumored to be about 5–10 years older than he said he was). Each of these descriptions of Paige deserves a more thorough explanation in order to better understand the phenomenal pitcher.

Veeck described Paige's pitches as having "blinding speed" in his younger days, yet only a "wrinkle of a curve." The curve, according to Veeck, did not develop fully until Paige was 54 years old. A passage from Veeck's autobiography explained in further detail the style of the great Satchel Paige:

> He had all kinds of different deliveries. He'd hesitate before he'd throw. He'd wiggle the fingers of his glove. He'd wind up three times. Satch was always a practicing psychologist. He'd get the hitters overanxious, then he'd get mad, and by the time the ball was there at the plate to be swung at, he'd have them way off balance.
>
> His greatest asset, though, was his control. One of his barnstorming gags was to set up a one-by-two plank behind home plate and stick four tenpenny nails into it. Then he'd drive the nails into the board by pitching from the mound. And never take more than ten pitches. That's control, man. One of my own unfilled ambitions is to start a game with an entire team of midgets and let them go a couple of times around the batting order, walking endlessly. Another of my unfilled ambitions is to pitch Satchel Paige against that same team of midgets. Satch, I think, is the only pitcher alive who could get the ball consistently into that tiny strike zone.[14]

There are other stories about Paige's control and his complete confidence in his own pitching ability. In his youth when he was playing semipro ball in Mobile, Alabama, Paige supposedly called the outfielders on the team in since he was confident not only that he could get the batter out, but that the batter wouldn't even make contact with the ball. This is something that Paige reportedly did often, but only if the team he was playing for had a safe lead. In addition to dramatics like this, Paige would also make promises such as that he would strike out the first six or the first nine in a game, and then would follow through on his promise.[15] It is difficult to know the accuracy in claims such as these, but Paige himself discussed these events in his autobiography *Maybe I'll Pitch Forever*. Paige told a story of how the defense fell apart around him when he played with a semipro league in Mobile, Alabama, in 1926. With the bases loaded and a one-run lead, Paige claimed he called in his outfielders and struck out the batter for the final out of the inning. He also claimed that when he played for friend and manager Alex Herman on the Chattanooga Black Lookouts in the Negro Southern League, he called in the outfield with some regularity. Paige said that he and Herman performed the trick to draw fans to the game, yet only did it when their team was safely in the lead. He also discussed a gag he once performed where he lined up 10 pop bottles in front of home plate and knocked the bottles over with pitches. In his autobiography, Paige claimed that he could "nip frosting off a cake with his fastball." Paige also corroborated Veeck's claim that his curve did not develop until later in his life, and said that his fastball was so good there was no need for a curveball early in his career.[16] Paige's autobiography was not published until 1961, meaning that some of the events he discussed in the book took place as much as 35 years earlier. It is possible that there are some distortions and inaccuracies when recalling events that took place so many years before.

Paige's attitude and personality drew almost as much attention as his pitching abilities. Many teams in the Negro Leagues considered him an unreliable contract jumper because he would go from team to team, regardless of whether or not he still had a contract with a team. In 1938, he was even banned by the Negro National League because of his willingness to cut out of a contract.[17] At times in the early 1940s many players, both white and black, threatened to travel to Mexico to play because of the promise of more money. Paige was completely aware of the crowds he brought to the Negro Leagues and would often exploit that if given the opportunity. He realized the significance of the East-West game to the owners from a financial standpoint and he also realized that many of the fans were coming to the game to see him. In the early 1940s he demanded a share of the profits, something players did not always receive, for playing in the game. At first, they played just for the honor and later played for around $50 and travel fees to the game, but Paige wanted more. At first the owners obliged, giving only Paige more money, something that many sportswriters claimed was unfair to the other players. By 1944, however, the owners refused to give Paige a greater share of the profits from the game and he threatened to pull out of the event. Paige tried one last ditch effort, claiming that all of the proceeds from that year's game should be given to the Army-Navy Relief Fund since the country was in the midst of World War II. The Negro League owners not only balked at this idea, but then declared Paige ineligible to play in that year's East-West game.[18]

The game drew enough national attention that the *New York Times* covered the game, yet did not dedicate an excessive amount of space to it. Annually a small story would run in the *Times* regarding the battle between the East-West all-stars, providing a recap of the major action and in some years a box score containing the statistics of the players' performance in the game.

An article from the August 14, 1944, edition of the *New York Times* addressed the Paige controversy along with a summation of the game. "Leroy (Satchel) Paige, legendary Negro pitcher, did not play for the West today as a result of a dispute over distribution of receipts. Paige, who said he demanded the receipts should be turned over to charity, unsuccessfully attempted to get other all-stars to withdraw from the game."[19] The way this article addresses the disagreement, Paige is painted in a favorable light. The owners are depicted as greedy, not just for keeping the proceeds from being donated to charity but from preventing the popular Paige from pitching in the annual all-star game. Throughout World War II, the Kansas City Monarchs, Paige's Negro League team at the time, drew crowds better than most other Negro League teams, with an average of 6,000 to 7,000 fans per game. When Paige pitched there were sometimes as many as 30,000 to 40,000 fans in attendance, with a relatively equal number of whites and blacks in the stands.[20] That both whites and blacks were fans of Paige may be why the *New York Times* was more likely to be forgiving of Paige, yet more critical of the Negro League team owners.

Chester Washington, a sports writer from the *Pittsburgh Courier*, addressed this swell in crowd figures when he expressed excitement to learn that Paige was returning to the Pittsburgh Crawfords in 1936. Washington wrote that the return of Paige "will greatly enhance the drawing power of this already popular club," and that Gus Greenlee "says Satch is worth every penny he's spent on him." Washington also says, "Especially in the east, fans are practically Crawford crazy, and when Satch sweeps into town with them, it will be like the coming of the circus."[21] This article by Washington emphasizes the drawing power of Paige and how much extra money he could earn for a team's ownership. It also compares the popularity of Paige to the coming of a circus, another example of Negro League baseball being more like an entertainment spectacle than a legitimate sporting event.

Paige was not always depicted as so altruistic in newspaper stories like the *Times* article, however. In an article from 1943, Wendell Smith paints Paige as a "loafer" and is fairly hard on the pitcher for not showing up when he was to make a scheduled appearance. Paige had earned a reputation for standing up scheduled appearances.

> Leroy (Satchel) Paige made suckers out of 10,000 people Wednesday night at Forbes Field! He made 'em turn out ... stand in line ... and then crane their necks like a flock of kangaroos, looking for him after they had paid out their hard-earned dough to see him pitch against the Homestead Grays.
> The "Great Satchel" ... the man who has received more than any other player in the history of Negro baseball for doing less ... didn't feel like putting on his uniform Wednesday night.... So he just lolled around in the dressing room while his mates were out on the field taking a shellacking from the Homestead Grays.

The article goes on to suggest that Paige claimed he didn't show up because he was not scheduled to pitch anyway, yet the article asserts that fans would not have been upset if Paige had a legitimate excuse for not showing up. Smith then attacks the image of Paige as the ceaseless barnstormer with a rubber arm, calling reports of the famous player's having pitched in 100 games "publicity hooey." Paige in fact "coasted," Smith contends, earning some $15,000 for "approximately 15 ball games."[22]

This article is very interesting for the way it plays on prejudicial stereotypical attitudes regarding African Americans. At this point in time Paige was playing for the Kansas City Monarchs, a team that has a history of white ownership. This article implies that through Paige's laziness and shifty attitude he was taking advantage of the white owners of the Monarchs by earning more than any other player while doing less than these other players. Paige was the big drawing card, the star of the league that attracted both black and white fans. This could be the reason that these stereotypes were directed toward him, yet not toward other Negro League players.

The other interesting fact about this article is that it was written by Wendell Smith, a prominent African American sportswriter with the weekly *Pittsburgh Courier* in the 1930s and 1940s. In addition to his position as a sportswriter with the *Courier*, Smith maintained a close relationship with Jackie Robinson, the first baseball player to break the color line in the white major leagues. It is difficult to imagine why Smith may have wanted to depict Paige as an unsavory character within the context of the Negro Leagues, but one can theorize about Smith's motives. Starting in the early 1940s, Smith began a push to convince white major league teams to accept an African American player to end segregation. It is entirely possible that Smith recognized the potential controversy with Paige and wanted to draw attention to less controversial Negro League players in the hopes that one player would soon be able to integrate the major leagues. Once Paige himself was brought to the Cleveland Indians during the 1948 season, he maintained his reputation as a playboy and as a player that neglected to show up at the ballpark when he was supposed to. Supposedly Cleveland manager Lou Boudreau's patience had worn thin regarding Paige, and there were rumors that he would not be brought back to Cleveland after the 1949 season. Regarding this scenario, Smith is especially harsh, saying, "If you were Satchel Paige would you represent your people admirably or would you remain Satchel Paige?" Smith once wrote that Paige "should not be allowed to jeopardize men like Larry Doby, Jackie Robinson, and Roy Campanella, all of whom have acquitted themselves as gentlemen on and off the field."[23] These quotes show that Smith did have some apprehension that Paige's attitude could end up jeopardizing young African Americans hoping to integrate the white major leagues.

One Negro League teammate of Paige's from the Birmingham Black Barons and the Pittsburgh Crawfords in the early 1930s had this to say about Paige as a teammate:

> We'd leave the hotel, go to the ballpark — no Satchel. Fifteen minutes before gametime, somebody would say "Hey, Satchel just came in the dressing room." He was always full of life. You'd forgive him for everything because he was like a great big boy. He could walk in the room and have you in stitches in ten minutes' time. He'd warm up by playing third base or clowning with somebody and then he'd go out and pitch a shutout. How could you get mad at a guy like that?[24]

This quote shows that even some of Paige's own teammates saw him as someone who liked to have fun and was never extremely serious about playing the game, or at least not as serious as some of the other players were. It is interesting that this was the most popular of all of the Negro League players, the one whose mere presence could boost game attendance by the thousands on days that he pitched.

Smith and another prominent African American could also be somewhat critical of the Negro Leagues in general. The first African American in the major leagues, Jackie Robinson, had his own column in the *Pittsburgh Courier* throughout the 1947 season, the season he integrated the major leagues. In one of these columns, Robinson weighs in on the Cleveland Indians' addition of Larry Doby, the second African American to enter the major leagues and the first in its American League.

> I am sure Larry is going to like being in the big leagues. I know that I sure do. It's plenty tough up here, but there's nothing like it. One thing he is sure to find out quickly and that is that there is a great difference between the majors and the Negro National League. I don't mean that the Negro National League is a great deal inferior. They play good ball and they play hard. But I think the big difference is experience. In the majors you seldom have an easy day. Every day you face a pitcher, for instance, who is good. He knows exactly what he's doing and I have found that most of them are very smart. They make very few mistakes. They've been schooled for years on baseball technique and know the game inside and out.[25]

It is surprising to find Jackie Robinson making a statement about experience compared to the Negro Leagues and the white major leagues. Even though Robinson only spent a year with the Kansas City Monarchs, he still had to know that many of the Negro League players not only played almost every day during the season, but would often barnstorm during the off-season in the United States, Caribbean and South America. Not to say that there were no white players who participated in off-season baseball, but for Robinson to imply this makes the Negro League players sound inexperienced, which they were not. Robinson played with Satchel Paige on the Monarchs, so he obviously knew that there were intelligent Negro League pitchers who knew exactly what the opponent was doing. Take Hilton Lee Smith, who also pitched for the Monarchs, for example. Alex Radcliffe of the Chicago American Giants once said, "The hardest pitcher in baseball for me to hit was Hilton Smith of Kansas City, and there were very few pitchers I respected." Often overshadowed by Paige, Smith was well respected by fellow baseball players, including Paige. In fact, in 1942 when Paige was questioned about the possibility of signing African American players to the major leagues, he suggested Smith as a good candidate for success. It was even Smith that recommended Robinson to the Kansas City Monarchs after he saw him play during winter league baseball.[26]

In a *Pittsburgh Courier* column from 1940, the writer Randy Dixon is very critical of the Negro National League, at one point writing, "Does the league accomplish anything at its meetings? No, the league does not accomplish anything at its meetings? [*sic.*] The age of miracles is past."[27] While one may think that it is another instance of the *Courier* making a lazy reference to something involving the Negro Leagues, Dixon later reveals that the meetings are closed to reporters and is very critical of this fact. It is possible that *Courier* columnists (like Dixon and Smith) were critical of the Negro Leagues simply because they would not grant them access to meetings and the inner workings of teams. When Robinson spent his first spring training in Florida with the Brooklyn Dodgers, Smith stayed with Robinson and was granted great access to the young second baseman. Smith's files at the National Baseball Hall of Fame and Museum in Cooperstown, N.Y., show a record of correspondence between Robinson and Smith and also Smith and Branch Rickey, the general manager of the Brooklyn Dodgers that signed Robinson. Since he was treated with a more open attitude by the Dodgers, it might mean he has less bitter feelings toward them than toward the Negro League teams that shut reporters out of meetings.

There are other instances of Smith criticizing the African American community, however. In a 1938 *Courier* column, Smith is very critical of African Americans for attending white major league games while they still refused to integrate.

> Why we continue to flock to major league ball parks, spending our hard earned dough, screaming and hollering, stamping our feet and clapping our hands, begging and pleading for some white batter to knock some white pitcher's ears off, almost having fits if the home team loses and crying for joy when they win, is a question that probably never will be answered satisfactorily. What in the world are we thinking about anyhow?[28]

When black fans eagerly supported these white teams even though they would not integrate, Smith said they were almost betraying the Negro Leagues by not providing them more support. So even though he is actually more supportive of the Negro Leagues than he is in some of his other columns, Smith still offers a form of criticism to the African American community in general.

Despite critiques, the 1940s led to a surge in popularity of the Negro Leagues. The Kansas City Monarchs saw a great increase in attendance during the war, despite the fact that it is estimated that more than one million African Americans left to fight in World War II, including at least 14 Monarch players.[29] Despite this fact, what probably led to the increase in popularity and overall attendance is the fact that more African Americans had slightly more disposable income to attend games. The need for workers in defense factories led to more African American employment, with most probably earning higher wages than they had prior to the war. Because owners like Wilkinson of the Monarchs made wartime adjustments such as shifting game times around to accommodate swing-shift workers and allowing all soldiers in uniform to get into games for free, fans could more easily attend games. Mary Jo Weaver, who was named "Miss Monarch" in 1940, said, "I don't think there was a black person in Kansas City that would miss a game." The only other team that Kansas City had to offer at this point was a New York Yankees minor league club. While this team introduced some star players, these players were always brought very quickly to New York to play with the major league club. One also has to consider the increase in the African American population in most Northern cities during the 1940s, due to the migration of many Southerners to the North. A large percentage of Negro League teams were in the North, and these Southern migrants may have chosen to attend these games as a form of entertainment.[30]

Also gaining in popularity during the 1940s were the off-season barnstorming teams. Paige first teamed with famous major league pitcher Dizzy Dean as each man would preside over his own barnstorming team in cross-country competition. Immediately following World War II, it was Paige and pitcher Bob Feller who became known for their barnstorming tours. In 1948, Paige and Feller would pitch together on the world champion Cleveland Indians team, but prior to that they were known for their barnstorming. The two men and their teams flew across the country in two Flying Tiger aircraft left over from the war and called their tour the Paige/Feller All-Stars. The teams played 32 games in 26 days and drew over 400,000 fans during their 1946 tour. The barnstorming players made more money than white major league World Series players and were so popular that baseball commissioner Kenesaw Mountain Landis issued a ban on barnstorming until the 1946 World Series between the St. Louis Cardinals and Boston Red Sox was over. To this act, a sportswriter from the *Kansas City Call*, an African American paper, said,

"Can't have the Negro ball player show up the whites, y'know." When the barnstorming tour was complete, many of the black stars would fly to Los Angeles to form Chet Brewer's Kansas City Royals in the California winter league. At times entertainers Cab Calloway and Lionel Hampton would show up, put on uniforms and serve as coaches to the delight of the fans.[31]

Another Negro League team existed during this time period that provided a great deal of entertainment to fans. The Indianapolis Clowns was a team often compared to the Harlem Globetrotters, a team that attempted to entertain not only through their play but also through their on-field antics. During the 1930s and 1940s, some of the antics the Clowns took part in were wearing grass skirts, "painting their bodies in a storybook approximation of cannibals" and using such names as Selassie, Mofike, Wahoo and Tarzan.[32] Some did not agree with the concept of the team, also referred to as the Ethiopian Clowns, because it just perpetuated negative black stereotypes. For example, at one point Wendell Smith said that the Clowns' antics were little better than "minstrel shows," and said he believed that most African Americans disagreed with the concept behind the team. However, the Clowns drew large crowds despite a ban from the Negro American and Negro National Leagues barring competition against them. One person admitted, "Whether some of us like the white chalk put on the players' faces or not (another one of the clowns' antics), the Clowns prove, from the crowds they draw, that they have something the public wants."[33]

Larry Doby, a former player for the Negro National League Newark Eagles and in 1947 the first African American to integrate the all-white American League, weighed in on his opinion of the Clowns during a 2001 interview with former Major League Baseball commissioner Fay Vincent. Doby said the Negro Leagues were often painted by some as being about clowning and showmanship and he believed that misconception came from the Clowns. Doby expressed worry that children might see a team like the Clowns and think that all of the Negro Leagues were like that if they didn't know the appropriate history. He compared most Negro League teams to white major league teams such as the New York Yankees or Giants and the Brooklyn Dodgers. He believed that the barnstorming tours of Paige and Feller were important because they showed that there was talent among both white and black players. Doby said black players had to get away from the ideal of that comical mold, saying, "I would be the world's worst actor if I have to act that way."[34] This shows that many African American players wanted to be taken seriously and wanted to escape the stereotype of African Americans associated with clowning and minstrel shows.

With the integration of the white major leagues in 1947, the Negro National League and the Negro American League experienced the beginning of their decline. Prior to that, the Negro Leagues had enjoyed a great amount of success and an increase of attendance brought about by an increase in African American population in the North, as well as an increase in disposable income among African Americans during World War II. Drawing fans to the games were events such as the East-West All-Star Game and colorful and talented players like Josh Gibson and Satchel Paige. Regardless of this surge in popularity, the Negro Leagues and players like Paige still had to battle with an image of teams that were not as serious as the white major league teams and players who were often more concerned with clowning and antics then they were with serious baseball. Teams like the Indianapolis Clowns encouraged myths such as these. Despite this fact, the Negro Leagues were still extremely popular with both whites and blacks, primarily because of the talent they showcased and because of the popularity of baseball with the American public.

Notes

1. Bob Williams, "Sports Rambler," *Call and Post,* 5 May 1945, 6B.
2. Janet Bruce, *The Kansas City Monarchs: Champions of Black Baseball* (Lawrence: University Press of Kansas, 1985), 75.
3. Ibid, 68–69, 72.
4. Rob Ruck, *Sandlot Seasons: Sport in Black Pittsburgh* (Urbana: University of Illinois Press, 1993), 156.
5. Jack Connelly, *Baseball's Dark Past,* Race and Ethnicity: African Americans file, National Baseball Hall of Fame and Museum, Cooperstown, N.Y.
6. Nat Trammell, "Baseball Classic-East vs. West," *Colored Baseball and Sports Monthly,* 1 October 1934, 6, in *The Unlevel Playing Field: A Documentary History of the African American Experience in Sport,* ed. David K Wiggins and Patrick B. Miller (Urbana: University of Illinois Press, 2003), 101.
7. Larry Lester, *Black Baseball's National Showcase: The East-West All-Star Game, 1933–1953* (Lincoln: University of Nebraska Press, 2001), 294, 301, 313, 321.
8. Robert Peterson, *Only the Ball Was White* (Englewood Cliffs, N.J.: Prentice Hall, 1970), 98–101.
9. Louis Effrat, "Negro Star Game to American Loop," *New York Times,* 30 July 1947, 24.
10. "2 Negro Leagues in All-Star Game," *New York Times,* 24 August 1948, 29.
11. Peterson, *Only the Ball Was White,* 98–101.
12. Bill Veeck and Ed Linn, *Veeck — As in Wreck* (New York: Bantam, 1962), 184.
13. Neil Lanctot, *Negro League Baseball: The Rise and Ruin of a Black Institution* (Philadelphia: University of Pennsylvania Press, 2004), 104–105.
14. Veeck and Linn, *Veeck — As in Wreck,* 186.
15. Peterson, *Only the Ball Was White,* 141.
16. LeRoy (Satchel) Paige with David Lipman, *Maybe I'll Pitch Forever* (New York: Grove Press, 1961), 29–30, 41, 34–35, 38.
17. Ibid, 136–137.
18. Bruce, *The Kansas City Monarchs,* 103.
19. "West Nine Takes Negro Game by 7–4," *New York Times,* 14 August 1944, 9.
20. Bruce, *The Kansas City Monarchs,* 100.
21. Chester L. Washington, "Satchel's Back in Town," *Pittsburgh Courier,* May 9, 1936, in *The Unlevel Playing Field: A Documentary History of the African American Experience in*

Sport, ed. David K Wiggins and Patrick B. Miller (Urbana: University of Illinois Press, 2003), 98.

22. Wendell Smith, "Paige 'Thumbs Nose' at His Public Here," 1943, Wendell Smith Papers, Folder 3, National Baseball Hall of Fame and Museum, Cooperstown, N.Y.

23. Jules Tygiel, *Baseball's Great Experiment: Jackie Robinson and His Legacy* (New York: Oxford University Press, 1983), 234.

24. Peterson, *Only the Ball Was White*, 141–142.

25. Jackie Robinson, "Jackie Robinson Says: Larry Doby Is a Good Ball Player; Glad to See Him with Cleveland," *Pittsburgh Courier*, 12 July 1947, 15.

26. Jim "Mudcat" Grant with Tom Sabellico and Pat O'Brien, *The Black Aces: Baseball's Only African American Twenty-Game Winners* (Farmingdale, N.Y.: The Black Aces, LLC, 2006), 89–91.

27. Randy Dixon, " The Sports Bugle," *Pittsburgh Courier*, 3 February 1940, Effa Manley Papers, Folder 3, National Baseball Hall of Fame and Museum, Cooperstown, N.Y.

28. Wendell Smith, "A Strange Tribe: On the Loyalties of Black Fans," *Pittsburgh Courier*, 14 May 1938, in *The Unlevel Playing Field: A Documentary History of the African American Experience in Sport*, ed. David K Wiggins and Patrick B. Miller (Urbana: University of Illinois Press, 2003), 135–137.

29. Bruce, *The Kansas City Monarchs*, 98.

30. *Ibid.*, 100–101, 106.

31. *Ibid.*, 104–105.

32. Peterson, *Only the Ball Was White*, 204.

33. Lanctot, *Negro League Baseball*, 108–110.

34. *Larry Doby: National Baseball Hall of Fame and Museum, Inc.*, Fay Vincent Oral History Collection, 3 hrs, 2001, National Baseball Hall of Fame and Museum, Cooperstown, N.Y., videocassette 1.

13

Jackie Robinson: The Desegregation of Baseball and the Fight for Civil Rights

Jared Evan Furcolo Wheeler

This is a game played with a cork ball, which is wound tightly in yarn and covered by two layers of leather stitched together two hundred and sixteen times. This is a game played with an expertly carved wood bat shaped to perfection by the hands of a craftsman. This is a game that blooms in the spring, thrives in the summer, and dies with the falling autumn leaves. This is America's game. This is baseball.

Albert G. Spalding characterized the game of baseball in his 1911 book *America's National Game*. "I claim that Base Ball owes its prestige as our National Game to the fact that as no other form of sport it is the exponent of American courage, confidence, combativeness; American dash, discipline, determination; American energy, eagerness, enthusiasm; American pluck, persistency, performance, American spirit, sagacity, success; American vim, vigor, virility."[1] But all Americans were not treated equally. African Americans were largely excluded from baseball, American's national pastime.

Baseball truly became our national game on April 15, 1947, when Jackie Robinson of the Brooklyn Dodgers broke the racial barrier that had kept African Americans from playing major league baseball for sixty years. Robinson's peaceful resistance and his will to stand up for the equality of his race extended beyond the game of baseball and helped influence other African Americans to fight for their cause during the civil rights movement.

The rookie receiving advice from the star, as Jackie Robinson laughs at something Satchel Paige told him.

The African American people have long struggled to obtain civil rights within American society. The oppression of African Americans started with the institution of slavery by America's earliest settlers. African Americans were held in bondage and given few, if any, social or civil rights. Slavery expanded with the creation of the cotton gin by Eli Whitney in 1793, when the South became a huge distributor of cotton and integral to the U.S. economy. The ideas and laws behind slavery conflicted with the ideological beliefs of many Northern liberals. War was the result.

One reason the American Civil War was fought was to determine the social status of slavery within American society. In 1863, under the Emancipation Proclamation, President Lincoln certified the freedom of the enslaved. In 1865, the Thirteenth Amendment was ratified, forever forbidding slavery in the United States.

The end of slavery forced African American people to assimilate into a white American society that was not interested in including them. Jim Crow laws were created, and these kept African Americans from obtaining civil and social rights. The Supreme Court case of Plessy v. Ferguson, in 1896, instituted the system of racial segregation. Segregation became a common practice within all areas of American society, including baseball.

The hope of African Americans to participate in white professional baseball diminished in April 1887 in Newark, New Jersey, where the Chicago White Stockings and the Newark team of the Eastern League faced off. Newark's pitching star was thirty-five-game winner George Stovey, a light-skinned Negro from Canada. Adrian "Cap" Anson was Chicago's captain, and the greatest player of his day. Rather then play against Stovey, he stomped off the field, his walk setting a pattern that would last for exactly sixty years.[2] Anson set a trend that day, and the owners established an unwritten agreement barring African Americans from playing white organized professional baseball.

Prior to Anson's stand for the segregation of baseball, a few African Americans had the opportunity to play within an organized professional setting. "Back in 1872 Bud Fowler, a Negro, broke the color line and became the first man of his race to play in organized ball."[3] Fowler was successful and established himself within white integrated leagues, playing ten of his twenty-year career in them. "Other blacks followed Fowler, and in 1884 two brothers from Ohio, Weldy and Moses Fleetwood Walker, briefly crashed the major leagues with Toledo of the old American Association."[4]

African Americans felt the harsh discrimination and responded by forming their own Negro leagues. Even so, there were still those who tried to sneak African Americans into white organized baseball. John McGraw was one of the greatest coaches in the history of the game. Famous for his intense style of play and short temperament, McGraw believed that if someone could play baseball, no matter the color of his skin, he was going to try to get them to play. In 1902 McGraw tried to sign Charley Grant to play second base for his Baltimore Orioles. McGraw passed Grant off as an Indian, "Chief Tokahoma," which "worked fine until the Orioles reached Chicago for an exhibition and every black in town turned out to cheer on Charley Grant." Charles Comiskey, the White Sox manager, was immediately suspect, and Grant was sent back to the Negro Leagues.[5] Several other attempts to desegregate baseball were tried but all failed until 1947, when Jackie Robinson took the first base position at Ebbets Field in Brooklyn.

Jackie Robinson was born on July 31, 1919, in Cairo, Georgia. When Robinson was six months old, his sharecropper father deserted his family and moved to Florida. To escape from discrimination in the South, Jackie's mother picked up and moved her family to Pasadena, California, hoping to give her kids a better life. Discrimination was still felt by the Robinsons in California, but there were more opportunities for Jackie to succeed. Robinson was a four-sport star in high school, which eventually earned him an athletic scholarship to the University of California as Los Angeles. "Robinson proceeded to rewrite the UCLA record books over the next two years, becoming the first letter man in the school's history. In basketball, he twice led the conference in scoring; in track, he won the national long jump championship; in football, he was an All-American halfback, averaging twelve yards per carry. Ironically his weakest sport was baseball. His base stealing and fielding were very good, but his batting average was mediocre."[6]

Robinson left school his senior year in order to make money to support his mother and his future wife and kids. In the spring of 1942, Robinson's plans were put on hold as the United States Army drafted him to fight in World War II. Robinson's time in the army helped shape his character as a strong African American man. The Army was segregated, and during his stint, Robinson faced prejudice and even several confrontations. "His handling of the situations revealed the character of the man who would carry the hopes of many Americans."[7] Robinson was stationed on Southern bases and felt the effects of segregation heavily, since he was not allowed to participate in the activities that whites could. Robinson did not stand for the unfair treatment of African Americans by whites. "Robinson was returning from town to base by bus one day when the driver suddenly stopped and ordered him to sit in the back. Robinson refused, knowing the driver's request was a violation of a federal ruling against segregated buses on army bases."[8] He received an honorary discharge due to this incident. Robinson returned home in 1945, and he began playing baseball for the Kansas City Monarchs in the Negro League and came to the attention of Branch Rickey.

Rickey was in charge of the Brooklyn Dodgers of the National League. Rickey saw the injustice of segregation and discrimination, and he used his Christian background to denounce the unfair and unequal treatment of African Americans in a free American society. Rickey also believed that desegregation would be good for baseball and for the economic growth of the game. "Rickey recognized that there was an untapped well of talent remaining in the country: black players who had demonstrated in the Negro Leagues that they could play baseball on a par with the best major leaguers. Rickey was determined to mine this 'black gold' first, even if it meant defying the baseball establishment in the process. He ordered the scouting of the Negro Leagues during the war, looking for the right player to be the first black on the Dodgers."[9] Rickey believed that it would take someone special to be able to peacefully handle the immense amount of hatred that would be thrown at him and still perform to the best of his ability. Rickey found these attributes in Jackie Robinson. "Rickey wanted the first black he signed to be capable of dealing with any amount of pressure and stress. Indeed he wanted someone whose competitive instincts would enable him to respond affirmatively to stressful situations. In Robinson, Rickey found a suitable candidate."[10]

On October 23, 1945, Jackie Robinson signed a contract to play for the Brooklyn Dodgers farm club in Montreal. Rickey believed that placing Robinson in Montreal would allow him to perform to his highest capabilities while in a more receptive environment. Robinson played the 1946 season in Montreal, helping them win a championship by leading the league in many offensive and defensive categories.

In 1947, Robinson made the Dodgers ball club out of spring training and seemed prepared both mentally and physically to play. On April 15, 1947, the Brooklyn Dodgers took the field, and Jackie Robinson joined them as the first African American to play organized white baseball in the twentieth century. Although Rickey received heavy amounts of criticism from his colleagues and employees, he and Jackie Robinson successfully and peacefully integrated the game of baseball. This marked Robinson as not just a baseball player, but also an activist, inspiring African American people.

As the color barrier began to dissolve, Robinson faced many trials from fans, players, and even teammates. Robinson heard the worst racial remarks and received the worst treatment from the Philadelphia Phillies and their coach, Ben Chapman, a native of Alabama, at Ebbets Field in 1947. Dodgers owner Bob Carpenter urged Rickey to bench Robinson, and "Carpenter's close friend general manager Herb Pennock phoned Rickey to tell him not 'to bring that nigger here' to Shibe Park."[11] Robinson reacted peacefully towards the harsh racial comments made by the Phillies; he had to in order for him to succeed. Robinson explained how he wanted to crack but did not.

For one wild and rage-crazed minute I thought, "To hell with Mr. Rickey's noble experiment. It is clear it won't succeed.... What a glorious, cleansing thing it would be to let go." To hell with the image of the patient black freak I was supposed to create. I could throw down my bat, stride over to the Phillies dugout, grab one of those white sons of bitches and smash his teeth in with my despised black fist. Then I could walkaway from it and I would never become a sports star. But my son could tell his son someday what his daddy could have been if he hadn't been too much of a man.[12]

Robinson's patience was tested both on and off the playing field. When the team traveled, Robinson encountered hotels that would not house him. Robinson's family was threatened, and he received death threats. Prior to the Dodgers' visit to Cincinnati, Robinson received letters that said if Robinson attempted to play at Cincinnati's Crosley Field, a group by the name of the Travelers was going to try to kill him. The FBI quickly took hold of the situation and scouted out the field. "Brooklyn Dodger baseball star Jackie Robinson's life was threatened today in letters received by the Cincinnati Baseball Club, and police searched the area of Crosley Field before and during the double header. They found nothing and expressed the opinion that the letters were from a crank."[13]

On the field, opposing players went out of their way to inflict pain on him. Ken Burns describes an incident that occurred in St. Louis, where the anti–Robinson feeling was strong: "During the game, Enos Slaughter, out at first by at least ten feet, nonetheless jumped into the air and deliberately laid open Robinson's thigh with his spikes."[14]

Robinson handled the racial slurs and attacks peacefully and with dignity, making himself a hero throughout the African American community. Through his experience in baseball, Robinson sparked a revolution that would help end segregation and unfair treatment of the African American people in all areas of American life.

The integration of baseball and the heroism of Jackie Robinson helped encouraged members of the civil rights movement in the 1950s and 1960s. After Robinson retired in 1956 (one year before the beloved Dodgers left Brooklyn), he used his influence as the first African American baseball player to help strengthen the fight for civil rights. Robinson became a spokesperson for the civil rights movement, becoming a symbol of hope for the African American people.

Robinson took the position of vice-president at a popular restaurant chain called Chock Full o' Nuts. Robinson was hired by a white businessman by the name of Bill Black. Bill Black was owner and founder of Chock Full o' Nuts Corporation and was known for giving African Americans the opportunity to work. "Mr. Black was considered guilty of racial discrimination in hiring. The majority of his employees were blacks. A few racists referred to his company as, 'Chock Full o' Niggers.' Mr. Black once faced the charge that he was discriminating against whites."[15] Bill Black hired African Americans because they were capable of doing the job, not because of their skin color. While Robinson worked for the Chock Full o' Nuts Corporation, the NAACP approached him to assist with their fund-raising activities.

The National Association for the Advancement of Colored People, NAACP, was founded in 1909. It began as a nonprofit organization to help minority groups obtain equality in all social spheres. "The NAACP has as its mission the goal of eliminating race prejudice and removing all barriers of racial discrimination through democratic processes."[16] Robinson was approached by Roy Wilkins, the executive secretary of the NAACP, who asked if Robinson would be willing to participate in the annual Freedom Fund Drive. Robinson received approval from Bill Black to participate, joining arms with Wilkins in helping the fight for social equality.

The Freedom Fund Drive was a national effort to raise major funds to further NAACP activities. Robinson, along with activist Frank Williams, began speaking in front of various crowds, asking them to donate money towards the fight for civil rights. People responded to Robinson, and the NAACP raised one million dollars in donated funds. Robinson wrote, "Our NAACP fund-raising tour was only the beginning of a protracted drive for the organization. We were gratified to learn that the year of our tour was the first year the NAACP had ever raised a million dollars, and we are determined to continue working as a team."[17] Robinson saw the effect he had on the African American people, and he believed that he had the opportunity to continue to make a bigger impact in the fight for racial equality because of how he was perceived by people. Robinson said, "I felt I had a debt to my people and I wanted to volunteer my services at the same time to the organization I believed was helping them the most."[18]

Robinson also became politically active, publicly supporting the candidate who would stand up for African Americans and their search for equality. Robinson corresponded frequently with political figures that supported the civil rights movement. In August 1957, Jackie Robinson sent a telegram to President Eisenhower's assistant, Fred Morrow, expressing his thoughts about the weaknesses of the 1957 Civil Rights Act. Robinson did not want Eisenhower to sign the bill because it incorporated social limitations for African Americans. Robinson wrote, "I am opposed to the Civil Rights bill in its present form. I have been in touch with a number of my friends and we disagree that half a loaf is better than none. We have waited this long for a bill with meaning and can wait a little longer."[19]

Jackie Robinson was heavily inspired by the popular civil rights activist

Martin Luther King, Jr. and his tactic of peaceful resistance. Robinson used the same approach to succeed in being the first African American in baseball. Robinson knew how hard it was to not be filled with hatred and anger, and he was amazed by King and his attitude towards the white man. "King was well prepared for his part in the war; the weapon would be the white man's Christianity. He knew his people, and he could bring the old cadences of the Southern Negro preacher the new visions of the social gospel which demanded change in America."[20] King used his Christian ideals to help African Americans obtain certain civil and social rights.

King was a main target of racial hatred during the civil rights movement, just as Jackie Robinson was during his baseball career. King did not believe physical retaliation was the answer. After the Ku Klux Klan bombed King's home, a mob of African Americans congregated in front of his porch waiting to seek retaliation. King replied to them:

> Don't get panicky. If you have weapons take them home. We cannot solve this problem through retaliatory violence. We must love our white brothers no matter what they do to us.... Jesus still cries out in words that echo across the centuries: "Love your enemies; bless them that curse you; pray for them that despitefully use you." This is what we must live by. We must meet hate with love.[21]

King was successful in granting the African American race a foothold within society by not retaliating with violence but with love. King realized that the African American race had to live in harmony with the white race. If the African American race responded in violence it would just add fuel to the fire preventing growth of the civil rights movement. Jackie Robinson took the same approach as Martin Luther King, Jr. in his fight for civil rights. Robinson believed that races should unite and work together, and he took a stand against African American nationalists.

When a group of African American nationalists from the Harlem section in New York wanted to prevent a white Jewish man from opening up a steakhouse in the neighborhood, Robinson described the reason: "The nationalists did not want the white merchant to come to the street with his low-priced steaks because it would hurt the black restauranteur who was selling steaks for a higher price."[22] Robinson strongly disagreed with the African American nationalist group's anti–Semitism. Robinson quickly spoke out against these tactics, stating, "All my life we have been fighting against this same thing as it applies to the Negro.... It is a matter of principle. Black supremacy is just as bad as white supremacy."[23] After Robinson's statement, the nationalists began to picket the Chock Full o' Nuts Corporation.

Jackie Robinson also frequently spoke out against Malcolm X, another prominent figure of the civil rights movement, because of his tactics of violence. Malcolm X saw the unequal, unjust position of the African American in the United States as the fault of the white man. Malcolm believed and preached the use of violence by the African American against the white race to overcome the oppression. "Malcolm X stood apart, dimly perceived as a racist and demagogue inflaming the black lumpenproletariat to revenge its grievance in blood."[24] Malcolm X believed Robinson was being used by the white man and targeted him as a moderate black. Malcolm X wrote Robinson a letter labeling him a man who succumbed to the ideals of the white man. "You stay as far away from the Negro community as you can get, and never take an interest in anything in the Negro community until the white man himself takes an interest in it. You, yourself, would never shake my hand until you saw some of your white friends shaking it."[25]

Many other African Americans followed Robinson's lead and joined the battle for civil rights. As a young child, Russell C. Campbell's father, Rev. Stephen Campbell, took him to see Jackie Robinson play. Campbell told of the influence Robinson had on him in an interview:

> It goes without saying that the trail blazers in the "Revolution" of social change, made an impact on many of us, who were a part of the Movement. As a child, my father would take me to baseball games and I did, indeed, see the great Jackie Robinson play. My older brother was a member of a southern black league team and often told me of the pain and arrows associated with the racist environment dealing with that experience. Mr. Robinson was somewhat of a passive-aggressive character, in my view, but made a difference from which the Revolution can, and was built. We in the Movement saw Jackie Robinson as a part of the necessary foundation on which Revolutions are developed.[26]

Campbell was a high school student in Detroit, Michigan, when he became a member in the NAACP youth council. The duty of the NAACP youth council was to organize and support demonstrations such as picketing stores in downtown Detroit. Campbell enrolled at Morehouse College in Atlanta to be on the front lines of the civil rights movement. When Campbell arrived at Morehouse in the fall of 1961 he quickly joined a group called the Committee on Appeal of Human Rights, or COAHR. COAHR was a nonviolent organization whose members consisted of mainly college students. Soon Campbell was elected vice chairman of COAHR, and he joined their efforts with other civil rights groups such as the SNCC and SCLC. Campbell became an activist in several demonstrations and protests, some of which led to his arrest. Campbell even worked with Martin Luther King, Jr. at the Albany, Georgia, demonstration. Campbell continued the activist work begun by Jackie Robinson, a founder of the revolution for civil rights and equality.

Another African American heavily influenced by the work of Jackie Robinson was William A. Johnson, Jr. Johnson is a huge Dodger fan because his favorite player, Jackie Robinson, played his entire career with them. In

January 1994, Johnson was inaugurated mayor of the city of Rochester in New York. Johnson became the sixty-fourth mayor of Rochester and the first African American to have this position.

Johnson attended Howard University in Washington, D.C., earning B.A. and M.A. degrees in political science. After graduation, Johnson was involved in developing programs to help the growth and progress of the African American community. Johnson became president and CEO of the Urban League of Rochester, where he instituted the Salute to Black Scholars program. This program recognized outstanding academic achievement amongst African American high school students. Johnson was very involved in improving the quality of education within the Rochester public school system.

In 1996, Johnson was recognized by the National Urban League with the Whitney M. Medallion for his achievements and services within the Urban League of Rochester. In 1999, Johnson was named one of the top ten public officials in an issue of *Governing Magazine*. In 2006, Johnson completed his third four-year term as mayor.

Johnson saw Robinson as a pioneer of the civil rights movement, and expressed this in a recent interview:

> The whole fate of black America was resting on the shoulders of Jackie Robinson. The world was counting on him to fail and react negatively but he beat his enemies and helped advance the black race in American society. We always give Martin Luther King, Jr. credit for changing life for black America. Robinson does not really get much credit but he was a pioneer. If Robinson would have failed it would have set back the Civil Rights movement.[27]

Jackie Robinson fought for African American equality both on and off the baseball field. In 1947, the nation watched as Robinson broke the color barrier in baseball when he stepped on the diamond for the Brooklyn Dodgers. His peaceful resistance to hate and racial inequality provided African Americans with a different and effective strategy for addressing segregation. After his retirement, Robinson used his public image to advance equal rights and help create a better society for the future of the African American race in American society. He remains a symbol of reform, peace, and progress within the African American culture and American society as a whole. Jackie Robinson desegregated America's national pastime and was instrumental in desegregating America as a nation. By playing America's national pastime, he was able to unite the nation.

Notes

1. Albert G. Spalding, *America's National Game* (1911), 2–3.
2. John Holway, *Voices from the Great Black Baseball Leagues* (New York: Dodd, Mead, 1975), 2.

3. Holway, *Voices*, 1.
4. Holway, *Voices*, 1.
5. Holway, *Voices*, 2.
6. John Grabowski, *Jackie Robinson* (New York: Chelsea House, 1991), 15.
7. Grabowski, *Jackie Robinson*, 17.
8. Grabowski, *Jackie Robinson*, 18.
9. John Rossi, *The National Game* (Chicago: Ivan R. Dee, 2000), 154.
10. G. Edward White, *Creating the National Pastime* (Princeton: Princeton University Press, 1996), 154.
11. Bruce Kuklick, *To Everything a Season* (Princeton: Princeton University Press, 1991), 147.
12. Ken Burns, *Baseball* (New York: Random House, 1994), 291.
13. FBI Files, "Jackie Robinson," http://foia.fbi.gov/robinson/robsn3.pdf (accessed 8 April 2003).
14. Burns, *Baseball*, 289.
15. Jackie Robinson, *I Never Had It Made* (New York: Ecco [HarperCollins], 1995), 125
16. National Association for the Advancement of Colored People, "NAACP Leadership," http.www.NAACP.org/leadership/index.html (accessed March 28, 2003).
17. Robinson, 129.
18. Robinson, 126.
19. Jackie Robinson to Fred Morrow, 13 Aug 1957, Dwight D. Eisenhower Library, http://www.archives.gov/digital_classroom/lessons/jackie_robinson.
20. Jon Meacham, *Voices in Our Blood* (New York: Random House, 2001), 375.
21. Robinson, *I Never Had It Made*, 211.
22. Robinson, 146.
23. FBI Files, "Harlem Pickets Switch Tactics," 1 August 1952, http://foia.fbi.gov/robinson (accessed 15 April 2003)
24. David Gallen and Peter Goldman, *Malcolm X: As They Knew Him* (New York: Carroll & Graf, 1992), 213.
25. Robinson, 178.
26. Russell Campbell, "Civil Rights Movement," 2 March 2003, e-mail to author.
27. Mayor William A. Johnson interviewed by Kenneth Dean, "Jackie Robinson," personal interview, 20 February 2003.

14

Integration and the Homestead Grays

Nathan Lovato

Many regard the Homestead Grays as the most successful team put on the field during the reign of the Negro Leagues in America, roughly 1920 to 1960. The Grays' only competition for this honor is the Kansas City Monarchs. The Grays originated in 1910 as the Homestead Blue Ribbons. Their purpose was to give the black mill laborers of Homestead, Pennsylvania, recreation when they were not working.[1] This collection of players was mostly African American steel mill workers. However, by 1911, their best player and eventual owner, Cumberland "Cum" Posey was not a steel mill worker. He came from a wealthy family and was able to buy his way onto the club. The Grays were a barnstorming act from their inception until 1929 when they joined the American Negro League (ANL). The Grays played games wherever they could against all kinds of competition. For example, during the 1925 and 1926 seasons, the Grays unbelievably had a combined record of 236–30–11.[2] Had the white Washington Senators signed key members of the black Homestead Grays prior to 1945, the Senators, not the Brooklyn Dodgers, would have been the first modern team to integrate in major league baseball. This paper will primarily look at why integration attempts by the Washington Senators failed even after 1940 when the Grays moved to Washington permanently. Before the primary issue is delved into, a look at some early integration of baseball is presented to provide some context.

Early integration is hard to assess because the records are scarcer and news articles did not always address the issue. One player we do know about

Homestead Grays of 1939

The Homestead Grays had a star-studded lineup that any major league manager would have been envious of. Top row, from left to right: Josh Gibson, Edsall Walker, David Whatley, Roy Welmaker, Arnold Waite, Henry Spearman, Ray Brown, Jim Williams, Robert Roy Gaston and Roy Partlow; front row, Jerry Benjamin, Speck Roberts, Lou Dula, Vic Harris, Buck Leonard, Sam Bankhead, and Jelly Jackson.

is Fleet Walker. On May 1, 1884, Moses "Fleetwood" Walker played his first game in an integrated league as catcher for the Toledo ball club of the American Association. He went 0 for 3. For the rest of the 1884 season, Walker played in another forty-two games and batted .263.[3] In 1887, Walker and fellow black player George Stovey joined the Newark Ball Club of the International League. On July 14, the Newark Little Giants played an exhibition game with the all-white Chicago White Stockings. Before the game, Chicago's captain, Adrian "Cap" Anson, made some comments about not playing if Stovey played, at which time Stovey and Walker were forced to sit the bench for the game to avoid a forfeit and loss of revenue from the game. The International League voted in a "gentleman's agreement" to no longer sign black players following this incident and others like it. Due to Anson's harsh comments, and the International League's decision, African Americans were relegated to playing segregated baseball for over a half century. According to *Sol White's History of Colored Base Ball*, the Argyle Hotel of Babylon, Long Island, New York, formed the first professional "all colored base ball" team in 1885.[4] It was organized by the Argyle's headwaiter, Frank Thompson.

Although there were attempts made at integrating baseball between 1885 and 1920, none were successful. John McGraw, the legendary manager of the New York Giants, tried to pass off light-skinned blacks as Hispanics or Cubans but this did not work. Most famously, in 1901 McGraw tried to sign Charlie Grant, a middle infielder. McGraw changed Grant's name to Charlie Tokahoma. Supposedly, "Tokahoma" hailed from the Cherokee Nation. Soon after this shenanigan was orchestrated, it was outed by one of Grant's friends when he gave Grant some congratulations. Grant would never play for McGraw as himself or Charlie Tokahoma.[5] More of these attempts were also made. In 1911, the Cincinnati Reds signed Armando Marsans and Rafael Almeida. Many questions abounded from the Cincinnati media about the origins of these two men. In response to these comments, the Cincinnati administration commented that the two men were "as pure white as Castile soap."[6] In 1914 Dolf Luque, a Cuban pitcher, was signed by the Boston Braves. Luque started off poorly, but then came into his own. The New York *Age* wrote in regards to integration, "It would not be surprising to see a Cuban a few shades darker breaking into the major leagues."[7] Because of his exploits, Luque would become the first Hispanic star in the majors. Although it was in the Pacific Coast League and not the majors, the last African American to play in white, "organized" baseball was Jimmy Claxton of the Oakland Oaks. Claxton was passed off as a Native American from an Oklahoma Indian tribe. Supposedly, the Oaks' owner was a member of the same tribe. Claxton, a crafty left handed pitcher only played for the Oaks for six days (May 28 to June 2, 1916). Claxton's demise was helped, some suggest, when the Zeenut candy company rushed printing his baseball cards.[8] Because of problems like these no colored man would play in the major leagues for another thirty-one years. Also because of these happenings, it was more apparent that the only practical solution for blacks playing professional baseball was for them to have their own segregated league. This is where Andrew Foster stepped up to the plate.

In 1920, Chicago American Giants owner and manager Andrew "Rube" Foster created and became commissioner of the Negro National League (NNL). The NNL lasted until 1930 and was primarily a Midwestern based league. During this time, the American Giants became the preeminent team of the NNL. By 1923, another Negro League had been formed on the East Coast to combat Foster's NNL when Ed Bolden established the Eastern Colored League (ECL) which catered to the region's black population.[9] The formation of these leagues was made possible because a large number of blacks had migrated to northern cities like Chicago, Detroit, New York, Pittsburgh, and Washington, D.C.

Both the NNL and ECL extended invitations to the Grays, but Cumberland Posey was more than content to keep the Grays independent, for Posey felt he could make more money running the Grays that way. By 1930, Posey had begun to amass a collection of players that any major league owner would later envy. Posey had numerous players that could flat out play, but the two that stood out by the end of their careers were Walter "Buck" Leonard and Josh Gibson. These two were so good that they earned the monikers of the "black Lou Gehrig and the black Babe Ruth," respectively. These men were so good that maybe the monikers should be reversed. Posey had such an eye for talent that he could not pass up either of the two players. According to Brad Snyder's *Beyond the Shadow of the Senators*, Ben Taylor, manager of the ECL's Baltimore Stars, discovered Leonard in 1933 on a sandlot in Leonard's hometown of Rocky Mount, North Carolina.[10] Leonard played with the Stars for the 1933 season and then met with Posey in New York. From 1934 to 1948, Leonard was a fixture in the Grays' lineup. On the other hand, the more notable (arguably) and mythical (definitely) figure in the history of the Homestead Grays is Josh Gibson. Gibson's professional career supposedly started in Pittsburgh in 1930 when he went to a Grays game. One legend has it that the regular catcher for the Grays had a broken finger, and Cum Posey signed Gibson out of the grandstands.[11]

President of the Negro National League, Rube Foster.

Throughout the 1930s, the Grays played their weekday games in Homestead and their weekend games at Forbes Field in Pittsburgh. Playing in Pittsburgh allowed Posey to make a bigger income from the gate receipts. This was all well and good for the Grays, but something about Washington, D.C., was beckoning Posey to have the Grays play some of their games there. Griffith Stadium was set in the largest black neighborhood in Washington, D.C., LeDroit Park. Because of this, the Senators had a very loyal black following. Posey thought that this could work to the Grays' advantage. In 1940, Cum Posey struck a deal with the Senators' owner, Clark Griffith. The terms of the deal were that when the Senators were out of town, the Grays would play their weekday and Saturday games in Homestead and Pittsburgh. After the Saturday game concluded, the Grays would get in a bus and drive six hours to Washington and play a double-header at Griffith Stadium on Sundays.[12] The rule of the time was that Griffith Stadium was segregated, even though there were no written laws on the books; this is just the way it was. For Senators games, black fans were relegated to seats in the right field pavilion of Griffith Stadium. However for the Grays games, there was no segregated seating. Eventually, all of the Grays games would be played in Washington. However, during the first season of playing in the nation's capital, the Grays had worse attendance than they had in Homestead or Pittsburgh, averaging four to five thousand fans in their first season in Washington.[13] Perhaps this was because the fans were still supporting the Senators even though they had fallen on hard times. This is where the fight for the Senators to integrate began, with Sam Lacy, a black journalist from Washington, D.C., leading the way.

The physical and cultural geographies of Washington, D.C., give an interesting spin to the idea of the Washington Senators being the primary integrators of the sport. At the time, Washington was regarded as "First in War, First in Peace, and Last in the American League."[14] Integrating would have done the lowly Senators some good. The nation's capital is below the Mason-Dixon Line; therefore, culturally, it is Southern. Conversely, due to its status as the nation's capital, and its transient population of politicians, Washington is a Northern city. Washington had a population that was almost fifty percent black. This made Washington, D.C., a melting pot. During the era of the Negro Leagues, however, Jim Crow laws were in full effect in the South and even in Washington. Public places like restaurants and hotels were openly segregated while others like Griffith Stadium were covertly segregated. Because of this, racism was the norm.

The perceived anti-racist and pro-integration attitude shown by Clark Griffith was another reason that Cumberland Posey chose to take the deal that would make the Homestead Grays the largest baseball draw in Washington. In 1937, Sam Lacy procured an interview with Clark Griffith where Griffith stated about integration, "The time is not far off when colored players will take their places beside those of other races in the major leagues."[15] This gave hope to people like Sam Lacy who were championing the cause. The years 1937 to 1945 were the heyday of the Homestead Grays when they won seven out of nine pennants. The Grays had signed star players like James "Cool Papa" Bell and Martin Dihigo. The Grays were the New York Yankees of the Negro Leagues. Add to this the fact that the Senators were in shambles and the black community of D.C. had warmed up to and even begun to relish the Grays. Then throw in the comments made by Clark Griffith to Sam Lacy. Reintegration of the Washington Senators and major league baseball seemed to be in the cards. Another thing that gave the members of the Grays hope was one of Clark Griffith's practices. Griffith did not believe in using a farm system like other ball clubs did. Instead, he would sign light-skinned South Americans (most commonly Venezuelans), Cubans or other Caribbean-born players.[16] He did this because it was cheaper. Griffith would do anything to save or make a buck. This is the true reason why Griffith allowed the Grays to rent Griffith Stadium — so he could end up in the black rather than the red.

The national scene was also being primed to think that re-integration was going to happen. In 1937, Chester L. Washington, the sports editor of the *Pittsburgh Courier,* sent telegrams to William Benswanger, owner of the Pittsburgh Pirates, and Pie Traynor, the skipper of the Pirates, suggesting some Negro League players that could help out the hapless Bucs.[17] Three of the players Washington suggested: Josh Gibson, Buck Leonard, and Ray Brown, were members of the Grays. Traynor did not say a thing about this proposal, but Benswanger would later say that a "number of Negro Leaguers were good enough to play in the majors."[18] Even though Benswanger was in favor of integrating, he did not want to be the trailblazer. Benswanger did go so far as to offer tryouts to three Negro League players for the Pittsburgh Pirates in 1942. He later reneged on his offer due to pressure from the media.

While all of this had been going on, Lacy was in Chicago fighting for integration there. He left Chicago in 1943 and returned to Washington to continue the fight. By 1944, the Grays were playing full-time in Washington. Josh Gibson and Buck Leonard wanted to play in the majors and even approached Griffith about that possibility. Again, Griffith had no intention of signing them because he was too busy making money with them in a separate league.[19] The Grays were starting to out-draw Griffith's Senators, especially when Satchel Paige and his Kansas City Monarchs came to Washington.[20] At this time with the talent Posey amassed, the Grays had the potential to annihilate Griffith's lowly Senators. Lacy tried to use all this drawing power to convince major league baseball that the time to integrate had arrived.

Sam Lacy wanted to keep the fight going. He had a meeting set up with MLB Commissioner Kenesaw Mountain Landis. Clark Griffith and Connie Mack, the owner/manager of Philadelphia Athletics, were also in attendance. It was widely known that Landis and Mack were not in favor of integration, even if they never openly showed this attitude. They were regarded as two of the most racist men in baseball. After hearing some of the testimony presented at the meeting, Mack and Griffith came to the conclusion that the integration movement was "a Communistic plot to overthrow Baseball."[21] Nothing came of these meetings as a result. Major league baseball was still no closer to integrating.

Cumberland Posey was not helping the cause. He thought that the owners of the Negro League teams should be more worried about "protecting their investment"[22] rather than being part of a humanitarian mission to see integration happen. During the 1944 season, the games the Grays played at Griffith Stadium were sparsely attended. The black citizens of D.C. and the followers of the Grays were becoming disenchanted with Posey's lack of commitment, yet the Grays were still winning championships. It is ironic to see a team not get much support yet be good enough to win championships year in and year out. The players the Grays had on their roster did not worry about whether they were going to play ball in the majors; they played to their fullest potential to win games and championships.

By 1946, Branch Rickey had signed Jack Roosevelt "Jackie" Robinson to play in the Brooklyn Dodgers organization. Robinson was playing for the Montreal Royals (Brooklyn's Triple-A affiliate). This integrated minor league baseball. On April 15, 1947, Robinson took his position at Ebbets Field to break the color barrier once again. However, Branch Rickey and the Brooklyn Dodgers should not have been the first modern team to integrate the major leagues. With all of his comments praising African Americans, the flagship integrator should have been Clark Griffith. According to Brad Snyder in "When Segregation Doomed Baseball in Washington," "In 1978, Calvin Griffith (Clark's nephew) revealed his real reason for moving the original Washington Senators to Minnesota. Calvin Griffith said, 'The trend in Washington is all colored. Black people don't go to ball games.'"[23] Once a racist seed is planted and weeds start growing, it is hard to kill.

It is unfortunate that the majority of players that played for the Homestead Grays and for the rest of Negro League baseball never experienced playing in the majors. If they had, it would have put many a white in the minor leagues, but the level of play would have been greater. Even more unfortunate is that Josh Gibson and Buck Leonard never played for the Washington Senators. Who knows, maybe we would be talking about Barry Bonds breaking Josh Gibson's home run record if they had. If Clark Griffith had stuck to his guns and integrated the Senators, they would have rivaled the New York Yankees in terms of pennants won after 1935. Nothing can be done now about that. Without people like Sam Lacy, Wendell Smith, Lester Rodney and Branch Rickey, the integration of professional baseball could have been stymied longer than it was.

Notes

1. Brad Snyder, *Beyond the Shadow of the Senators: The Untold Story of the Homestead Grays and the Integration of Baseball* (Chicago: McGraw-Hill Books, 2003), 36.
2. *Ibid.*, 38.

3. Lawrence D. Hogan, *Shades of Glory: The Negro Leagues and the Story of African American Baseball* (Washington D.C.: National Geographic Society and the National Baseball Hall of Fame and Museum, 2006), 43.
　4. Jerry Malloy, *Sol White's History of Colored Baseball, with Other Documents on the Early Black Game, 1886–1936* (Lincoln: University of Nebraska Press, 1995), 8.
　5. Geoffrey C. Ward and Ken Burns, *Baseball: An Illustrated History* (New York: Alfred A. Knopf Press), 86.
　6. *Ibid.*, 112.
　7. *Ibid.*, 112.
　8. *Ibid.*, 112.
　9. Neil Lanctot, *Negro League Baseball: The Rise and Ruin of a Black Institution* (Philadelphia: University of Pennsylvania Press, 2004), 5.
　10. *Ibid.*, 25.
　11. *Ibid.*, 39.
　12. *Ibid.*, 88.
　13. *Ibid.*, 88.
　14. Brad Snyder, "When Segregation Doomed Baseball in Washington," 16 February 2003, *Washington Post*, D-3.
　15. Snyder, "When Segregation Doomed Baseball."
　16. Snyder, *Beyond the Shadow...*, 58.
　17. Hogan, *Shades of Glory*, 328.
　18. *Ibid.*, 328.
　19. Snyder, "When Segregation Doomed Baseball."
　20. *Ibid.*
　21. Snyder, *Beyond the Shadow...*, 180.
　22. *Ibid.*, 206.
　23. Snyder, "When Segregation Doomed Baseball."

15

"We Can't Never Lose": The *Bingo Long Traveling All-Stars & Motor Kings* 30 Years Later

Raymond Doswell

The year 2006 marked the 30th anniversary of the premiere of the only major theatrical treatment solely dedicated to black baseball history—*The Bingo Long Traveling All-Stars & Motor Kings.* Based on the historical fiction of novelist William Brashler, *Bingo Long* stands among the earliest and most often referenced interpretations of African American baseball during American segregation. In some respects, *Bingo Long* was a cinematic and cultural triumph when it first appeared in July 1976. Established entertainment giant Motown, the industrial heart of African American music, saw Brashler's story of a rebellious 1930s traveling exhibition team as a promising gamble for its fledgling film division. They got the backing of Universal Studios to film on location in the state of Georgia, only a few years removed from its "Jim Crow Era" past. *Bingo Long* attempted to exalt a troubled but heroic past for African Americans, far different from the gritty "blaxploitation" films also popularized in the 1970s.

For over 30 years, the film has been universally praised for offering a rare glimpse into baseball history, and universally scorned for its emphasis on comedic elements in black baseball, clowning and stereotyped images. Yet, in spite of the volumes of historical information produced since, *Bingo Long* remains an essential and primary interpretation of the Negro Leagues for many in the general public, much to the chagrin of the film's critics. That speaks to the power of cinema in interpreting history and, to some degree, the enduring qualities of what the creators of *Bingo Long* presented. This paper will examine the genesis of the film project, the unique baseball aspects and personalities within the film, and touch upon critiques of the film from various perspectives.

A Novel Idea

In 1970, Iowa Writer's Workshop alumnus William Brashler searched for a subject for his first novel. Inspired in part by athletes he had come to know from his work with a semiprofessional basketball team — former college and fringe professional players, African American men who exuded spirit and camaraderie, great athleticism, and weariness from missed opportunities and dreams deferred — Brashler found his muse for a short story. Novelist and teacher Bill Fox, who had interviewed Negro Leagues players, saw his basketball story and asked him to consider black baseball as his next subject. Fox shared taped interviews with Leroy "Satchel" Paige, which opened up a new world for Brashler. The publication of Robert Peterson's *Only the Ball Was White* gave him a new foundation to work from. Finally, he sought out former ballplayers, most notably James "Cool Papa" Bell, to round out his research. Bell was extremely generous with both time and information. The result was the creation and publication of *The Bingo Long Traveling All Stars & Motor Kings* in 1973.

In the novel, the team works through various misadventures — battling bad luck and racism with athletic skill and humor — while barnstorming the country to escape an oppressive owner from the Negro baseball leagues. The Bingo Long character is a power-hitting catcher with movie star charisma. He motivates and cajoles renegade members of the Louisville Ebony Aces away from the merciless Sallison Potter, local mortician and the team's owner. His teammate, Leon Carter, has all the pitching prowess of a Satchel Paige. Carter is often the voice of dissention and reason to balance Long's exuberance and adventuresome spirit. The rebels are secretly funded by one of Potter's rival team owners as they set out on the road with an uncertain future. They balance shadow ball and clowning with serious play, and make it from Louisville, through the upper Midwest and into Kansas City to challenge the vaunted Kansas City Monarchs, before the team begins to disband on the dirt roads of rural Kansas. Throughout the trip, they experience the lows of violence in a brothel, to the highs of getting their comeuppance against Potter. Ultimately, the adventure ends in a whimper, as the team runs out of meal money and their best young player, "Esquire Joe" Calloway, is recruited to play in the major leagues.

Movies and Myth-making

Young Hollywood producer Rob Cohen convinced Motown Records founder Barry Gordy to invest in the rights to turn Brashler's gritty baseball novel into a feature film. Cohen was hired to lead Motown's film division, which had already scored success with *Lady Sings the Blues*. The popular film earned soul-singing superstar Diana Ross an Academy Award nomination in the lead role and earned emerging actor Billy Dee Williams the moniker of "the black Clark Gable." Motown film projects, such as *Lady Sings the Blues* (1972), *Mahogany* (1975) and *The Wiz* (1978), were intended to have crossover appeal—featuring black stars and black subjects palatable to all cultures. This approach contrasted with the more aggressive and often militant black films of the 1970s such as *Shaft*, *Super Fly* and *Black Caesar*.

"Movies should operate as myth; they should have certain purity. But the tendency today is to overcomplicate in the name of truth, realism, art and life," Cohen told the *Los Angeles Times*. With this mantra Cohen engaged writers Matthew Robbins and Hal Barwood, who teamed on *The Sugarland Express* (1974), to rework the novel into a humor infused script with a heroic ending. Cohen boastfully declared that the retelling of *Bingo Long* on screen would "set the myth of black ballplayers firmly and forever. Although it is based on basic fact, the facts have been loosely interpreted in the best traditions of the movies."

Cohen almost secured *Sugarland's* wunderkind young director Stephen Spielberg to oversee the project, but the success of Spielberg's next film, *Jaws*, gave him freedom to work on more of his own projects. British television director John Badham (who would later direct *Saturday Night Fever*) ultimately landed the assignment, overcoming some ignorance about baseball and the American South to complete filming in about 3 months on location in rural Georgia.

The project secured talents such as Billy Dee Williams, veteran stage actor James Earl Jones, superstar comedian Richard Pryor, talented Broadway actors, and former baseball people to bring *Bingo Long* to life. The Long and Carter characters are switched, so that Long becomes the pitcher, making Billy Dee Williams the Paige-like iconic figure, and James Earl Jones the power hitting and often sullen catcher with an intellectual interest in W.E.B Du Bois. Both play for Potter's *St. Louis* Ebony Aces before breaking away to form the All-Stars. The edginess of 1939 segregated America as showcased in Brashler's novel was transformed into a PG rated adventure tale with slapstick escapades, a violent knife attack, a glimpse of rural black life, and a heroic late inning victory. The All-Stars victory came in an exhibition game against the best of the Negro Leagues. The victory earned them a spot in the

Leagues once held by Potter's Aces. One of the issues that immediately surfaced after the film came out was why the changes in setting? How much did the interpretation of the leagues change with this new venue?

On the Set

The cast and crew survived many pitfalls—the humid Georgia summer, inconsistently running old cars and motorcycles, a near disastrous collision of vehicles, a nagging merchant who tried to squeeze the production team for money and fees to keep his properties visually on screen, and an almost freshly painted municipal stadium that needed to remain old looking—to complete the film. With a production investment that reached close to $3,000,000 from Universal Studios, *Bingo Long* became the most expensive "black film" produced at that time.

"We have a real uphill battle trying to make high budget black films because there has never been such a thing as a high budget black film," producer Cohen told the *Los Angeles Times* after a number of Motown film projects, including *Bingo Long*, appeared to be several months behind initial production schedules. "We aren't making 'Super Fly' or the story of violent high school kids in Detroit strung out on dope for a budget of $500,000. We are making classy films with glamour and love that whites and blacks can identify with," Cohen explained.

Cohen's high-minded endeavor seemed to fascinate the film media, especially the *Los Angeles Times*. The *Times* gave *Bingo Long* extensive coverage during its production and release. Reporters went on location to capture the enthusiasm of the project through detailed interviews with James Earl Jones, Billy Dee Williams, director John Badham and the talented baseball extras starring in the film. The coverage clearly showed the commitment everyone had to the film and to Cohen's attempt at making groundbreaking entertainment. Williams noted the importance of the film in interpreting the segregated past. "It's not just about baseball—it has a universal feeling," he explained. "It's every man's experience, every man's struggle. And the beautiful thing about it is that here you're dealing with the humor of all that pain."

Among the baseball people in the film was the charismatic, pioneering major league black umpire Emmett Ashford. Ashford told the *Los Angeles Times*, "it has been said down through the years, that I should have gone into show business." He had done some television work in Los Angeles with various roles, but this was his first film role. He worked on location in Macon, Georgia, for three weeks. Even though this was his first film, he was already typecast as the umpire.

Leon "Daddy Wags" Wagner was best known as an outfielder for the

Giants, Cardinals, Angels and Indians for 12 years in the 1960s. After baseball, he settled in Los Angeles and fell into acting. He landed a role in the Oscar nominated *Woman under the Influence* as a construction worker. His baseball play, however, led him to the *Bingo Long* project, where he grossed $10,000 for 8 weeks' work, compared to his top salary of $47,000 as a ballplayer. Of his acting Wagner explained, "It's all natural ability. I'm a free agent now. I have talent, I work hard, and I'm not camera shy. I performed before 30,000–40,000 people when I was 19. The acting secret is to be yourself. I play it like I'm rapping with the dudes at the bar. I want people to look up at the screen and say. 'Hey, man. That's Daddy Wags being Daddy Wags.'"

The fact that *Bingo Long* was being filmed in the previously segregated South was not lost on the cast and crew. Generally speaking, Macon and Savannah, Georgia, welcomed the crew with open arms. They also welcomed the thousands of dollars the project poured into those communities. On the DVD re-release of the film, Badham praised the authenticity of the extras that joined the cast, both white and black. In rural black areas, the community members spontaneously created a "second line" when the All-Stars paraded down the street. Badham also noted how some people got too deep into their parts. After reviewing one scene where white fans launched boos at the All-Stars, one actor's face was so convincing in his venom that he looked as if he could eat through glass. "I should have calmed that actor down," Badham lamented.

Still, good memories prevailed. People came out to watch and be supportive. Ashford noted how Richard Pryor organized baseball contests for the young people in Macon. Wagner recalled the star treatment they received as first rate. He also joked that Pryor and Billy Dee Williams had hundreds of female fans outside their hotel room doors, while he only had about ten.

James Earl Jones brought his extended family to the location and they loved Savannah. "We gave them hotel rooms and they sort of hung out and watched the filming and flirted with the ballplayers and the ballplayers flirted with my cousins," he recalled. "Going through Georgia was a lot of fun in real life. People who would join on the roadside would become a part of the movie in different neighborhoods in Macon. I really got to know America a little better during the shooting of that movie."

The final baseball element of the film, which may have been a blessing and a curse, was that the producers found Ed Hamman and the last remnants of the Indianapolis Clowns to participate. Since the beginning of black baseball, there have been teams or performers who added vaudeville-like antics to their baseball play as extra entertainment, and the Clowns were chief among them. The Clowns played baseball and delighted fans from the late 1930s through the 1960s, criss-crossing the country in various incorporations inside and outside of the professional Negro Leagues structure. The team members involved with the filming included "Birmingham Sam" Brison, Jophery Brown, a one armed player named Steve Anderson and a dwarf named Dero Austin, who would pop out of suitcases for Clowns games in the 1960s. The players were as equally enthusiastic as the actors were to be part of the project. "Just making this movie is like doing my life story," noted Brison. "This is more truth than anybody has ever seen in their life. This picture scares me." It is that truth, within the context of the Clown teams, that makes the film controversial for many observers.

Hamman helped manage the Clowns with Syd Pollock and eventually became owner of the team in the 1950s–1960s. Hamman was also a skilled baseball clown and helped develop a number of routines, sight gags, and comedic devices that the team popularized — such as specially designed percussion fireworks. An ardent self-promoter, he joined the film crew as "technical advisor," but never received a film credit. Hamman and his ballplayers flawlessly created the shadow ball routines and clowning for the film. Director Badham was among the few filmmakers in history to capture shadow ball and other pantomime routines. However, the emphasis on the clowning antics placed it outside the context of the 1939 setting the film was trying to create. The Clowns represented by these actors were a post 1950s barnstorming team, and this weighted the film heavily towards comedy. By this later date in the Clowns history they had become more entertainers than professional ballplayers, which had not been true in their earlier history.

Reviews and Reflections

The critiques of the film were mixed but mostly positive. *The New York Times* noted that the film managed "to provoke a lot of sober subsidiary response that, happily, never [got] in the way of the show." *The Kansas City Times* called the film "freewheeling entertainment and not a history lesson." *The Los Angeles Times* proclaimed it a "jackpot," "a two popcorn box action thriller laced with comedy" which demonstrated an "appreciation for the brotherliness of adversity."

Upon the film's release, audiences responded well to the film's exuberance, humor and music, but did not make it a blockbuster. Later that summer, the film had to compete against what would become an iconic baseball movie, *The Bad News Bears*, and an iconic sports film, the Academy Award winning *Rocky*.

In spite of modest success, *Bingo Long*, now available on DVD and VHS, has over the years consistently ranked high on several lists of all-time favorite baseball films and received several screenings at baseball themed film festivals and programs. It seemed that Rob Cohen's prophecy about the film came to pass because, after 30 years, *Bingo Long* remains the only major film with a nationwide theatrical release to deal with this era of black baseball. Thus, a lot of weight was placed on the film as truth to baseball fans, disappointing some historians and former Negro Leagues veterans alike. For some, the film's emphasis on the clowning and barnstorming aspects of black baseball misrepresented the true story. Upon seeing the famous scene where the All-Stars learn to drum up support for their team by parading into a town and dancing, the legendary Satchel Paige recoiled, "I never danced in no street!" Even though he enjoyed the film, noted critic Roger Ebert crystallized these opinions in his review, "We understand, as we're meant to, that they're 'Uncle Tomming' to survive. What we don't quite understand is why their behavior is supposed to be as funny today as it was meant to be then."

Every Negro League veteran and fan wanted to embrace the film with the same enthusiasm demonstrated by Sam Brison, but not everyone was convinced. Reflecting on the film's legacy, James Earl Jones understood the disappointment of the players. "They wanted the heroism to be celebrated. This movie was not about celebrating anybody's heroism," he stated. "I suppose the people who were unsung, and they had not been sung, believe me, by the general press or the general audience, and they thought 'well here's a chance maybe that I can get my time in the sun,' and they didn't. I can understand that it was disappointing for them. But that's not what we set out to do."

Jones, however, rebuts Ebert's critique as a bit unfair. "Who said it was meant to be funny? I don't think that 'cake walking' down the street is meant to be funny, then or now. It's meant to attract attention," he explains. "That team couldn't afford radio commercials. They had to attract the audience by doing unusual stuff, like firecrackers hidden in the ball. Leon, my character, was sour the whole time. He didn't think any of it was funny or fun. He thought it was crappy behavior to go out there and ride his awkward motorcycle down the street with a bunch of clowns. He was the worst proponent of that. He didn't like doing it." It is this balance and context Jones described that was, in his view, missed by critics. The critics did not understand the context in which many of the antics originally took place. That lack of understanding caused them to describe as humorous many actions that were simply a form of publicity originally.

Legacy

Today, Negro Leagues history has reached an apex in popularity. The Negro Leagues Baseball Museum thrives in Kansas City and has a number of traveling exhibits on tour. Baseball fans make Negro Leagues apparel part of their game day wardrobe. The National Baseball Hall of Fame has new exhibits and new inductees connected to the Negro Leagues. Negro Leagues tribute days at major baseball stadiums draw large numbers of fans to honor former players and enjoy nostalgic uniforms. Research in African American baseball has reached new levels of scholarship in recent years. There have also been a handful of fictionalized novels using the Negro Leagues as the setting. Yet, since 1976, no one has taken the challenge to present a major feature film with black baseball as the primary theme.

However, there have been television movies and documentary film projects undertaken, such as cable giant HBO's *Soul of the Game* (1996). *Soul* took great license with historical events and time lines, but created an interesting and entertaining character study of black baseball's three most influential figures—Paige, Gibson, and Jackie Robinson. *Finding Buck McHenry* (2003) was cable channel Showtime's effort to take a moderately popular children's book of the same title and illuminate Negro Leagues history. A struggling young baseball player learns lessons of history and life from a man he suspects to be a lost veteran of the Negro Leagues, who happens to work at his school. Both projects have had modest success, leaving television over theaters to perhaps become the most viable option for new projects on the Negro Leagues. With these types of successes and the interest that exists in the Negro Leagues its history is not done being told on film.

At the end of *Bingo Long*, the two main characters embrace their on-field victory and new fortune with a bit of cautious optimism, as they know the end of the Negro Leagues is near. Long turns to Leon Carter, declaring that as long as they work together, "We can't never lose." In spite of the cinema drought, interest in Negro Leagues baseball remains high. With continued scholarship, research and education, an inspired filmmaker may soon arrive to take Negro Leagues baseball to the broadest possible audiences, for which we all will be the winners.

Notes

1. See William Brashler, *The Bingo Long Traveling All Stars & Motor Kings* (Champaign: University of Illinois Press, 1993), vii–xv.
2. Gregg Kilday, "Movie Notes: Mowtown Simplifies the Complex," *The Los Angeles Times*, 3 August 1974, A7.
3. Mary Murphy, "Movie Call Sheet: Spielberg Set for New Project," *The Los Angeles Times*, 10 January 1975, G12.
4. Hal Erickson, *Baseball in the Movies: A Comprehensive Reference*, 1915–1991 (Jefferson, N.C.: McFarland, 1991), 77–78; Hollie West, "Nostalgia on the Basepaths: Black League Has Its Innings in 'Bingo,'" *The Los Angeles Times*, 14 September 1975, S1 and S30.
5. Mary Murphy, "Movie Call Sheet: Motown Firms Film Commitment," *The Los Angeles Times*, 3 September 1975, G14.

6. West, "Nostalgia," S30.
7. Dave Distel, "Makes Movie Debut: Ashford Behind Plate in Front of the Camera," *The Los Angeles Times*, 30 January 1976.
8. "Scores in 'Bingo Long': Wagner's Batting 1,000 in Acting League," The *Los Angeles Times*, 20 August 1976, F10.
9. Director's commentary, *The Bingo Long Traveling All-Stars & Motor Kings*, Universal Studios, DVD, 2001.
10. James Earl Jones, interview with Raymond Doswell, June 2006.
11. West, "Nostalgia," S30; see also Alan Pollack, *Barnstorming to Heaven: Syd Pollock and His Great Black Teams* (Alabama: 2006).
12. For historic footage of Reece "Goose" Tatum and the Indianapolis Clowns, see "Negro Leagues Baseball (1946)" in *Treasures from American Film Archives: 50 Preserved Films*, DVD (National Film Preservation Board, 2000), program 3.
13. Vincent Canby, "Film on Black Baseball Is a 'Bingo,'" *The New York Times*, 17 July 1976, 10; Dennis Stack, "Film of the Day," *The Kansas City Times*, 14 July 1976; Charles Champlin, "Critic At Large: 'Bingo' Hits the Jackpot," *The Los Angeles Times*, 16 July 1976, B1.
14. Brashler, xiv; Roger Ebert, "The Bingo Long Traveling All-Stars and Motor Kings," *Chicago Sun Times*, 16 July 1976.
15. James Earl Jones, interview with Raymond Doswell, June 2006.
16. *Ibid*.

Appendix A: A Satchel Paige Chronology

Larry Lester

July 7, 1906—Leroy Robert Paige is born in Mobile, Alabama.

May 1, 1926—Satchel Paige, 19 years old, makes his debut in the Negro Southern League, pitches Chattanooga Black Lookouts to a 5–4 win over the Birmingham Black Barons.

April 29, 1929—Satchel Paige, for the Birmingham Black Barons, fans 17 Cuban Stars for a 6–2 win.

May 29, 1929—Satchel Paige fans 18 Nashville Elite Giants in a 14-inning game. He allows 9 hits, 4 walks and 6 runs.

July 14, 1929—Satchel Paige strikes out 17 Detroit Stars in a 5 to 1 win.

September 2, 1929—A unique day in black baseball history. Two pitchers, Slap Hensley and Satchel Paige, pitch in both games of a double header. Hensley, pitching for the St. Louis Stars vs. the Kansas City Monarchs, pitches one inning of relief for Rosey Davis, yielding three hits and two runs, for no decision. He starts the second game and pitches a complete seven innings, giving up nine hits and three runs, to pick up the win. Meanwhile at Rickwood Field in Birmingham, Alabama, Paige starts and finishes nine innings, yielding eight hits, striking out four and three walks and two runs, to pick up the win. In the second game, he relieves for two and ⅔ innings, yielding no runs for his second win that day.

October 5, 1930—Willie Foster of the Chicago American Giants wins 6–1 over Earl Whitehill and the American League All-Stars. The major league squad includes sluggers Harry Heilmann, Art Shires, Charlie Gehringer and

Rickwood Field was one of the many parks Satchel Paige pitched in over the years while traveling across the country playing for the Monarchs.

pitcher Lefty O'Doul. The next day, Satchel Paige defeats the All-Stars, giving the American Giants three out of four wins.

May 30, 1932—The Homestead Grays and the Pittsburgh Crawfords engage in a triple-header at Forbes Field in Pittsburgh. The Crawfords are the home team for the first two games, with the Grays serving as home team for the finale. The Crawfords win the morning game 4 to 1; and the afternoon game, 10 to 0, a five-hitter by Satchel Paige. The Grays captured the twi-lighter, 9 to 2. Britt who caught the first two games, pitches the third game, a two-hitter for the Grays' win.

July 8, 1932—Pittsburgh Crawford Satchel Paige pitches the first of two career no-hitters. Paige strikes out 11 New York Black Yankees, walking three in defeating them in the second game of the double header.

July 14, 1933—Sug Cornelius and the Chicago American Giants defeat Satchel Paige and the Pittsburgh Crawfords to claim the first-half Negro National League title.

November 12, 1933— Playing for the Royal Giants in the California Winter League, Satchel Paige is honored with his own day at White Sox Park in Los Angeles, California. His Giants defeat Joe Pirrone's All-Stars and their ace southpaw Larry French, of the Pittsburgh Pirates, 5–0. The Giants lose the second game of the double header, 4–1. Paige receives numerous gifts at the ceremony between the games.

July 4, 1934— Pittsburgh Crawford Satchel Paige pitches a no-hitter against the Homestead Grays, striking out 17 batters. Winning 4–0, only a walk and an error prevented a perfect game. Paige boasts, "It got so I could nip frosting off a cake with my fastball."

July 7, 1934— Satchel Paige hits a single on his birthday, breaking up Chicago American Giant Sug Cornelius's no-hitter in the tenth inning to start a three-run-rally to win the game. After Paige's single, Josh Gibson hits a single and Judy Johnson triples, providing the nucleus for a 3–0 win.

August 10, 1934— Satchel Paige of the House of David defeats former teammate Chet Brewer and the Kansas City Monarchs, 2–1, to capture the championship game of the *Denver Post* Tournament. The Monarchs are the first black team invited to the coveted tournament.

August 26, 1934— The second annual East-West All-Star game is held in Comiskey Park in Chicago, Illinois. Ches Williams collects three hits, including a double for the East squad. Mule Suttles also gets three hits, including a triple for the West team. Satchel Paige, for the East, pitches four innings in picking up the victory, while Willie Foster, last year's winner, takes the 1–0 loss.

September 8, 1934–Two of black baseball's finest hurlers, Satchel Paige and Slim Jones, meet in the second game of a four-team doubleheader at Yankee Stadium. Paige of the Crawfords and Jones of the Stars battle to a 1–1 deadlock that is halted after nine innings due to darkness. Jones whiffs nine, allowing three hits and one unearned run, while Paige fans 12, giving up six hits and a run in the first inning. Years later, many players claim this was the greatest game ever played. Attendance was estimated at 30,000.

October 20, 1934— Satchel Paige out-battles Dizzy Dean of the Cleveland Rosenblums, 4–1, in an exhibition game in Cleveland. Paige strikes out 13 in six innings and allows no hits. Dean reminisces, "If Satch and I were pitching on the same team, we'd cinch the pennant by fourth of July and go fishing until the World Series."

October 26, 1934— LeRoy Robert Paige and Janet Howard are married in Pittsburgh, Pennsylvania. Famed toe-tapper Bill "Bojangles" Robinson serves as Paige's best man.

June 6, 1935— Chet Brewer of the Kansas City Monarchs and Satchel Paige of Bismarck pitch eight innings of scoreless baseball in Winnipeg, Canada. Paige strikes out 18 Monarch batters.

June 16, 1935— In a rematch, Satchel Paige of Bismarck defeats Chet Brewer and the Kansas City Monarchs, 2–1. Paige strikes out 12 Monarchs, allowing only two Monarchs to reach second base. Catcher Quincy Trouppe, of Bismarck, throws out three runners attempting to steal second base.

September 15, 1935— Satchel Paige of Bismarck (North Dakota), pitching in relief, wins both games of a double header against the House of the David to win the *Denver Post* Tournament.

July 25, 1936— The Pittsburgh Crawfords defeat the Philadelphia Stars in both games of a doubleheader by scores of 6–4 and 8–5. Satchel Paige wins the first game, fanning 15, while Willie Foster, making his first start for the Crawfords, wins the second.

April 22, 1937— The Crawfords team continues to be dismantled when Satchel Paige, along with the recently traded Josh Gibson, jump to the Dominican Republic.

September 13, 1937— Joe DiMaggio tells Lester Rodney of the *New York Daily Worker* that "Satchel Paige is the greatest pitcher I ever batted against."

September 16, 1937—*The New York Daily Worker* publishes an article titled, "Paige Asks Test for Negro Stars." Many fans thought Paige was apolitical but he proudly boasts, "Let the winners of the World's Series play [the Negro League All-Stars] just one game at Yankee Stadium — and if we don't beat them before a packed house they don't have to pay us!" Paige's challenge was never accepted.

September 19, 1937— Twenty-year old schoolboy Johnny Taylor of the Negro League All-Stars pitches a no-hitter over Satchel Paige's Santo Domingo All-Stars at the Polo Grounds before 22,500 fans, for a 2–0 win.

July 2, 1939— Joe Louis, Cab Calloway, and Bojangles Robinson are honored guests at the double header at Yankee Stadium and offer their selections to baseball's Hall of Fame. Louis picks Mule Suttles, Fats Jenkins, Satchel Paige, Josh Gibson and Willie Wells. Calloway selects Paige, Gibson, Jenkins, Bullet Rogan, and Frank Duncan. Bojangles names Cannonball Dick Redding, Oscar Charleston, and Jose Mendez.

August 17, 1939— Janet Howard Paige files for separation from Leroy "Satchel" Paige on the grounds of desertion. In 1943, she is awarded a cash settlement of $1,500 by a Chicago Circuit Court. (See also July 23, 1943, and October 26, 1934.)

October 1, 1939— Hilton Smith of the Kansas City Monarchs holds the Satchel Paige All-Stars to four hits. The Monarchs defeat the All-Stars, 11–0. Paige's All-Stars included Frazier Robinson at catcher, Herb Souell, Newt Joseph, George Giles, Mex Johnson and Jesse Douglass. Paige only lasted four innings against the powerful Monarchs.

December 3, 1939— Satchel Paige, pitching for Guayama in Puerto Rico, strikes out 17 batters en route to a 1–0 win over Mayaguez and pitcher Bud Barbee. It would be 14 years later when Bill Turley for San Juan duplicated the feat in the Puerto Rican League.

June 5, 1940—The media reports that Lee Wilkinson, brother of J.L. Wilkinson and Newt Joseph, former Monarch, are organizing the Satchel Paige All-Stars. Paige had been rumored to be under contract with the Newark Eagles and scheduled to report on this day. Instead, Paige and his all-stars appear in Richmond, Virginia, against the Brooklyn Royal Giants on Sunday, June 9.

July 20, 1940—Ed Herr, scout for the Cleveland Indians, writes to Sam Lacy about the color barrier in major league baseball: "Judging by what the big leagues are paying for pitching talent now, I would place a collective price tag of a quarter million dollars on the colored hurling corps of Satchel Paige's All-Stars of a few years back."

September 14, 1940—Satchel Paige of the Kansas City Monarchs strikes out 10 Chicago American Giant batters in five innings of a game stopped because of darkness.

March 10, 1941—Press release via telegraph from San Juan, Puerto Rico, concerning Satchel Paige states: "Satchel Paige, colored baseball star, has been fined $25 and given a year's suspension by Carlos Garcia de Noceda, president of the Puerto Rican Semi-Pro League, it was announced today. Garcia said that he found that Paige, while pitching for Guayama, deliberately used tactics designed to delay the game and cause Ponce [Lions] to lose. Paige once went so far as to throw the ball far over the outfielder's head. Paige joined Guayama of the Puerto Rican Winter League, 1939/40, and led the team to first place with a 39–17 won-lost record. Paige is leading the league with 19 victorias [wins] and 208 ponchadoes [punch outs]. Fortunately—because Paige has been the league's best drawing card—the suspension does not take effect until the season closes less than two weeks from now."

May 11, 1941—Satchel Paige, property of the Kansas City Monarchs, pitches for the N.Y. Black Yankees against the Philadelphia Stars in a game at Yankee Stadium. Paige is paid $100 by each club. A regularly scheduled league game is cancelled and caused a furor throughout the league. Jim Semler and Eddie Gottlieb were responsible for booking this gate attraction.

June 30, 1941—The Puerto Rico Sports Commission lifts its year-long ban on Satchel Paige for delaying a game while pitching for Guayama. The team appealed the suspension and won a reversal of the $25 penalty. (See March 10, 1941.)

September 14, 1941—A reported 39,500 Detroit fans watch Satchel Paige of the Monarchs pitch a six-hitter to defeat the Chicago American Giants.

October 14, 1941—Satchel Paige and Bob Feller engage in a pitching duel of fireball pitchers at Sportsman Park, in St. Louis, before 10,124 fans. Feller's All-Stars win 4–1.

May 24, 1942— Before 29,000 at Wrigley Field, Satchel Paige pitches six innings, giving up two hits and a run, with teammate Hilton Smith shutting out the Dizzy Dean All-Stars the last three innings for a 3–1 victory.

May 31, 1942— Before 22,000 at Griffith Stadium, Satchel Paige pitches five innings to defeat the Dizzy Dean All-Stars 8–1. Dean pitches the first inning only, giving up three hits and a run. A week earlier, Paige won a 3–1 game at Wrigley Field. Judge Landis prohibits a scheduled July 4 match up because the first two games outdrew major league games.

August 2, 1942— In a twin-bill at Yankee Stadium, Kansas City Monarch pitchers Satchel Paige and Hilton Smith combine for a one-hit shutout over the New York Cubans, for a 9 to love win. In the nightcap, the Philadelphia Stars defeat the Baltimore Elite Giants, 7–4, as Henry Spearman's grand slam sparks the Stars' attack.

September 14, 1942— The Homestead Grays in an attempt to win a World Series game against the Kansas City Monarchs recruits four players for game four. With Lennie Pearson (1b), Ed Stone (rf) and Leon Day (p) from Newark, and Bus Clarkson (ss) from the Philadelphia Stars, they beat Satchel Paige's team, 4–1. Leon Day fans 12 in beating Satchel Paige and the Monarchs 4–1. The Monarchs protest, contending that Day and three other players were picked up from other teams. The Monarchs' protest is upheld. Day's win is reversed (or thrown out), and the Monarchs sweep in four games.

July 18, 1943— Satchel Paige Day is celebrated at Wrigley Field in Chicago. Paige, on loan from the K.C. Monarchs, pitches for the Memphis Red Sox, defeating the New York Cubans, 1–0, before 20,000 fans. Paige fans seven, walks two and does not allow a ball to be hit out of the infield. Porter Moss hurls two-hit ball in the last four frames. The Birmingham Black Barons and the Cincinnati Clowns team up for the first game of the double header.

July 23, 1943— The Kansas City Call reports that Janet Howard Paige has filed for divorce from Leroy Paige on the charge of desertion and names Lucy Figueroa as a correspondent. The petition for divorce states that Paige earns approximately $40,000 annually from playing baseball and owns property valued at $25,000 with a collection of antiques and curios valued at about $30,000. (See April 17, 1939, and October 26, 1934.)

November 7, 1943— In Hollywood, California, Satchel Paige of the Baltimore Colored Giants defeats Bob Newsom and Joe Pirrone's All-Stars, 11–8.

July 2, 1944— Legend has it that Paige often loaded the bases intentionally, called in the outfield, sat his infielders down, and then struck out the side, but never in a league game. At Ebbets Field against the New York Cubans he attempts the fabled feat, with some refinement. Before approximately

14,000 fans, Paige matches wits with West Indian ace Victor Greenidge. Having to pitch on a moment's notice, Paige normally would pitch only three innings. He was scheduled to pitch again two days later (on July 4) against the Bushwicks, a strong semi-pro team, in Dexter Park.

However, the fans are treated to 11 innings of superb pitching from the legend. Paige strikes out 15 Cubans, and in the ninth inning he fills the bases deliberately, with no outs. The Cubans had scored an unearned run in the fifth, on a fielding error, two stolen bases, and a passed ball by catcher Sammie Haynes. The Monarchs open the ninth inning leading 2 to 1, when Hector Rodriguez slaps a single to center. Next Showboat Thomas hits a fly to center that is muffed by outfielder Hilton Smith, normally a pitcher, which allows the speedy Rodriguez to score. With the score tied, 2–2, next to bat is Louis Louden, followed by the always dangerous duo of Pancho Coimbre and Tetelo Vargas. All three men were perennial all-stars at Comiskey Park. Coimbre and Vargas would later be elected to the Puerto Rican Baseball Hall of Fame.

Paige intentionally walks Louden and Coimbre to load the bases and the drama is on.

To the fans' delight he strikes out Vargas. With one out, another all-star performer, Rogelio Linares, comes to bat. Linares hits a hard grounder to Herb Souell at third, who fires to Frank Duncan (who had replaced Haynes as catcher) for the second out of the inning. Rabbit Martinez, who made 10 all-star appearances, flies out to end the threat.

The Monarchs score a run in the eleventh inning to capture a 3 to 2 victory.

October 5, 1945— The Satchel Paige All-Stars defeat the Bob Feller All-Stars 4–2, before 20,000 fans in Wrigley Field. Paige gives up two hits, one run and fanned 10 batters in five innings.

October 13, 1945— Outfielder Johnny Davis of the Newark Eagles hits a three-run homer to help the Satchel Paige All-Stars defeat the Bob Feller All-Stars.

October 12, 1947— Lahoma Brown from Langston, Oklahoma, and Leroy "Satchel" Paige are married in Hays, Kansas.

November 2, 1947–In the warmth of Los Angeles, Satchel Paige and Bob Feller go the distance in a challenge game of all-stars. Paige pitches a shutout, winning 8–0.

July 7, 1948— Bill Veeck signs 42-year-old Satchel Paige to a Cleveland Indian contract. Critics claim it is another publicity stunt by Veeck. Paige adds, "Age is a question of mind over matter. If you don't mind, it doesn't matter."

July 9, 1948— Satchel Paige from the Kansas City Monarchs pitches his first major league game for the Cleveland Indians. Paige recalls, "I can remember catcher Jim Hegan reaching over and grabbing a towel to wipe off the plate. I told him there weren't no need of doing anything like that. I gave him this gum wrapper and told him to lay it the long way of the home plate. After I split that wrapper a few times with my fast ball, they sort of decided I still had my control." Paige enters the Indians' 73rd game of the season in the fifth inning, down 4–1, after pitcher Bob Lemon had been removed for a pinch-hitter. He pitches two scoreless innings, holding the St. Louis Browns to two singles and strikes out one batter. Paige is later lifted for a pinch hitter, roommate Larry Doby. Paige added, "I wasn't afraid of anybody I'd seen in that batter's box. I'd been around too long for that. I wasn't as fast as I used to be, but I was a better pitcher. If I couldn't overpower them, I'd out cute them." The Indians lose the game to the Browns, 5–3. Lemon is credited with the loss.

July 15, 1948—Satchel Paige becomes the first black pitcher to win a major league ball game. He relieves Bob Lemon and pitches the final three and a third innings for his first major league victory. Hank Majeski ties the score with a two-run home run. Paige allows three hits and no more runs to gain the victory.

July 18, 1948—Satchel Paige relieves Bob Feller in the sixth inning with one hitless inning. Paige does not receive a decision for his work.

July 19, 1948—Steve Gromek picks up a win, after Satchel Paige pitches two innings of relief, giving up three hits and three walks, plus a wild pitch en route to an 11-inning victory over the Washington Senators.

July 21, 1948—Satchel Paige pitches one inning of hitless ball in the second game of a Yankee doubleheader.

July 22, 1948—Satchel Paige pitches two innings, fanning Joe DiMaggio, giving up one hit, as the Cleveland Indians lose to the New York Yankees, 6–5.

July 25, 1948—Satchel Paige pitches two more innings (one hit) of relief, yielding a homer to Joe's brother Dom DiMaggio. Paige's Indians are shutout, 3–0.

July 30, 1948—Satchel Paige pitches four and two-thirds innings in relief of Steve Gromek and Don Black. He gives up four hits and two runs. Paige, in his longest stint of the season, is credited with his only loss of the season.

August 3, 1948—Paige gets first starting pitching assignment versus the Washington Senators, before 72,434 fans. The attendance sets a record for a night game in Cleveland history. He wins 5–3.

August 8, 1948—Satchel Paige pitches one and a third innings to pick up a victory against the Yankees. He yields two hits in the 8–6 victory.

August 11, 1948—Satchel Paige relieves Bob Lemon and pitches two and two-thirds innings for a save. He gives up a two-run single to the St. Louis Browns' Hank Arft.

August 13, 1948— Satchel Paige becomes the first black pitcher to throw a nine-inning shutout in the American League. At age 42, Paige shuts out the Chicago White Sox, 5–0, before a sellout crowd of 51,013 at Comiskey Park. Paige gives up five hits in only his second start since joining the team.

August 20, 1948— Satchel Paige pitches his second straight shutout, a three-hitter, in a 1–0 win over the White Sox in Cleveland's Municipal Stadium, before a record night game crowd of 78,382 fans.

August 24, 1948— Satchel Paige starts and pitches only two and two-thirds innings in Fenway Park. He gives up five hits and three runs in the 9–8 loss. Paige's scoreless streak of 26 innings is stopped in the second inning.

August 27, 1948— Satchel Paige pitches one inning of relief against the N.Y. Yankees, in a 7–2 loss.

August 30, 1948— Satchel Paige starts and pitches his first complete major league game (see entry for Aug. 13, 1948). The Indians take a 10–1 victory over the Washington Senators at Griffith Stadium.

September 4, 1948— Satchel Paige starts and pitches four innings. He is relieved in the fifth inning, as the Indians win 6–4.

September 8, 1948— Satchel Paige pitches one inning and walks four batters. The Indians defeat the Detroit Tigers 8–7 in 11 innings.

September 9, 1948— Satchel Paige relieves Bob Feller and gives up three hits and two walks in one and a third innings. Paige blows the save.

September 12, 1948— Satchel Paige starts and pitches four innings, yielding five hits and two walks. Paige strikes out six batters as the Tribe wins 6–4 over the St. Louis Browns.

September 14, 1948— Satchel Paige pitches two hitless innings of relief as the Indians lose to the Yankees, 6–5. This game concludes Paige's first season in the majors. In 72 and two-thirds innings, Paige pitches in 21 games. This includes seven starts and 14 relief appearances. He compiles a 6–1 win-loss record and an ERA of 2.48.

October 10, 1948— Paige becomes the first black player to pitch in the World Series for the Cleveland Indians, when he works two-thirds of an inning in relief.

February 9, 1951— The St. Louis Browns sign the ageless Satchel Paige, at 45. Paige last pitched for the Cleveland Indians in 1949.

May 20, 1951— Satchel Paige rejoins the Negro Leagues, this time with the Chicago American Giants. He pitches four innings, gave up one hit, strikes out three, walks none, as his team beats the Black Barons, 6–3 on opening day in Chicago. At bat, he hits into a double play and has a single.

July 14, 1951— After pitching for Bill Veeck in Cleveland in 1948, and the Chicago American Giants earlier in the season, Satchel Paige rejoins Veeck with the St. Louis Browns. To make room on the roster, utility infielder John

Berardino is taken off the active list and named coach. Coach Fred Hofmann goes back on the road as a scout.

June 30, 1952—Satchel Paige is named to the American League All-Star team.

August 6, 1952—Satchel Paige at 46, becomes the oldest pitcher in the majors to pitch a complete game or a shutout. He beats Virgil Trucks and the Detroit Tigers 1–0 in 12 innings.

March 14, 1956—Satchel Paige signs with the Birmingham Black Barons at age 50 to do a little pitching and managing.

April 29, 1956—Satchel Paige, now with the Miami Marlins of the International League, after only four days of training, pitches a four-hit, 3–0 shutout over Montreal, in a seven-inning contest.

August 7, 1956—The largest crowd in minor league history, 57,713 fans, watches 51-year-old Satchel Paige pitch for the Miami Marlin. The Marlins host Columbus of the International League in a game played in the Orange Bowl.

August 13, 1956—Satchel Paige, now in his fifties pitches a one-hitter to blank Rochester, 4–0. The seven-inning victory raises Paige's record to 10–3 and lowers his ERA to 1.50.

July 14, 1958—In *Newsweek* magazine, Satchel Paige spins his philosophy: "I used more psychiatry than I used to. I stares at them, slaps some rosin around and by the time I lets go those batters' legs starts to wobble.... I ain't never thrown an illegal pitch. The trouble is once in a while I tosses one that ain't been seen by this generation."

August 23, 1959—Satchel Paige, pitching for the Havana Cubans, plays the Kansas City Monarchs at Ebbets Field in New York. Paige, who gives his age as "between 40 and 60," yields one earned run, while striking out four in three innings. Paige wears a White Sox uniform sent to him by owner Bill Veeck.

August 24, 1961—Ageless Satchel Paige signs with Portland. In 25 innings for the Beavers, he compiles a 2.88 ERA.

January 30, 1965—The National Baseball Congress in Wichita, Kansas, names Satchel Paige the all-time outstanding player.

September 25, 1965—The city council of Kansas City, Missouri, proclaimed this day as Satchel Paige Day. Satchel Paige pitches his last major league game at the age of 59, for the Kansas City Athletics. He pitches three innings against the Boston Red Sox, giving up one hit and no runs. Paige later claims the secret of success was to "just take the ball and throw it where you want to. Throw strikes. Home plate don't move."

August 6, 1968—Serving as a deputy sheriff in Kansas City, Missouri, Leroy Satchel Paige loses his democratic primary bid for the State Legislature to political veteran Leon M. Jordan. Paige only gathers 382 votes against 3,870 votes for Jordan.

August 12, 1968— Satchel Paige is signed by the Atlanta Braves as a pitching coach. He needs 158 days to qualify for the major league pension plan. Braves president William Bartholomay assigns Paige his retirement age — number 65 — as his jersey number.

May 25, 1970— Satchel Paige is honored in Springfield, Illinois, during Satchel Paige Day before a minor league game between the Springfield Redbirds and Wichita Aeros. Paige received congratulatory letters and telegrams from President Ronald Reagan, Illinois governor James Thompson and other dignitaries.

August 9, 1971— Satchel Paige is inducted into the National Baseball Hall of Fame.

January 26, 1972— Satchel Paige makes a guest appearance on the popular Ralph Edwards' *This Is Your Life* television show.

July 29, 1974— Satchel Paige, James "Cool Papa" Bell and Normal "Tweed" Webb appear on Joe Garagiola's *Baseball World Show* on NBC-TV.

May 31, 1981— The made-for-television movie *Don't Look Back* starring Louis Gossett, Jr., as Satchel Paige and Beverly Todd as his wife Lahoma makes its debut on national television.

June 5, 1982— Satchel Paige Memorial Stadium, located at 48th and Swope Parkway, is dedicated in Kansas City, Missouri. It will be the home of little league baseball teams and special events.

June 8, 1982— Perhaps the world's greatest pitcher, Satchel Paige dies in Kansas City, Missouri.

Appendix B: Milestones, Achievements and Records from Kansas City's Blackball Past

Larry Lester

1924   The first Colored World Series is played between the Kansas City Monarchs and the Hilldale Club from Darby, Pennsylvania. The Monarchs, led by future Hall of Famers Bullet Rogan and Jose Mendez, win the 10-game series, five games to four with one tie.

1925   The Hilldale Club, from Darby, Pa., wins the Colored World Series, defeating the Kansas City Monarchs, five games to one.

1930   The Kansas City Monarchs play their first game under the lights in Enid, Oklahoma. This is five years before the first major league night game would be played at Crosley Stadium in Cincinnati, Ohio, in 1935.

1941   Catcher Frank Duncan, Sr., and pitcher Frank Duncan, Jr., become the first father and son to play on the same team, the Kansas City Monarchs, in the same year — fifty years before the Ken Griffey family made major league history.

1942   The Kansas City Monarchs, led by Buck O'Neil, sweep the Homestead Grays in four games to capture the Negro League World Series.

1946   The Newark Eagles with Monte Irvin, Larry Doby and Leon Day defeat the Kansas City Monarchs in seven games to capture the Black World Series title.

1950   Ernie Banks starts his professional baseball career with the Kansas City Monarchs before being drafted into the U.S. Army.

1953   The first woman in professional baseball, Toni Stone, joins the Indianapolis Clowns. She joins the Kansas City Monarchs the following season.

1956   Buck O'Neil becomes the first black scout in the major leagues for the Chicago Cubs.

1962 Buck O'Neil becomes the first black coach in major league baseball, with the Chicago Cubs.

1964 Norm Bass, former Kansas City A's pitcher, from 1961 to 1963, plays one game at defensive back for the Denver Broncos in 1964.

1965 Satchel Paige, of the Kansas City A's, becomes the oldest pitcher, at 59, to start a major league game, pitching three innings against the Boston Red Sox, giving up one hit.

1971 Paige becomes the first player to go into the Cooperstown National Baseball Hall of Fame as a Negro Leaguer.

1977 Frank White, Kansas City Royals, becomes the first black player to win the Gold Glove Award at second base in the American League.

1979 The Alcorn Braves basketball team becomes the first historically black institution invited to the NIT. The Braves are led by coach David Whitney, former Kansas City Monarch.

1980 Kansas City Royals centerfielder Willie Wilson becomes the first American League batter to collect 100 hits from each side of the plate, collecting 230 hits in total. He is also the first player with more than 700 (705) at-bats in a season.

1980 Frank White, of the Kansas City Royals, is the first major league player to win the ALCS Most Valuable Player award.

1980 U.L. Washington and Frank White form the first African American double play combination in American League history.

1982 The first Negro League player to be selected to the National Baseball Hall of Fame, Satchel Paige, dies in Kansas City, Missouri.

1990 The Negro Leagues Baseball Museum, Inc., in Kansas City, Missouri, is created in the historic 18th and Vine area.

1994 Hal McRae is the last manager of the Kansas City Royals with a winning record (64–51, this season, 286–277 overall).

1994 John "Buck" O'Neil is named to the Missouri Sports Hall of Fame.

1998 Wilber "Bullet" Rogan, former pitcher, outfielder and manager for the Monarchs, is inducted to the National Baseball Hall of Fame in Cooperstown.

2001 Hilton Lee Smith, former pitcher for the Monarchs, is inducted to the National Baseball Hall of Fame in Cooperstown.

2001 Buck O'Neil Way is dedicated in Kansas City, Missouri, becoming the first street named after a former Negro Leaguer.

2006 Former Monarchs Andy Cooper, Willard Brown, and owner J.L. Wilkinson are inducted to the National Baseball Hall of Fame in Cooperstown.

Note: These are merely some key dates and events chosen by the conference planning committee representing black baseball in Kansas City. This is not intended to chronicle every significant and/or meaningful moment in the history of American baseball. More detailed information describing the history of black baseball can be found in the 2006 Jerry Malloy Negro League Research Conference booklet.

Kansas City's Black Players

National Hall of Famers and Their Seasons in Kansas City   *Halls and Induction Years*

1. Ernie Banks, 1950, 1953 — (U.S.—1977)
2. Bernardo Baro, 1930 — (Cuba—1945)
3. James "Cool Papa" Bell, 1932, 1934 — (U.S.—1974)
4. Willard "Home Run" Brown, 1935–43, 1946–51, 1958 — (Puerto Rico—1991, U.S.—2006)
5. Andy Cooper, 1928–29, 1931–39 — (U.S.—2006)
6. Willie Foster, 1931 — (U.S.—1996)
7. Francisco "Pancho" Herrera, 1952–54 — (Cuba—1997)
8. John Henry "Pop" Lloyd, 1921 — (U.S.—1977)*
9. Jose Mendez, 1920–26 — (Cuba—1939, U.S.—2006)
10. Leroy "Satchel" Paige, 1935–36, 1939–48 — (U.S.—1971, Puerto Rico—1996)
11. Agustin Parpetti, 1921 — (Cuba—1962)
12. Bartolo Portuondo, 1920–22 — (Cuba—1985)
13. Jackie Robinson, 1945 — (U.S.—1962)
14. Jose Rodriguez, 1920 — (Cuba—1951)
15. Wilber "Bullet" Rogan, 1920–38 — (U.S.—1998)
16. Cristobal Torriente, 1926 — (Cuba—1939, U.S.—2006)
17. Bob Thurman, 1949 — (Puerto Rico—1991)
18. Hilton Smith, 1936–48 — (U.S.—2001)
19. Norman "Turkey" Stearnes, 1931, 1934, 1938–40 — (U.S.—2000)
20. Willie "Devil" Wells, 1932, 1934 — (U.S.—1997)
21. J.L. Wilkinson, 1920–48 — (U.S.—2006)

*Lloyd played briefly with the Monarchs in the 1921 postseason series against the Kansas City Blues.

Former Negro League players who played major league baseball for Kansas City teams

Major League Years with the Athletics	NL Career & Major NL Team
1. Harry "Suitcase" Simpson, 1955–1958	1946–48, Philadelphia Stars
2. Jose Guillermo "Pants" Santiago, 1956	1947–48, New York Cubans
3. Bob Boyd, 1961	1946–50, Memphis Red Sox
4. Bob Trice, 1955	1948–50, Homestead Grays
5. John Wyatt, 1961–1966	1953–55, Indianapolis Clowns
6. Satchel Paige, 1965	1926–60, Kansas City Monarchs

Major League Years with the Royals	NL Career & Major NL Team
7. George Spriggs, 1969–70	1959–60, Kansas City Monarchs

A record 21 former Monarchs played for major league teams— The players and their debut dates:

1. Jackie Robinson	Brooklyn Dodgers	April 15, 1947
2. Hank Thompson	St. Louis Browns	July 17, 1947

3. Willard Brown	St. Louis Browns	July 19, 1947
4. Satchel Paige	Cleveland Indians	July 9, 1948
5. Quincy Trouppe	Cleveland Indians	April 30, 1952
6. Connie Johnson	Chicago White Sox	April 17, 1953
7. Ernie Banks	Chicago Cubs	September 17, 1953
8. Gene Baker	Chicago Cubs	September 20, 1953
9. Curt Roberts	Pittsburgh Pirates	April 13, 1954
10. Elston Howard	New York Yankees	April 14, 1955
11. Bob Thurman	Cincinnati Reds	April 14, 1955
12. John Kennedy	Philadelphia Phillies	April 22, 1957
13. Frank Barnes	St. Louis Cardinals	September 22, 1957
14. Pancho Herrera	Philadelphia Phillies	April 14, 1958
15. Hank Mason	Philadelphia Phillies	September 12, 1958
16. George Altman	Chicago Cubs	April 11, 1959
17. Lou Johnson	Chicago Cubs	April 17, 1960
18. Walt Bond	Cleveland Indians	April 19, 1960
19. J.C. Hartman	Houston Colt .45s	July 21, 1962
20. George Spriggs	Pittsburgh Pirates	September 15, 1965
21. Ike Brown	Detroit Tigers	June 17, 1969

Monarchs East-West All-Stars

In 1936, the Kansas City Monarchs, not a member of any league, had a record 11 players make an appearance in the East-West classic. Players with "(2)" beside their name indicate they played in both games that year.

Total participants — 131 players

1934
Brewer, Chester Arthur "Chet" — p

1936 — RECORD 11 PLAYERS
Allen, Newton Henry "Colt" — 2b/ss
Brown, Willard Jesse "Home Run" — ss
Cooper, Andrew L. "Andy" — p
Dwight, Edward Joseph "Eddie" — cf
Else, Harry "Speed" — c
Harris, Chick "Popsicle" — 1b
Kranson, Floyd Arthur — p
Milton, Henry William "Streak" — cf
Patterson, Andrew Lawrence "Pat" — 2b
Rogan, Wilber "Bullet" — lf
Taylor, Leroy — rf

1937
Allen, Newton Henry "Colt" — 2b/ss
Brown, Willard Jesse "Home Run" — lf
Mayweather, Eldridge E. "Chili" — ph

Milton, Henry William "Streak" — ph
Smith, Hilton Lee "Smitty" — p

1938
Allen, Newton Henry "Colt" — 2b
Johnson, Byron "Mex," "Jew Baby" — ss
Milton, Henry William "Streak" — rf
Smith, Hilton Lee "Smitty" — p

1939
Milton, Henry William "Streak" — rf
Smith, Hilton Lee "Smitty" — p (2)
Stearnes, Norman Thomas "Turkey" — rf
Strong, Theodore Roosevelt "Ted," "T.R." — 1b/ss (2)

1940
Greene, James Elbert "Joe," "Pea" — c
Milton, Henry William "Streak" — rf
Smith, Hilton Lee "Smitty" — p

1941

Allen, Newton Henry "Colt" — ss
Paige, Leroy Robert "Satchel" — p
Smith, Hilton Lee "Smitty" — p
Strong, Theodore Roosevelt "Ted," "T.R." — rf

1942

Brown, Willard Jesse "Home Run" — lf (2)
Greene, James Elbert "Joe," "Pea" — c (2)
O'Neil, Jr., John Jordan "Buck" — 1b (2)
Paige, Leroy Robert "Satchel" — p
Smith, Hilton Lee "Smitty" — p
Strong, Theodore Roosevelt "Ted," "T.R." — rf (2)

1943

Brown, Willard Jesse "Home Run" — cf
O'Neil, Jr., John Jordan "Buck" — 1b
Paige, Leroy Robert "Satchel" — p
Williams, Jesse Horace "Bill" — ss

1944

Serrell, Bonnie Clinton "El Grillo" — 2b

1945

McDaniels, Booker Taliaferro "Cannonball" — p
Robinson, Jack Roosevelt "Jackie" — ss
Williams, Jesse Horace "Bill" — 2b

1946

Renfroe, Sr., Othello Nelson "Chico" — ss
Scott, John — lf

1947

Abernathy, Robert William "James" — lf
Smith, John Ford "Geronimo" — p
Souell (Cyrus), Herbert "Herb," "Baldy" — 3b (2)

1948

Brown, Willard Jesse "Home Run" — cf (2)
LaMarque, James Harding "Lefty" — p (2)
Souell (Cyrus), Herbert "Herb," "Baldy" — 3b (2)

1949

Brown, Willard Jesse "Home Run" — 3b, lf
LaMarque, James Harding "Lefty" — p
O'Neil, Jr., John Jordan "Buck" — ph
Richardson, Noval Eugene "Gene," "Britches" — p

1950

Cooper, Thomas Roger "Tom" — c/rf
Johnson, Jr., Clifford "Connie" — p
Souell (Cyrus), Herbert "Herb," "Baldy" — 3b

1951

Brewer, Sherwood "Woody" — 3b
Cooper, Thomas Roger "Tom" — c/1b
Smith, Theolic "Fireball" — p
Williams, Jesse Horace "Bill" — 2b

1952

Baylis, Henry "Hank" — 3b
Henderson, James "Duke" — cf
Jackson, Isiah "Ike" — c
Jackson, Jr., John W. "Stony" — p
Phillips, Jr., Richard Albaso "Dick" — p

1953

Armenteros, Juan — c
Banks, Ernest "Ernie" — ss
Baylis, Henry "Hank" — 3b
Brewer, Sherwood "Woody" — 2b
Cooper, Thomas Roger "Tom" — lf
Herrera, Juan Francisco "Pancho" — 1b
Jackson, Jr., John W. "Stony" — p
Johnson, Ernest D. "Schooley" — rf

1954

Nunez, Dagoberto — lf
Herrera, Francisco "Pancho" — 1b
Armenteros, Juan — c
Mason, Hank "Pistol" — p

1955

Whitney, David L. — lf
Cartmill, Al — 2b
Hartman, J.C. — ss
Baylis, Henry "Hank" — 3b
Armenteros, Juan — c

Paige, Leroy Robert "Satchel" — p
Maroto, Ricky — p

1956
Bond, Walt — lf
Carpenter, Andrew — p
Eliott, Eugene — 3b
Jackson, A.J. — p (2)
Jones, Bill — lf
Kennedy, John — ss
Maroto, Ricky — cf (2)
McKnight, Ira — rf/3b/c (2)
Montgomery, Joe — rf
Robinson, James — 3b

1957
Evans, John — 3b
McKnight, Ira — c
Robinson, James — 2b
White, Willie — 1b
Wilson, Bob — cf
Winston, John "Booby" — p

1958
Cain, Marion "Sugar" — p
Grigsby, Aubrey — p
Hubbard, Palmer — pr

Jarvis, Gideon — lf/3b
McKnight, Ira — c
Robinson, James — ss
Self, John — 1b
Tidmore, Ozzie — 2b
Washington, Willie — 3b
White, Willie — rf

1959
Dancey, Nate — inf
Gilbert, Paul — 1b
Hubbard, Palmer — of
Mitchell, Jessie — lf
Taylor, Tommy — p
Washington, Willie — 3b
Winston, John — p

1960
Brown, Issac "Ike" — ss
Dancey, Nate — 2b
Franklin, Leon — p
Grant, Calvin Lewis — p
Hubbard, Palmer — cf
McKnight, Ira — 3b
Miller, Mel — of
Taylor, Tommy — p
Williams, Frank — rf

Kansas City Monarchs Season-by-Season Records

Negro National League

Year	W-L	Finished	Managers
1920	41–29	tied for second place, 3½ games back	Jose Mendez
1921	50–31	second, half a game back.	Mendez
1922	46–33	tied for second	Sam Crawford
1923	57–33	first — No WS played	Crawford
1924	55–22	first	Mendez
		World Series, defeated Hilldale Giants, 5-4-1.	
1925	62–23	second, 2½ games back	Mendez
		Playoffs, defeated St. Louis Stars, 4–3	
		World Series, lost to Hilldale Giants, 5–1	
1926	57–21	first	Bullet Rogan
		Playoffs, lost to Chicago American Giants, 5–4	
1927	54–29	second, 4 games back	Rogan
1928	50–31	second, 10½ games back	Rogan
1929	62–17	first — no WS played	Rogan
1930	39–26	third, 15½ games back	Rogan
1931 to 1936, barnstorming			

Negro American League

1937	first place, won-lost record not known — no WS played		Andy Cooper
1938	32–15	first — no WS played	Cooper
1939	28–14	first — no WS played	Cooper
1940	first place, won-lost record not known — no WS played		Cooper
1941	first place, won-lost record not known — no WS played		Cooper
1942	first place, won-lost record not known		Frank Duncan
	World Series, defeated the Homestead Grays, 4–0		
1943	fourth place, won-lost record not known		Duncan
1944	23–42	last place, 22½ games back	Duncan
1945	32–30	fourth place, 17½ games back	Duncan
1946	43–14	first	Duncan
	World Series, Lost to Newark Eagles, 4–3		
1947	38–22	second, 7½ games back	Duncan
1948	41–25	second, 10 games back	Buck O'Neil

Negro American League, West Division

1949	54–37	first — no WS played	O'Neil
1950	52–21	first — no WS played	O'Neil
1951	42–28	first — no WS played	O'Neil
1952	23–26	fourth, 8½ games back	O'Neil
1953	56–21	first — no WS played	O'Neil
1954	23–43	last , 20½ games back	O'Neil
1955	first place, won-lost record not known		O'Neil
1956	finish & won-lost record not known		Jelly Taylor
1957	place & won-lost record not known		Dizzy Dismukes
1958	30–24	first — no WS played	Dismukes
1959	finish & won-lost record not known		Willie Washington
1960	finish & won-lost record not known		Sherwood Brewer

Appendix C: Rosters of Kansas City's Black Teams

Leslie A. Heaphy

Rosters are compiled by the editor from a variety of sources. They are not necessarily complete, just the best effort to find as many names as possible.

Jenkins Sons (1906–07)
Dorsey, Roy (1906–07)
Evans, Frank (1907)
Houston, William (1906–07)
Lee, Fred (1907)
Lindsay, Bill — p (1907)
McAdoo, Tully (1907)
McCampbell, Ernest (1906–07)
McCampbell, Tom (1906–07)
Page, Gertha (1906)
Pullam, Arthur "Chick" (1907)
Stearman, Tom — of (1906–07)
Wilkins, West (1906–07)

Kansas City All-Nations
Blukoi, Frank — 2b
Coleman, Clarence — c
Crow, Sam — 3b
Donaldson, John — p/of
Evans, Frank — of/3b
Hernandez, Ricardo "Chico" — 1b
McNair, Hurley — of
Mikado, Jap
Mendez, Jose — p/ss
Rogan, Wilber "Bullet Joe" — p/ss/of
Torriente, Cristobal — of
Turner, B. — 1b
Wilkins, Wesley — p
Wilkinson, J.L. — p

Kansas City Colored Giants
Jackson, William "Ashes" — 3b
Lindsay, Robert "Frog" — ss
Rogan, Wilber "Bullet Joe" — p
Skinner, Floyd — util

Kansas City Giants
Binga, William — 3b
DeMoss, Elwood "Bingo" — 2b

Evans, Frank — 3b/of
Foster, Albert "Red" — 1b
Hardy, Arthur
Jackson, Wilbur "Ashes" — 3b
Johnson, Topeka Jack
Lee, Fred
Lindsay, William "Bill" — p
Lindsay, Robert "Frog" — ss
McAdoo, Dudley
McCampbell, Ernest
McCampbell, Tom
Neal, George — 2b
Norman, Jim — mgr
Payne, Felix
Pettus, Zack — c
Pulliam, Chick — c
Rogan, Wilber — p
Robinson, Robert "Ginny"
Smith, Tobe
Smith, Worthy
Stearman, Tom — of
Tenny, William — c
Wakefield, Bert — of
Wilkins, Wesley — of
Williams, Dee

Kansas City Monarchs

Abernathy, James — cf (1945)
Adams, Packinghouse — 3b (1938)
Alexander, Joe — c (1950)
Alexander, Ted — p (1943–44, 1946–47)
Allen, Newt — ss/2b (1922–44)
Alsop, Clifford — p (1920, 1922)
Anderson, Theodore "Bubbles" — 2b (1922–24)
Armenteros, Juan — c (1953–55)
Baker, Gene — ss (1948–50)
Bankhead, Sam — (1934)
Banks, Ben — 2b (1951–52)
Banks, Ernie — ss (1950, 1953)
Barbee, Quincy — of (1949)
Barnes, Ed — p (1937–38)
Barnes, Frank — p (1949–50)
Barnes, V. — 2b (1940)
Barnhill, Herbert — c (1943)
Bartlett, Homer — p (1924–25)
Baro, Bernardo — of (1920)
Bayliss, Henry — 2b (1951–55)

Bell, Clifford — p (1921–22, 1924–27, 1932)
Bell, James "Cool Papa" — of (1932, 1934)
Bell, William — p (1923–30, 1932)
Bell, William "Lefty" — p (1949–54)
Bennette, George — of (1922)
Bennett, Willie — of (1953, 1955)
Bergin, Jim — 1b (1949)
Berry, John Paul — 1b (1935–36, 1945)
Berry, Mike — p (1947)
Betts, Russell — p (1950–51)
Beverly, Charles "Lefty" — p (1931–35)
Bibbs, Rainey — 3b (1938–41)
Blackburn, Hugh — p/1b (1920)
Blattner, Frank — 2b/1b/of (1921)
Blukoi, Frank — 2b (1920)
Bobo, Willie — 1b (1924)
Bowe, Randolph — p (1938–39)
Boyd, Ollie — of (1933)
Bradley, Frank — p (1937–42)
Breda, Bill — of (1950–51)
Bremer, Eugene — p (1935, 1937)
Brewer, Chet — p (1925–35, 1937, 1940–41)
Brewer, Sherwood — 2b (1953–55)
Broadnax, Maceo — p (1932)
Brooks, Jesse — 3b (1937)
Brown, Ray — p (1928, 1931)
Brown, Willard — of (1935–43, 1946–52)
Bryant, Allen "Lefty" — p (1940–41, 1943, 1946–47)
Bumpus, Earl — p/rf (1944)
Byas, Richard "Subby" — of (1931)
Carlyle, Sylvester "Junius" — inf (1945)
Carr, George "Tank" — inf/of (1920–22)
Carter, William — c (1922)
Cartmill, Alfred — 2b (1949, 1951, 1955)
Caruthers, — p (1935)
Chretian, Ernest — of (1949–50)
Clay, William — p (1932)
Clifford, Luther — c (1949)
Collins, Gene — p (1947–51)
Cooper, Alfred "Army" — p (1923, 1928–31)
Cooper, Andrew "Andy" — p (1928–30, 1932–41)
Cooper, Tom — of/1b (1947–53)
Cordova, — 3b (1921)
Cox, Roosevelt — 3b/c (1938)

Crawford, Sam — p/mgr(1920–24, 1934–35)
Creacy, Dewey — 3b (1924)
Currie, Rube — p (1920–23, 1932)
Curry, Lacy — ss (1949)
Cyrus, — 3b (1939)
Daniels, Cliff–p (1956)
Davis, James — p (1921)
Davis, Lee — p (1945)
Davis, Roosevelt — p (1930)
Dawson, Johnny — c (1938, 1941–42)
Dean, Nelson — p (1925–26, 1932)
Decuir, Lionel — c (1939–40)
Dewitt, Fred — c (1922, 1925, 1927)
Diggs, Leon — of (1956)
Dismukes, William "Dizzy" — mgr (1941–42)
Donaldson, John — p/of (1920–25, 1931, 1934)
Douglas, Jesse — 2b (1937, 1940–41)
Douse, Joe — p (1952–53)
Drake, William "Plunk," "Bill" — p (1922–25)
Duffy, Bill — c (1947)
Duncan, Frank — c/mgr (1920–34, 1937–38, 1941–47)
Duncan, Frank III — p (1941, 1946, 1949)
Duncan, Melvin — p (1950–51, 1954–55)
Dwight, Eddie — of (1928–29, 1933–37)
Edwards, William — p (1944)
Elliott, Eugene — 3b (1956)
Else, Harry — c (1936–38)
Evans, Frank — p/of
Everett, Clarence — inf (1927)
Everett, Curtis — of (1950–51)
Fagan, Bob — 2b (1920–22)
Favor, Thomas "Monk" — inf/of (1947)
Flores, Conrad — p (1954)
Foreman, Sylvester "Hooks" — of/c (1920–22, 1925, 1927, 1933)
Foreman, Zack — p (1921)
Foster, Willie — p (1931, 1934)
Fowlkes, Samuel — p (1950)
Garner, — of (1949)
Gaston, Isaac — util (1949)
Giles, George — 1b (1927–29, 1932–34)
Gillard, Luther — of (1938)
Gilmore, James — p (1954–55)
Gisetaner, Willie "Lefty" — p (1922–23)

Glass, Carl — p/1b (1927)
Gordon, Herman — 2b
Goshay, Samuel — of (1949)
Gray, Chester — c (1945)
Gray, Roosevelt "Chappy" — 2b
Greene, James "Joe" — c/of (1939–43, 1946–47)
Green, Willie — (1924)
Hall, Charley — util (1948)
Hamilton, Jim — ss (1946)
Harding, Hallie — of (1928–31)
Hardy, Paul — c (1939, 1942)
Harper, Dave "Chick" — of (1920–21, 1944–45)
Harris, Chick — of/p (1931–32, 1934, 1936)
Harris, Curtis — 1b (1936)
Harrison, Tomlini — p (1930)
Hartman, J.C. — ss (1955)
Hawkins, Lemuel — 1b/of (1920–27)
Hayes, Jimmy — c (1949)
Haynes, Sammy — c (1943–45)
Henderson, James — of (1949, 1952–53)
Herrera, Francisco "Pancho" — c/1b (1952–54)
Hicks, Wesley — of (1931)
Hill, Fred (1924)
Hood, Dozier — p (1945)
Hopwood, — of (1928)
Horn, Herman "Doc" — of/3b (1951, 1953–54)
Hoskins, Bill — of (1943)
Howard, Elston — c (1948–50)
Howard, Herb — of/p (1948)
Hubbard, Larry — inf/of (1946)
Hughes, Lee — p (1950)
Hunt, Leonard — of (1949–51, 1953)
Hunter, Bertrum — p (1932, 1934)
Hutchinson, Willie — p (1939, 1941)
Jackson, Isiah — of/c (1951–53)
Jackson, John — p (1951–53)
Jackson, W. — p (1938–39)
Jamerson, Londell — p (1950–51)
Johnson, Byron "Mex" — ss (1937–40)
Johnson, Clifford "Connie" — p (1940–42, 1946–50)
Johnson, Ernest — p (1949–50, 1953–54)
Johnson, Leonard — p (1948)
Johnson, Oscar "Heavy" — of/c (1922–25)

Johnson, Robert — p (1944)
Johnson, Roy — 2b (1920–22)
Johnston, Wade — of (1923–27)
Joseph, Newt — 3b (1922–35)
Kennedy, John — ss (1956)
Kennedy, Ned — p (1954)
Kenyon, Harry — p/of (1928)
King, Leonard — of (1921)
Kranson, Floyd — p (1935–40)
Laflora, Louis — of (1925)
LaMarque, James "Jim" — p (1942, 1944–51)
Landers, Robert — p (1949, 1951–52)
Lane, Alto — p (1931)
Livingston, L.D. — of (1928–31)
Lloyd, John Henry "Pop" — ss (1921)
Locke, Eddie — p (1944–45, 1949, 1951)
Long, Emory "Bang" — of (1945)
Long, Tom — c (1926)
Mack, John — p (1945)
Maddox, Vernon — p (1956)
Madison, Robert — ss/p (1935–36)
Manese, Ed (1924)
Marcell, Everett — c/p (1939)
Markham, John — p (1930, 1937–40)
Maroto, Enrique — of (1954–56)
Marshall, Jack — p (1922, 1924)
Marshall, William — 2b (1938)
Marvin, Alfred — p (1938)
Mason, Henry "Hank" — p (1951–52, 1954)
Massingale, — of (1945)
Matchett, Jack — p (1939–45)
Mays, Dave — of (1937)
Mayweather, Eldridge — 1b (1935–38)
McCall, William — p (1924)
McCallister, Mike — of (1921)
McDaniels, Booker — p (1940–45, 1947, 1949, 1952)
McDaniels, Fred — of (1944)
McHenry, Henry — p (1930–31, 1937)
McInnis, Gregg — p (1942)
McMullin, Clarence — of (1945–46)
McNair, Hurley — p (1920–27, 1934)
Mendez, Jose — p/inf/mgr (1920–26)
Miller, Dempsey — p (1926)
Miller, Percy — ss (1922)
Milton, Henry — 2b/of (1935–40)
Mitchell, Robert "Bob" — p (1954)

Mitchell, George — p (1927)
Montgomery, Joe — of (1956)
Moody, Lee — 1b/3b (1944–47, 1949)
Moore, Walter "Dobie" — ss (1920–26)
Moreland, Nate — p (1945)
Morris, Harold "Yellow Horse" — p (1924, 1936)
Moses, C. — p (1938–40)
Mosley, C.D. — p (1938)
Mothell, Carroll "Dink," "Deke" — 2b/3b (1920–21, 1924–34)
Muir, Walter (1920)
Napoleon, Larry — p (1946–47)
Norman, Garrett — of (1933)
Nunez, Berto — p (1953–54)
O'Neil, John "Buck" — 1b/mgr (1938–43, 1946–55)
O'Neill, Charles — c (1922)
Orange, Grady — 2b (1926–27, 1931)
Paige, Leroy "Satchel" — p (1935–36, 1939–47, 1950, 1955)
Parpetti, Augustin — 1b (1921)
Patterson, Andrew "Pat" — 3b (1936, 1941)
Peeples, Nat — of (1949–51)
Pierre, Joseph — inf (1950–51)
Phiffer, Lester — 3b (1951–52)
Phillips, Dick — p (1954)
Phillips, Norris — p (1942–43)
Pointer, Robert — p (1950)
Porter, Merle — 1b (1949–50)
Portuando, Bartolo — 3b/2b (1920–22)
Primm, Randolph — p (1926)
Radcliffe, Theodore "Ted," "Double Duty" — c (1945)
Ragland, Hurland — p (1921)
Ray, John — of (1945)
Ray, Otto — c/of (1920–22)
Redd, Eugene — 3b (1922)
Redus, Wilson "Frog" — of (1930)
Renfroe, Othello "Chico" — inf/of (1945–47, 1953)
Richardson, Gene — p (1947–53)
Rile, Ed — p (1921)
Rivers, Bill — of (1944)
Roberts, Curt — 2b (1947–50)
Robinson, Frazier — c (1939, 1942–43)
Robinson, Jackie — ss (1945)
Robinson, Neil — of (1939)
Rochelle, Clarence — p (1944)

Rodriquez, Jose — c
Rogan, Wilber "Bullet Joe" — p/mgr (1920–33, 1935–38)
Rogers, William — of (1931)
Rowan, Bill — of (1951–52)
Russell, Branch — of/3b (1922)
Sanderson, Johnny — ss (1947)
Saunders, Bob — p (1926)
Scott, John — of (1945–48)
Scroggins, John — p/of (1947)
Segula, Percy — p (1921)
Serrell, William "Bonnie" — 1b (1942–45, 1949–51)
Simms, Bill — of (1937–38, 1941–43)
Smaulding, Owen — p (1927)
Smith, Eugene — p (1941)
Smith, Fred — c (1946)
Smith, Hilton — p (1937–48)
Smith, John Ford — p (1941, 1946–48)
Smith, Monroe — of (1944)
Smith, Theolic — p (1945, 1949)
Snead, Sylvester — of/2b (1941)
Souell, Herb — 3b/inf (1940–51)
Starks, Leslie — of (1933)
Stearnes Turkey — of (1931–34, 1938–40)
Stockard, Theodore — 2b (1937)
Stone, Toni — 2b (1954)
Strong, Ted — p (1937–39, 1941–42, 1946–47)
Stubblefield, Mickey — p (1948–49)
Surratt, Alfred "Slick" — inf/of (1949–51)
Sweatt, George — of /1b(1921–25)
Taborn, Earl — c (1946–51)
Taylor, John "Red" — p (1921–22)
Taylor, Leroy — of (1928–30, 1932, 1934–36)
Taylor, Raymond — c (1938, 1944)
Taylor, Sam — c (1953–54)
Thomas, Dan — 2b (1922)
Thomas, Walter — of/p (1936, 1944–45)
Thompson, Henry "Hank" — 2b (1943, 1945–48)
Thompson, Dick — inf (1954)
Thompson, Samuel "Sad Sam" — p (1931–32, 1941)
Thurman, Bob — p/of (1949)
Torriente, Cristobal — of (1926)
Treadway, Elbert — p (1939–40)
Trent, Ted — p (1932, 1936)

Trouppe, Quincy — of/p (1932, 1934–36)
Turner, Bob — c (1946)
Tyler, Bill — p (1927)
Tyler, Eugene — p (1943)
Tyson, — c (1941)
Vanever, Bobby — inf (1944)
Vaughn, Harold — of (1926–27)
Waldon, Ollie — of (1944)
Walker, George — p (1939–43, 1945, 1950–52)
Ward, Britt — c (1944)
Ware, — 1b (1941)
Washington, Edgar "Blue" — 1b
Washington, Lafayette "Fay" — p (1945)
Watson, Amos — p (1946)
Webster, Ernest — p (1954)
Webster, Jim "Double Duty" — p/c (1936)
Wells, Willie — ss (1932, 1934)
White, Eugene — 1b (1956)
White, Bill "Willie" — p (1952)
Whitney, — of (1955)
Williams, Eli — of
Williams, F. — of (1927)
Williams, Felix — of (1949–51, 1953–54)
Williams, Henry — c (1922–25)
Williams, Jessie H. — 2b/ss (1939–46, 1951)
Williams, Leroy — ss (1950–51)
Willis — of (1949)
Wilson, Herbert — p (1928–29)
Wilson, Woodrow "Lefty" — p (1936–37)
Wright, Bill — of (1948)
Wylie, Enloe — p (1944–47)
Young, Edward "Pep" — c (1944)
Young, Leandy — of (1940, 1945)
Young, Maurice — p (1927)
Young, Tom — c (1925–29, 1931–35, 1941)
Young, William — p (1927)

Kansas City Royal Giants

Bell, — of
Booker, Dan — p
Brewer, Chet — p
Brewer, Sherwood — 2b
Brown, Barney — p
Buckley, Cody — p
Childs, Charles — p
Gessup, Gentry — p

Harriston, —c
Haywood, Buster—c
Johnson, Jack—of
Kellman, —3b
Lamarque, James "Lefty"—p
Marquez, Luis—of
Meckling, S.—c
Milliner, Eugene—of
Neal, —2b
Norman, Jim—inf
Paige, Satchel—p
Pulliam, Chick—c
Robinson, —of
Souell, Herb—3b
Stearman, Tom—of
Steele, Ed—of
Taylor, T.—2b
Ware, Archie—1b
Williams, Jesse—ss

Kansas City Royals—winter

Bassett, Pepper—C
Brewer, Chet—p
Dandridge, Ray—2b
Hairston, Sam—c
Hoskins, Bill—of
Hyde, Cowan "Bubba"—of
Mackey—C
Mathis, Verdell—p
Moody, Lee—1b
Moreland, Nate—p
Neil, Ray—2b
Nelson, Clyde—3b
Serrell, Bonnie—1b
Simms, —of
Smith, Hilton—p
Steele, Ed—of
Wells, Willie—ss
Williams, Johnny—p
Williams, Jesse—ss
Wright, —of

Kansas City Tigers

Black, Troy—p/of
Countee, Othello—ss

Currie, Reuben "Rube"—p
Davis, Arthur—of
Duncan, Frank—c/1b
Dwight, Eddie—of
Ewing, Dorsey—of
Ewing, William—of
Gray, Roosevelt "Chappy"—c/1b
Henderson, Arthur "Rats"—2b
Nealy, R.J.—of
Ragland, Hurland—p
Redd, Eugene—2b
Smith, Leander—of
Smith, Raymond—util
Webb, Floyd—mgr

Original KC Monarchs

Evans, Frank
Houston, William
Lee, Fred
Lindsay, Bill—p
Lindsay, Robert "Frog"
McAdoo, Tully
McCampbell, Ernest
McCampbell, Tom
Pullam, Arthur "Chick"
Wakefield, Bert
Wilkins, West

Paige's All-Stars

Bankhead, —ss
Bell, Cool Papa—of
Brewer, Chet—p
Matlock, —p
Paige, Satchel—p
Palm, Clarence—c
Parnell, Red—of
Patterson, —p
Perkins, —of
Scales, George—3b
Spearman, Al—of
Thomas, Dave "Showboat"—1b
Williams, Jesse—2b

Appendix D: A Biographical Dictionary of Select Kansas City Monarchs

Leslie A. Heaphy

Allen, Newton Henry ("Newt," "Colt")
b. 19 May 1901, Austin, Texas
d. 9 June 1988, Cincinnati, Ohio
Ht. 5' 8", wt. 170 lbs.

Newt Allen was one of those rare players who played his entire career with one team. In his case, Allen spent over twenty years as a player with and manager of the Kansas City Monarchs. Hailing from the Lone Star state, Allen played for a number of semipro teams before landing with the All-Nations and then the Monarchs.

Allen was a switch hitter who rarely struck out and was not the batter you wanted to see coming to the plate in a clutch situation. He also loved to disrupt the game with his base running, making it tough for fielders trying to turn the double play. He was described by one teammate as a scrappy ball player, doing whatever it took to help his club win. He became the regular second baseman for the Monarchs in 1924 as he impressed the team not only with his clutch hitting but his play around the bag. He managed to beat out George Sweatt for the starting job.

Allen helped the Monarchs to their first World Series title in 1924. He hit .275 in ten games with eight runs scored and two RBIs but made three

Captain, manager and infielder Newt Allen poses for the cameras in Kansas City.

errors in the field. The Monarchs' usually steady fielding was more than a little suspect in the Series as they made 23 miscues as a club against Hilldale's 18.[1]

Allen played in four East-West games, in 1936, 1937, 1938 and then in 1941. He got 15 at-bats and unfortunately never got a hit.[2] He made the teams more for his defensive play. Allen also managed the Monarchs starting in 1937 while still playing second base. He led the club to five pennants in the Negro American League. He resigned as manager going into the 1942 season and Dizzy Dismukes took over. Allen stayed on at second base.

While never a power hitter Allen cemented his place on the Monarchs' roster with his defensive play and his leadership qualities. He was often voted team captain by his teammates and was always a fan favorite. In 1941 the team planned a tribute to their manager before a game against the St. Louis Stars.[3] Allen played in 914 games during his long career, hitting a respectable .287 with 561 runs scored. He walked 312 times to go with his 1,017 hits.[4] When the *Pittsburgh Courier* came out with their poll of the best players in the Negro Leagues in 1952 Allen appeared on the second team as a utility player.

Bell, William, Sr.

b. 31 August 1897, Galveston, Texas
d. 16 March 1969, El Campo, Texas
Ht. 5' 9", wt. 180 lbs

William Bell pitched for fifteen seasons in the Negro Leagues, completing eight of those with the Kansas City

Monarchs. After leaving the Monarchs he played for six more teams before retiring in 1937. He compiled a lifetime record of 124–48 while completing nearly 75 percent of the games he started. Bell could be called the workhorse of the staff.

Bell's best season with the Monarchs came in 1924 as he helped them make it to the first colored World Series. Bell had an 11–2 record and an ERA of 3.72. He relied on excellent control and a wicked curveball to get batters out. In 1926 he pitched 190 innings and had a 15–6 record with a 2.45 ERA.

Bell's career numbers included 225 games pitched, with an ERA of 3.20. He completed 122 games of the 164 he started. He kept opposing hitters guessing with 543 strikeouts but he also walked 306.[5] His career numbers earned him the chance to be considered for election to the Baseball Hall of Fame in 2006.

Brewer, Chester Arthur ("Chet")

b. 14 January 1907, Leavenworth, Kansas
d. 26 March 1990, Whittier, California
Ht. 6' 4", wt. 185 lbs.

Chet Brewer became a standout pitcher for the Kansas City Monarchs, depending on a variety of pitches to get out the opposing hitters. He did not have as many deliveries as Satchel Paige but he did have a spitter, a wicked changeup, a fastball with some life in it and even an overhand drop. Some opposing batters claimed that Brewer made his reputation on the spitter and an emery ball; that he relied on illegal pitches for his wins. Whether he did or not there is no doubt that Brewer belonged among the talented pitchers on the Monarchs staff.

Brewer pitched in the Negro Leagues for twenty-five years, twelve of those with the Monarchs. He also spent five seasons with the Cleveland Buckeyes, joining them in 1946 following their World Series victory in 1945. His career numbers include 208 games with a 90–64 record. His lifetime ERA of 2.89 showed how tough it was to get a hit off him when he had his best stuff. Brewer also spent some time with the Washington Pilots and Potomacs when the Monarchs left the Negro Leagues to barnstorm in the early 1930s.

Chet Brewer had one of the best years of his career in 1929 when he pitched in 23 games and compiled a 17–3 record. His dominance on the mound helped the Monarchs win the Negro National League pennant that season. In Brewer's first full year with the Monarchs in 1926 he went 13–2 with an amazing 2.05 ERA. He pitched 140 innings and only gave up thirty-two earned runs. Brewer also pitched in two East-West games during his career, in 1934 and in 1947.

He pitched six innings total, giving up four hits and only one earned run.[6]

Brewer played many winter seasons in Latin America. He was elected to the Mexican Baseball Hall of Fame in 1966 in honor of his play in the Mexican leagues. In fact he was once praised as one of the best pitchers to head south of the border. In one five game stretch he gave up only two runs on seven hits and struck out 42 batters. Reporter Alfred Bland said, "Like a shot from a cannon Brewer exploded his fastball into the waiting mitts of the catchers. His elusive curves broke with unprecedented sharpness. He never let up. He was invincible."[7] When he did not venture south for the winter Brewer pitched in the winter leagues in California for teams such as Bakersfield, the Cleveland Giants and Wilson's Elite Giants. He compiled a 43–15 record pitching against white and black teams.

After retiring following the 1945 season Brewer went on to manage and then scout for the Pittsburgh Pirates from 1957 to 1974. In 1950 Brewer managed the Porterville club in the California League. He also started a youth baseball league where he lived in California to introduce youngsters to the game of baseball.[8]

Monarchs pitcher Chet Brewer pitching south of the border in 1948.

Brown, Willard Jessie ("Homerun")

b. 26 June 1915, Shreveport, Louisiana
d. 4 August 1996, Houston, Texas
Ht. 5' 11½", wt. 195 lbs.

Catcher Sammy Haynes called Brown a "Sunday Player."[9] He said he could play on any day, but on Sundays when the crowds came out he shone brighter than usual for the Kansas City Monarchs. The brightness of his career ended with a final glory in 2006 with Brown's induction into the National Baseball Hall of Fame. He had already been inducted into the Puerto Rican Hall of Fame in 1991 because of seasons like 1950 when he hit .360 with 16 homers for the Santurce club, according to the *Chicago Defender*.[10]

Brown played for fifteen years in the Negro Leagues as well as five years in the minors and another ten seasons in Puerto Rico. He hit .351 lifetime with the Monarchs since that was his only team in the Negro Leagues. He hit sixty-seven home runs that can be accounted for in box scores of league games. Brown played in eight East-West games hitting .250 with six hits. In contrast to his All-Star struggles at the plate Brown hit .320 in the postseason with four homers and 20 RBIs.[11]

Brown often showed up in the newspapers as the leading hitter for the Monarchs. For example, in a 1946 game at the Polo Grounds before nearly 18,000 fans Brown gave them a real show. He provided Paige and Hilton Smith all the offense they needed as he hit two three-run homers to beat the New York Cubans 11–0. In another 1946 game Brown hit two homers to help the Monarchs defeat the Cincinnati Crescents 6–5.[12]

In 1947 Brown had a chance to play for a short stint with the St. Louis Browns in the American League (AL). He played in only 21 games and hit .179 but he got the chance. He did hit the first home run by a black player in the AL on August 13, 1947.[13]

Brown returned to the Monarchs lineup in 1948. By mid-season the *Defender* reported Brown in fine form, as he was hitting .343. He helped his club beat the 1947 Champion Cleveland Buckeyes in a mid-season series to maintain their hold on second place. Brown hit two homeruns in the series to keep the Buckeyes in third place. Kansas City fans were glad to have their hard-hitting center fielder back.[14]

Cooper, Andrew Lewis ("Andy")

b. 24 April 1898, Waco, Texas
d. 3 June 1941, Waco, Texas
Ht. 6' 2", wt. 220 lbs.

Getting batters to swing at junk became Andy Cooper's specialty when he pitched for both Detroit and Kansas City. He served as the anchor for both staffs during his career and finally received the recognition he deserved with his election to the National Baseball Hall of Fame in 2006. Cooper pitched from 1920 to 1939, joining the Monarchs in 1928.

In the mid–1920s Cooper dominated hitters in the league while pitching for Detroit. In 1923 he went 15–7 with 68 strikeouts. He bettered that mark in 1925 at 11–2 with a 2.81 ERA while in 1926 he pitched 184 innings and only walked 34 batters. He started the 1928 season with a 10-0 shut out over the Cleveland Tigers. Cooper pitched a two-hitter with eight strikeouts. Eddie Dwight provided all the offense he needed. Cooper then came back the next time and defeated the Tigers again by a score of 4–3. Again Eddie Dwight scored the winning run on a squeeze play.[15]

With the Monarchs Cooper had one of his best years in 1929 when the Kansas City club won the pennant. Cooper had a 13–3 record that year with a 2.86 ERA. He struck out 50 batters in just 148 innings. In 1931 Cooper found himself pitching in the California Winter League and then a series in Honolulu with the Philadelphia Giants. The Giants came out of the series at 8–1 with Cooper pitching and playing some first base. In 1936 Cooper pitched for the Monarchs in the semipro tournament in Bismarck against another Monarch pitcher, Hilton Smith. The Bismarck series was a national tournament teams were invited to play in.[16]

Cooper only made one All-Star appearance, in 1936. He pitched in one inning and had an uneventful outing. Though he dominated for many years his lack of All-Star appearances can be easily explained because the East-West classics did not begin until 1933, and his career was winding down by then. He also managed the West squad in the 1938 contest. He had a strong team made up of a number of his Monarchs including Henry Milton, whom he used to replace Willard Brown, who was in a slump at the time.[17]

Cooper's career numbers included a 116–57 record with an ERA of 3.24. In addition to starting 175 games Cooper also was one of the early relievers in the game, compiling 29 saves in a league that rarely kept those kinds of records.[18]

Donaldson, John Wesley

b. 20 February 1892, Glasgow, Missouri
d. 12 April 1970, Chicago, Illinois
Ht. 6' 0", wt. 185 lbs.

Growing up in rural Missouri, John Donaldson quickly became a familiar name all over the Midwest. After graduating from Evans School in 1910 he began his baseball career in 1911 and continued pitching to large crowds until he retired in 1938. W.A. Brown signed Donaldson to pitch for his Tennessee Rats and he quickly began appearing under headlines touting him as one of the best strikeout pitchers of the day. J.L. Wilkinson stepped in and signed him away from the Rats, getting him to anchor the staff of his new team, the All-Nations.

The All-Nations traveled all over and attracted a lot of attention because of their skills as well as the unique makeup of the team. Wilkinson not only signed Donaldson but a variety of others of varying backgrounds as well, including Carrie Nation, the club's female first baseman. Wilkinson advertised the team well, sending out advance notices to let towns know they were coming so they could come out and watch Donaldson pitch. The All-Nations arrived in town with their own band and a variety of other acts to entertain the fans before the game. Once the game was under way, no extra entertainment was necessary as Donaldson led the way to victory after victory.

During his years with the All-Nations opposing batters described him as "a wonder." Donaldson pitched against a variety of hitters including major leaguers such as Hal Chase and Earl Smith, who "marveled at his burning speed, remarkable control and baffling curves."[19]

In 1913 Donaldson was joined on the All-Nations staff by Wilkinson's newest addition, the great Cuban sensation Jose Mendez. Together the two made the All-Nations nearly unbeatable. Donaldson would regularly record 11, 13, 16 and over 20 strikeouts in games against opponents like the Peerless Chains and the Indianapolis ABCs. In a 1923 victory over the Peerless Chains Donaldson won 6–3 with 13 strikeouts.[20] In 1916 a *Defender* reporter claimed Donaldson had struck out 240 in twelve games. In an eighteen inning game in Sioux Falls he was credited with 35 strikeouts and another 27 in a twelve inning game a couple of days later.[21]

Putting together Donaldson's record during his long career has been difficult because so much of it came before he joined the Monarchs and the NNL in 1920. After serving in World War I Donaldson returned to baseball and the Wilkinson fold. Wilkinson was beginning a new venture by joining the newly created Negro National League in 1920. Donaldson stayed with the Monarchs until 1923 when he left to join the Bertha Fishermen in Minnesota.

He made a great deal of money playing for the Bertha club before returning to the Monarchs in the 1930s. Donaldson finally called it quits after the 1938 season. He went to work for the Post Office until the late 1940s when he signed on with the White Sox as a scout and then he continued to coach kids in the Chicago area until he died in 1970.[22]

According to the statistics that have been created for Donaldson he earned the moniker the papers gave him as the greatest colored pitcher ever. He recorded 235 wins against 84 losses with an ERA of 1.37. He struck out 3,832 batters and completed 86 shutouts. He had six no-hitters to his credit, including three consecutively. In addition to being a phenomenal pitcher Donaldson also helped himself with the bat, hitting .334 in over 1,800 at-bats.[23] He was also chosen as one of the top pitchers in the Negro Leagues in the 1952 *Pittsburgh Courier* poll. He ranked in the same company with Willie Foster, Satchel Paige, Bullet Joe Rogan and Smokey Joe Williams. Numerous managers and owners such as John McGraw often lamented the fact that they could not sign Donaldson due to his color. McGraw stated, "If Donaldson were a white man or if the unwritten law of baseball didn't bar negroes from the major leagues, I would give $50,000 for him and think I was getting a bargain."[24]

Duncan, Frank Lee, Jr. ("Dunk")

b. 14 February 1901, Kansas City, Missouri
d. 4 December 1973, Kansas City, Missouri
Ht. 6' 0", wt. 170 lbs.

Considered one of the best backstops to ever play the game, Frank Duncan enjoyed a long and illustrious career with the Kansas City Monarchs and a number of other clubs. He started his career with the Monarchs and almost immediately got to play in the Negro League World Series in 1924. Later he came back to manage the Monarchs for a time in the 1940s.

Long-time Monarchs catcher Frank Duncan posing here for the Santa Clara team.

On the way to winning the 1924 World Series Duncan played in seventy games and hit .267. While he had no home runs he did drive in 37 runs. Behind the plate he only made five errors, showing why pitchers liked having him behind the plate.[25]

Known best for his defensive skills, Duncan made any runner think twice before trying to steal on him. Pitchers loved having him behind the plate because he caught a great game and knew all the batters. He also made hitters nervous with all his talk behind the bag. At the plate Duncan did not have a lot of power but relied on spraying line drives around the field. He did get chosen for the East-West Game in 1938 while playing with Chicago. His son Frank III later pitched for Baltimore in the mid-1940s. They actually played together in an exhibition game in 1941.

Hawkins, Lemuel

b. 2 October 1895, Macon, Georgia
d. 10 August 1934, Chicago, Illinois
Ht. 5' 10", wt. 185

Though he began his career in the U.S. Army playing for the 25th infantry team, Hawkins made his mark as the first baseman for the Kansas City Monarchs in the 1920s. He played alongside Dobie Moore for the army and then with the Monarchs. He became captain of the team and led them to the first Negro League World Series in 1924.

Known as a tough hitter Hawkins generally batted lead-off, making contact and rarely striking out. He never liked to lose and had a fiery temper on and off the field. Hawkins got a chance to put his knowledge to work as a manager in 1929 when he was offered the reigns of the Shreveport Sports in the Texas-Oklahoma-Louisiana League. The club's owners gave Hawkins free reign to secure whatever players he needed to make them competitive against the Tulsa Black Oilers, Dallas Black Giants and other league entrants.[26]

Hawkins's infamous temper and desire to be the best got him in some trouble with the law after his baseball career ended. He ended up spending two years in Leavenworth State Prison for his part in a robbery of a church after earlier being cleared of murder charges after a card game. He died unexpectedly when he got shot in a robbery gone bad in 1934.

Johnson, Byron ("Mex")*

b. 16 September 1911, Little Rock, Arkansas
d. 24 September 2005, Denver, Colorado

Born in Little Rock, Ark., on Sept. 16, 1911, Byron "Mex" Johnson, the grandson of a former slave, did not enjoy the traditional fairy tale sports life of being born and raised with his sport of choice as an accelerant to propel him to professional greatness. These times were different, as a person's skin color and socioeconomic status strongly dictated what his hobby would be. However, when Johnson was old enough to play baseball, he played with anything and everything that he could get his hands on that remotely resembled a baseball, bat and bases. "My first ball is the same Coca-Cola bottle cap you see today," Johnson said. "People ask me when did I start to play baseball. I tell them, I don't ever remember not playing baseball."[27] Even late in his life at an advanced age, Johnson showed the animated, vibrant personality that made him a favorite of players and coaches alike. When questioned of the origin of his unusual nickname, "Mex," he said "When I was a kid, somebody bought me a big old Mexican hat. And it was way wide, and it had lots of red tassels, little red balls all around it. I wore it all the time, riding around with my old pet goat."[28]

Johnson enjoyed a career that was not necessarily marked by longevity, but he playing the starring role of a supernaturally gifted defender on the baseball diamond. Vacuum-like defensive exploits at shortstop earned Johnson the moniker of "The Vacuum Cleaner," from Ted "Double-Duty" Radcliffe. Many see Johnson as the Ozzie Smith of the 1930s, capable of catching the ball before the crack of the bat reached the spectators. Johnson was quoted, "I could play shortstop, period. I didn't think anybody could hit the ball by me. They told me they had never seen anybody make the double play the way I could."[29] The major difference between the two, sans Smith's back flips as he ran to his position, was money. Smith made millions and will probably be a first-ballot hall of famer, while Johnson left the Kansas City Monarchs to become a teacher in Arkansas. Johnson may have loved baseball, but the game of baseball did not fully return the gesture. Johnson realized he could not go any higher than his current standing as an African-American athlete in the segregated United States and was resolved to go on with his life without baseball.

In the summer of 1933, Johnson began managing and playing professional ball in his hometown of Little Rock with the DuBisson Tigers, a team sponsored by a local mortuary, which was also the funeral home that had

*This profile contributed by Michael Harkness-Roberto

buried his mother over a decade earlier. The Tigers traveled all over the South, including New Orleans, where he was spotted by Wiley College football coach Fred "Pop" Long, who was impressed with Johnson's tremendous arm strength and supposed bulky athletic build, despite being 5' 8" and 145 pounds. This lack of supposed bulk drew the ire of Coach Long, when he realized that he had given a full football scholarship to a young man that was dwarfed by many if not all of his teammates. Long soon realized, however, that under the small stature was an intellect that was unmatched by any athlete in the sporting world.[30]

At Wiley, an all-black Methodist school known for outstanding scholastics and a superb football team, Johnson earned a teaching degree and immediately received a job teaching biology and coaching football at his alma mater, Paul Laurence Dunbar High School, in Little Rock. In 1936, Johnson was formally asked to play for the Monarchs, an offer that he rejected in order to stay and teach at Dunbar. Johnson actually gave up playing in order to focus on teaching science. Ironically, Johnson loved butterflies, in particular the Monarch. One year later, the Monarchs pursued Johnson again, and after discussions with his family, he decided to accept the offer and become a Kansas City Monarch. Upon his advent with the Monarchs, Hall-of-Famer Joe "Bullet" Rogan, whom Johnson credited as being the one who taught him how to hit a curveball, mentored Johnson in the game of baseball.[31]

On his first day in a Monarch uniform in 1937, Johnson met Willard Brown, the Monarchs' power hitting everyday shortstop. Johnson believed he had little chance of supplanting such a great talent as Brown. Nevertheless, the Monarchs' white owner, J. Leslie Wilkinson, still wanted to take a look at Johnson's abilities and asked him to try out during the middle of a game despite riding a train the entire night before. Player-manager Andy Cooper relented to Wilkinson's wishes and placed Johnson in the lineup, where the ever-graceful shortstop effortlessly fielded a hard grounder and instantly started a magnificent double play with a swift toss to second. By the time he got back to the dugout, he had the job stolen from their regular shortstop Brown, who was consequently moved to the outfield.[32]

One particular story involving Johnson's introduction to the league was his encounter with the Chicago American Giants' surly first baseman, "Big" Ed Young. Standing 6' 2" and weighing 210 pounds, Young was a formidable force, especially for a tiny rookie like Johnson. In their first meeting, Young after getting a base hit was easily out on the ensuing double play, but Young tried to spike Johnson. Johnson looked up before the attempted spiking, halting Young, who retreated back to his dugout. Later in that game, the same situation occurred, only this time Johnson threw at Young's head, taking Young's hat to first with the ball to complete yet another double play. After the game at a local diner, Young found Johnson eating dinner and confronted him. Johnson was sure he was going to endure the beating of his life. However, the confrontation simply amounted to Young saying hello and promptly leaving.[33]

The highlight of Johnson's playing career was his selection to the 1938 East-West All-Star Game. More than 30,000 fans crammed into Chicago's Comiskey Park to see the contest that rivaled the buzz produced by the World Series. Johnson thrived on the pressure of the game, playing flawless defense for nearly 8 innings and producing a base hit in a 5–4 West victory. The hit earned Johnson a bat, which was one of the few keepsakes he hung onto. The bat in question belonged to teammate Turkey Stearnes, someone who was known to be stingy with his bats. However, Stearnes relented and promised Johnson that he could keep it if he came through with a base hit.[34]

In 1939 and 1940, Johnson traveled the nation and played on Satchel Paige's All-Star team, which regularly barnstormed against white "all-star" teams put together by Dizzy Dean or Bob Feller. It was not unusual for a team to play 250 games in a season, which provided extreme wear and tear on the careers of many players. On some Sundays, the players endured four games back to back.[35] Surviving records of these contests, which can be quite rare, and other exhibition games, produced by baseball historian John Holway, show the black stars winning over 60% of the hundreds of games played up until 1947. Jackie Robinson joined the Brooklyn Dodgers in 1947, breaking the long-standing color line and essentially ending the Negro Leagues, as many of its best players signed major league contracts, thereby also ending much of the barnstorming.

It may be believed that team harmony played a factor in the relative success the Paige All-Stars had against the major leaguers. While Feller chose players from both the American and National leagues, Paige's All-Stars were essentially an extension of the Kansas City Monarchs. With the team dominated by the Monarchs, team spirit and unity made these outstanding athletes into a coherent unit. Johnson later remarked, "We weren't only as good as them, we were better. They finally had to recognize that. It wasn't that we weren't good enough; they just never gave us a chance. That is the way we had to play. I had some good days and some bad days, because white fans would always come and watch us play, but we couldn't go to their restaurants to eat a good meal. But that was the way we had to play if we wanted to play at all."[36]

Johnson was drafted by the army in 1941 and served in Europe until 1945. Upon returning from the war, Johnson returned to teaching, a noble profession that he enjoyed during the baseball off-seasons as well. Regrettably, Johnson's devotion to education and civil rights would be severely tested.

Johnson would be directly affected by one of the more significant moments of the civil rights movement when his niece, Carlotta Walls, received death threats when she helped integrate Arkansas' Little Rock Central High School. In 1958, one year after the integration at Central and ensuing threats, Johnson was forced to move his family to Denver, Colorado. Nevertheless, such incidents would come to a gradual end, enabling Negro League players such as Johnson to receive the recognition they truly deserved.

The man that proudly stated that he barnstormed with Satchel Paige was honored in 1996 with a display of a Hitter's Hands bronze at the Denver studio of Raelee Frazier. One other casting of Johnson's hands around a bat was placed in the Negro Leagues Baseball Museum in Kansas City in the fall of 1995.[37] Despite his playing days with the famous Kansas City Monarchs, his times with Paige and his reputation as a great defensive player, one would be hard pressed to find any mementos from his playing days at his former residences. In fact, his favorite memorabilia was not from his baseball days, but a plaque celebrating his hole-in-one on the 17th hole at Indian Tree Golf Course in 1993 on his 81st birthday.[38] Johnson also traveled around the country with baseball researcher Jay Sanford sharing his stories about black baseball.

In Johnson's recently produced biography by Jan Sumner, former president Bill Clinton shared his thoughts of the inspirational Monarch; "Byron Johnson spent his life striving for greatness, both athletically and intellectually, and striving to instill it in others. He was a pioneer, paving the way for African Americans to enjoy equal rights and equal opportunities. Without Negro Leaguers like Byron demonstrating the extent of their skills, Major League Baseball would have taken much longer to integrate. Without educators like Byron, our nation's young people would not have had desperately needed role models to mold their characters and challenge their intellects. I am grateful for his inspiring life."[39] Johnson died September 24, 2005, at the age of 94; his daughter Jacquelyn Benton confirmed shortly after his death that he had had prostate cancer.

Johnson, Clifford ("Connie")

b. 27 December 1922, Stone Mountain, Georgia
d. 25 November 2004, Kansas City, Missouri
Ht. 6' 4", wt. 200 lbs.

Connie Johnson pitched for the Kansas City Monarchs throughout the 1940s. His tenure was interrupted from 1943 to 1945 when he served in World War II. Johnson was a big, powerful right-hander with excellent control and a variety of pitches. He pitched for one year with the Crawfords before joining the Monarchs, immediately helping them win the NAL championships in 1941 and 1942. He was 2–2 and 3–0 in the two series.[40]

He came back to the Monarchs after his military stint ended and immediately posted a 9–3 record in 1946. His best season came in 1950 when he was 11–2 with a 2.17 ERA. Johnson's control and power earned him a shot in the white organized leagues from 1951 through 1961. In describing how he came to be signed by the White Sox Johnson told researcher Eric Enders that it just happened. It was not something he planned or expected. According to Johnson,

> a kid brought me a telegram one day, he said, "Here, Connie, I've got a telegram for you." I got it, read it, and he sat there looking at me — he knew what was in it, you know. I told him it wasn't nothing. He said, "You sure it ain't nothin?" I said the White Sox just called me. "The White Sox just called you! And you ain't gonna look more expressive than *that*? Man!" And that's all there was to it, they bought me. When I left the Monarchs, I knew they wouldn't be in it too much longer. They didn't have any of the *real* good ballplayers anymore like they had before. All of them were going to the majors, or Puerto Rico, or Cuba, places like that.[41]

He played parts of five seasons in the major leagues and finished with a record of 40–39 with one save. He pitched for the White Sox and the Orioles in 123 games. He had 34 complete games and a final ERA of 3.44. He did not hit much while in the majors, getting to bat only 126 times with a .169 average. In one game in 1955 Johnson helped the White Sox beat the Indians 6–0. He struck out twelve batters and gave up only six hits en route to the victory.[42]

Johnson also pitched in Cuba and toured with Roy Campanella's all-star team in 1954. Wherever he played Johnson quickly became a fan favorite and was always well-liked by his teammates. He was selected twice to play in the East-West Classic, in 1940 and again in 1950 when he got the victory.

Joseph, Walter Lee ("Newt")

b. 27 October 1899, Birmingham, Alabama
d. 18 January 1953, Kansas City, Missouri
Ht. 5' 7", wt. 165

A fiery player and dangerous hitter is how his teammates would describe their third baseman Newt Joseph. He joined the Monarchs in 1921, and though he had a tough start at the plate he quickly developed into a feared hitter. His fielding at the hot corner made him a regular right away though he did not start his career as an infielder. Joseph began his ball playing as a catcher and even did a little pitching before finding a permanent home at third with Kansas City.

Joseph provided the Monarchs with their voice on the field, loving to rile up the opposing team with his chatter. He made it tough for opposing hitters when he played in tight to guard against the bunt. This also made it easier for him to steal signs which he did on a regular basis. His teammate Newt Allen once stated that if you gave him two or three innings he could steal the opposing team's signs. He had a great throw to first when he charged the ball, making it nearly impossible for hitters to get the jump on him.

In the 1924 World Series for Kansas City Joseph played in ten games and hit only .132. He did hit one home run and score six runs. He really was not on the roster for his hitting but rather his fielding and his intensity. Occasionally he did have flashes of power as he showed in an exhibition game in 1930 against the Port City Sand Crabs of Galveston. Joseph hit three home runs in a contest the Monarchs won 17–4 with Bell and Brewer combining for the win.[43]

Joseph was also a business man, owning the Paseo Taxi Cab Company, which later became the Monarch Cab Company. He initially started the venture with catcher Frank Duncan and then kept it going himself. He also spent some time as the manager of Satchel Paige's traveling all-star team toward the end of his playing career as well as managing a team called the Little Monarchs in 1939.

McNair, Allen Hurley ("Mack")

b. 28 October 1888, Marshall, Texas
d. 2 December 1948, Kansas City, Missouri
Ht. 5' 4", wt. 160

Roaming the outfield for the Monarchs, Hurley McNair covered a lot of ground and always kept the base runners honest. At the plate he loved to hit for power and surprised many pitchers the first time they faced him because of his small size. He was a tough player to strike out, walking a great deal instead.

From 1920 through 1927, he batted .320 with the Kansas City Monarchs, playing on the 1923–25 championship squads. During the 1924 season leading to the World Series victory over Hilldale, McNair played in 72 games and hit .353 while scoring 65 runs. He hit eight home runs while driving in 55 runs. He even led the club in home runs in 1927, which was unusual since he was not known as a power hitter. In games on July 8, 1922, and on July 9, 1927, McNair helped the Monarchs by hitting for the cycle.[44]

Before joining the Monarchs and helping them establish their dominance in the NNL, McNair had played since 1912 with the Gilkerson Union Giants, the Chicago Giants and the American Giants. After his playing career ended McNair continued to work in the Negro Leagues as an umpire.

Mendez, Jose de la Caridad ("El Diamante Negro")

b. 19 March 1887, Cardenas, Cuba
d. 31 October 1928, Havana, Cuba
Ht. 5' 8", wt. 170

Jose Mendez had a long and storied baseball career in Cuba and the United States. His achievements led to his election to the Cuban Hall of Fame in 1939 and to the National Baseball Hall of Fame in 2006. In his first season in the Cuban League in 1908 Mendez showed what teams could expect for years to come as he fashioned a 9–0 record to help his Almendares club win the pennant. He debuted in the U.S. that same year with the Brooklyn Royal Giants. Later that winter Mendez pitched 25 consecutive scoreless innings against the Cincinnati Reds on their tour of Cuba, thereby establishing himself as a star.

The 1912 papers referred to Mendez as "the Black Mathewson" after he beat the great Christy Mathewson on the Giants trip to Cuba. Mathewson called Mendez a "great pitcher" and said he would be a star if he could play in the majors. He had great control and incredible speed on his fastball, and could field his position better than any pitcher around.[45]

In 1914 after developing some arm trouble Mendez moved to shortstop and joined Wilkinson's All-Nations team along with other greats such as John Donaldson. In a three game series versus the ABCs in 1916 Mendez made some spectacular plays at shortstop to help Donaldson and company pull off all three wins. He was flawless in the field and even added a couple of hits at the plate.[46]

Mendez stayed with Wilkinson and his newly created Monarchs club in the NNL in 1920. He split his time with the Monarchs as a shortstop, pitcher and playing manager. In 1924 he helped the Monarchs to their World Series victory by going 2–0 with a shutout in the final game. His final victory came after he had had surgery and been ordered by doctors not to pitch. He beat Hilldale 5–0 on a three-hitter. He managed the Monarchs to three straight pennants from 1923–25. His Negro League career ended in 1926 and he died in 1928 of pneumonia after pitching in the 1927 Cuban league.

In describing how Mendez came to be such a dominant pitcher one historian had the following to say:

They said that Jose Mendez's fastball came from the sugarcane fields of Cuba. The right-handed star of Cuban and Negro Leagues was only 5-foot-8 and when he burst onto the scene at age 21, he might not have weighed more than 155 pounds. But reportedly by chopping sugarcane, he developed broad shoulders, a powerful arm and forceful fingers. The result was a fastball that danced in the strike zone and crushed bats.[47]

In his seven seasons as a pitcher for the Monarchs, Mendez had a 27–12 record. His ERA was 3.52 and he struck out 147 batters while walking only 59. Jose Mendez became an international star hurling teams in the U.S. and Cuba to numerous championships. Though small in stature, Mendez made up for it in heart and his desire to win.[48] When he died in 1928 the papers described him as one of the best ever. Many of his former teammates took up a collection to present to his wife Marcelina in honor of his exploits.[49]

Moore, Walter ("Dobie")
b. 1893, Atlanta, Georgia
d. 1 December 1977, Mableton, Georgia
Ht. 5' 11", wt. 230

Though his career got cut short due to a gunshot wound Moore put together stellar numbers while he was playing. Moore spent his career with the KC Monarchs after having served in the army along with fellow Monarchs Rogan and Lem Hawkins. Many consider Moore to be one of the best shortstops that ever played in the Negro Leagues though he actually began his career as a catcher. The Monarchs developed a formidable infield with Moore and Newt Allen anchoring the center.

Moore played for seven years with the Monarchs in addition to two winters in Cuba before his career ended. He had incredible numbers during that period, hitting .346 lifetime while displaying some power with thirty-two home runs. He helped the Monarchs to two pennants and a World Series victory with his clutch hitting. In 1924 Moore hit .352 with 56 RBIs to lead the Monarchs into the World Series. Moore helped them win the final game of the series by scoring the first of five runs in an 8th inning rally. He hit .272 in the postseason with six RBIs.[50]

Moore displayed a lot of hustle on the field and a fiery attitude that occasionally got him in trouble. Owner J.L. Wilkinson fined Moore following one game against Detroit when he went into the stands after a fan because he did not like comments being made about his playing.[51]

Mothell, Carroll Ray ("Deke," "Dink")

b. 16 August 1897, Topeka, Kansas
d. 24 April 1980, Topeka, Kansas
Ht. 5' 10", wt. 175

Dink Mothell played for fifteen seasons in the Negro leagues and spent most of those years with the Monarchs. He started his career in 1914 with the Topeka Giants. As a member of the Kansas City club beginning in 1920, Mothell proved valuable because he could play nearly every position on the field and play it well. He had good range and speed when he patrolled the outfield and he could go deep in the hole at short to throw runners out. The only trouble he seemed to have was in turning a quick double play.

At the plate he generally batted in the lower half of the order since he did not have a lot of power. One of his best seasons came in 1926 when he hit .301 while playing second base. He got a lot of extra-base hits because of his aggressive base-running style. His desire to get on base at any cost moved him up in the batting order as his career progressed.

Mothell helped the Monarchs establish their dominance in the 1920s. He played in 70 games and hit .284. The only position he did not play during the season was shortstop. He even pitched one complete game, giving up only three runs and earning the victory. He played a lead role in their 1924 final victory over Hilldale in the World Series. While Mendez picked up the victory Mothell knocked in 2 of KC's five runs in their 8th inning rally. He played in seven games in the Series, hitting .154 in 13 at-bats.[52]

Later with the Cleveland Stars Mothell went through a stretch where he hit safely thirteen times in 46 at-bats while hitting second in the order. He was signed by the Stars because of his versatility on the field even though it was 1932 and this was near the end of his career. Mothell closed out his playing days with the Monarchs in 1934 and got the chance to play in the *Denver Post* tournament.

O'Neil, John Jordan ("Buck")

b. 13 November 1911, Carrabelle, Florida
d. 6 October 2006, Kansas City, Missouri
Bats R, throws R
Ht. 5' 10", wt. 190 lbs.

A player, manager, scout and coach, John Jordan "Buck" O'Neil had a long and storied baseball career. Though he began playing with the Miami Giants, O'Neil spent almost his entire playing and managing career with the

Kansas City Monarchs. He was their mainstay at first base in the late 1930s and most of the 1940s, with only a short hiatus when he served in World War II. When Andy Cooper put O'Neil at first base he shifted Ed Mayweather to the outfield to make room.

O'Neil helped the Monarchs win the 1942 World Series, hitting .353 and fielding superbly. The Monarchs again made the Series in 1946, losing to the Newark Eagles despite O'Neil hitting .333. His postseason numbers stood at .325 in twenty-one games. O'Neil also played in three East-West classics and managed the western squad in four other contests. In eleven at-bats O'Neil had no hits but did knock in one run.

As a player O'Neil ended his career with a .288 average, batting in the lower half of the order for the Monarchs during much of his playing career because he did not have a lot of power. O'Neil was a contact hitter and won a batting title in 1946 with a .350 average. In 1946 O'Neil traveled with the Satchel Paige All-Stars, getting a chance to play against major league players.

O'Neil's managerial duties began in 1948 after he took over from another long-time Monarch, Frank Duncan. He remained at the helm through the 1955 season. The Monarchs won four league titles under the direction of their skipper, though they never won a World Series. One of the reasons for the lack of a Series title is that after 1950 there were few postseason tournaments played, as the league declined in numbers of teams and players. After baseball integrated in 1947 the future of the Negro Leagues became uncertain and teams began to fold. The Monarchs were sold outright to T.Y. Baird in 1948, for example.

Monarchs first baseman Buck O'Neil doing some stretching before a game.

In 1956 O'Neil moved on to a new phase of his career as a scout for the Chicago Cubs. As a scout O'Neil saw lots of stars and signed a number of future players to their first contracts. He changed duties for the Cubs in 1962 when he was signed as their first African American coach. After leaving the Cubs organization in 1988, O'Neil returned to Kansas City, where his professional playing career had begun. His national prominence rose when he helped narrate the Ken Burns PBS special on baseball. He helped organize the Negro Leagues Museum in 1990 and served as board chairman through 2006. O'Neil served until 2001 on the Veterans' Committee for the Baseball Hall of Fame, helping to ensure the election of a number of the stars from the Negro Leagues. Countless other honors have been awarded to O'Neil for his lifetime commitment to baseball and the Negro Leagues. O'Neil died in Kansas City at the age of 94. The Negro Leagues Museum is trying to raise the money to build an education and research center to be named in O'Neil's honor.

Richardson, Norval Eugene ("Gene")

b. 26 January 1928, San Diego, California
d. 1 August 1997, Paradise Hills, California
Ht. 5' 10", wt. 160 lbs.

Gene Richardson joined the Monarchs pitching staff in 1947 and pitched on and off for Kansas City for the next eight seasons. He called it quits after the 1953 campaign. A left-handed pitcher, Richardson had average stuff but good command of his pitches. He never dominated the staff but did attract the attention of the Boston Braves in 1949, although little came of their interest immediately. Richardson helped the Monarchs through the beginning of the lean years for the Negro Leagues as more and more players found their way into white organized ball and teams folded each season.

Richardson nearly got a tryout with the San Francisco Seals in 1948. The local papers in Oakland reported that Richardson and Curtis Roberts were invited to a tryout by the Seals general manager Charles Grahm, Jr. The tryout was later denied by manager Lefty O'Doul and team president Charles Grahm, Sr.[53]

Richardson played briefly with the Denver Bears of the Class A Western League in late 1949 and 1950 before being released in June. Richardson had been sent to the Bears by the Braves organization. The Braves liked his numbers in 1949 as Richardson struck out 126 hitters in 24 games while compiling a 14–5 record and an ERA of 2.57.[54]

Richardson rejoined the Monarchs after his short minor league stint in

1950. In 1953 he compiled a 7–1 record by the middle of the season to help manager Buck O'Neil lead this young squad.

Rogan, Charles Wilber ("Bullet Joe")

b. 28 July 1893, Oklahoma City, Oklahoma
d. 4 March 1967, Kansas City, Missouri
Ht. 5' 7", wt. 170

Called by many the best pitcher in the Negro Leagues, Wilber Rogan enjoyed a long and distinguished career with the Kansas City Monarchs. A native of Oklahoma, Rogan played on a number of local clubs, playing whatever position his club needed. He began his career with the Pullman Colts in 1908 as a catcher. After two stints in the army Rogan became a pitcher. When he joined the Monarchs staff in 1920 he quickly became their anchor as well as a much feared batter at the plate.

Rogan developed a devastating array of pitches that kept hitters off-balance and guessing. In addition to three different types of curveball, he had a spitter, a forkball and a palm ball. Rogan also helped his cause at the plate with some power but more importantly as a dangerous man to have at bat in clutch situations.

One of the highlights of his career came in 1924 when he helped the Monarchs beat Hilldale to win the first Negro League World Series. Hilldale's batters only hit .251 against Rogan in the Series with only one home run given up to Judy Johnson. Rogan pitched in four games, completing three of them and compiling a 2–1 record with a 2.57 ERA. At the plate Rogan helped the cause by hitting .372 with 13 hits in 40 at-bats. His thirteen hits led all Monarchs batters in the series.[55]

The following season Rogan continued his brilliant pitching. He compiled a 14–2 record that included four shutouts and fourteen complete games. When he was not on the mound Rogan could also be found patrolling the outfield because of his bat. In a 1922 win over Detroit, Rogan played right field and hit a three run homer to help the Monarchs to a 10–8 victory. Rogan had three putouts in the field and no errors.[56]

Rogan pitched for the Monarchs from 1920 through 1938, almost exclusively. He pitched in 209 games, completing 132 of his starts. His record stood at 116–50 when he stopped pitching. He struck out an amazing 855 batters and walked 361 in 1444 innings. He also played and batted even when he did not pitch. He came to the plate 2022 times in his career and hit .338. While he did not have a lot of power he made good contact and he drove in 251 runs. With his hitting prowess Rogan often batted cleanup for the Monarchs. His

Future Hall of Famer Bullet Joe Rogan warming up before a game.

skills at the plate and on the mound earned him Hall of Fame honors in 1998.[57] Rogan also earned mention in the 1952 *Pittsburgh Courier* poll of the best players in the Negro Leagues. He is on the first team with Paige, Donaldson, Smokey Joe Williams and Willie Foster.

Rogan also did some umpiring in the league. He worked with "Little Boy" Goodman in the 1940 East-West Classic.[58] League president J.B. Martin liked to rotate the assignment for the big game so that the better umpires got the chance to call the game. Martin encouraged teams to use former players such as Rogan because they knew the game and the rules.

During the off-season Rogan often pitched in the winter league in California. Playing for the Los Angeles White Sox in 1920 and 1921, Rogan was joined by Lem Hawkins, John Donaldson, George Carr, Dobie Moore and Hurley McNair as they dominated the teams they played. One of the advantages they had was the fact that so many of them played together during the regular season. Rogan and Carr also played for the Philadelphia Colored Royal Giants later in the 1920s in the same league.

Smith, Hilton Lee ("Smitty," "No Run")
b. 27 February 1907, Sour Lake, Texas
d. 18 November 1983, Kansas City, Missouri
Ht. 5' 11", wt. 185 lbs.

Hilton Smith grew up in the shadow of Satchel Paige, a shadow he never seemed able to step out of. Paige was the showman and Smith his backup. During much of his baseball career with the Monarchs Smith came in to pitch after Paige started a game. He would pitch five or six innings of brilliant ball though most people only remembered seeing Satchel pitch.

Smith relied on his curveball to get batters out. Just as Paige had a variety of pitches and deliveries, Smith could throw a variety of curveballs. He learned so well that in his first game with the Monarchs Smith threw a no-hitter in 1937. Smith's reputation as the star of the Monarchs staff grew quickly after that. He remained as the mainstay of the staff until Paige came on the scene again in 1941 and overshadowed Smith's steady performances.

In 1935 Smith pitched in the National semipro tournament for Bismarck. He helped lead them to victory by out-pitching Andy Cooper. Manager Babe Mohn wanted his ace on the mound against the KC star.[59]

Smith pitched for the Monarchs from 1937 through 1948, compiling a 71–31 record. He pitched over 800 innings and had a career 1.68 ERA. His control was impeccable as he walked only 96 batters while striking out 470. He had eight straight seasons where he never threw a wild pitch and only hit three batters over that same stretch.[60]

In looking over Smith's career one can find a number of games to highlight starting with an 8–0 shutout over the Toledo Crawfords in 1939. Smith gave up five hits but struck out 12 en route to the complete game win. In a benefit game in 1942 Smith and Paige combined for a one-hitter to beat Jefferson's barracks. Smith pitched six innings of no-hit ball before giving way to Paige. The hitting star in the game was Willard Brown with two homers. Smith combined with teammate Booker McDaniels in 1945 for a 4–0 shutout over the Cincinnati Clowns, with Jackie Robinson providing all the runs they needed on his inside-the-park home run.[61]

Monte Irvin described Smith as a fine pitcher and a finer gentleman after he was elected to the Baseball Hall of Fame. Irvin stated, "He had one of the finest curveballs I ever had the displeasure to try and hit. His curveball fell off the table."[62] Smith could fool batters with many pitches.

After his baseball career ended in 1949 Smith went to work for Armco Steel in Kansas City. He died in 1983 without ever really knowing if people knew what he had done on the baseball diamond. Though his career was validated with his induction into the Baseball Hall of Fame in 1998, Hilton Smith never lived to see that day.

Monarchs pitcher Hilton Smith showing off the form that earned him induction into the Baseball Hall of Fame.

Taylor, Leroy

b. 11 August 1902, Marshall, Texas
d. 7 March 1968, Santa Monica, California

Known as a speedy outfielder who played for a number of teams during his career, Leroy Taylor had his longest tenure with the Kansas City Monarchs. He could cover a lot of ground and he had a strong arm. He used his speed at the plate to make up for his lack of power. Taylor developed proficiency with the hit and run and sacrificing runners.

Taylor's best season came in 1929 when he hit .355 in the fifth slot in the Monarchs' batting order. The Monarchs went on to win the NNL championship that year. When the Monarchs left the league after the 1930 season, Taylor drifted a bit, playing wherever he found a chance until he rejoined his KC teammates in 1932. His name appeared in a few box scores for the Monarchs through the 1936 season before he called it quits.

Williams, Jesse Harold

b. 22 June 1913, Henderson, Texas
d. 27 February 1990, Kansas City, Missouri
Ht. 5' 11", wt. 160 lbs.

Jesse Williams anchored the middle of the infield for the Monarchs throughout the 1940s. He could field anything that came his way at short and throw batters out from deep in the hole. He made turning a double play look easy from both second and short. His prowess in the field was recognized in 1943 and 1945 when he played in the East-West classic.

At the plate Williams did not have much power but he could bunt and he loved being up in clutch situations. He generally batted near the bottom of the batting order. In the All-Star games he hit .500 and drove in four runs. In the 1942 World Series Williams led the Monarchs with a .471 average.[63]

Before Williams became the starting shortstop for the Monarchs in 1940 he had played for the Mineola Black Spiders. He spent his first season with the Monarchs in 1939 as a utility player before winning the starting job. When Jackie Robinson joined the club in 1945 Williams switched to playing second base so Robinson could play short, and they made quite a double play combination.

Williams played a couple of winter seasons in Mexico and Cuba in the late 1940s and one winter in the California league. Williams ended his playing career with one season in Vancouver and then six at-bats in the Texas League. Injuries and age limited his opportunities and he finally retired during the 1954 season.

Young, Thomas Jefferson ("Tom")
b. 1902, Tatum, Oklahoma
d. unknown
Ht. 6' 0", wt. 190 lbs.

Tom Young spent most of his baseball career with the Kansas City Monarchs. He caught for them while they were in the Negro Leagues and when they barnstormed as an independent club in the 1930s. When he first joined the Monarchs Frank Duncan was still doing most of the catching and so Young served as his backup. As Duncan's playing time lessened and he took on more managerial duties, Young caught more regularly. He had a pretty solid arm behind the plate and made contact at the plate. He provided the KC club with a solid left-handed hitter in their lineup. Young provided his pitchers with a big target behind the plate but for all his size he could also move.

In 1935 Young caught 70 of the 79 games the Monarchs had played by mid-July. He was in the lineup regularly because he was hitting well and showing some real power. His manager, Sam Crawford, liked his hustle and desire to win.[64]

One of the highlights of his career came in 1939 when he caught a no-hitter thrown by Chet Brewer, while they were both playing in Mexico.[65] For a short time in 1927 Young's brother Maurice found a spot on the Monarchs pitching roster, making them one of the few family pitching-catching teams in the leagues.

Endnotes

1. Larry Lester, *Baseball's First Colored World Series* (Jefferson, N.C.: McFarland, 2006), 185, 187, 197.
2. Larry Lester, *Black Baseball's National Showcase* (Lincoln: University of Nebraska Press, 2001), 411.
3. *Chicago Defender*, 9 August 1941.
4. National Baseball Hall of Fame, http://www.baseballhalloffame.org.
5. National Baseball Hall of Fame, http://www.baseballhalloffame.org.
6. Lester, *Black Baseball's National Showcase*, 440; National Baseball Hall of Fame Web site.
7. Alfred Molly Bland, "South America Praises Chet Brewer," *Chicago Defender*, 23 February 1935, 16.
8. Dwight Chapin, "The Bad Old Days...," *Los Angeles Times*, 13 January 1977, D1.
9. Larry Lester and Sammy Miller, *Black Baseball in Kansas City* (San Francisco: Arcadia, 2000), 52.
10. *Chicago Defender*, 18 February 1950.
11. National Baseball Hall of Fame, http://www.baseballhalloffame.org.
12. *Chicago Defender*, 13 April and 20 July 1946.
13. Lester and Miller, *Black Baseball in Kansas City*, 40; *New York Times*, 14 August 1947.
14. "Monarchs Beat Buckeyes Twice," *Chicago Defender*, 19 June 1948, 10.
15. "Monarchs in Two Wins from Clevelanders," *Chicago Defender*, 19 May 1928, 8.
16. "Smith Will Pitch against Monarchs," *The Bismarck Tribune*, 11 August 1936, 6; "Royal Giants Nip Hawaiian Braves, 5–0," *Chicago Defender*, 4 July 1931, 9.

17. John Lake, "East-West Game Sunday; Expect Record Crowd," *Chicago Defender*, 20 August 1938, 9.
18. National Baseball Hall of Fame Web site.
19. "John Donaldson, Pitcher, Has Big Following in West," *Chicago Defender*, 22 May 1926, 10.
20. Russell Cooper, "Restoration of a Lost Legacy," *Columbia Tribune*, 11 June 2005.
21. "All-Nations Tackle the American Giants," *Chicago Defender*, 23 September 1916, 5.
22. "John Donaldson Succumbs," *Chicago Defender*, 18 April 1970, 33.
23. Biography of Donaldson, National Baseball Hall of Fame, http://www.baseball halloffame.org.
24. "Famous Negro Pitcher Here," *Los Angeles Times*, 16 February 1917.
25. Lester, *Baseball's First Colored World Series*, 224.
26. "Lem Hawkins Now Manager of Shreveport," *Chicago Defender*, 18 May 1929, 8.
27. Eric Eames, "Byron Johnson: Remembering the Negro Leagues at 92," *The Metropolitan* 25, no. 29 (April 24, 2003): 95–96.
28. Scott Johnson, "Satchel, Buck and Me: Byron Johnson and the Kansas City Monarchs," *New Odyssey: African- American Issues in the Urban West*, Fall 1992, 19.
29. Jim Armstrong, "Oppressed knock down door to success," *The Denver Post*, 28 March 1999.
30. Jan Sumner, "Legacy of a Monarch" (Denver: Jadan Publishing, 2005), 38–39.
31. Nick Wilson, "Voices from the Pastime" (Jefferson, N.C.: McFarland, 2000), 132–33.
32. Johnson, "Satchel, Buck and Me," 132.
33. Sumner, "Legacy of a Monarch," 56–58.
34. Joe Moran, "Spotlight: Talkin' Baseball," *Rocky Mountain News*, 5 April 1994.
35. Michael Romano, "81-year-old plays on field of dreams," *Rocky Mountain News*, September 1992.
36. Eames, "Byron Johnson," 95–96.
37. Bud Wells, "Negro League days draw recognition for Johnson," *Rocky Mountain News*, 8 February 1996.
38. Jerry Crasnick, "Sharing Memories of the Negro Leagues," *Denver Post*, 22 July 1996.
39. Sumner, excerpt of foreword by President Bill Clinton.
40. James Riley, *The Biographical Encyclopedia of the Negro Leagues* (New York: Carroll and Graf, 1994), 430.
41. Eric Enders interview with Connie Johnson, 8 March 2000, http://www.ericenders.com/conniejohnson.htm.
42. Riley, 431; "Connie Johnson," Historic Baseball, http://www.historicbaseball.com/players/j/johnson_connie.html; "Connie Johnson and the Chisox," True Baseball, http://www.truebaseball.com/cj791955.htm.
43. Lester, *Colored World Series*, 71; "K.C. Monarchs Still Showing Good Form," *Chicago Defender*, 19 April 1930, 9.
44. "Negro Leagues Baseball," Out of the Shadows, http://outoftheshadows.net/cycle.htm; Lester, *Baseball's First Colored World Series*, 224; *Chicago Defender*, 8 July 1922, 10.
45. "American Ball Players Claim Jose Mendez, Cuba's 'Black Mathewson,' Is Pitching Marvel," *Washington Post*, 21 January 1912, S4.
46. "Taylor's Team Defeated Twice," *Chicago Defender*, 23 September 1916, 5.
47. Thomas Harding, "Mendez Dominated as Pitcher, Manager," http://mlb.mlb.com/NASApp/mlb/news/article.
48. National Baseball Hall of Fame, http://www.baseballhalloffame.org.
49. "Jose Mendez, Ball Player, Dies in Cuba," *Chicago Defender*, 10 November 1928, 9.
50. *Chicago Defender*, 5 September 1942, 24; National Baseball Hall of Fame Web site.
51. *Chicago Defender*, 8 July 1922, 10.
52. *Chicago Defender*, 5 September 1942, 24; Lester, *Colored World Series*, 42–43, 86.
53. R.V. Tyson, "Negro Players Are Barred by S.F. Seals," *Chicago Defender*, 7 March 1948, 11.
54. "Denver Releases Gene Richardson," *Chicago Defender*, 29 July 1950, 18.
55. Lester, *Baseball's First Colored World Series*, 185, 196, 243.
56. "Detroit Won 2 Games from the Monarchs," *Chicago Defender*, 8 July 1922, 10.

57. Lawrence D. Hogan, *Shades of Glory*, National Geographic, 2006, 185, 396–97, 407–08.
58. "Rogan Is Selected Umpire," *Chicago Defender*, 17 August 1940, 23.
59. "Hilton Smith to Pitch One Game for Monarchs Sunday," *The Bismarck Tribune*, 23 July 1938.
60. Hogan, *Shades of Glory*, 408–09.
61. *Chicago Defender*, 19 August 1939, 10; 25 July 1942, 19; 19 September 1942, 23; 28 April 1945, 7.
62. Hilton Smith Bio, National Baseball Hall of Fame, http://www.baseballhalloffame.org.
63. Riley, *Biographical Encyclopedia*, 852–53.
64. "Kansas City Monarchs in West; Triumph," *Chicago Defender*, 20 July 1935, 14.
65. Riley, *Biographical Encyclopedia*, 891.

Bibliography: Black Baseball in Kansas City

Leslie A. Heaphy

All Nations Team

"ABC Team and the All Nations in Tie Game." *Chicago Defender*, 6 October 1917, 10.
"All Nation Team Doing Great Work." *Chicago Defender*, 7 October 1916.
"All Nations Hand Bull Moosers Double Drubbing." *Chicago Defender*, 23 September 1916.
"All Nations Lose Game to Michigan City Team." *Chicago Defender*, 11 May 1918, 9.
"All Nations Tackle the American Giants." *Chicago Defender*, 23 September 1916.
"All Nations Team Plays in Duluth." *Northwestern Bulletin*, 23 June 1923, C6.
"All Nations Wallop the Brandeis Team." *Chicago Defender*, 23 September 1916.
"Bismarck Beats All-Nations Again; Tunes Up for Crucial Series." *Bismarck Tribune*, 17 July 1936.
"Bismarck Loses to All-Nations in Cold Game Here Last Night." *Bismarck Tribune*, 9 June 1928, 8.
"Bismarck Nine Trims All-Nations 3 to 2 in Thrilling Game Here." *Bismarck Tribune*, 21 July 1933.
"Bismarck Nips All-Nations 5 to 4 in Opener of Three-Game Series." *Bismarck Tribune*, 29 August 1933, 6.
"Colorful All-Nations Nine Will Play Bismarck Club Here Tonight." *Bismarck Tribune*, 20 July 1933.
"Giants Win in the Seventh; Score 3–2." *Chicago Defender*, 5 August 1916, 7.
"K.C. All-Nations to Meet Local Team on Sunday and Monday." *Lima News*, 3 July 1927, 11.
"Kansas City All-Nations Club Meets Bismarck Team Here Tonight." *Bismarck Tribune*, 8 June 1928.
"Kansas City All-Nations Team Takes Twelve Inning Struggle from Lima, 6–2." *Lima News*, 20 June 1927.
"Kansas City All-Nations Will Meet Lima Nine on Home Grounds Sunday." *Lima News*, 10 June 1927, 11.
"St. Louis Giants vs. All Nations." *Chicago Defender*, 14 October 1916.
"Taylor Takes Two Games from All Nations." *Chicago Defender*, 8 September 1917, 9.
"Union Giants Whip the All Nations Club." *Chicago Defender*, 25 September 1915, 7.

Allen, Newton Henry ("Newt")

"Allen Sure to Start in Ball Classic." *Chicago Defender*, 30 July 1938, 9.
Allen, Newt. Interview by John Holway, n.d. Interview T208, transcript. University of Missouri, Archives and Manuscript Division, St. Louis, Missouri.
Dixon, Phil. "Newt Allen, Great Star of the

Monarchs Dies in Cincinnati." *Kansas City Call,* 17 June 1988, 12.
Holway, John B. "Negro League Veterans Pick an All-Time Team." *The Sporting News,* 5 July 1982, 37.
"Kansas City Allen Quits as Manager." *Chicago Defender,* 4 April 1942, 19.
Kleinknecht, Merl F. "Allen, Newton Henry 'Newt.'" In *Biographical Dictionary of American Sports, Baseball,* ed. David L. Porter. Westport, Conn.: Greenwood Press, 2000, 15.
McClean, Tony. "Negro League Spotlight: Newt Allen, Second to None." *Sun Reporter,* 1 September 2005.
"Newt Allen." In *Baseball: The Biographical Encyclopedia,* ed. David Pietrusza, Matthew Silverman, and Michael Gershman. Kingston, New York: Total Sports Publishing, 2000, 17.
Steele, David. "Negro Leaguers Seek Entry into Hall." *USA Today Baseball Weekly,* 16 August 1991, 17.

Baird, Tom

"Coming of Major League Baseball to Kansas City Will Help — Baird." *Chicago Defender,* 15 January 1955, 10.
Cowans, Russ. "Baird on First Assignment." *Chicago Defender,* 22 February 1956, 22.
"Former Owner of Monarchs Dies in Sleep." *Chicago Tribune,* 3 July 1962, A3.
"Negro Pro Baseball Team Demands $50,000 Payment for Robinson's Signature." *Nevada State Journal,* 25 October 1945, 10.
T.Y. Baird Papers. Kansas Collection, Spencer Research Library, University of Kansas Libraries, Lawrence, Kansas.

Baltimore Black Sox

"Baltimore Black Sox Loom as Dangerous Ball Club." *Norfolk Journal and Guide,* 10 May 1930.

Brewer, Chet

"Brewer Talks Turkey; May Play for Cole's Giants." *Chicago Defender,* 2 February 1935.
"Chet Brewer." In *Baseball: The Biographical Encyclopedia.* Ed. by David Pietrusza, Matthew Silverman, and Michael Gershman. Kingston, New York: Total Sports Publishing, 2000, 124.
Ellenbecker, Phil. "Brewer: Cooperstown Bound?" *Leavenworth Times,* 30 August 1987, 8A.
Etkin, Jack. "Chet Brewer." *Innings Ago* (January 1978): 46–51.
Holway, John B. "Chet Brewer: Just as Good as Satchel?" *Sporting News,* 28 November 1983, 56.
_____. "Papa Chet, Monarch of L.A.: An Interview with Chet Brewer." *Baseball History* (Spring 1986): 52–69.
Lester, Larry. "Brewer, Chester Arthur 'Chet.'" In *Biographical Dictionary of American Sports, Baseball,* ed. David L. Porter. Westport, Conn.: Greenwood Press, 2000, 143–144.
Maly, Ron and Holway, John. "Baseball's Great Brewer Joins Register Hall." *Des Moines Sun Register,* 1 April 1984.
Rae, Lorne. "It Was a Real Baseball." *Saskatchewan History,* January 1991, 16–20.
Young, A.S. "Doc." "Chet Brewer: Death of a Negro League Superstar." *Los Angeles Sentinel,* 12.

Brown, Willard Jessie

Brown, Willard. Interview by Bill Marshall, 22 June 1982. Interview 820H116 Chan 97. A.B. Chandler Oral History Project, University of Kentucky Library, Lexington, Kentucky.
Cottrol, Bob. "Historically Speaking ... Willard Brown." *Black Sports,* 1 March 1975, 50–51.
_____. "Willard Brown, He Lasted Only Six Weeks." *Black Sports* 4 (March 1975), 50- 51.
Etkin, Jack. "Willard Brown Found St. Louis Browns a Step Down from Monarchs." *Kansas City Star,* 25 July 1985.
"50,000 Watch 3d Army Nine Score, 9 to 2." *Washington Post,* 3 September 1945, 6.
Floto, James. "Willard Brown." *Diamond Angle* 4 (February 1993): 29–30.
"Kansas Tornado Is Willard Brown." *Chicago Defender,* 23 July 1949, 15.
Kleinknecht, Merl F. "Brown, Willard Jessie." In *Biographical Dictionary of American Sports, Baseball,* ed. David L. Porter. Westport, CT: Greenwood Press, 2000, 162–163.
Lacy, Sam. "Looking 'Em Over." *Baltimore Afro-American,* 6 August 1947.
Letlow, Paul J. "Former Monarchs Considered for Hall." *The News Star,* 12 January 2006.
_____. "Monarchs' Brown Headed to Hall of Fame." *The News Star,* 30 July 2006.
_____. "Which Brown Would Show Up? Former Monroe Monarch Was Aloof but Quite Talented." Thenewsstar.com, Feb 27, 2006.

McConnell, Jim. "Baseball's Dark Past." *Pasadena Star-News*, reprinted in *Grandstand Baseball Annual* (1998).
"71st Division Wins ETO Game by 9 to 2." *New York Times*, 3 September 1945, 20.
"Sport." *Time*, 28 July 1947, 37.
Tygiel, Jules. "Those Who Came After." *Sports Illustrated*, 27 June 1983, 40–48.
Waggoner, Glen. "It's Never Too Late to Start Doing the Right Thing." *USA Today Baseball Weekly*, 20 May 1992, 22.
"Willard Brown." In *Baseball: The Biographical Encyclopedia*. Ed. David Pietrusza, Matthew Silverman, and Michael Gershman. Kingston, New York: Total Sports Publishing, 2000, 136.
"Willard Brown Finds Pitching on Island Good." *Chicago Defender*, 18 February 1950, 16.
"Willard Brown Hits Two Home Runs." *Chicago Defender*, 13 April 1946, 10.
"Willard Brown Holds Bat Lead." *Chicago Defender*, 7 July 1951, 17.
Wilson, Walt. "Willard Brown, a Forgotten Ball Player: He Hit a Milestone Home Run." *The National Pastime*, January 2004.

Cooper, Andrew

"Cincinnati 9 Battles Andy Cooper's K.C." *Chicago Defender*, 22 May 1937, 13.
Lake, John. "Andy Cooper Will Manage West's Game." *Chicago Defender*, 20 August 1938, 9.
"Monarchs Hurler." *The Bismarck Tribune*, 11 August 1936.

Denver Post *Tournament*

Kreck, Dick. "Post Tourney Blazed Trail of Equality." *Denver Post*, 30 June 2003.

Donaldson, John Wesley

"ABCs Come for Another Series." *Chicago Defender*, 13 July 1918, 9.
Addison, Justin. "Glasgow Celebrates John Wesley Donaldson Day." *The Democrat Leader*, 15 June 2005.
"A Legend of the Past Gets Shot at Hall." *Star Tribune Weekly*, 7 December 2005.
"Chi Sox Sign Donaldson as Talent Scout." *Chicago Defender*, 9 July 1949, 16.
Cooper, Russell. "Glasgow Honors Donaldson." *Columbia Tribune*, 12 June 2005.
_____. "Restoration of a Lost Legacy." *Columbia Tribune*, 11 June 2005.
"Donaldson Again Pitches the ABCs to Victory." *Chicago Defender*, 1 June 1918, 9.
"Donaldson Beaten." *Chicago Defender*, 6 October 1917, 10.
"Donaldson Blanks the Brandeis; Whiffs Nineteen." *Chicago Defender*, 23 September 1916.
Falkoff, Robert. "Donaldson Made Most of Opportunities." MLB.com, 9 February 2006.
"Famous Negro Pitcher Here." *Los Angeles Times*, 16 February 1917.
"Glasgow Born Baseball Great." *The Glasgow Missourian*, 17 July 2003.
Gorton, Peter. "One of the World's Greatest Baseball Pitchers of All Time." *The Kenmare News*, 22 February 2006.
Hill, Justice B. "Is Donaldson Worthy of Hall Induction?" MLB.com, 31 July 2006.
"John Donaldson Again Playing for Bertha Team." *Northwestern Bulletin*, 30 April 1927, C4.
"John Donaldson Beaten; Royals Take Second." *Chicago Defender*, 6 July 1918, 9.
"John Donaldson, Pitcher, Has Big Following in West." *Chicago Defender*, 22 May 1926, 10.
"John Donaldson Succumbs." *Chicago Defender*, 18 April 1970, 33.
"John Donaldson Turns Down Offer of $10,000." *Chicago Defender*, 24 February 1917, 2.
"John Wesley Donaldson Day" Program and Exhibit. Glasgow Community Museum, 12 June–10 July 2005, Glasgow, Missouri.
Litke, Jim. "Remembered at Last." *The Indianapolis Star*, 28 September 2004.
"Memorial Honors Three of Negro League's Best." *The Tribune*, 27 September 2004.
"Minnesota Teams Features John Donaldson." *Northwestern Bulletin*, 14 June 1924, C2.
"Negro a Wizard Pitcher." *Lincoln Daily News*, 26 May 1915, 7.
"Negro Nine Faces David Outfit Here." *The Bismarck Tribune*, 28 August 1929, 8.
Pride, Karen. "Negro League Players Gravesites Honored." *Chicago Defender*, 27 September 2004.
Rand, Michael. "A Legend of the Past Gets Shot at Hall." *Star Tribune*, 7 December 2005.
"Recognition for Three Negro League Stars." *Chicago Sun-Times*, 27 September 2004, 6.
Skipper, John. "Baseball Great Once Pitched in Mason City." *Globe Gazette*, 2 March 2006.
"Taylor and His Gang Is Next Attraction." *Chicago Defender*, 8 June 1918, 9.
"Taylor's Team Defeated Twice." *Chicago Defender*, 23 September 1916, 5.
"Three Great Pitchers Are Barred from Big Leagues Because of Color." *Syracuse Herald*, 16 June 1915.

Wronski, Richard. "A Fan's Tribute to Legends of Negro Leagues." *Chicago Tribune*, 25 September 2004, 1, 8.

Duncan, Frank

"Duncan, Giles and Several Others Gone." *Chicago Defender*, 13 April 1935, 16.
Holway, John B. "Historically Speaking ... Frank Duncan, the Complete Catcher." *Black Sports Magazine* (December 1973): 22–23, 54.
McClean, Tony. "The Negro Leagues: Gone but Not Forgotten; Remembering Frank Duncan." BlackAthleteSportsNetwork.net, 19 April 2004.
Riley, James A. "Duncan, Frank." In *Biographical Dictionary of American Sports, Baseball*, ed. David L. Porter. Westport, Conn.: Greenwood Press, 2000, 419–420.

Hawkins, Lemuel

"Lem Hawkins Now Manager of Shreveport." *Chicago Defender*, 18 May 1929, 8.

Johnson, Byron ("Mex")

"A Life Worth Remembering: Ex-Negro League Player Johnson Celebrated." *Rocky Mountain News*, 29 September 2005.
Berger, Jody. "Portrait of a Black Baseball Pioneer." *Rocky Mountain News*, 12 July 2003, 11B.
"Byron Johnson of Negro Leagues Dies." *Associated Press*, 27 September 2005.
Crasnick, Jerry. "Sharing Memories of the Negro Leagues." *Denver Post*, 22 July 1996, 1D, 6D.
Etkin, Jack. "A Life Worth Remembering." *Rocky Mountain News*, 29 September 2005.
"Former All-Star Carried Legacy of Black Baseball." *The Denver Post*, 27 September 2005.
Johnson, Scott. "Satchel, Buck and Me." *New Odyssey* (September 1992): 19–21.
"Memorial for Negro Leaguer Johnson Is Today." *USA Today*, 28 September 2005.
Sanchez, Robert. "Big-time Win for Negro League Players." *The Denver Post*, 10 December 2004.
_____. "Former All-Star Carried Legacy of Black Baseball." *Denver Post*, 27 September 2005.
_____. "Stats Cover the Bases, Put Crown on Careers." *Denver Post*, 10 December 2004, 1A, 4A.

"Shortstop for Negro Leagues' K.C. Monarchs." *Chicago Sun-Times*, 30 September 2005.
Sumner, Jan. *Legacy of a Monarch: An American Journey*. Denver, Colo.: Jadan Publishing Co., 2005.

Johnson, Clifford ("Connie")

Allen, Tracy. "Rites Today for Monarchs Star Pitcher Connie Johnson." *The Kansas City Call*, 3 December 2004.
Dickson, Albert. "Clifford 'Connie' Johnson, Jr." *Sporting News* 221, no. 15 (14 April 1997): 36.
Funeral Program. Kansas City, Missouri. 3 December 2004.
Kelley, Brent. "Connie Johnson Remembers His Pitching Days." *Sports Collectors Digest*, 15 June 1990, 26–263.
Marazzi, Rich. "Negro Leaguer Connie Johnson Had Two Separate (and Maybe Even Equal) Careers." *Sports Collectors Digest*, 16 August 1996, 90–91.
"The Negro Baseball Leagues." Oral interview with Buck O'Neil, Woody Smallwood, Connie Johnson, and Hank "Pistol" Mason. Kansas City, Mo.: NoirTech Research, Inc.
Player Panel including Connie Johnson, Jesse Rogers, and Al Surratt. June 1996. SABR 26 Convention. Kansas City, Missouri.
Player Panel including Bill Cash, Connie Johnson, Butch McCord, Al Surratt, and Tom Turner. June 21, 1997. SABR 27 Convention. Louisville, Kentucky.
Posnanski, Joe. "Johnson's Pitching, and Spirit, Were Ageless." *Kansas City Star*, 1 December 2004.
_____. "Negro Leagues Great Connie Johnson Recalls Facing Ted Williams." *Kansas City Star*, 22 June 2001.
True Baseball. http://www.truebaseball.com/connie/career.htm. See section about the career of Connie Johnson.

Joseph, Newt

"Birmingham Presents Game to Kansas City Monarchs as Pitchers Walk Batters." *Chicago Defender*, 27 June 1925, 9.
"K.C. Monarchs Team Reorganized." *Chicago Defender*, 4 July 1931, 8.

Kansas City

Adler, Eric. "In 'Fuzzy' World, Chatty Pets Have Negro League Names." *The Kansas City Star*, 17 March 2001.

Allhoff, Fred. "Thunder Over Kansas City." *Liberty*, 17 September, 1938, 4–8.

Boyce, David. "Kansas City Team Is a Prince of an Idea." *Kansas City Star*, 21 July 1996.

De Angelo, Dory. *What About KC!* Kansas City, Missouri: Two Lane Press, Inc., 1995.

Goldman, Stuart. "Municipal Stadium Marked for History." *The Kansas City Star*, 7 April 2000, D5.

Karlen, Neal. "Kansas City: Culture in Many Forms." *The New York Times*, 8 April 2001, 6, 21.

Heaphy, Leslie A., ed. *The 9th Annual Jerry Malloy Negro League Conference Booklet*. Jefferson, N.C.: McFarland, 2006.

Lester, Larry, and Miller, Sammy J. *Black Baseball in Kansas City*. Chicago, Ill.: Arcadia Publishing, 2000.

Kansas City Monarchs

"American Giants Play Paige and Kansas City in Detroit August 6." *Chicago Defender*, 5 August 1944, 7.

"Another Record Crowd Due When Barnstormers Tangle at Moana." *Nevada State Journal*, 6 August 1940, 10.

"Barons Lose to Kansas City." *Chicago Defender*, 9 June 1945, 7.

"Baseball Leagues Open Season, May 4." *Chicago Defender*, 3 May 1947, 20.

Basenfelder, Don. "Paige Is Hero as KC Wins Flag Here." *Philadelphia Record*, 30 September 1942.

"Bat Bombardment by Mendez and Company Puts St. Louis Stars Down; Losers 4 Times." *Chicago Defender*, 12 September 1925, 9.

"Bathing Beauty Contest in Kansas City August 11." *Chicago Defender*, 10 August 1940, 22.

"Big Crowd Sees Monarchs Annex 10-Inning Battle." *Great Bend Daily Tribune*, 5.

"Birmingham Divides with Kansas Citians." *Chicago Defender*, 11 July 1942, 20.

"Birmingham to Battle Strong K.C. Monarchs." *Chicago Defender*, 29 May 1937, 14.

"Booker McDaniels Back with Monarchs." *Chicago Defender*, 26 February 1949, 14.

Brown, Samuel. "Memphis in 8–3 Win Over K.C. Picked." *Chicago Defender*, 29 April 1939, 8.

Bruce, Janet. *The Kansas City Monarchs: Champions of Black Baseball*. Kansas: University Press of Kansas, 1985.

"Bucks Beat Monarchs Twice, 1 to 0; 5 to 4." *Pittsburgh Courier*, 29 May 1943.

Campbell Janet Bruce. "Beyond the Box Score, the Kansas City Monarchs." *History News* 47 (March–April 1992): 6–8, 10–11.

"Capacity Crowds Expected at Clash of Barnstormers." *Nevada State Journal*, 2 August 1939, 3.

"Chairmakers Meet Colored Team Here on Monday Night." *Sheboygan Press*, 13 June 1936, 14.

"Chairs Battle Kansas City Monarchs Tonight." *Sheboygan Press*, 2 July 1937, 16.

Chaudhuri, Nupur. "We All Seem Like Brothers and Sisters." *Kansas History* (Winter 1991): 270–288.

"Chicago American Giants, Monarchs Divide Honors." *Chicago Tribune*, 21 May 1945, 22.

"Chicago at Home, Loses to Monarchs." *Indianapolis Recorder*, 2 June 1928.

"Chicago Giants and Kansas City Play Two Today." *Chicago Tribune*, 30 May 1943, A3.

"Chicago in 2 Wins Over Kansas City." *Chicago Defender*, 31 July 1943, 11.

"Chicago Opens League Race in Kansas City." *Chicago Defender*, 5 May 1945, 7.

"Chicago Opens League Season in Kansas City." *Chicago Defender*, 14 May 1938, 8.

"Chicago Wins 2 from Kansas City to Move into 2nd Place." *Chicago Defender*, 1 September 1945, 7.

"Cincinnati and Kansas City Divide Pair." *Chicago Defender*, 12 June 1937, 14.

Clark, William E. "Hilldale Nine Wins Opening Game in Colored World Series from Monarchs of Kansas City, but Lose the Second." *New York Age*, 10 October 1925.

"Clowns, Kansas City Play in Texas and Oklahoma." *Chicago Defender*, 24 April 1948, 11.

"Colored Clubs Divide 2 Games Here Sunday." *The Bismarck Tribune*, 25 July 1938, 6.

"Colored Nines to Open World Series Today." *Chicago Tribune*, 19 September 1937, B4.

"Colorful Kansas City Monarchs Win Initial Counter with Reno Larks." *Nevada State Journal*, 27 July 1941, 31.

"Coming of Major League Baseball to Kansas City Will Help — Baird." *Chicago Defender*, 15 January 1955, 10.

Cowans, Russ J. "Monarchs Have Youth." *Chicago Defender*, 4 July 1953, 24.

"Cubans Meet K.C. Monarchs." *Chicago Defender*, 14 July 1945, 7.

"Cubans Put Another Dent in Monarchs." *Chicago Defender*, 22 May 1926.

"Dallas Fans to Honor Monarch Stars, July 8." *Pittsburgh Courier*, 3 July 1943.

Dixon, Phil. *The Monarchs: 1920–1938*. Sioux Falls, S.D.: Mariah Press, 2001.

Dukes, Howard. "Contributions Made in Later Years Also Valuable." *South Bend Tribune*, 9 September 2001.

(Kansas City Monarchs, continued)
"Eagles Make First Trip to Kay Cee." *Chicago Defender,* 6 August 1949, 15.
Edwards, Milton. "Monarchs Oldtimers Play Ball in Exhibition Game at Paige Stadium." *Kansas City Call,* 14–20 September 1984, 13, 24.
"18,000 See Kansas City Lose to Chicago, 6 to 2." *Chicago Defender,* 2 June 1945, 7.
"Elites Meet Kansas City." *Chicago Defender,* 30 April 1949, 15.
Enright, James. "The Kansas City Monarchs." *The Sporting News,* 31 December 1958, Section 2, 8.
"Ethiopian Clowns to Play Monarchs 8–19." *Twin City Leader,* 10 August 1940, C3.
"Ethiopian Clowns to Play Monarchs 6–27." *Twin City Leader,* 21 June 1941, C4.
Etkin, Jack. *Innings Ago.* Kansas city, Mo.: Normandy Square Publications, 1987.
_____. "Memories of Early Days with Monarchs Still Fresh for Two Survivors." *Kansas City Star,* 23 July 1985, 1C, 3C.
_____. "Willard Brown Found St. Louis Browns a Step Down from Monarchs." *Kansas City Star,* 25 July 1985.
"Fay Says." *Chicago Defender,* 30 June 1951, 17.
"Fine Crop of Young players Win for KC." *Chicago Defender,* 4 July 1953, 23.
Forbes, Frank. "Grays Vs. Monarchs in Kansas City Sunday." *Chicago Defender,* 19 September 1942, 23.
_____. "Kansas City Monarchs Go Down Before Black Yanks." *Chicago Defender,* 13 July 1946, 11.
"Fort Leavenworth at Kansas City." *Chicago Defender,* 7 August 1945, 7.
"14,457 See K.C. Monarchs Beat Cleveland." *Chicago Defender,* 22 May 1948, 11.
"Gala Four-Team Twin Bill at Wrigley Field." *Chicago Defender,* 5 September 1942, 23.
"Gamblers Meet Monarchs Again in Rubber Tilt." *Reno Evening Gazette,* 28 July 1949, 22.
"The Gift of Life." Wilkinson File. Research Library, National Baseball Hall of Fame and Museum, Inc., Cooperstown, New York.
"Grays Defeat Kansas City." *Chicago Defender,* 30 June 1945, 7.
"Hard-hitting Stars to Play with Monarchs." *Washington Post,* 15 June 1942, 18.
"Here's Monarchs Battery." *Mansfield News-Journal,* 31 July 1941, 12.
"History of Monarchs Formed Two Years ago." *Twin City Herald,* 23 July 1932, C1.
"Hitting Spree to Kansas City, 19–3." *Chicago Defender,* 20 June 1925.
Holway, John B. *Bullet Joe and the Monarchs.* Washington, D.C.: Capital Press, 1984.

_____. "Kansas City's Mighty Monarchs." *Missouri Life,* March–June 1975, 83–87, 89.
"In K.C. Beauty Contest Aug. 18." *Chicago Defender,* 17 August 1940, 24.
"Indians Meet Kansas City Monarchs Monday." *Oshkosh Northwestern,* 8 May 1935, 15.
"Inter-League Four-Team Bill Takes Kansas City, Barons East." *Chicago Defender,* 11 August 1945, 7.
"Israelite Davis Meet Kansas City Monarchs Here Today." *Helena Daily Independent,* 18 July 1936.
"Johnston Blossoms Out as Pitcher When Rogan's Crew Walks Off with 8–3 Game." *Chicago Defender,* 17 April 1926.
"Kansas Citians Beat Chicago." *Chicago Defender,* 17 July 1948.
"K.C., Beaten by Cuban stars, Comes Back to Cinch the First Half of League Race." *Chicago Defender,* 10 July 1926.
"KC Connection Began Baseball's Globalization." *Kansas City Star,* 26 October 2004.
"K.C. Monarchs and Chicago American Giants in Houston." *Chicago Defender,* 31 March 1945, 7.
"K.C. Monarchs Defeat Clowns." *Chicago Defender,* 22 April 1944, 9.
"K.C. Monarchs Shine on Tour of Canada and West." *Chicago Defender,* 11 July 1936, 14.
"K.C. Monarchs to Rebuild." *Chicago Defender,* 13 April 1935, 16.
"K.C. Monarchs Triumph Over 'Davids.'" *Chicago Defender,* 1 September 1935, 11.
"Kansas City and Chicago Divide Pair." *Chicago Defender,* 3 September 1938, 9.
"Kansas City and Chicago Tie in 17th." *Chicago Defender,* 18 September 1937, 21.
"Kansas City and Clowns in Dallas Sunday Night." *Chicago Defender,* 21 August 1943, 19.
"Kansas City and Clowns Split Two." *Chicago Defender,* 16 June 1945, 9.
"Kansas City and Fosters Divide Bill." *Chicago Defender,* 7 June 1924.
"Kansas City and Hilldale Tied in World Series Play." *Chicago Defender,* 18 October 1924.
"Kansas City and Paige at Yankee Stadium June 17." *Chicago Defender,* 16 June 1945, 9.
"Kansas City and Paige Here Sunday, May 10." *Chicago Defender,* 9 May 1942.
"Kansas City and Paige Swipe Double-Header." *Chicago Defender,* 16 May 1942.
"Kansas City Allen Quits as Manager." *Chicago Defender,* 4 April 1942, 19.
"Kansas City at Cleveland." *Chicago Defender,* 14 June 1947, 20.
"Kansas City at Memphis." *Chicago Defender,* 21 June 1947, 11.
"Kansas City at Memphis June 2." *Chicago Defender,* 1 June 1946, 11.

"Kansas City at Memphis Sunday." *Chicago Defender*, 14 April 1945, 7.
"Kansas City Back Again for 4 Games." *Chicago Defender*, 18 June 1938, 8.
"Kansas City Baseball Heroes of Old Cherish Their Memories of the Way It Was." *Kansas City Star*, 21 July 1985, 1, 7.
"Kansas City Beaten Twice by Cleveland." *Chicago Defender*, 29 May 1943, 11.
"Kansas City Beats Cuban Stars Three." *Chicago Defender*, 7 August 1926.
"Kansas City Breaks Even in Two Games." *Chicago Defender*, 4 July 1925.
"Kansas City Club Here for 5-Game Series with Foster." *Chicago Defender*, 8 July 1922.
"Kansas City Divides Two with Chicago." *Chicago Defender*, 6 August 1938, 8.
"Kansas City Divides with Black Barons." *Chicago Defender*, 14 April 1945, 7.
"Kansas City Grabs 1st World Series Game." *Chicago Defender*, 28 September 1946, 11.
"Kansas City Has Some Fun with Chicago." *Chicago Defender*, 4 June 1938.
"Kansas City Heads East for Invasion." *Chicago Defender*, 12 June 1943, 19.
"Kansas City in 6 to 2 Victory Over Am. Giants." *Chicago Defender*, 12 May 1945, 8.
"Kansas City in Two Victories." *Chicago Defender*, 19 May 1945, 7.
"Kansas City Is After Sox Park for Home Tilts." *Chicago Defender*, 3 October 1931, 9.
"Kansas City Is Beaten by Memphis." *Chicago Defender*, 21 April 1945, 7.
"Kansas City Is Beaten in 11th by Poor Throw." *Chicago Defender*, 7 July 1923.
"Kansas City Is Here Aug. 24." *Chicago Defender*, 25 August 1945, 7.
"Kansas City Is Shut Out by Padrone." *Chicago Defender*, 7 June 1924.
"Kansas City Just Too Much for American Giants; Fans Puzzled About Chicago Team." *Chicago Defender*, 12 June 1926.
"Kansas City Knocks the Detroit Stars Over for Four Straight Victories." *Chicago Defender*, 14 August 1926.
"Kansas City Monarchs and Chicago in Crucial Series." *Chicago Defender*, 1 July 1939, 9.
"Kansas City Monarchs Beat American Giants, 5 to 0." *Chicago Tribune*, 19 June 1938, A2.
"Kansas City Monarchs Come for Five-Game Series with Foster's American Giants." *Chicago Defender*, 4 July 1925.
"Kansas City Monarchs Down Chairmakers by 5–1 Score." *Sheboygan Press*, 16 June 1936.
"Kansas City Monarchs Greatest of Colored Teams in Baseball Today." *Helena Daily Independent*, 29 June 1936.
"Kansas City Monarchs in Charity Game." *Chicago Defender*, 18 July 1942.
"Kansas City Monarchs in Lone Star State." *Chicago Defender*, 6 April 1940, 22.
"Kansas City Monarchs in West; Triumph." *Chicago Defender*, 20 July 1935, 14.
"Kansas City Monarchs Invade New York July 20." *Chicago Defender*, 19 July 1941, 23.
"Kansas City Monarchs Invade Philly, Brooklyn." *Chicago Defender*, 22 June 1940, 24.
"Kansas City Monarchs Look Like Champs; Win All Games." *Chicago Defender*, 27 April 1935, 17.
"Kansas City Monarchs Meet East Helena on July 1st." *Helena Daily Independent*, 28 June 1936.
"Kansas City Monarchs Oppose Bismarck Here Tonight." *The Bismarck Tribune*, 15 June 1934.
"Kansas City Monarchs Play Davids Here at 6:30 Today." *Helena Daily Independent*, 23 July 1935.
"Kansas City Monarchs Play House of David Tonight." *Nevada State Journal*, 6 August 1940.
"Kansas City Monarchs Play Indianapolis Clowns in Stadium Here Saturday Night." *Zanesville Signal*, 19 August 1951, 3.
"Kansas City Monarchs Sell Outfielder, Catcher to Yankees." *Chicago Tribune*, 29 July 1949, B6.
"Kansas City Monarchs Set A.B.C.'s Down, 9 to 3." *Indianapolis Star*, 30 May 1921.
"Kansas City Monarchs Swamp Chairs 20 to 4." *Sheboygan Press*, 3 July 1937, 2.
"Kansas City Monarchs Tip Chairmakers by 8–2 Score." *Sheboygan Press*, 17 June 1938, 12.
"Kansas City Monarchs to Rebuild." *Chicago Defender*, 13 April 1935, 16.
"Kansas City Monarchs to Train in Louisiana." *Chicago Defender*, 28 March 1942, 19.
"Kansas City Monarchs Trail American Giants." *Chicago Defender*, 30 April 1938, 8.
"Kansas City Monarchs Versus Harold's Club Tonight." *The Journal*, 15 June 1949, 8.
"Kansas City Monarchs Win American League Playoff." *Chicago Defender*, 9 September 1939, 8.
"Kansas City Monarchs Win First Half in NAL." *Chicago Defender*, 16 July 1955, 10.
"Kansas City Monarchs Win in the Fifteenth, 6–5." *Chicago Defender*, 27 May 1939, 10.
"Kansas City Monarchs Win World Championship." *Chicago Defender*, 10 October 1942, 23.
"Kansas City Monarchs Win World Series." *Chicago Defender*, 25 October 1924.
"Kansas City on Top, 2–1." *New York Times*, 18 September 1946, 34.

(Kansas City Monarchs, continued)
"Kansas City Opens with Birmingham." *Chicago Defender*, 10 May 1941, 22.
"Kansas City Plays Bucks in Cleveland." *Chicago Defender*, 5 June 1943, 21.
"Kansas City Plays Newark in N.Y. on August 24." *Chicago Defender*, 23 August 1941, 24.
"Kansas City Plays St. Louis." *Chicago Defender*, 26 September 1925.
"Kansas City Pries League Lid Off with 13 Inning Win." *Chicago Defender*, 27 May 1922.
"Kansas City Ready for Classic with Chicago." *Chicago Defender*, 15 May 1937, 13.
"Kansas City Ready to Greet Monarchs." *Chicago Defender*, 8 May 1937, 14.
"Kansas City–St. Louis Games Play by Play." *Chicago Defender*, 26 September 1925.
"Kansas City Splits Even with Memphis." *Chicago Defender*, 23 May 1942, 20.
"Kansas City Splits with Clowns; Grab League Title." *Chicago Defender*, 7 September 1946, 11.
"Kansas City Stopped by Fort Wayne." *Chicago Defender*, 24 May 1924.
"Kansas City Swipes One from Detroit." *Chicago Defender*, 30 May 1925.
"Kansas City Takes Five Straight from Rube Foster's American Giants." *Chicago Defender*, 6 June 1925.
"Kansas City Took Last of Series." *Chicago Defender*, 23 May 1925.
"Kansas City Vs. Cubans on June 27." *Chicago Defender*, 26 June 1943, 11.
"Kansas City Vs. Grays at Pittsburgh, June 26." *Chicago Defender*, 23 June 1945, 7.
"Kansas City Victor Over Detroit, 10–1." *Chicago Defender*, 17 May 1924.
"Kansas City Wins 8 to 4 Over Raleigh." *Chicago Defender*, 31 May 1958, 24.
"Kansas City Wins Five Games from Birmingham." *Chicago Defender*, 19 September 1925.
"Kansas City Wins 4 to 0 from Cincinnati Clowns." *Chicago Defender*, 28 April 1945, 7.
"Kansas City with Bell on Mound Downs Wichita, 6–2." *Chicago Defender*, 6 August 1927.
"Kansas City Won First World Series in 1924." *Chicago Defender*, 5 September 1942, 24.
"Kansas City Won World Series from Hilldale by Winning Deciding Game." *Chicago Defender*, 25 October 1924.
"Kansas City's Chances Bright." *Chicago Defender*, 29 March 1947, 19.
"Kay Cees Have Many Hurlers." *Chicago Defender*, 1 April 1944, 9.
"Kay Cees Trounce Bears." *Chicago Defender*, 20 July 1940, 24.
"K.C. Monarchs Defeat Clowns." *Chicago Defender*, 22 April 1944, 9.

Kerkhoff, Blair. "Monarchs Were Kansas City's First Champions." *Kansas City Star*, 26 June 1999.
"Kessenich to Hurl Against Monarchs Tonight." *Sheboygan Press*, 15 June 1936.
Kline, Betsy. "At the Right Moment, KC Monarchs and Other League Teams Gave Their Best." *Kansas City Star*, 29 August 1983.
"Larks Trailing Monarchs 2–0 in 3 Game Series." *Reno Evening Gazette*, 28 July 1941, 9.
"Leading Negro Teams in 2 Wichita Games." *The Great Bend Daily Tribune*, 4 June 1953, 7.
"Lima All-Stars, Monarchs Play Here Wednesday Night." *The Lima News*, 14 August 1960.
McMahon, David R. "Kansas City Monarchs." In *Encyclopedia of Ethnicity and Sports in the United States of America*, ed. George Kirsch et al. Westport, Conn.: Greenwood Press, 2000, 266–267.
Mehl, Ernest. "Negro League Era Fading with Breakup of Monarchs." *The Sporting News*, 8 February 1956, 15.
"Memphis, Kansas City at Detroit Sunday." *Chicago Defender*, 21 July 1945, 7.
"Memphis Takes Twin Bill from Kansas City, Paige." *Chicago Defender*, 5 August 1944, 7.
"Monarch Club Had New Ideas in Baseball." *Berkshire Evening Eagle*, 15 August 1952, 20.
"Monarch Game Begins Sunday at 2:30 at Paige Stadium." *Kansas City Call*, 7–13 September 1984, 13–14.
"Monarch Players Gain in East-West Game Poll." *Chicago Defender*, 5 July 1941, 23.
"Monarch Recruits Have Good Records in Semi Pro Ranks." *Kansas City Call*, 5 March 1927.
"Monarchs and Clowns Have Good Combinations." *Chicago Defender*, 7 June 1952, 18.
"Monarchs and Clowns Shift Training Bases." *Chicago Defender*, 21 March 1953, 22.
"Monarchs and Clowns to N.Y." *Chicago Defender*, 14 September 1946, 11.
"Monarchs and Fosters Off to Kansas City for 5 Games." *Chicago Defender*, 5 June 1926.
"Monarchs Beat Red Sox, 8–7." *Chicago Defender*, 15 April 1939, 8.
"Monarchs Beaten in Twin Bill by Indianapolis A's." *Chicago Defender*, 16 June 1923.
"Monarch's 'Big Five' Stand at Top of Negro American League Pitchers." *Chicago Defender*, 8 July 1950, 17.
"Monarchs, Bucks in Night Game, August 8." *Chicago Defender*, 5 August 1944, 7.
"Monarchs, Clowns Tie Major League Records." *Chicago Defender*, 15 May 1948, 10.
"Monarchs Cop League Title by 2–1 Count." *Chicago Defender*, 25 September 1937, 20.

"Monarchs Defeat House of David Before Large Crowd." *Reno Evening Gazette*, 6 August 1941, 13.
"Monarchs Expect 18,000 at Opener." *Chicago Defender*, 23 May 1953, 23.
"Monarchs Face Giants Today; Paige to Pitch." *Chicago Tribune*, 30 May 1945, 29.
"Monarchs Face Negro Giants in Opener Today." *Chicago Tribune*, 9 May 1948, A6.
"Monarchs Find New Ace Shortstop in Hartman." *Chicago Defender*, 6 August 1955, 11.
"Monarchs Get Help." *Chicago Defender*, 29 April 1950, 17.
"Monarchs Homerun Beats Chicago." *Indianapolis Recorder*, 16 June 1928.
"Monarchs in Houston." *Chicago Defender*, 14 May 1949, 14.
"Monarchs, in Philly, Face Hard Fight." *Chicago Defender*, 10 October 1925.
"Monarchs in Triple Win Over St. Louis." *Chicago Defender*, 23 May 1295.
"Monarchs in 2 Games with Blount's Men." *Chicago Defender*, 7 June 1924.
"Monarchs Keep Up Win Streak on Tour of States." *Chicago Defender*, 18 July 1936, 15.
"Monarchs Lose to Toledo." *Chicago Defender*, 12 August 1939, 8.
"Monarchs Open at Home against Stars, May 22." *Chicago Defender*, 21 May 1949, 14.
"Monarchs Open Spring Training with Many New Faces in Lineup." *Chicago Defender*, 5 May 1956, 19.
"Monarchs Play Lexington Park." *Twin City Herald*, 15 July 1938, C3.
"Monarchs Play Stars on May 8." *Chicago Defender*, 7 May 1949, 15.
"Monarchs Plus Paige to Play Clowns Aug. 27." *Chicago Defender*, 22 August 1942, 19.
"Monarchs Rally Beats Chicago." *Indianapolis Recorder*, 23 June 1928.
"Monarchs, Red Sox Play Here." *Council Bluffs Nonpareil*, n.d.
"Monarchs Sold." *Washington Post*, 18 February 1956, 37.
"Monarchs Split Twin Bill." *New York Times*, 31 May 1945, 20.
"Monarchs Stop A.B.C.'s in Two Straight Games." *Chicago Defender*, 1 July 1922.
"Monarchs Tie in 14 Innings." *Chicago Defender*, 7 April 1945, 7.
"Monarchs to Battle Clowns at Miners Park Here Tonight." *Joplin Globe*, 10 September 1954, 6A.
"Monarchs to Be Honored Today." *The Kansas City Star*, 30 July 2006.
"Monarchs to Play Chi. Giants in St. Paul." *Twin City Herald*, 8 July 1939, C5.
"Monarchs to Play Ethiopian Clowns." *Twin City Leader*, 21 June 1941, C4.

"Monarchs to Play Here Friday Night." *Sheboygan Press*, 1 July 1937, 30.
"Monarchs to Play Miami Clowns." *Twin City Leader*, 24 August 1940, C3.
"Monarchs to Play Red Sox on May 19th." *Chicago Defender*, 18 May 1940, 23.
"Monarchs to Play Stars Sept. 11." *Chicago Defender*, 27 August 1955, 10.
"Monarchs to Play Three Games in Oklahoma." *Chicago Defender*, 31 May 1941, 24.
"Monarchs Trainer." *Kansas City Call*, 17 November 1926.
"Monarchs Trim Red Sox, 3–0." *Chicago Defender*, 18 May 1946, 11.
"Monarchs Vs. Clowns Sunday." *Chicago Defender*, 28 April 1945, 7.
"Monarchs Will Be in Perfect Condition." *Kansas City Call*, 2 March 1928.
"Monarchs Will Meet Chicago in a Twin Bill." *Chicago Defender*, 17 June 1950.
"Monarchs Win at Lexington Park." *Minneapolis Spokesman*, 15 July 1938, C7.
"Monarchs Win, 5 to 2." *New York Times*, 5 July 1958, 12.
"Monarchs Win Over Memphis." *Atchison Daily Globe*, 16 July 1953.
"Monarchs Win Playoff for League Title." *Chicago Defender*, 3 October 1925.
"Monarchs Win 2 Games from Chicago Giants." *Chicago Defender*, 24 June 1950, 16.
"Monarchs Win World Series." *Chicago Defender*, 25 October 1924.
Montre, Lorraine Kee. "Life with Monarchs Made Players Feel Like Kings." *St. Louis Post-Dispatch*, 9 August 1993.
"Morris Tames Kansas City Monarchs." *Bismarck Tribune*.
"Negro Champions Play Here Today." *New York Times*, 29 June 1958, S6.
"Negro Players are Barred by S.F. Seals." *Chicago Defender*, 7 March 1948, 11.
"New York Yankees Yank Two From Kansas City Monarchs." *Chicago Defender*, 6 August 1949, 1.
"Newark Ties Kansas in World Series." *Chicago Defender*, 28 September 1946, 11.
"Paige and Kansas City Defeat Newark Eagles." *Chicago Defender*, 30 August 1941, 23.
"Paige and the Monarchs Trim Memphis Sox." *Chicago Defender*, 28 July 1945, 7.
"Paige Stars as Monarchs Win in Yankee Stadium." *Pittsburgh Courier*, 3 July 1943.
Penn, Steve. "A Legacy One Shoe at a Time." www.KansasCity.com, 1 June 2004.
"Plan Gala Day for Kansas City's Opener." *Chicago Defender*, 17 May 1941, 22.
Posnanski, Joe. "KC's All-Time Baseball

(Kansas City Monarchs, continued)
Team." *The Kansas City Star*, 13 July 2003, C1, C8, C10.
"Rain Halts Kansas City Bathing Beauty Contest." *Chicago Defender*, 17 August 1940, 23.
"Rain Halts Teams After 2-Game Play." *Chicago Defender*, 26 September 1925.
Reece, L.V. "Satchel and His Fellow Monarchs." *Sportland* (Summer 1946): 19–22.
"Remains with Kansas City." *Chicago Defender*, 25 April 1942, 20.
Riley, James. "The Dean of the Monarchs." *Old Tyme Baseball News* 4 (Fall 1991): 31.
"Royals to Face Monarchs Tonight at Moana, Opening Six-Day Baseball Program." *Reno Evening Gazette*, 28 July 1939, 17.
"St. Louis Wins from Kansas City; Beaten by Cleveland." *Chicago Defender*, 1 July 1939, 9.
Sanchez, Robert. "Big-time Win for Negro League Players." *The Denver Post*, 10 December 2004.
"Satchel Paige and Kansas City Here Sunday, Monday." *Chicago Defender*, 29 May 1943, 11.
"Satchel Paige Rejoins the Monarchs." *Chicago Defender*, 11 June 1955, 11.
Schlegel, W.R. "Kansas City Runs Riot to Beat Memphis Twice." *Chicago Defender*, 31 May 1947, 11.
"Stars, K.C. Play in Grand Rapids." *Chicago Defender*, 9 June 1956, 17.
"Stars, Monarchs Fight for Lead." *Chicago Defender*, 16 June 1956, 17.
"Strong Kansas City Club Here for 4-Game Series." *Chicago Defender*, 26 May 1923.
Taylor, Jeff. "Past Is Relived as Monarchs Take the field." *Kansas City Times*, 10 September 1984, B3.
"Team in a Reunion." *Kansas City Times*, 9 March 1945.
"Ten Monarchs Return for Stadium Finale." *Kansas City Times*, 24 September 1971.
"They Treated 'Em Awful Rough in Kansas City." *Chicago Defender*, 12 June 1926.
Tolmon, Rosetta. "Allen 'Sports' Bryant Remembers the Monarchs." *Kansas City Call*, 15 June 1984, 36.
"Town-Team Baseball and the Kansas City Monarchs." In *Sleeper Cars and Flannel Uniforms: A Lifetime of Memories from Striking Out the Babe to Teeing It Up with the President*, ed. Elden Auker and Tom Keegan. Ill.: Triumph Books, 2001, 93–98.
Trussel, Robert. "'Monarchs' Hits for Cycle." *Kansas City Star*, 4 March 2004.
"Twenty-Five Negroes Have Baseball Calibre to Make Major Leagues." *Lowell Sun*, 30 July 1942, 9.
"25th Infantry Ball Players Join Monarchs." *Chicago Defender*, 1 April 1922.
"27,500 See Kansas City and Paige Defeat Cubans." *Chicago Defender*, 26 July 1941, 23.
"Twinight Bill Set Tonight." *Washington Post*, 16 August 1945, 11.
"Twins to Use Ace Pitcher in Big Game." *The Herald-Press*, 14 September 1945, 7.
Twyman, Gib. "Former Monarchs Gather, Recall Negro League Glory Days." *Kansas City Star*, 9 September 1984, 6.
Young, William and Nathan. "The Story of the Kansas City Monarchs." *Your Kansas City and Mine*. Self-published, 1950. 68–70, 127–128.
"Youngsters Lift Kaycees to Top Berth." *Chicago Defender*, 9 July 1949, 14.

Mendez, Jose

"American Ball Players Claim Jose Mendez, Cuba's 'Black Mathewson,' Is Pitching Marvel." *Washington Post*, 21 January 1912, S4.
"Jose Mendez, Ball Player, Dies in Cuba." *Chicago Defender*, 10 November 1928, 9.

Paige, Leroy ("Satchel")

Abel, Rick E. "Last Respects to Baseball's Legendary Satchel Paige Is Paid by Hundreds Saturday." *Kansas City Call*, 18 to 24 June 1982, 1–2.
"Actor Satch." *Ebony*, December 1959, 109, 112, 114.
"Ageless Satchel Paige." *Chicago Defender*, 31 August 1968, 10.
Ainslie, Peter. "In Kentucky: Memories of Black Baseball." *Time*, 10 August 1981, 4–5.
"All-Stars, Giants Mix." *Los Angeles Times*, 1 December 1935, 21.
"American Giants Play Paige and Kansas City in Detroit August 6." *Chicago Defender*, 5 August 1944, 7.
Anderson, Dave. "Looking Back at Satchel." *New York Times*, 10 June 1982, 29.
Argetsinger, Amy. "New Paige Park a Tribute to the Old Days of Black Baseball." *Washington Post*, 22 September 1996.
Armstrong, Jim. "Negro League's Hidden Talent Labored on Fields of Dreams." *The Denver Post*, 28 March 1999.
"Around the Majors." *Washington Post*, 8 June 1999, D6.
"Baseball Hall to Select Negroes." *Salisbury Daily Times*, 4 February 1971.
Basenfelder, Don. "Paige Is Hero as KC Wins Flag Here." *Philadelphia Record*, 30 September 1942.

Berger, Wally, and George Snyder. "An Encounter with the Great Satchel Paige." *The Diamond Angle,* Winter 2001, 17–19.

"Black Hall of Famers Get Special Berth, Satchel Paige First In." *Jet*, 25 February 1971, 52–53.

Blumenstock, Kathy. "Paige Dies, Legendary Pitcher, 75." *Washington Post*, 9 June 1982, D1-D2.

"The Brainiest Man in Baseball: Leroy 'Satchel' Paige..." *Ebony* (August 1952): 26–28, 30, 34.

"Braves Hire Satchel Paige." *Chicago Defender*, 13 August 1968, 26.

"Brooklyn Defeats Paige." *Chicago Defender*, 1 June 1940, 23.

Brown, Garry. "Incomplete Team." *New York Times*, 31 October 1999, SP17.

Brown, George F. "Satchel Paige Tells the World You Don't Have to Get Old." *Sepia* (December 1961): 51–54.

Bryson, Bill. "Clubhouse Was Satchel's Bullpen." *Baseball Digest*, 1 July 1961, 89–90.

Burnes, Brian. "It Ain't Restful: The Legend Rambles On." *Boston Phoenix*, 15 July 1993, 8–9, 14–16.

_____. "The Legend Gains on Satchel Paige...." *Kansas City Star Magazine*, 20 July 1980, 6–10, 13.

Cannon, Jimmy. "Endless Road for Satchel." *New York Post*, 16 August 1955. Reprinted in *New York Post*, 25 May 1997, 92.

Casey, Phil. "Doctor Backs Satch's Advice: 'Think Cool.'" *Washington Post*, 11 May 1963, B30.

"Catching Satchel, Rooming with Jackie." *Detroit Free Press*, 10 January 1991.

Catlin, Roger. "Staging Satchel." *The Record*, 6 November 1997, YT-3.

"Chicago Fans Honor Satchel Paige Who Wins 4–2." *Chicago Defender*, 1 August 1942, 19.

"Chicago to Honor Satchel Paige Sunday." *Chicago Defender*, 25 July 1942, 19.

Clark, John L. "Satchel Paige: The Life History of the Great Pitcher." *Chicago Defender*, 20 June 1942, 19.

"Cleveland Signs Paige for Relief." *Pottstown Mercury Sports*, 8 July 1948, 18.

"Cleveland's Heavy Hitting Keeps Paige Out of Action." *The Berkshire Evening Eagle*, 9 July 1948, 16.

"Cleveland Indians Sign Satchel Paige." *Chicago Defender*, 10 July 1948.

"Clowns to Show Off Bonus Pitcher Here." *Chicago Defender*, 10 August 1963, 20.

"Coast Stars Blast Paige." *Los Angeles Times*, 15 November 1943, A9.

Cobbledick, Gordon. "Old Satch: He's Really Got It." *Sport* 5 (December 1948): 32–35.

_____. "Satch a Match for the Hall of Fame." *Baseball Digest* 11 (October 1952): 31–33.

Cohane, Tim. "Ancient Satchel." *Look* 17 (7 April 1953): 65–66.

Condon, David. "Satchel Paige: A Legend Is Gone." *Chicago Tribune*, 9 June 1982, D1, D3.

Considine, Bob. "On the Line." *Lowell Sun*, 14 August 1942.

"Cop Socks Satchel Paige." *Cleveland Call and Post*, 18 August 1945.

Cowans, Russ. "Glory Comes Late to Ol' Satch Via His Untiring Arm." *Chicago Defender*, 9 October 1948, 13.

_____. "Old Satch Says He's on Last Legs." *Chicago Defender*, 21 March 1953, 24.

Crasnick, Jerry. "Bouton to get 'Eternal' Notoriety." *The News and Observer* (Raleigh, N.C.), 29 July 2001, B1–B2. Satchel Paige Was also inducted into Shrine of the Eternals.

Creamer, Robert. "Fine Paige out of History." *Sports Illustrated* (June 1981): 55.

Cronin, Don. "Ex-Players Take a look at 'Life in the Negro Leagues.'" *Chronicle-Telegram*, 25 April 1981, B-3.

Cuhaj, Joe and Tamra Carraway-Hinckle. "Leroy 'Satchel' Paige and the Negro Leagues." In *Baseball in Mobile*. S.C.: Arcadia Publishing, 2003.

Cummiskey, Joe. "Baseball's Greatest Drawing Card." *Negro Digest*, August 1944, 69–70.

Daley, Arthur. "Satch Proved Self in Brief Role." *Baseball Digest* 9 (May 1950): 55–57.

_____. "Sports of the Times." *New York Times*, 8 July 1948, 30 and 19 February 1950, S2.

Day, John C. "Buck Leonard's Homerun and Pitching of Paige Feature Game." *Chicago Defender*, 2 August 1941.

"Dean Vs. Paige on Menu Today at Cubs' Park." *Chicago Tribune*, 24 May 1942, A2.

Dokes, David. "Looking Back on Satchel Paige." *Great Moments in Sports-Baseball Magazine* (May 1988): 6–10.

Donovan, Richard. "The Fabulous Satchel Paige." *Collier's* 131 (30 May, 6 and 13 June 1953): 54–59.

Dukes, Howard. "Contributions Made in Later Years Also Valuable." *South Bend Tribune*, 9 September 2001.

Durso, Joe. "Satchel Paige, Black Pitching Star Is Dead at 75." *New York Times*, 9 June 1982, 48.

Dye, Robert. "Satchel Paige Is the Best." *Kansas City Times*, 4 October 1971.

Dyer, Braven. "Lou Reveals 'Saga of Satch.'" *Los Angeles Times*, 5 June 1960, H2.

_____. "'Satch' Through with Baseball?" *Los Angeles Times*, 8 November 1958, A1.

(Paige, Leroy "Satchel," continued)
"18,000 Watch Grays Blast Satchel Paige." *Washington Post*, 25 June 1945, 9.
"East Is Not Sorry that Satchel Paige Is Gone." *Chicago Defender*, 13 May 1939, 10.
Einstein, Charles. *The Baseball Reader— Satchel Paige*. Bonanza Books, 1984.
Elderkin, Phil. "Hurler Satchel Paige: Pitching Wonder Who Never Looked Back." *Christian Science Monitor*, 14 June 1982, 16.
"Everybody Wants Satchel Paige, Nobody His Salary." *Chicago Defender*, 9 February 1935, 16.
"Ewell Blackwell Pitches for All-Star Nine Tonight." *Los Angeles Times*, 23 October 1947, A11.
"Fabulous Satchel Paige Signed by Indians." *Los Angeles Times*, 8 July 1948, A9.
"Feller Again Beats Paige's Ball Club." *Chicago Defender*, 25 October 1947, 20.
"Feller All-Stars Here." *New York Times*, 4 October 1946, 18.
"Feller All-Stars Whip Paige, 4–2." *Los Angeles Times*, 3 October 1945, A7.
"Feller Hurls Against Paige Here May 31." *Washington Post*, 23 May 1942, 23.
Finger, Bill. "Passing in Review." *Call and Post*, 16 June and 27 October 1934.
Fitzgerald, Ed. "Let's Get Old Satch Into the Hall of Fame." *Sport* 13 (November 1952): 16–19.
"Florals Face Paige Stars in 2 Games." *Chicago Tribune*, 15 August 1937, A4.
Floto, James. "Profile #14—Satchel Paige." *Diamond Angle* (Winter 1991): 12–17.
Forbes, Frank. "Paige Faces Cubans in New York Sunday Aug. 2." *Chicago Defender*, 1 August 1942, 21.
Fox, William Price Jr. "A Conversation with Satchel Paige." *Holiday* (August 1965): 18, 24–26, 28–29.
_____. "The First Time I Met Satchel Paige." http://www.sportsjones.com/sj/442.shtml.
_____. *Satchel Paige's America*. Alabama: University of Alabama Press, 2005.
Freeman, Barney. "Paige's Feat Again Raises Negro Question." *Berkshire Evening Eagle*, 1 October 1942, 16.
Friedman, Dan. "Satchel Paige: Life and Times of an 'Ordinary' Man." *The Record* (Hackensack, N.J.), 15 February 1998.
Frommer, Harvey. "Satchel Paige." www.baseballlibrary.com.
"Giants, All-Stars Split." *Los Angeles Times*, 16 October 1933, 10.
Gietschier, Steven P. "The Short, Sweet Indian Summer of Satchel Paige." *Timeline*, April–May 1989, 44–53.
Gilbert, Thomas. "Satchel and Josh: African-American Baseball in the 1930s." In *The Good Old Days, Baseball in the 1930s*. New York: Franklin Watts, 1996, 125–140.
Gildea, William. "Paige Admits He's Feeling His Age." *Washington Post*, 29 April 1969, D2.
Goldgaber, Arthur. "He Pitched Over the Plate with Pinpoint Accuracy." *Investor's Business Daily*, 27 January 2006, A04.
Gottlieb, Jeremy. "A Pitch for the Home Team." *The Boston Globe*, 4 December 2005, 12.
Grady, Sandy. "The Return of Satchel Paige." *Baseball Digest*, 1 October 1968, 32–35.
Grayson, Harry. "Against Big Leaguers Paige Would Bear Down." *The Signal Sports*, 7 July 1943, 9.
Gustkey, Earl. "Satchel Paige Breaks Own Rule and Looks Back." *Baseball Digest* 39 (March 1980): 78–82.
"Hall of Fame for Paige." *The Coshocton Tribune*, 8 July 1971, 3-B.
"Hall of Famer Satchel Dies but Won't Be Forgotten." *Gettysburg Times*, 9 June 1982, 13.
Harmon, Willie Bea. "Sportorial: Was Paige Missed?" *Kansas City Call*, 18 August 1944.
Harrison, Roscoe. "Satchel Paige Runs for Missouri Legislature." *Jet*, 8 August 1968, 50–54.
Herskowitz, Mickey. "Paige Near the End of the Book." *Baseball Digest* 23 (April 1964): 46–48.
Hickok, Ralph. "Biography of Satchel Paige." In *Who's Who of Sports Champions*. New York: Houghton Mifflin Company, 1995.
Higgins, Chester A. "History of the Negro Leagues." *The Sun Reporter*, 8 June 1995.
"Highlights from '77 Interview of Satchel Paige." AZCentral.com, 2 August 2006.
Hill, Justice B. "Paige Family Remembers Satchel." www.MLB.com, 8 July 2006.
_____. "Statue of Paige a Moving Tribute." MLB.com, 28 July 2006.
"Hollywood Grabs Satchel Paige's 'Face' for Film." *Chicago Defender*, 18 October 1958, 18.
Holway, John. *Josh and Satch: The Life and Times of Josh Gibson and Satchel Paige*. Westport/London: Meckler Publishing, 1991.
Holway, John B. "Cool Papa, Biz and Satch." *LA Weekly*, 15 May 1992, 41–42.
_____. "The Kid Who Taught Satchel Paige a Lesson." *Baseball Research Journal* 16 (1987): 36–44.
_____. "Negro League Reunion: Paige and Pals." *Washington Post*, 28 June 1981, A1.
_____. "Paige Helped Change Baseball, and World." *Washington Post*, 13 June 1982.
_____. "Paige's Four Day Rider Does Job." *Washington Post*, 7 July 1991, D3.

Holway, John with James "Joe" Greene. "I Was Satchel's Catcher." *Journal of Popular Culture* VI (1972): 157–170.
"How Good Was Paige?" *Stevens Point Daily Journal*, 10 August 1971.
Humphrey, Kathryn Long. *Satchel Paige*. New York: Franklin Watts, 1988.
"'I Keep Coming Back,' Says Pitching Marvel Satchel Paige." *Chicago Defender*, 31 August 1968, 16.
"Immortal: Satchel Paige." *Kennebac Journal*, 27 March 1973, 9.
Jarrett, Vernon. "Business Acumen of Satchel Paige." *Chicago Tribune*, 13 August 1971, 19.
_____. "Satchel Paige's Great Day." *Chicago Tribune*, 11 August 1971, 18.
Jenkins, Lee. "Satchel Paige Readies Arm for 24th Year." *Chicago Defender*, 12 March 1960, 25.
Johnson, Scott. "Satchel, Buck and Me." *New Odyssey* (Fall 1992): 19–21.
Jones, Carmen. "Monument Honors Satchel Paige, Wife." *Kansas City Call*, 10 August 1989, 1, 4.
"Jumping Ball Players May Be Sent Home." *Chicago Defender*, 10 July 1937, 20.
Kahn, Dean. "Black Baseball Made Its Mark." *The Bellingham Herald*, 24 February 2002, A1–A2.
Kalb, Elliott. "Satchel Paige." In *Who's Better, Who's Best in Baseball*. New York: McGraw-Hill, 2005, 107–111.
"Kansas City and Paige Here Sunday, May 10." *Chicago Defender*, 9 May 1942.
"Kansas City and Paige Swipe Double-Header." *Chicago Defender*, 16 May 1942.
"Kansas City and Paige at Yankee Stadium June 17." *Chicago Defender*, 16 June 1945, 9.
Kaplan, Janice L. "One 'Diamond,' Many Facets." *The Washington Post*, 1 February 2002.
Kearns, James S. "Ol' Satch Gets New Pitches, Scheme of Life." *Chicago Daily News*, 21 May 1941.
Kee, Lorraine. "Battling Balls, Battling Racism." *St. Louis Post-Dispatch*, 23 March 1994.
Kemp Jon. "Satchel Paige, 75, Master of Mound and Bon Mot, Dies." *Los Angeles Times*, 9 June 1982, B1.
Kennedy, Bob. "As Good as Satchel Paige." *The Portsmouth Herald*, 18 September 1943, 5.
Kerrane, Kevin. "Satchel Paige." In *The World of Baseball: The Hurlers*. Redefinition Books, 1990, 108–09.
Kirshenbaum, Jerry, ed. "A Most Unnatural Natural." Obituary. *Sports Illustrated*, 21 June 1982, 9.
Koppett, Leonard. "Looking Back, Paige Says He's Proud." *New York Times*, 10 August 1971, 26.
Lardner, Rex. "The Ageless Satchel Paige." *Sport* (January 1969): 44–47.
"Law Tells Satch — 'Win or Jail.'" *Ebony* (September 1958): 77–78, 80.
Lawson, Ed. "20,000 See 'Satch's' Team Lose in 12th." *Washington Post*, 14 August 1942, 22.
Lebovitz, Hal. "The Day Old Satch Made the Majors." *Sport* 24 (September 1957): 70, 74.
_____. *Pitchin' Man*. Cleveland, Ohio: Cleveland News, 1948.
"Lemon's All-Stars Nip Paige's Royals, 7–6." *Los Angeles Times*, 16 October 1950, C4.
"Lemon's Stars Tackle Paige and Co. in Tilt." *Los Angeles Times*, 31 October 1948, 31.
Lemperle, Dominique. "Sonora Volleyers with Golden Valley Title." *Union Democrat*, 20 September 2005.
"Leonard, Paige Top Negro League Stars." *The Record* (Hackensack, N.J.), 8 June 1999.
"Leroy Robert (Satchel) Paige." *Washington Post*, 10 June 1982, A16.
Lester, Larry. "Leroy Robert 'Satchel' Paige." In *Unions to Royals: The Story of Professional Baseball in Kansas City*. Missouri: AG Press, 1996, 22–23.
_____. "Leroy "Satchel" Paige." *Black Sports, the Magazine* (April 2005): 20–22.
_____. "Satch vs. Josh." *National Pastime* (June 1993): 30–33.
Lewis, Allen. "For Satchel It Was Always in the Bag." *Baseball Digest* (August 1960): 10.
Lewis, Franklin. "Fast or No, It's Still Satchmo." *Baseball Digest* 10 (October 1951): 35–36.
Lewis, Lloyd. "Hesitation Ball." *Negro Digest* (November 1944): 37–38.
_____. "Keep Movin'." *Chicago Daily News*, 20 September 1940.
Lind, Angus. "Saluting 'Satchel' Paige." *New Orleans Times-Picayune*, 6 July 2005, 1.
Lipman, David. "Maybe I'll Pitch Forever." *Negro Digest* (November 1944): 37–38.
Macht, Norman. *Satchel Paige*. New York: Chelsea House Publishers, 1991.
Marasco, David. "Before Jackie." *Diamond Angle* (Spring 1998): 11.
_____. "The Travellin' Man Goes to Portland." *The Diamond Angle* (May–June 1996): 27–28.
McClean, Tony. "Satch, Josh and the Summer of '42." *Pittsburgh Courier*, 6 August 2006.
McGinn, Gerald A. "Satchel Paige Shows He Still Has His Stuff." *Washington Post*, 6 July 1966, D4.
McGuff, Joe. "'Inner' Paige Usually a Closed Book." *Kansas City Star*, 9 June 1982, 1A, 6A.

(Paige, Leroy "Satchel," continued)
_____. Commentary: "Paige Made Pitching the Consummate Show." *Kansas City Times*, 9 June 1982, D1–D2.
McKenzie, Rob. "Boy, Could Satchel Ever Talk." *National Post* (Canada), 23 July 2005, WP14.
Mellinger, Sam. "The Majors: Rounding the Bases, Truth, Reasons, More." *Kansas City Star*, 14 May 2006.
"Memphis Takes Twin Bill from Kansas City, Paige." *Chicago Defender*, 5 August 1944, 7.
Menna, Larry K. "Paige, Leroy Robert ('Satchel')." In *Encyclopedia of Ethnicity and Sports in the United States of America*, ed. George Kirsch et al. Westport, Conn.: Greenwood Press, 2000, 350–351.
Mills, Prentice. "Satchel Paige, the Great Integrator of the Game." *Black Ball News* (May–June 1992): 2–8.
Mims, Linda. "The Great 'Satchel' Paige." *Sacramento Observer*, 23 August 1995.
Miranda, Fausto. "Satchel Paige Recibio su Premio ... Tarde." *El Nuevo Herald*, 1 October 1995.
"Monarchs Get Satchel Paige." *New York Times*, 18 May 1961, 43.
Monroe, Al. "Willie Foster Loses Contest to S. Paige." *Chicago Defender*, 1 September 1934.
Moore, James. "Baseball's Oldest Rookie." *Newsweek*, 25 October 1999, 50–52.
"Morning Briefing." *Los Angeles Times*, 10 June and 19 July 1982, OC-B2.
Morten, Baker E. "Stepin' Fetchit Eyes Movie on Satchel Paige." *Chicago Defender*, 14 May 1960, 18.
Mortenson, Tom. "Pitching Paige." www.beckett.com, 60.
"Moviemakers Plan Life Story of Legendary Black Pitcher." *Tri-City Herald*, 8 August 1974, 28.
Munhall, Jack. "Paige, Grays Beat Stars, 8–1, Before 22,000." *Washington Post*, 1 June 1942, 17.
"Munns, Satchel Hook Up Today in Mound Duel." *Los Angeles Times*, 10 November 1935, 24.
Murray, Jim. "Move Over Satchel." *Los Angeles Times*, 12 August 1971, F1.
_____, "Satchel Paige: A Virtuoso in a Cow Pasture Waiting for Place in Baseball Hall of Fame." *Milwaukee Journal*, 24 June 1964.
"Negro Teams Play 2 Today in Cubs' Park." *Chicago Tribune*, 15 August 1943, A5.
"Negroes to Honor Stars." *New York Times*, 2 July 1939, S2.
Newman, Fred. *Satchel: A Requiem for Racism.* Castillo Theatre, New York City, New York, 16 January–1 March 1998.

"Now Pitching: Satchel Paige." *New York Times*, 12 June 1965, 25.
Nunn, William. "'Satch' Stop 'Big Bad Men' of West Team." *Pittsburgh Courier*, 1 September 1934.
"Ol' Satchel Wow 'Em in 'Debut.'" *Los Angeles Times*, 26 September 1965, C4.
"Old Age, High Pay Strike Out Paige." *New York Times*, 27 January 1954, 32.
"Old Satch Paige, Great Negro Pitcher Signed by Cleveland, Says 'Batters Can't Scare Me — I've Been Around Too Long.'" *Washington Post*, 8 July 1948, 17.
"Ole Satch Voted Place in Pilots Hall of Fame." *New York Times*, 14 May 1967, S5.
"Ole Satchel Paige Can Sit Pretty in Bull-Pen Now." *Washington Post*, 26 June 1952, 16.
"One Thing Is Certain: Satchel Oldest Rookie in History." *Council Bluffs Nonpareil*, 8 August 1948, 23.
O'Neil, John "Buck." "Unforgettable Satchel Paige." *Reader's Digest* 124 (April 1984): 89–92.
Otto, Solomon, with John Solomon Otto. "I Played Against 'Satchel' for Three Seasons: Blacks and Whites in the 'Twilight' Leagues." *Journal of Popular Culture* 7 (1974).
Page, Don. "Satchel Paige: His Bag Is Pitching." *Los Angeles Times*, 17 August 1968, B2.
"Paige Agrees to Pitch for Negro Giants." *Chicago Tribune*, 8 May 1951, C6.
"Paige All-Stars Defeat Florals Twice, 2–0 and 11–0." *Chicago Tribune*, 16 August 1937, 23.
"Paige and Day to Pitch in Negro All-Star Clash." *Chicago Tribune*, 31 July 1943, 14.
"Paige and E. Chicago Team Lose to Detroit." *Chicago Defender*, 31 July 1943, 11.
"Paige and Monarchs Defeat Philadelphia." *Chicago Defender*, 23 June 1945, 7.
"Paige and Monarchs Play All-Stars Sunday." *Chicago Defender*, 27 September 1941, 23.
"Paige and Monarchs Trim Memphis Sox." *Chicago Defender*, 28 July 1945, 7.
"Paige Answers Call for Help from Bismarck." *Bismarck Tribune*, 3 September 1943.
"Paige Attracts Throng of 10,800." *Los Angeles Times*, 25 October 1943, A9.
"Paige Beats Newsome as Nines Split Pair." *Los Angeles Times*, 4 December 1933, 9.
"Paige Becomes Father 7th Time." *Washington Post*, 18 October 1965, C2.
"Paige Conquers Thurston." *Los Angeles Times*, 11 December 1933, 12.
"Paige Defeats Black Yankees." *Chicago Defender*, 18 August 1945, 7.
"Paige Fills a Chapter in Attendance Record Book." *Call and Post*, 6 September 1948.

"Paige Gets $1,000 Pitch but There's Catch to It." *New York Times*, 14 January 1969, 48.
"Paige Has Fast Ball Team." *Chicago Defender*, 17 June 1939, 8.
"Paige Has His Night, Wins for Browns, 6–3." *New York Times*, 29 July 1952, 26.
"Paige Here Tonight." *Washington Post*, 12 July 1951, 16.
"Paige Holds Barons to One Hit." *Chicago Defender*, 26 May 1951, 16.
"Paige Hurls First Game of Season — and Wins." *Chicago Defender*, 1 June 1946, 11.
"Paige Hurls Kansas City to Victory." *Chicago Defender*, 16 August 1941, 21.
"Paige in Detroit Sunday." *Chicago Defender*, 31 August 1940, 22.
"Paige in Hall of Fame." *The Coshocton Tribune*, 10 February 1971, 2-B.
"Paige Inducted into Hall." *The Frederick Post*, 10 August 1971, B-1.
"Paige Insists He'll Quit After This Year." *Los Angeles Times*, 10 March 1953, C2.
"Paige Is First Star of Old Negro Leagues to Be Selected for Hall of Fame." *New York Times*, 10 February 1971, 52.
"Paige Is Here on Sept. 22." *Chicago Defender*, 21 September 1940, 22.
"Paige, Monarchs Play Clowns in St. Louis Aug. 30; Then Kansas City." *Chicago Defender*, 31 August 1946, 11.
"Paige Named Full-Fledged Hall of Famer." *Syracuse Post-Standard*, 8 July 1971, 16.
"Paige Not in Accident." *New York Times*, 3 November 1953, 39.
"Paige of History." *Daily News*, 11 August 1991, 63.
"Paige Pitches and Chicago Loses 9–3." *Chicago Defender*, 14 September 1940.
"Paige Pitches, Wins 2–1." *Chicago Defender*, 28 September 1940, 22.
"Paige Reinstated After 'Resigning' from Miami." *Washington Post*, 16 August 1958, A12.
"Paige Shows Fine Form in Spring Camp." *Chicago Defender*, 29 May 1954, 23.
"Paige Signs Salina Pact." *Chicago Defender*, 23 June 1960, A26.
"Paige Stadium Dedication Sunday." *Kansas City Call*, 9–15 September 1983, 1–2.
"Paige Stops Grays 11 to 3 for Monarchs." *Washington Post*, 11 August 1943, 14.
"Paige Sure Bet as Hall of Famer Selectee Today." *The Progress*, 9 February 1971, 10.
"Paige to Face American Giants in Detroit Aug. 6." *Chicago Defender*, 29 July 1944.
"Paige to Hurl for Monarchs Against Grays." *Washington Post*, 20 Jun 1943, R2.
"Paige to Hurl in Toledo Wednesday." *Chicago Defender*, 22 May 1943, 21.

"Paige to Pilot and Pitch." *New York Times*, 15 March 1956, 51.
"Paige to Pitch for Chi. Giants." *Portland Press Herald*, 8 May 1951, 12.
"Paige to Pitch for East Vs. West Game." *Chicago Defender*, 26 July 1941.
"Paige to Pitch in East-West Battle Today." *Chicago Tribune*, 31 July 1955, A4.
"Paige Tops Black Yanks." *New York Times*, 13 August 1945, 14.
"Paige Vs. Dean at East Chicago July 8." *Chicago Defender*, 7 July 1945, 7.
"Paige Vs. 1965 Red Sox." *New York Times*, 3 August 1968, 12:2.
"Paige Vs. Roy Henshaw, Parmalee Sunday, June 4." *Chicago Defender*, 3 June 1944, 9.
"Paige Voted Best Ever in NBC Ranks." *Chicago Tribune*, 20 December 1964, B2.
"Paige Whiffs Eighteen." *Los Angeles Times*, 23 October 1933, 13.
"Paige Whips Black Yanks." *Chicago Defender*, 10 August 1946, 11.
"Paige Will Hurl Here August 31." *Chicago Defender*, 9 August 1941, 23.
"Paige Will Pitch in Cuban Circuit." *Bismarck Tribune*, 11 June 1937, 10.
"Paige Will Pitch in Grays-Monarchs Twin Bill Sunday." *Washington Post*, 22 June 1945, 11.
"Paige Wins as Giants Divide Double-Header." *Los Angeles Times*, 11 November 1935, A10.
"Paige's Farewell on Sunday." *New York Times*, 8 August 1945, 26.
"Paige's Monarchs on Top." *New York Times*, 18 June 1945, 12.
"Paige's Monarchs Play Here Tuesday Night." *Washington Post*, 6 September 1942, 2.
"Paige's Team Tops Dean's All-Stars." *New York Times*, 25 May 1942, 19.
Paige, Leroy. Interview by J.R. Wright, n.d., Private Collection, Kalamazoo, Michigan.
Paige, Leroy "Satchel," as told to David L. Lipman. *Maybe I'll Pitch Forever*. New York: Doubleday and Co., Inc., 1962.
Paige, Satchel. "Did Some Boxin' with the Crawfords." *Cleveland News*, 4 August 1948, 11.
_____. "Don't Throw Curves in Mexico." *Cleveland News*, 10 August 1948.
_____. "Duel with Josh Gibson — to the Finish." *Cleveland News*, 6 August 1948.
_____. "Fans Want 'Clews.'" *Cleveland News*, 28 July 1948.
_____. "Gotta Stick with Bob, He'll Come 'Round." *Cleveland News*, 12 August 1948.
_____. "He's 'Trunk' Paige to Red Caps." *Cleveland News*, 22 July 1948.
_____. "I Haven't Showed All My Pitches." *Cleveland News*, 11 August 1948.

(Paige, Leroy "Satchel," continued)
___. "I Was a Rookie at Play in 'Hookie.'" *Cleveland News*, 2 August 1948, 11.
___. "Let's Talk About My Feet." *Cleveland News*, 27 July 1948.
___. "Satch Is Born Rock." *Cleveland News*, 29 July 1948.
___. "Sniff When You Buy a Goat." *Cleveland News*, 30 July 1948.
___. "They Had to Ask My Ma." *Cleveland News*, 3 August 1948.
Paige, Satchel, as told to Ernest Mehl. "My Biggest Baseball Day." *Negro Digest* (May 1943): 7–10.
Penn, Steve. "A Grave Baseball Mystery." *Kansas City Star*, 13 April 2006.
___. "Daughter Teaches Lore of a Legend." *Kansas City Star*, 26 March 2001.
___. "Homerun Efforts for a Hometown Park." *The Kansas City Star*, 5 March 2001.
___. "Stadium Named for Paige Awaits Repair." *Kansas City Star*, 30 October 1997.
"The People Speak." *Chicago Defender*, 19 August 1958, A11.
Peterson, Robert. "The Greatest Battery Ever." *Boys' Life* (April 1971).
"Pittsburgh Crawfords Split Twin Bill with Cincinnati; Satchel Paige in First Tilt." *Norfolk Journal and Guide*, 24 April 1937, 17.
Posnanski, Joe. "How Good Was Satchel Paige?" *Kansas City Star*, 8 June 2003.
___. "Paige Proves Truth Can Be Inconvenient." *Kansas City Star*, 2 July 2006.
Povich, Shirley. "Clowning Delayed Negroes' Start in Majors." *Washington Post*, 11 May 1953, 8–9.
___. "Satch Paige a Very Special Case in Baseball." *Washington Post*, 18 May 1953, 11.
"Profiles of Prominent Negro Leaguers: Leroy Satchel Paige." *St. Louis Post-Dispatch*, 4 February 2001.
Rae, Lorne. "It Was a Real Baseball." *Saskatchewan History* (January 1991): 16–20.
Ray, Bob. "He's Just a Big Man from the South." *Los Angeles Times*, 12 November 1933, E6.
Rea, E.B. "Crawfords' Mound Ace Injured in Auto Crash." *Norfolk Journal and Guide*, 24 April 1937, 17.
Reaves, Jospeh A. "Cooperstown Will Hear Paige's Voice in the Air." *Courier News*, 2 August 2006.
Reece, L.V. "Satchel and His Fellow Monarchs." *Sportland* (Summer 1946): 19–22.
Reilly, Edward J. "Paige, Leroy." In *Baseball, An Encyclopedia of Popular Culture*. Calif.: ABC-CLIO, 2000, 229.
"Retire? 'Old' Satch Not Ready Yet." *Chicago Sun-Times*, 20 January 1957, 73.

Roberts, M. B. "Paige Never Looked Back." http://www.ESPN.com, 11 November 1999.
Rogosin, Donn. "Satch vs. Josh — Classic Duel at Large." *The Sporting News*, 18 July 1981, 48.
Rubin, Robert. *Satchel Paige, All Time Baseball Great*. New York: G.P. Putnam's Sons, 1974.
Ruck, Rob. "Paige, Leroy 'Satchel.'" In *Biographical Dictionary of American Sports, Baseball*, ed. David l. Porter. Westport, Conn.: Greenwood Press, 2000, 1165–1167.
Rusk, Howard A., MD. "The Waste of the Aged." *New York Times*, 25 August 1968, 15.
Sambol, Richard. "Satchel Paige School Will Unveil Statue of Its Namesake." The *Kansas City Star*, 18 March 2001, 15.
"Satch Hurls 3-hit, 1–0 Win." *Washington Post*, 21 August 1948, 10.
"Satch Makes the Big Leagues." *Life*, 26 July 1948, 49–50ff.
"Satch Paige Earns Starting Role Against Nats Sunday." *Washington Post*, 17 July 1948, 10.
"Satch Paige Jumps Club." *Chicago Defender*, 6 August 1958, A24.
"Satch, Pro in '26, Pays Fan Who Proves It." *Washington Post*, 24 August 1948, 16.
"Satch Signs Up." *Los Angeles Times*, 10 February 1952, B10.
"Satch the Sage." In *The Best Man Plays, Major League Baseball and the Black Athlete, 1901–2002*, by Andrew O'Toole. Jefferson, N.C.: McFarland, 2003, 25–53.
"Satchel and Pillette in Duel Today." *Los Angeles Times*, 17 November 1935, 24.
"Satchel-Foot Paige's Former Batterymate Says Grays' Brown Will Upset Celebrated Pitcher." *Washington Post*, 16 June 1942, 23.
"Satchel Hurls for Cleveland Indians." *Chicago Defender*, 17 July 1948, 10.
"Satchel Is Still a Big Draw." *Chicago Defender*, 10 January 1957, 23.
"Satchel Loses Wager; Played Pro Before '27." *Lincoln Journal*, 24 August 1948.
"Satchel Made Victim of No-Hit Contest." *Chicago Defender*, 25 September 1937, 20.
"Satchel Needs a Gripsack for All His Records." *Chicago Tribune*, 11 July 1943, A3.
"Satchel Saved by Homer in Ninth." *Los Angeles Times*, 25 November 1935, A11.
"Satchel Shows His Stuff Before 1,200." *The Lima News*, 1 July 1961, 8.
"Satchel Snares Sixth Victory from Nats, 10–1." *Los Angeles Times*, 31 August 1948, C1.
"Satchel the Great." *Time*, 19 July 1948, 56–57.
Satchel Paige. Files. Kansas City Public Library, Kansas City, Missouri.
"Satchel Paige." In *Baseball: The Biographical Encyclopedia*. Ed. David Pietrusza, Matthew

Silverman, and Michael Gershman. Kingston, New York: Total Sports Publishing, 2000, 860.
"Satchel Paige." In *The 100 Greatest Baseball Players of the 20th Century Ranked*, by Mark McGuire and Michael Sean Gormley. Jefferson, N.C.: McFarland, 2000, 97–98.
"Satchel Paige, a Lively 52 (?), Says Ball Is 'Livelier, All Right.'" *New York Times*, 18 August 1961, 24.
"Satchel Paige, Ace Negro Pitcher, Signed by Indians for Relief Role." *New York Times*, 8 July 1948, 26.
"Satchel Paige and Kansas City Here Sunday, Monday." *Chicago Defender*, 29 May 1943, 11.
"Satchel Paige Appears with Globetrotters." *Washington Post*, 14 December 1964, C5.
"Satchel Paige at Stadium Today for 29th Negro All-Star Game." *New York Times*, 20 August 1961, S2.
"Satchel Paige Beaten by Willis on Coast." *Chicago Defender*, 9 March 1935, 16.
"Satchel Paige Dies of Heart Attack." *The Frederick News*, 9 Jun 1982, C-3.
"'Satchel' Paige Dies of Heart Attack." *The Frederick Post*, 9 June 1982, D-3.
"Satchel Paige Eyes Return to Majors." *Chicago Defender*, 25 July 1959, 23.
"Satchel Paige Fails to Appear After League Acts." *New Jersey Herald News*, 2 July 1938, 7.
"Satchel Paige Fans Nine Batters in N.Y. Game." *Chicago Defender*, 17 May 1941, 22.
"Satchel Paige Gets Test at Hollywood Today." *Los Angeles Times*, 14 November 1943, 23.
"Satchel Paige Hands Beating to Dizzy Dean." *Chicago Tribune*, 22 October 1934, 17.
"Satchel Paige Helps Chicago Giants Win 2." *Chicago Tribune*, 21 May 1951, C4.
"Satchel Paige Holds St. Louis Browns Runless." *Chicago Defender*, 17 July 1948.
"Satch Paige Hurls Again Tonight at Griffith Stadium." *Washington Post*, 16 September 1954, 34.
"Satchel Paige in Hall of Fame; Wants a Manager's Job." *Jet*, 26 August 1971, 50–52.
"Satchel Paige in Hospital." *New York Times*, 27 March 1969, 61.
"Satchel Paige Is 44." *New York Times*, 18 July 1948, S2.
"Satchel Paige Is Hard Man to Really Pin Down." *Chicago Defender*, 16 August 1958, 24.
"Satchel Paige Is Making the Rounds." *Chilicothe Constitution*, 10 June 1981.
"Satchel Paige, Josh Gibson Among Top Black Athletes to Be Studied for Hall of Fame." *The Gettysburg Times*, 4 February 1971, 12.
"Satchel Paige Leads Monarchs to 8–3 Victory." *Chicago Tribune*, 1 September 1941, 27.
"Satchel Paige Loses as Bosox Nab Twin Bill." *Los Angeles Times*, 25 August 1952, C2.
"Satchel Paige May Pitch Chicago League Opener." *Chicago Defender*, 6 May 1939, 10.
"Satchel Paige May Switch to Coaching Job." *Chicago Tribune*, 22 March 1959, A2.
"'Satchel' Paige Mystifies Royals." *Nevada State Journal*, 6 August 1940, 10.
"Satchel Paige Named to Cooperstown Hall." *Nevada State Journal*, 10 February 1971, 13.
"Satchel Paige Not Eligible for 1940 East-West Baseball Classic." *Chicago Defender*, 3 August 1940, 24.
"Satchel Paige of Samurai." *Los Angeles Times*, 13 November 1973, D10.
"Satchel Paige on Trotter's Bill Wednesday." *Chicago Defender*, 29 December 1964, 25.
"Satchel Paige Philly Stars Tackle Cubans." *Chicago Defender*, 8 July 1950, 17.
"Satchel Paige Pitches for Mixed Team." *Minneapolis Spokesman*, 6 September 1935, C2.
"Satchel Paige Pitches His Best Game for Title Down in Old San Domingo." *Kansas City Times*, 26 March 1943.
"Satchel Paige Rejoins the Monarchs." *Chicago Defender*, 11 June 1955, 10.
"Satchel Paige Returns to Crawfords." *Chicago Defender*, 2 May 1936, 13.
"Satchel Paige Returns to Organized Baseball." *New York Times*, 26 August 1961, 10.
"Satchel Paige Returns to Wrigley Field for Sunday's Bargain Bill." *Chicago Defender*, 14 August 1943, 11.
"Satchel Paige Sharp in Six-Inning Stint." *Los Angeles Times*, 5 September 1961, C2.
"Satchel Paige Signs, Jumbles Brown Records." *Chicago Tribune*, 10 February 1952, A6.
"Satchel Paige Signs as Manager of Barons." *Mansfield News Journal*, 15 March 1956, 16.
"Satchel Paige Signs to Pitch for Newark Eagles." *Chicago Defender*, 20 January 1940, 23.
"Satchel Paige Stars; Memphis Nine Wins, 1 to 0." *Chicago Tribune*, 19 July 1943, 21.
"'Satchel' Paige Still Has Pitching Savvy, Scribe Discovers." *Chicago Defender*, 9 July 1966, 18.
"Satchel Paige Still Leads East-West Game Poll." *Chicago Defender*, 12 July 1941, 23.
"'The Satchel Paige Story' Hollywood's Next Mixed Film." *Chicago Defender*, 29 October 1949, 26.
"Satchel Paige Story Pix to Include Spring Training." *Chicago Defender*, 24 January 1953, 22.
"Satchel Paige Tells the World ... 'You Don't

(Paige, Leroy "Satchel," continued)
Have to Get Old.'" *Sepia*, December 1961, 51–54.
"Satchel Paige to American League." *Chicago Defender*, 29 June 1940.
"Satchel Paige to Hurl Against Giants Sunday." *Chicago Defender*, 7 September 1940, 20.
"Satchel Paige to Hurl for Kansas City Against Giants." *Chicago Defender*, 21 September 1935, 13.
"Satchel Paige to Pitch." *New York Times*, 17 June 1945, S4.
"Satchel Paige to Pitch for Miami Club Again." *Los Angeles Times*, 6 February 1958, C6.
"Satchel Paige to Receive Sheepskin." *Chicago Defender*, 30 July 1960, 24.
"Satchel Paige Turns Movie Actor: "You Get to Sit a Lot, Pay Is Good."'" *Washington Post*, 21 December 1958, C5.
"Satchel Paige Twirls for Royal Giants Today." *Los Angeles Times*, 14 October 1934, E4.
"Satchel Paige Unbeaten on Coast; Hero of League." *Chicago Defender*, 2 February 1935, 17.
"Satchel Paige, Using 'My Nuthin' Ball,' Tames Chicago Giants in 4-Inning Stint." *New York Times*, 21 May 1951.
"Satchel Paige Walks Out on Miami Marlins." *Chicago Defender*, 16 August 1958, 24.
"Satchel Paige Whips House of David Nine." *Chicago Defender*, 21 September 1935, 14.
"Satchel Paige Will Be Barred From N.N. League." *Norfolk Journal and Guide*, 8 May 1937, 18.
"Satchel Paige Will Hurl at Griffith Stadium." *Washington Post*, 16 August 1959, C5.
"Satchel Paige Will Manage, Play in Alaska." *Washington Post*, 28 August 1965, E2.
"Satchel Paige Wins in Nat'l Semi-Pro 1st Round Play." *Chicago Defender*, 3 September 1960, 24.
"Satchel Paige Writes Own Story." *Chicago Defender*, 20 March 1962, 22.
"Satchel Paige's All-Stars Lose to Monarchs." *Washington Post*, 21 August 1959, C6.
"Satchel Paige's 3-Game Stand May Set Mark." *Washington Post*, 11 August 1942, 18.
"Satchelfoots." *Time*, 19 July 1948, 56–57.
"Says Satchel Signed with Western Loop Team in Big Surprise Action." *New Jersey Herald News*, 29 April 1939, 8.
Scheuer, Philip K. "Old Satch's Advice Found Sound by Chief of MGM." *Los Angeles Times*, 9 January 1955, D3.
Seeman, Bruce Taylor. "Satchel's Pitch for Living Well: Live Smart." *The Star-Ledger*, 20 April 2004, 19, 29.
Segreti, James. "Satchel Paige Pitches, Grins and Conquers." *Chicago Tribune*, 23 September 1940, 21.
Shane, Ted. "Satchel Man." *Reader's Digest* 54 (June 1949): 39–42.
Shirley, David. *Satchel Paige: Baseball Great*. New York: Chelsea House, 1993.
Shrine of the Eternals. Induction Day Program. Pasadena, Calif. 29 July 2001. Inductees included Satchel Paige.
Silverman, Al. "Satchel Paige Sounds Off." *Sport*, November 1972, 44–46.
"Slow: Satchel Paige." *New Yorker*, September 1952, 32–33.
Spilde, Tony. "Baseball, Bismarck and Boundaries Broken." *The Bismarck Tribune*, 18 September 2005.
"Sports Gossip." *Mansfield News-Journal*, 4 August 1941, 10.
"The Sports Immortals: Satchel Paige." *Mansfield News-Journal*, 19 April 1973, 37, and *The Frederick News*, 21 March 1973, B-3.
Stainbeck, Berry. "Dang! Nobody Liked Hitting His Ole Trouble Ball." *Panorama* (September 1980): 82–85.
Stann, Francis. "Satchel Paige-Hall of Famer." *Baseball Digest* (January 1972): 78–79.
Sterry, David, and Arielle Eckstut, eds. *Satchel Sez: The Wit, Wisdom and World of Leroy "Satchel" Paige*. New York: Three Rivers Press, 2001.
Tammeus, William D. "A Giant Is Returned to Earth." *Kansas City Star*, 13 June 1982, A1, A18.
"Theolic Smith, Satchel Paige Star as Monarchs, Bucks Split." *Pittsburgh Courier*, 12 June 1943.
"This Week in Baseball." *Jet*, 12 February 2001, 20. A look back at Paige's election to the Hall of Fame.
Torriero, E.A. "We Lost Satchel: KC Neighbors Shed Tears as Legendary Baseball Player Dies." *Kansas City Times*, 9 June 1982, A1, A12.
Trabal, Ismael. "Milito en 8 Equipos de las Ligas Negras, Satchel Paige." *Deportiva*, 18 March 2000.
"27,500 See Kansas City and Paige Defeat Cubans." *Chicago Defender*, 26 July 1941, 23.
Veeck, Bill. "The Ageless Nomad of Baseball." *Chicago Tribune*, 25 March 1962, E6.
Veeck, Bill, and Ed Linn. "Baseball's Own Paul Bunyan: Satchel Paige." *Chicago Tribune*, 20 July 1962, C1.
———. "Unforgettable Satchel Paige Was Above Race, Prejudice." *Washington Post*, 10 August 1962, D4.
"Veteran Satchel Paige Is Signed by Cleveland Club." *Coshocton Tribune Sports*, 7 July 1948.
Wade, Dick. "Paige Packs Cooperstown." *Kansas City Times*, 9 August 1971.

———. "Satchel Looks Back." *Kansas City Star*, 9 August 1971.
Walburn, Lee. "Satchel Might Be Gaining on Us." *Atlanta*, August 1980, 79ff.
Washington, Chester. "Interview with Johnnie Craig." *Pittsburgh Courier*, 24 April 1937.
Webber, H.B. "Paige Deal Hangs Fire with Owners." *Norfolk Journal and Guide*, 23 April 1938, 7.
Wheatley, Tom. "Who Was Satchel Paige and Why Do They Still Talk About Him?" *Beckett Monthly* (September 1989): 75–77.
White, Gordon S. Jr. "Mr. Paige Keeps 'Em Low and Away at Stadium." *New York Times*, 21 August 1961, 27.
Whiteside, Larry. "Catching a Negro League Legend by the Tale." *Boston Globe*, 20 August 1991.
"White Racism Kept Them Out of Big Leagues." *Jet*, 22 July 1971, 48–49.
"Winter Baseball Season on Today." *Los Angeles Times*, 24 October 1943, 19.
"With No Baseball, It's Mighty Lonesome Winter for Ol' Satch." *The Bismarck Tribune*, 3 January 1949.
Wolf, Al. "Paige Touted the Greatest." *Los Angeles Times*, 2 April 1961, G2.
Woodward, Stanley. "Satchel's Ambition." *Negro Digest*, August 1943, 41–43.
"World Series stars to Play in Exhibition Game." *Cleveland Call and Post*, 20 October 1934.
Young, A.S. "A Black Athlete in the Golden Age of Sports." *Ebony*, March 1969, 122–132.
Young, Fay. "Paige Threatens Not to Hurl in All-Star Classic." *Chicago Defender*, 5 August 1944.
———. "'Satch' Baseball's Great Drawing Card." *Chicago Defender*, 28 May 1949, 20.
———. "Satchel Paige Magnificently Defeats Sox." *Chicago Defender*, 21 August 1948, 10.
———. "23,000 Watch Paige Subdue Clowns, 6–1." *Chicago Defender*, 7 September 1946, 11.
Young, Frank A. "48,000 See East All-Stars Beat Paige and West." *Chicago Defender*, 22 August 1942, 19.
———. "Satchel Paige Not Eligible for 1940 East-West Baseball Classic." *Chicago Defender*, 3 August 1940.
"Young Men Keep Paige from Majors." *Washington Post*, 17 July 1960, C3.

Robinson, Jackie

Adler, David A. *Jackie Robinson: He Was the First*. New York: Holiday House, 1989.

Albaugh, Dan. "Ben Chapman: Jackie Robinson's Worst Nightmare." *Sports Collectors Digest*, 26 September 1997, 146–147.
Albom, Mitch. "All Should Celebrate Robinson." *The Free Lance-Star* (Fredericksburg, Va.), 15 April 1997, B1, B5.
Allen, Harold C. "Jackie Robinson." In *Great Black Americans*. West Haven, Conn.: Pendulum Press, 1971, 97–126.
Allen, Lee, and Thomas Meany. "Jackie Robinson." In *Kings of the Diamond*. New York: G.P. Putnam, 1965, 130–133.
Allen, Maury. *Jackie Robinson: A Life Remembered*. New York: Franklin Watts, 1987.
Alvarez, Mark. *The Official Baseball Hall of Fame Story of Jackie Robinson*. New York: Little, Simon, 1990.
Amedio, Steve. "Fans Accepted Kalbaugh's Teammates in '46." *Schenectady Gazette* (N.Y.), 6 April 1997.
Anderson, Dave. "The Days That Brought the Barrier Down." *New York Times*, 30 March 1997.
———. "Erskine Recalls Lessons Learned from Jackie Robinson and His Own Son." *New York Times*, 14 February 2005, D8.
———. "Jackie Robinson, First Black in Major League Dies." *New York Times*, 25 October 1972.
———. "How the First Black Came to Brooklyn: A Scout Remembers." *New York Times*, 30 March 1997.
———. "Robinson Loved Playing in St. Louis." *New York Times*, 24 October 1985, 24.
———. "Robinson 'Stood Up for What He Believed.'" *New York Times*, 1 April 1997, B14.
Angell, Roger. "Designated Hero." *The New Yorker*, 15 September 1997, 82–88.
Appel, Marty. "True Blue." *Beckett Vintage Sports* (April 1997): 70–72, 74.
Araton, Harvey. "There's Room for More Than One Local Hero." *New York Times*, 27 April 1997.
Ardolino, Frank. "Breaking the Color Line: Five Film Representations of Jackie Robinson 1950–1992." *Aethlon* 13, no. 2 (Spring 1996): 49–60.
———. "Jackie Robinson Plays Football in Hawaii." *The National Pastime* 15 (1995): 68–70.
"Are They Ganging Up on Jackie?" *Our World* 9 (August 1954): 42–46.
Atkin, Ross. "The Enduring Legacy of Jackie Robinson." *Christian Science Monitor*, 28 February 1995.
Bacharach, Phil. "'He Had a Statement to Make.'" *Oklahoma Gazette*, 17 April 1997, 4–7.

(**Robinson, Jackie,** continued)
Bacon, John U. "Courage Under Fire." *The Detroit News,* 13 April 1997, 1A, 8A.
_____. "Robinson Helped White Americans Confront Prejudices, Weaknesses." *The Detroit News,* 13 April 1997, 8A.
_____. "Steal Away Home." *The Detroit News,* 13 April 1997, 1D, 11D.
"Bankhead, Doby, Campy, Robinson." *Our World* (April 1948): 46.
Barber, Walter "Red." *1947: When All Hell Broke Loose in Baseball.* New York: Doubleday, 1982.
_____. "Lead-Off Man." *New Republic,* 4 July 1983, 28–31.
"Baseball Great Honored." *The Daily Sun* (Ga.), 28 August 1997, A-3.
"Baseball Retires Number to Honor Jackie Robinson." *Akron Beacon Journal* (Ohio), 16 April 1997.
"Baseball to Honor Robinson." *Chicago Defender,* 6 March 2004, 42.
Baye, Betty Winston. "Remembering the Specialness of Jackie Robinson." Gannett News Service, 4 April 1997.
Beaton, Rod. "Players Hail Robinson Tribute." *USA Today,* 16 April 1997, C1.
Beaufort, John. "Jackie Robinson's Breakthrough." *Christian Science Monitor,* 1 December 1981.
Benjamin, Peter. "Then and Now." *New York Times Magazine,* 15 April 1962, 84–86.
Bennet, James. "Clinton Honors Robinson Amid Talks to Kids and Politicians." *New York Times,* 16 April 1997.
Berkow, Ira. "Dixie Walker Recalls Robinson Breakthrough." *New York Times,* 10 December 1981, 29.
_____. "Jackie Robinson, Who's That?" *New York Times,* 10 December 1989, S3.
_____. "Larry Doby: He Crossed Color Barrier, Only, He Was the Second." *New York Times,* 23 February 1997.
_____. "Larry Doby: An Overlooked Black Pioneer in the A.L." *Baseball Digest* (July 1997): 66–70.
_____. "No. Robinson Wasn't First." *The New York Times,* 6 April 1997, E3.
_____. "So Large a Sports Hero, He Filled the Screen." *New York Times,* 13 April 1997, 19.
Bernstein, Richard. "Admiring an American Hero from a Distance." *New York Times,* 17 October 1997.
"The Biggest Change of All." *The Detroit Free Press,* 28 March 1997, 12–15H.
Bims, Hamilton. J. "Black America Says Goodbye, Jackie." *Ebony* 28 (December 1972): 173ff.
Bock, Hal. "Baseball Honors Robinson." *Canton Repository* (Ohio), 16 April 1997, C1, C4.
_____. "Black Tips Hat to Robinson." *Massillon Independent* (Ohio), 16 April 1997.
_____. "In 1947, Baseball and America Changed Forever." *The Downtown* (Brooklyn, N.Y.), 28 March–3 April 1997, 1, 3.
_____. "Robinson's Legacy Lives On." *The Ann Arbor News,* 30 March 1997.
_____. "Slaughter: Spiking of Jackie Accidental." *The Record* (Hackensack, N.J.), 5 April 1997, S-3.
_____. "Two Have Gone Where No One Has Before." *Canton Repository* (Ohio), 15 April 1997, C1, C3.
Bodley, Hal. "Clinton: He'd Be Proud." *USA Today,* 16 April 1997, 3C.
Bondy, Filip. "Robby Still a Step Ahead." *NY Daily News,* 27 February 1997.
Bonner, Mary G. "Jackie Robinson." In *Baseball Rookies Who Made Good.* New York: Alfred A. Knopf, 1954, 131–139.
Bowen, C.D. "A Quarter Century: Its Human Triumphs." *Look,* 5 December 1961, 97 98.
"Branch Breaks the Ice: Brooklyn Signs Jack Roosevelt Robinson, Negro Shortstop." *Time,* 5 November 1945, 77.
Brandt, Keith. *Jackie Robinson: A Life of Courage.* Mahwah, N.J.: Troll Associates, 1992.
Brigham, Bob. "Welcome Home, Jackie." *The Diamond Angle* (Summer 1998): 14–15.
Briley, Ron. "Do Not Go Gently into That Good Night." In *Jackie Robinson: Race, Sports and the American Dream.* New York: M.E. Sharpe, 1998, 193–204.
_____. "Ten Years After: The Baseball Establishment, Race and Jackie Robinson." In *The Cooperstown Symposium on Baseball and American Culture, 1997.* Ed. Peter M. Rutkoff. Jefferson, N.C.: McFarland, 2001, 137–151.
Brockenbury, L.I. "Tales of Two Brothers, Jack and Mack Robinson." *Sepia* 10 (October 1962), 66–72.
Broeg, Bob. "Jackie Robinson." In *Superstars of Baseball,* 201–208. St. Louis: The Sporting News, 1971.
"Brooklyn Dodgers Sign First Negro to Play for Organized Baseball." *Life,* 26 November 1945, 133–134.
"Brooklyn's Three Brown Bums." *Our World,* 1 September 1946, 51–53.
Broom, Larry. "The Jackie Robinson Case." In *Sport and Society: An Anthology,* ed. J.T. Talamini and C.H. Page. Boston: Little, Brown and Co., 1973, 234–240.
Brosnan, Jim. "Jackie Robinson." In *Great Rookies of the Major Leagues.* New York: Random House, 1966, 9–25.
Brown, Jim. "Jim Brown Questions If It Was Robinson or Rickey Who Broke Baseball's

Color Barrier." *Los Angeles Sentinel*, 22 February 2006.
Brown, Joseph H. "Jackie Robinson's Spirit Lives On After 50 Years." *Tampa Tribune Times*, 5 October 1997.
Brown, Ray B. "Jackie Robinson." In *Contemporary Heroes and Heroines*. Detroit: Gale Research, 1990, 331–336.
Brown, William. *Baseball's Fabulous Montreal Royals*. Robert Davies Publishing, 1996.
Brubaker, J. "Small Beginning." *New Republic*, 9 June 1947, 38.
Brunt, Stephen. "Robinson Legacy Involves Issues Worth Examining." *The Globe and Mail*, 15 April 1997.
Burchard, S.H. "Jackie Robinson." In *Book of Baseball Greats*. New York: Harcourt, Brace, Jovanovich, 1983, 36–39.
Burnes, Brian. "Heroes in Another Field." *Kansas City Star*, 29 August 1983, 1B, 6B.
Burroughs, Todd. "Jackie Robinson and the Black Press." *Jackson Advocate* (Miss.), 20–26 March 1997, 2C, 4C.
Butler, Hal. "Jackie Robinson." In *Sports Heroes Who Wouldn't Quit*. New York: Julian Messner, 1978, 43–53.
"Buttoned Lip." *Newsweek*, 21 April 1947, 88.
Cable, Dale. *Jackie Robinson and the Integration of Organized Baseball*. Senior thesis, Allegheny College, Meadville, Pa., 1979.
Campbell, Bob. "Jackie Robinson Inspires New Plan." *The Star Ledger* (Newark), 2 March 1990, 41, 48.
"Can Jackie Make the Hall of Fame?" *Negro History Bulletin* 17 (October 1953): 6.
Caple, Jim. "The Legacy, Jackie Robinson." *St. Paul Pioneer Press*, 30 March 1997, 1–3N.
"Capture the Pioneer Spirit." *Instructor* 104, no. 3 (October 1994): 36.
Carpenter, Les. "Jackie's Test." *Seattle Times*, n.d.
Carpozi, George Jr. "A Commemorative Tribute to an American Hero." Vol. 1, no. 1. New York: Princeton Publishing Co., 1997.
Carroll, Jeff. "A Tale of One City." *Northwest Indiana Times*, 22 September 2004.
Cauz, Louis. "Robinson Missed Managing in the Majors." *The Globe and Mail*, 15 April 1997.
Chass, Murray. "Standing by Her Man, Always with Elegance." *New York Times*, 16 April 1997, B11, B13.
Chenier, Robert P. *Before Jackie Robinson: African-American Athletes in Northern Ohio*. M.A. thesis, Kent State University, 1993.
Christopher, Peter. "Jackie Robinson Led the Way." *Scholastic News* 53, no. 5 (February 1997): 2–3.

Cipriano, Ralph. "Mural Lends a Larger-than-life Look at Legend's Legacy." *Philadelphia Inquirer*, 7 August 1997.
"Clinton Joins Celebration of Robinson." *Pittsburgh Post-Gazette*, 16 April 1997, D1, D3.
"Clinton to Attend Robinson Ceremony." *The Record* (Hackensack, N.J.), 26 February 1997, S-3.
Cohen, Barbara. *Thank You, Jackie Robinson*. New York: Lothrop, 1988. (Fiction)
Coleman, Leonard. "The Man Who Gave Baseball Its Soul." *The Sporting News*, 14 April 1997, 7.
____. "N.L. President Coleman Reflects on the Impact of Jackie Robinson." *Los Angeles Times*, 13 April 1997.
Collier, Gene. "Young Pirates Praise Robinson." *Pittsburgh Post-Gazette*, 16 April 1997, D-3.
Collins, Noelle. "Jackie's Year." *American Legacy* (Spring 1997): 20.
Conlin, Bill. "The Day That Changed the World." *Philadelphia Daily News*, 9 April 1997, 6–9.
____. "You Watched in Awe." *Philadelphia Daily News*, 9 April 1997, 20–21.
Cope, Myron. "Jackie Robinson." In *Great American Athletes of the 20th Century*, ed. Zanger Hollander. New York: Random House, 1966, 124–127.
"Cosby Pays Tribute to Jackie Robinson." *The Wichita Eagle*, 11 February 1997.
Cose, Ellis. "The House That Jack Built." *Newsweek*, 14 April 1997, 58.
Cossell, Howard. "Great Moments in Sport: Jackie Breaks the Barrier." *Sport* 31 (June 1961): 78–91.
Coutros, Pete. "Brooklyn, Waiting for Jackie Robinson." *New York Post*, 15 April 1997, 8, 125.
Craft, David. "A Swell Jackie Robinson Video and a Controversial 'Prime 9.'" *Sports Collectors Digest*, 26 September 1997, 156–157.
Creamer, Robert. "The Daring Jackie Robinson Had the Stamp of a Very Special Ballplayer." *Sports Illustrated* 1 November 1982, 99–100.
____. "Perspective." *Sports Illustrated*, 1 November 1983, 99–100.
Curvin, Robert. "Remembering Jackie Robinson." *New York Times Magazine*, 4 April 1982, 46.
Daley, Arthur. "Between Two Putouts." *Baseball Digest* (March 1957): 72–75.
____. "Jackie Robinson." In *Sports of the Times*, 113 115. New York: E.P. Dutton, 1959.
____. "Play Ball!" *New York Times*, 15 April 1947.
Daniel, Dan. "Negro Player Issue Heads for

(Robinson, Jackie, continued)
Showdown." *Sporting News*, 1 November 1945.
Davids, Hal. "The Court-Martial of Lt. Jackie Robinson: Fifty Years Later, a Defense Lawyer Remembers his Client — the Future Baseball Legend." *National Law Journal* 17, no. 3 (19 September 1994): A12.
Davidson, Margaret. *The Story of Jackie Robinson: Bravest Man in Baseball.* New York: Dell Publishing, 1988.
Davis, David. "Fifty Years Later." *LA Weekly*, 12–18 December 1997, 58.
Davis, Reyn. "He Played Here, Now He's in the Hall." *Winnipeg Free Press*, 11 March 1997, C1.
Dawidoff, Nicholas T. "Recalling Jackie Robinson; Carl Erskine Visits an Exhibition Celebrating His Teammate." *Sports Illustrated*, 28 September 1987, 70ff.
Deford, Frank. "Crossing the Bar." *Newsweek*, 14 April 1997, 53–55.
_____. "40 Years Later; What Began with Jackie Robinson Is Not Yet Done." *Sports Illustrated*, 22 December 1986, 172.
Delaney, Paul. "Rooting for What Really Mattered." *New York Times*, 20 April 1997.
Denenberg, Barry. *Stealing Home: The Story of Jackie Robinson.* New York: Scholastic Books, 1990.
Dexter, Charles. *Baseball Has Done It.* New York: Lippincott Co., 1964.
DiTrani, Vinny. "When Jackie Robinson Broke Down the Barriers." *Baseball Digest* 46 (August 1987): 64–69.
"Dodgers Call Up Jackie Robinson, Negro Infielder." *The Miami Herald*, 9 February 1997.
"The Dodgers Jackie Robinson: All-American Hero." *Los Angeles Sentinel*, 21 May 1997.
"Does the Best Team Win?" *Quick News Weekly*, 10 April 1950.
Dolgan, Bob. "Sportswriter Helped Robinson Face Hostility." *Cleveland Plain Dealer*, 27 April 1997, 5C.
Donnellon, Sam. "The Learning Process Continues." *Philadelphia Daily News*, 9 April 1997, 44–45.
_____. "The Ones Who Followed." *Philadelphia Daily News*, 9 April 1997, 42–43.
Dorinson, Joseph, and Joram Warmund. *Jackie Robinson: Race, Sports and the American Dream.* Armonk, N.Y.: M.E. Sharpe, 1998.
Dougherty, Bill. "The Jackie Robinson of Today." *Baseball Digest* 10 (July 1951): 25–27.
Douglass, Gualterio. "Se Espera Que Invitenal Circuito Mexicano." *Excelsior*, 6 March 1946, 14.
Dowling, Tom. "Jackie Robinson 25 Years Later." *Baseball Digest* 31 (March 1972): 72–75.
Doyle, Paul. "Walking in His Footsteps, Wearing 42." *The Hartford Courant*, 15 April 1997, G11.
Dreier, Peter. "Remembering Jackie Robinson." *Tikkun* (Mar./Apr. 1997): 32ff.
Drees, Jack and Mullen, Jim C. *Where Is He Now?* Jonathan David Publishers, 1973.
Duckett, Alfred. "The American Family Robinson." *Sepia* 22 (January 1973): 28–33.
Durslag, Melvin. "Leo Durocher and Jackie Robinson." *TV Guide*, 24 July 1965, 12–13.
Durso, Joseph. "Jackie Robinson and His Legacy." *New York Times*, 12 April 1987.
Dwyre, Bill. "Racing into History." *Los Angeles Times*, 15 April 1997.
Early, Gerald. "American Integration, Black Heroism, and the Meaning of Jackie Robinson." *The Chronicle of Higher Education*, 23 May 1997, B4–B5.
Edes, Gordon. "Opening a New, Wide World: Robinson's Impact Felt Well Beyond the Chalk Lines." *The Boston Globe*, 28 March 1997.
Editor, "A Day in the Life of Jackie Robinson." *Ebony*, 1 August 1958, 90–94.
"Editorial: Challenge to Jackie Robinson." *Sporting News*, 26 December 1956.
"Editorial: Chandler and the Negro Baseball Problem." *Sporting News*, 31 January 1946.
"Editorial: Montreal Puts Negro Player on Spot." *Sporting News*, 1 November 1945.
"Editorial: A Negro in the Major Leagues." *Sporting News*, 23 April 1947.
"Editorial: No Good from Raising Race Issue." *Sporting News*, 8 August 1942.
"El Peregrinaje de Jackie Robinson." *El Nuevo Herald*, 9 February 1997.
Eldridge, Larry. "The Legacy of Robinson and Aaron." *Christian Science Monitor*, 3 August 1982, 10.
Enders, Eric. "A Legacy Remembered." *Austin American-Statesman*, 15 April 1997, A1, A12.
Epstein, Samuel, and Sue. *Jackie Robinson*. Garrard Publishing Co., 1974.
Erskine, Carl. *What I Learned from Jackie Robinson*. New York: McGraw-Hill, 2005.
"Everybody's Hero." *Ebony*, 1 August 1959, 25–32.
Falkner, David. *Great Time Coming: The Life of Jackie Robinson from Baseball to Birmingham*. New York: Simon and Schuster, 1995.
Farr, Naunerle C. *Babe Ruth, Jackie Robinson*. West Haven, Conn.: Pendulum Press, 1979.
"Faster Than Jackie Robinson: Branch Rickey's Sermon's on the Mound." *New York Times*, 13 April 1997.

Fernandez, Bernard. "The Definition of Daring." *Philadelphia Daily News*, 9 April 1997, 22–23.
_____. "One Very Special Friendship." *Philadelphia Daily News*, 9 April 1997, 32–33.
"50 Years, Still Fears: Smithsonian Unveils Special Robinson Show." *Los Angeles Times*, 15 April 1997.
Fetter, Henry. "The Party Line and the Color Line: The American Communist Party, the Daily Worker and Jackie Robinson." *Journal of Sport History* (Fall 2001): 375–402.
Fisher, Marc. "Baseball Honors Robinson 50 Years after Debut." *Albany Times Union*, 28 February 1997, C1, C7.
_____. "Jackie Robinson's Continuing Star Power." *The Washington Post National Weekly Edition*, 14 April 1997, 17.
_____. "Robinson Honors Abound for 50-Year Anniversary." *Washington Post* 27 February 1997, C2.
"The Flaws in the Diamonds." *The Economist*, 18 January 1997, 81–83.
Flynn, James J. "Jackie Robinson." In *Negroes of Achievement in Modern America*. New York: Dodd, Mead, 1970, 121–137.
Foner, Henry. "A Celebration of Jackie Robinson." *Jewish Currents*, October 1997, 20.
Foster, Terry. "Jackson Calls for Scrutiny as Robinson Is Celebrated." *The Detroit News*, 16 April 1997.
Frassinelli, Mike. "In Robinson's Footsteps." *The Morning Call* (Allentown), 25 February 2002.
"Friends Recall Jackie Robinson." *Jet*, 16 November 1972, 51–57.
"From First to Fame: Jackie Robinson." *Ebony* 17 (October 1962): 85–86.
Frommer, Harvey. *Jackie Robinson*. New York: Watts, 1984.
_____. *Rickey and Robinson: The Men Who Broke Baseball's Color Line*. New York: Macmillan Publishing Co., Inc., 1982.
Furillo, Bud. "Jackie Robinson: Remembering the Man That Changed Baseball." *Dodger Blue* 7 (15 April 1987): 30.
Gaven, Michael. "Jackie Robinson's Sore Arm." *Baseball Digest* 14 (September 1955): 77–82.
Gelberg, Jon. "Widow Says Jackie Robinson Would Frown on '97 Situation." *Newark Star-Ledger*, 27 February 1997.
Germain, David. "Biopic on Jackie Robinson in the Works." Associated Press, 29 March 2005.
Gietschier, Steven P. "The Week That Was." *The Sporting News*, 14 April 1997, 61.
Gittrich, Greg, and Stephen McFarland. "Locals Say Bill Should Be There." *New York Daily News*, 10 February 1997.

"A Golden Night for Jackie." *NY Daily News*, 10 February 1997.
Golenbeck, Peter. *Bums*. New York: Putnam, 1984.
_____. *Teammates*. San Diego: Gulliver Books, 1990.
"Good Citizens Make Good Communities." *Scholastic*, 13 December 1950, 5.
Goren, Herb. "Are They Giving Jackie Robinson the Works?" *Baseball Digest* 14 (September 1955): 77–82.
_____. "Do the Dodgers Miss Jackie Robinson?" *Baseball Digest* 16 (August 1957): 51–55.
_____. "Jackie Robinson Himself Now." *Baseball Digest* 7 (October 1948), 65–69.
Grabowski, Jack F. *Baseball Legends: Jackie Robinson*. Intro. by Jim Murray. New York: Chelsea House, 1991.
Grady, Sandy. "We're All Robinson's Children." *USA Today*, 3 April 1997, 13A.
Grant, Adam. "Here's to You, Jackie Robinson." *Scholastic News* 20, no.9, 14 February 1997, 6–10.
Gray, Paul. "Busting the Color Line." *Time*, 20 October 1997, 107.
Greene, Carol. *Jackie Robinson: Baseball's First Black Major Leaguer*. Chicago: Children's Press, 1990.
Griffin, Richard. "Jackie Robinson: A Portrait in Courage." *Toronto Star*, 1 June 1996, B5ff.
_____. "Jackie Robinson's Real Anniversary." *World Press Review* 43, no. 8 (August 1996): 38ff.
Grimsley, William. "Jackie Robinson." In *101 Great Athletes*, 249–251. Bonanza Books, 1987.
_____. "Jackie Robinson Lists Negro All-Star Baseball Team on Back of Paper Napkin." *The Gettysburg Times*, 30 July 1972, 15.
Grisamore, Ed. "Robinson's Birthplace Just a Fading Memory." *Macon Telegraph* (Summer 1995).
Gross, Joe. "Sports Comment: Jackie Robinson Was Right Man to Complete Quest." *The Capital* (Annapolis, Md.), 9 February 2003, C11.
Gross, Milton. "The Emancipation of Jackie Robinson." *Sport*, 1 October 1951, 80–85.
_____. "Why They Boo Jackie Robinson." *Sport* 14 (February 1953): 10–13.
Gutman, Bill. *Famous Baseball Stars: Jackie Robinson*. New York: Dodd, Mead and Co., 1973.
"Guts Enough Not to Fight Back." *Akron Beacon Journal*, 13 April 1997.
Hageman, William. "Chicago's 55-Year-Old Secret: Jackie Robinson's Tryout with the White Sox." *Chicago Tribune*, 26 March 1997, 1, 7.

(Robinson, Jackie, continued)
Hagen, Paul. "The Greatest Second Baseman Ever?" *Philadelphia Daily News*, 9 April 1997, 24–25.
Halberstam, David. "Jackie Robinson." *Sport* 77 (December 1986): 10–14.
"A Half Century Later: An American Hero; The Jackie Robinson Story." *Los Angeles Sentinel*, 30 April 1997.
Hall, Alvin. *The Cooperstown Symposium on Baseball and American Culture 1997 (Jackie Robinson)*. Ed. Peter M. Rutkoff. Jefferson, N.C.: McFarland, 2000.
Hand, Jack. "Dodger Boss Confident Negro Star Will Click." *Washington Post*, 25 October 1945, 12.
Harris, Elliott. "Recollections of Robinson." *Chicago Sun Times*, 11 May 1997, 6A.
Harris, Mark. "Jackie Robinson: Major League Baseball's First Black." *TV Guide*, 6 August 1977, 10–14.
_____. "Where've You Gone, Jackie Robinson?" *The Nation*, 15 May 1995, 674.
Head, John. "Great Granddaddy Versus Jackie Robinson." *Southern Exposure* (Fall 1979): 14–18.
_____. "Incomparable: Tiger's Terrific, but He's Nothing Like Jackie." *The Atlanta Journal and Constitution*, 2 May 1997.
Heller, Dick. "Jackie Was in a League of His Own." *The Washington Times*, 16 April 1997, B1, B5.
Henerson, Evan. "Hitting with Power." *The Daily News of Los Angeles*, 28 September 2001, L16.
Henry, Patrick. "Jackie Robinson: Athlete and American Par Excellence." *The Virginia Quarterly Review* (Spring 1997): 189–203.
Herwig, Carol. "Recollections of Robinson Hit Shelves for Summer." *USA Today*, 18 April 1997.
Herzog, Brad. "A Homerun for the Ages." *Sports Illustrated*, 1 April 1996, 1ff.
Hewitt, Brian. "An Untold Story: Jackie Robinson and a Kid's Heart." *Chicago Sun Times*, 5 April 1987.
Hofmann, Rich. "Lessons of a Legend." *Philadelphia Daily News*, 9 April 1997, 3–5.
Holcomb, Todd. "'We Were Trailblazers for Jackie Robinson': Year of the Black Crackers; Moore, 80, Is Last Survivor of the '38 Team." *The Atlanta Journal and Constitution*, 27 June 1997.
Hollander, Zander. *Great American Athletes of the Twentieth Century*. New York: Random House, 1966, 124–127.
Holmes, Tommy. "'We Looked at Him and There He Was.'" *St. Louis Post-Dispatch*, 27 June 1949.

Holway, John B. "Before You Could Say Jackie Robinson: Black Players." *Look* 35, 13 July 1971, 46–50.
"Hot Stove League." *Time*, 6 February 1950, 69.
Hughes, Langston. "Jackie Robinson." In *Famous American Negroes*, 139–144. New York: Dodd, Mead, 1954.
"Humble Heroics." *Newsweek*, 9 February 2004, 12.
"Hurray for Jackie Robinson." *Negro History Bulletin* (January 1955): 93.
"In His Debt: The Legacy of Jackie Robinson." *Altoona Mirror* (Pa.), 16 April 1997, A5.
"An Interview with Jackie Robinson." *Black Sports* (August 1977): 8–11, 39, 60, 62.
"Jack Robinson, First Negro Ever Admitted to Organized Baseball Signed by Rickey." *The Herald-Press*, 24 October 1945, 7.
"Jackie: He Changed Baseball." *Philadelphia Daily News*, 9 April 1997, Special Section, 1–56.
"Jackie Can Play First Base and Bat Too." *Our World* (May 1947): 28–30.
"Jackie Robinson: Athlete and American Par Excellence." *Virginia Quarterly Review* (Spring 2006).
"Jackie Robinson: A Commercial Hit 50 Years Later." *New York Amsterdam News*, 3 May 1997.
"Jackie Robinson—Baseball Superstar." *Atlanta Inquirer*, 12 April 1997.
"Jackie Robinson 50th Anniversary Celebration." Commemorative Edition, New York Mets, 15 April 1997.
"Jackie Robinson: The First Black Man to Play Major League Baseball." *Washington Post Magazine*, 12 April 1987, 34A.
"Jackie Robinson Gave His Life for Integration, Says Negro Leagues Player." *Italian Voice*, 26 May 2005.
"Jackie Robinson: A Man for All Seasons." *Crisis* 79 (December 1972): 345–49.
"Jackie Robinson: The Man, the Athlete, the Legacy." *New York Daily News* Special Tribute, 13 April 1997.
"Jackie Robinson Paige's Protégé." *Waterloo Courier*, 25 October 1945, 13.
"Jackie Robinson Pitching." *Newsweek*, 1 August 1949, 18–19.
"Jackie Robinson Scores Big in Business." *Sepia* 15 (June 1966): 52–56.
"Jackie Robinson: Un Ejemplo Humano." *El Mundo* (Oakland), 17 April 1997.
"Jackie Robinson Was the Right Man to Complete Quest." *The Sunday Capital*, 9 February 2003, C-11.
"Jackie Robinson's All Stars Win." *The Berkshire County Eagle*, 19 October 1949.

"Jackie Robinson's Doubleplay." *Life*, 28 May 1950, 129–132.

"Jackie Robinson's Team Beats Major Leaguers, 10–5." *Chicago Defender*, 19 October 1946, 11.

"Jackie's Still Busting Records." *Post-Tribune* (Gary, Ind.), 18 July 1997.

Jewell, Anthony. "A Player Remembers: 50 Years After Jackie Robinson's Debut." *Los Angeles Sentinel*, 1 August 1996.

Johnson, Chuck. "Baseball Says Robinson's Number Belongs to Ages." *USA Today*, 16 April 1997, 1C.

_____. "Rachel Robinson's Memoirs Tell of Love at First Sight." *USA Today*, 16 April 1997, C2.

_____. "Robinson's Legacy Lives." *USA Today*, 18 December 1997, 9C.

_____. "Salute to Robinson Includes $1M Pledge." *USA Today*, 27 February 1997, 8C.

Johnson, Spencer. *The Value of Courage: The Story of Jackie Robinson.* La Jolla, California: Value Communications, 1977.

Kahn, Roger. "Jackie Robinson." *Sport* 71 (December 1971): 64–87.

_____. "The Jackie Robinson I Remember." *Philadelphia Daily News*, 9 April 1997, and in *Journal of Blacks in Higher Education*, Winter 1996–97, 88–93.

_____. "The Ten Years of Jackie Robinson." *Sport* 20 (October 1955): 12–13.

Kashatus, William. "Baseball's Noble Experiment." *American History* (April 1997): 32–37, 56–61.

Kauffman, Bill. "Jackie Robinson—Pioneer and Destroyer." *The American Enterprise* 8 (July/August 1997): 80–81.

Kavanaugh, Lee Hill. "Did You Hear Jackie Robinson Sell That Disc?" *Kansas City Star*, 1 November 1997, E5.

Kiley, Kathy. "Politicians Remember Robinson's Impact." *USA Today*, 3 March 2005.

Keiser, Bob. "Don Newcombe, Sammie Haynes Remember Jackie Robinson the Man." *Tribune News Service*, 22 April 1997.

Kelley, William G. "Jackie Robinson and the Press." *Journalism Quarterly* (April 1976): 137–139.

Kennedy, Kostya. "Rachel Robinson: Jackie's Widow Discusses Their Life Together." *Sports Illustrated*, 16 September 1996, 18.

Kindred, David. "An Eternal Gesture Will Get an Enduring Honor." *Austin American*, 9 April 2002.

_____. "Jackie Robinson: One Man, Alone." *The Sporting News*, 14 April 1997, 6.

Kisner, Ronald E., and M. Cordell Thompson. "Troubles Cease for Robinson After 53 Years." *Jet* 43, no. 7, 9 November 1972, 46–59.

Klein, Frederick C. "A Hero Beyond the Ballpark." *Wall Street Journal*, 17 October 1997.

Koenig, Bill. "Crossing the Line: The Day Jackie Robinson Rewrote History." *USA Today Baseball Weekly*, 9–15 April 1997, 8–11.

Kuenster, John. "Jackie Robinson: His National Import Was Greater than Ruth's." *Baseball Digest* 35 (July 1976): 14–20.

Lamb, Chris. "I Never Want to Take Another Trip Like This One: Jackie Robinson's Trip to Integrate Baseball." *Journal of Sport History* 24 (Summer 1997): 177–191.

Lardner, John. "Reese and Robinson: Team within a Team." *New York Times Magazine*, 10 September 1949, 17.

"Laurels and Leverage." *Time*, 28 November 1949, 40.

Lemke, Bob. "Robinson Commemoratives Expected to Flourish in '97." *Sports Collectors Digest*, 7 March 1997, 52–54.

Lester, Larry. "The Life of Jackie Robinson: His Hardships and Triumphs." Commemorative Program, April 15, 1997, 9, 11, 13.

Libby, Bill. "Jackie Robinson." In *Heroes of the Hot Corner*. New York: Watts, 1972, 83–85.

Lipsyte, Robert. "Three Anniversaries, and Three Heroes." *New York Times*, 28 December 1997, 11.

_____. "What Would Jackie Robinson Say Today? Plenty." *New York Times*, 6 April 1997, 9.

Litke, Jim. "Remembering Robinson ... and the Negro League Legacy." *North Jersey Daily Record*, 21 February 1997.

Lopez, John P. "He Was More Than Game." *Minneapolis Star Tribune*, 15 April 1997.

Lupica, Mike. "To Honor Jackie." *NY Daily News*, 10 February 1997, 2–3.

_____. "A Night for Remembering Robinson." *The Record* (Hackensack, N.J.) 16 April 1997, S-3.

_____. "Now Batting For Brooklyn..." *Esquire* (April 1997): 95–98.

Mann, Arthur. *The Jackie Robinson Story*. New York: Low, 1950 (reprint, New York: Grosset and Dunlap, 1951).

_____. "Jackie an Immortal, Mr. Rickey Knows." *Newsday*, 28 June 1962.

_____. "Say Jack Robinson: Meet the Dodgers' Newest Recruit." *Colliers*, 2 March 1946, 67–68.

_____. "Truth about the Jackie Robinson Case." *Saturday Evening Post*, 13 May 1950, 19–21, 36.

_____. "24 Letterman." *Negro Digest* (May 1946): 31–35.

(**Robinson, Jackie,** continued)
Marasco, David. "Before Jackie." *The Diamond Angle* (October 1998): 16.
Marsh, Michael. "Smith Helped Jackie Along." *Chicago Sun Times*, 30 March 1997.
Massaquoi, Hans. "The Breakthrough Stars." *Ebony* 47, no. 10 (August 1992): 44ff.
Mayo, Jonathan. "Robinson Foundation Jackie's Lasting Legacy." *New York Post*, 15 April 1997, 10.
Maxwell, Jocko. "Robinson's the Name for 1947." *Baseball Digest*, 10 April 1946, 57–58.
McCollum, Sean. "Jackie Robinson: Leading the Way." *Scholastic Update*, 11 April 1997, 18–19.
McGowan, Lloyd. "Robinson Rivets Royal Keystone Job on Hitting, Fielding and Base-Stealing." *The Sporting News*, 5 June 1946, 19.
Meany, Thomas, ed. "Baseball Is a Different Game Now." *Collier's*, 19 August 1955, 38, 40–41.
———. "Does Jackie Robinson Belong in the Hall of Fame?" *Sport* 24 (November 1957): 24–27.
———. "Jackie's One of the Gang Now." *Sport* 7 (August 1949): 24–27.
———. "What Chance Has Jackie Robinson?" *Sport* 2 (January 1947): 12–14.
Menna, Larry K. "Robinson, Jack Roosevelt ('Jackie')." In *Encyclopedia of Ethnicity and Sports in the United States of America*, ed. George Kirsch et al. Westport, Conn.: Greenwood Press, 2000, 385–387.
Mercantini, Jonathan. "Coming Home: Jackie Robinson and the Dodgers Face the Crackers." *Atlanta History* 41 (Fall 1997).
Metcalf, George R. *Black Profiles: Jackie Robinson.* New York: McGraw Hill, 1968.
"Monarch Club Owner Not to Protest Robinson Case." *Washington Post*, 26 October 1945, 14.
"Monarch Owner to File Protest." *Los Angeles Times*, 24 October 1945, 10.
"Montreal Signs Negro Shortstop." *New York Times*, 24 October 1945, 17.
Moore, Terrence. "Thanks, Jackie: Shea Become Center of a National Celebration." *The Atlanta Journal and Constitution*, 16 April 1997.
———. "Too Bad a Few Grumblers Fail to Appreciate Legacy." *The Atlanta Journal and Constitution*, 16 April 1997.
Morse, A.D. "Jackie Wouldn't Have Gotten to 1st Base Without the Determined Mothering of a Quiet Woman." *Better Homes and Gardens* (May 1950): 226.
Mortenson, Tom. "Robinson's Big League Debut Uneventful." *Sports Collectors Digest*, 7 March 1997, 12.

"Most Important Negro in Baseball." *Ebony* (May 1956): 100–104.
Murray, Arch. "How the Post Covered Jackie's First Game." *New York Post*, 15 April 1997, 7.
"Nation Remembers Jackie Robinson's Accomplishment." *Daily Press* (Williamsburg, Va.), 16 April 1997, A1.
Nazel, Joseph G., Jr. *Jackie Robinson: First of a Chosen Few.* Np., nd.
Neal III, La Velle E. "The Original Rally." *The Kansas City Star*, 30 March 1997, J-25.
"Negro Ball Head Offers No Protest." *Lincoln Journal*, 25 October 1945.
"Negro Owner Files Protest." *Lincoln Journal*, 25 October 1945.
Nelson, John. "Robinson Was Target of Conspiracy." *The Herald* (Everett, Wa.), 28 February 1997, 6C.
Newfield, Jack. "Courage Under Fire." *New York Post*, 15 April 1997, 2–3, 126.
"News and Views: Where Have You Gone, Jackie Robinson? In College Baseball the Diamonds Are Almost All White?" *Journal of Blacks in Higher Education*, 31 August 2001.
Newhan, Ross. "Rachel Robinson, She Played a Role, but Don't Believe She Pushed Him." *Los Angeles Times*, 31 March 1997.
Nightengale, Bob. "Here's to You, Jackie: No. 42 Retired." *Los Angeles Times*, 16 April 1997, C6.
———. "It's Not Dodgers' Night." *Los Angeles Times*, 16 April 1997, C1, C6.
———. "Rickey Should Be Remembered." *The Sporting News*, 2 April 1997.
———. "Robinson Plus 50 Adds Up to Discontent." *Los Angeles Times*, 15 April 1997.
"No. Robinson Wasn't First." *The New York Times*, 6 April 1999.
"No Protest Lodged in Robinson Case." *Reno Evening Gazette*, 26 October 1945.
Norwood, Stephen H., and Harold Brackman. "Going to Bat for Jackie Robinson: The Jewish Role in Breaking Baseball's Color Line." *Journal of Sport History* 26 (Spring 1999): 115–54.
O'Connell, T.S. "Jackie's Arrival Signaled the End of the Negro Leagues." *Sports Collectors Digest*, 7 March 1997, 100–103.
O'Connor, Jim. *Jackie Robinson and the Story of All-black Baseball.* New York: Random House, 1948.
Ogden, R. Dale, and J. Ronald Newlin. "Race and Sport in Indiana: Before and After Jackie Robinson." *Hoosierisms Quarterly* 1 (Summer 1996): 9–14.
Olsen, James T. "Jackie Robinson: Pro Ball's First Black Star." *Creative Education*, 1974, 29 pp.

Orr, Jack. *The Black Athlete: His Story in American History*. Lion Press, 1969.
_____. "Jackie Robinson, Symbol of the Revolution." *Sport* 29 (March 1960): 52–59.
Oursler, Fulton. "Rookie of the Year." *Reader's Digest* 52, January–June 1948, 34–38.
_____. "Why I Know There Is a God." *St. Louis Globe-Democrat*, 15 September 1950, 67, 84.
Overmyer, Jim. "Jackie Robinson Breaks the Big League Color Barrier." Temple Anshe Men's Club, Pittsfield, Mass., 6 April 1997.
Palant, Miriam. "Sweats, Shouts and Tears." *New York Post*, 14 May 1950, 24.
Park, Michael Y. "Robinson Statue Is Unveiled." *New Jersey Journal*, 26 February 1998, A1, A4.
Parsons, Dana. "For Lifelong Fan, Jackie Robinson Was a 'Cut Above.'" *Los Angeles Times*, 4 April 1997.
Pietrusza, David. "Robinson's Breakthrough Not First." *USA Today Baseball Weekly*, 10 February 1993, 28.
Pincham, R. Eugene. "Robinson's Milestone Should Be No. 1." *Chicago Sun-Times*, 7 March 2004.
Plaut, David. "Robinson Biography a Worthy Read." *USA Today Baseball Weekly*, 8 October–14 October 1997, 14.
"Player of the Half Century." *Sport* (September 1996): 18.
Pollack, J.K. "Meet a Family Named Robinson." *Parent's Magazine* 30 (October 1955): 46–47.
"Portrait of Jackie Robinson." *Life Magazine*, 21–28 April 1947.
Povich, Shirley. "Breaking the Barrier." *The Washington Post*, 7 April 1997.
Powell, Larry. "Jackie Robinson and Dixie Walker: Myths of the Southern Baseball Player." *Southern Culture* (Summer 2002): 56–71.
Pratkanis, Anthony R., and Marlene E. Turner. "Nine Principles of Successful Affirmative Action: Mr. Branch Rickey, Mr. Jackie Robinson, and the Integration of Baseball." *Nine* (Fall 1994): 36–65.
"A Rainbow Coalition in the Mets' Dugout Thinks About Jackie Robinson." *New York Times*, 2 March 1997.
Ralph, John. "Breaking Barriers: Remembering April 15, 1947." *Jackson Advocate*, 10–16 April 1997, 1–2C.
Rampersad, Arnold. *Jackie Robinson: A Biography*. New York: Alfred A. Knopf, 1997.
Rashad, Ahmad. "50 Years of Blacks in Sports." *Ebony* 51, no. 1: 156ff.
Reddy, Bill. "Keeping Posted with Bill Reddy." *Post-Standard*, 4 June 1945.

Reidenbaugh, Lowell. "Jackie Robinson." In *Cooperstown: Where Baseball's Legends Live Forever*. St Louis: The Sporting News, 1983, 221–222.
Reilly, Edward J. "Robinson, Jack Roosevelt." In *Baseball: An Encyclopedia of Popular Culture*. Calif.: ABC-CLIO, 2000, 226–28.
"Remembering Jackie and Martin." *The Morning Call*, 16 April 2005.
Resnick, Joe. "Jackie Robinson: He Paved the Way for Some of Baseball's Greatest." *Dodgers Scoreboard Magazine* (May 1987): 12–13.
Rice, Grantland. "The Emancipation of Jackie Robinson." *Sport* 11 (October 1951): 12–15.
"Riches for a Rookie." *Time*, 24 November 1947, 54.
Rickey, Branch B. "Rickey and Robinson, Two Men of Conviction, Took a Big Risk with Each Other." *The New York Times*, 3 August 1997, 21.
Ritter, Lawrence. "Jackie Robinson Breaks the Color Barrier." In *The Story of Baseball*. William Morrow, 1983, 43–58.
Rivers, Jeff. "With His Bat, He Bashed the White Lie." *The Hartford Courant*, 15 April 1997, G3.
Robinson, Jackie. File. Research Library, National Baseball Hall of Fame and Museum, Inc., Cooperstown, New York.
Robinson, Jackie. *Baseball Has Done It*. Ed. Charles Dexter. Philadelphia: Lippincott, 1964.
_____. "The Best Advice I Ever Had." *Reader's Digest* 72 (January–June 1958), 214–216.
_____. *Breakthrough to the Big Leagues: The Story of Jackie Robinson*. New York: Harper and Row, 1965.
_____. "A Kentucky Colonel (Pee Wee Reese) Kept Me in Baseball." *Look*, 8 February 1955, 82–84.
_____. "The Most Unforgettable Character I've Met." *Reader's Digest*, October 1961, 97–102.
_____. "My Own Story." *Ebony* 3 (June 1948): 19–24.
_____. "Now I Know Why They Boo Me." *Look* 19, 25 January–22 February 1955, 23–28.
_____. "What's Wrong with Negro Baseball?" *Ebony*, June 1948, 16–18.
_____. "Why I'm Quitting Baseball." *Look* 21, 22 January 1957, 91–92.
Robinson, Jackie, as told to Ed Reid. "Jackie Tells Own Story." *Washington Post*, 27 August 1949, 10–11.
Robinson, Jackie, with Alfred Duckett. *I Never Had It Made*. New York, N.Y.: G.P. Putnam's Sons, 1972.
Robinson, Jackie, with Wendell Smith. *My*

(Robinson, Jackie, continued)
Own Story. New York, N.Y.: Greenburg, 1948.
"Robinson Crosses Line in Daytona Beach." *Orlando Sentinel*, 16 September 1990, C16.
"Robinson for Merit." *Newsweek*, 22 August 1947, 80.
"Robinson Replies to Robeson and Others." *Christian Century*, 3 August 1949, 908.
"Robinson Wins Rickey Scouts' Endorsement." *Chicago Tribune*, 24 October 1945, 27.
Robinson, Rachel. "I Live with a Hero." *Negro Digest* (June 1951): 3–14.
Robinson, Rachel, and Lee Daniels. *Jackie Robinson: An Intimate Portrait*. New York: Harry N. Abrams, Inc., 1996.
Robinson, Sharon. *Stealing Home: An Intimate Family Portrait*. New York: Harper Collins, 1996.
Robinson, Sharon A. "Remembering Jackie Robinson." *Essence* 17 (April 1987), 49.
"Robinson's Legacy Dims on Diamond." *Philadelphia Inquirer*, 13 July 2004.
Roeder, Bill. *Jackie Robinson*. New York: A.S. Barnes, 1950.
Roeder, Bill, and R. Cousins. "All-Star Second Baseman." *Saturday Review of Literature*, 15 July 1950, 10.
"Rookie of the Year." *Time*, 22 September 1947, 70–76.
"Rookie Chases Robinson Off First." *Newport News*, 1 April 1953.
Rosenberg, I.J. "Judging Robinson by the Numbers." *The Atlanta Journal and Constitution*, 13 April 1997.
Rosenthal, Harold. "Are Robbie's Rough Days Over?" *Negro Digest* (September 1950): 19.
_____. "The Story Behind the Story." *The New York Times*, 4 May 1997.
Rothe, Emil H. "Jackie Robinson's Major League Debut." *Baseball Digest* 31 (December 1972): 82–88.
Rowan, Carl T., with Jackie Robinson. *Wait Till Next Year*. New York: Random House, 1960.
Rudeen, Ken. *Jackie Robinson*. New York: Crowell Co., 1971.
Russo, Neal. "Robinson Discovered at 14." *Baseball Digest* 18 (October 1959): 52–55.
Sabin, Francene. *Jackie Robinson*. Mahwah, N.J.: Troll Associates, 1985.
"Safe at First." *Our Sports* (January 1946): 10.
Sailer, Steve. "How Jackie Robinson Desegregated America." *National Review* 48, 8 April 1996, 38ff.
Sandomir, Richard. "A Dissident Can Now Embrace Robinson's Legacy." *New York Times*, 5 April 1997.
_____. "A Hard-Hitting Profile of Robinson on ESPN." *New York Times*, 28 February 1997, B9.
_____. "An Effort to Cherish the Memory of Jackie Robinson." *New York Times*, 23 February 1997.
_____. "Personal Memories of Robinson from Some of Those He Touched." *New York Times*, 4 April 1997.
_____. "In Print, Cheerleading and Indifference." *New York Times*, 13 April 1997, 9.
_____. "Robinson's Image Goes to Market." *New York Times*, 23 February 1997.
_____. "With a Modest Entrance, Robinson Stepped Quietly into History." *New York Times*, 16 April 1997, B1, B13.
"Says Negro 'Outstanding Prospect.'" *Waterloo Courier*, 25 October 1945, 13.
Schmuck, Peter. "Robinson's 42 Retired Forever." *Daily Press* (Va.), 16 April 1997, D1, D5.
Schoor, Gene. *Jackie Robinson, Baseball Hero*. New York: G.P. Putnam's Sons, 1958.
Scott, Richard. *Jackie Robinson*. New York: Chelsea House, 1987.
Serby, Steve. "Safe at Home." *New York Post*, 15 April 1997, 12.
Shapiro, Leonard. "Robinson Special: Old Footage, New Insight." *Washington Post*, 28 February 1997, D9.
Shapiro, Milton. *Jackie Robinson of the Brooklyn Dodgers*. New York: Julian Messner, 1973.
"Shea Ceremony Highlighted by Retirement of Robinson's Number." *The Virginian-Pilot*, 16 April 1997, C1, C7.
Sheed, Wilfred. "And Playing Second Base for Brooklyn ... Jackie Robinson." *Esquire* (December 1983): 82–86.
Sher, Jack. "Jackie Robinson: The Great Experiment." *Sport* 5 (October 1948): 30–33ff.
Shorto, Russell. *Jackie Robinson and the Breaking of the Color Barrier*. Millbrook Press, 1991.
Shouler, Kenneth. "Here's to You, Mr. Robinson." *Biography* (July 1997): 54–60.
Shropshire, Kenneth L. "Jackie Robinson's Legacy." *Emerge* (April 1997): 60, 62–63.
Shwedel, Ari. "Jackie's Legacy Lives in Brooklyn." *New York Post*, 7 April 1997.
Silary, Ted. "War of the Words." *Philadelphia Daily News*, 9 April 1997, 18–19.
Simons, William. "Jackie Robinson and the American Mind: Journalistic Perceptions of the Reintegration of Baseball." *Journal of Sport History* 12 (Spring 1985): 100–112.
Smallwood, John. "Our Chance to Know Him." *Philadelphia Daily News*, 9 April 1997, 48.
Smith, Claire. "Blacks Turning Away from

Baseball and Robinson's Dream." *New York Times*, 30 March 1997.

———. "Color Issue Extends to People in the Seats." *New York Times*, 10 April 1997, B11.

———. "A Grand Tribute to Robinson and His Moment." *New York Times*, 16 April 1997, B1, B13.

———. "Ripple of Recognition Follows Robinson." *New York Times*, 2 May 1997.

Smith, Ronald A. "The Paul Robeson-Jackie Robinson Saga and a Political Collision." *Journal of Sport History* 6 (Summer 1979): 5–27.

Smith, Wendell. "The Jackie Robinson I Knew." *Baseball Digest* 5 (February 1946): 19–21.

"Soul of the Game." *Image* (May 1996): 8–9, 18, 38.

"South Seeks Jackie." *Newsweek*, 19 April 1948, 82.

Spencer, Lyle. "Newk: Jackie Wouldn't Like State of Game." *New York Post*, 15 April 1997, 16–17.

Spink, J.G. Taylor. "Rookie of the Year." *Sporting News*, 17 September 1947.

"Sports Legend Jackie Robinson: His Greatest Victory." *Midweek TV Showcase*, 10 October 1990, 3.

"Stamp Honors Robinson Feats." *New York Times*, 16 June 1982, 27.

Steele, David. "Time Wasn't Right for Robinson to Join Sox." *USA Today Baseball Weekly*, 16 August 1991, 31.

Stone, Sgt. Robert. "Jackie Robinson, Pathfinder." *Baseball Digest* 32 (February 1946): 19–20.

Strauss, Joe. "Jackie Robinson: Baseball, Nation Celebrate Robinson's Breakthrough." *The Atlanta Journal and Constitution*, 23 March 1997.

Stutz, Howard. "Lou Dials Says He Could Have Preceded Jackie Robinson." *Las Vegas Sun*, 5 January 1986, 2C.

Suehsdorf, A.D. "Honus Wagner's Rookie Year." *The National Pastime* 6 (Winter 1987): 11–17.

"Summer of '47: Breaking the Barrier." *St. Louis Post-Dispatch*, 18 May 1997, B1–8.

Sunde, Scott. "Blazing a Long Trail." *Seattle Post-Intelligencer*, 15 April 1997, A1, A8.

"Thanks Jackie!" *Time for Kids*, 11 April 1997, 4ff.

Thompson, M. Cordell. "Jackie Robinson: The Man and the Legacy He Leaves." *Jet* 43, 16 November 1972, 12–18, 52–57.

Thorn, John, and Jules Tygiel. "The Signing of Jackie Robinson." *Sport Magazine* 79 (June 1988): 66, 69–70.

"Tribute to Jackie: Robinson Brothers Were Great Track Stars." *The Philadelphia Tribune*, 25 April 1997.

Turkin, Hy. "No Blackball for Jackie." *Negro Digest* (March 1946): 41–43.

Tygiel, Jules. "A Spectacular Season: Jackie Robinson Breaks Through." In *Baseball History from Outside the Lines: A Reader*, ed. John E. Dreifort. Lincoln: University of Nebraska Press, 2001.

———. *Baseball's Great Experiment: Jackie Robinson and His Legacy*. New York: Oxford University Press, 1983.

———. "Beyond the Point (Color Line) of No Return." *Sports Illustrated*, 20 June 1983, 40–43, 62–67.

———. "The Court-Martial of Jackie Robinson." *American Heritage* 35 (September–October 1984): 34–39.

Tygiel, Jules, ed. *The Jackie Robinson Reader*. New York: Dutton Books, 1997.

———. "Sit in Back of the Bus, Not Lt. Jackie Robinson." *Kansas City Star*, 7 October 1984.

———. "A Spectacular Season." *American Legacy* (Spring 1997): 8–10, 12–13, 16–18.

Unger, Norman. "Baseball 1980: 35 Years After Jackie Robinson." *Ebony* 35 (June 1980): 104ff.

"U.S. Negro League Is Launched with Brown Dodgers in Brooklyn." *New York Times*, 8 May 1945.

Vecsey, George. "A Role Model for the Ages." *Altoona Mirror* (Pa.), 15 April 1997, A5.

———. "In the Capitol Rotunda, It's Robinson by Acclamation." *New York Times*, 3 March 2005, D1, D7.

Voigt, David Q. "Robinson, Jack Roosevelt 'Jackie.'" In *Biographical Dictionary of American Sports: Baseball*, ed. David L. Porter. Westport, Conn.: Greenwood Press, 2000, 1302–1304.

———. "They Shaped the Game: Jackie Robinson." *Baseball History* 1 (Spring 1986): 5–22.

"Wait till Next Year." *Ebony* (September 1960): 89–94.

Waldman, Frank. "Jackie Robinson." In *Famous American Athletes of Today*. Boston: Page Series, 1949, 237–57.

Washburn, Pat. "New York Newspapers and Robinson's First Season." *Journalism Quarterly* 58 (1981): 640–644.

Weber, Bruce. "The Celebration Stirs Up Memories for Many Fans." *New York Times*, 16 April 1997.

Weidhorn, Manfred. *Jackie Robinson*. New York: Maxwell Macmillan International, 1993.

Weir, Tom. "The Lifetime of a Legend." *USA Today*, 14 April 1997, 3C.

(Robinson, Jackie, continued)
_____. "Negro Leagues Had Talent, but Fans Left to Follow Robinson." *USA Today*, 16 April 1997, C3.
Weiss, William J. "The First Negro in 20th Century Organized Baseball." *Baseball Research Journal* 8 (1979): 31–34.
Wendel, Tim. "Another Barrier Broken." *USA Today Baseball Weekly*, 26 February 4 March 1997, 10–13.
Whitaker, Charles. "Before Jackie..." *Ebony* 47 (August 1992): 32ff.
White, Jack E. "Stepping Up to the Plate." *Time*, 31 March 1997, 90.
Whiteside, Larry. "Long Before Jackie Robinson's Historic Debut with the Brooklyn Dodgers, Negro League Players Thrived in Anonymity — and Made His Signing Possible." *The Boston Globe*, 9 July 1999.
Wilbon, Michael. "Jackie Didn't Struggle in Vain." *The Washington Post*, 6 April 1997.
_____. "Robinson: A Man in Deed." *Washington Post*, 1 March 1997, H1.
_____. "Robinson's Legacy Goes Far Beyond the Ballparks." *Washington Post*, 1 March 1997, H1.
Williams, Dorothy. *The Jackie Robinson Myth*. MA thesis, Concordia University, Canada, 1999.
Williamson, Christine. "Teaming Up: American Century Helps Minority Scholarship Fund." *Pensions and Investments*, 16 November 1998.
Willis, George. "Jackie Still Making a Difference." *New York Post*, 15 April 1997, 4, 116.
_____. "Mr. Robinson's Neighbor." *New York Post*, 6 April 1997.
_____. "Robinson a Pioneer till the Day He Died." *New York Post*, 27 March 1997.
Wimbish, Ralph. "At Home with 'Mr. Robinson.'" *New York Post*, 15 April 1997, 112.
Wisensale, Steven K. "The Political Wars of Jackie Robinson." *Nine* 2, no. 1 (Fall 1993): 18–28.
Young, A.S. "Doc." "The Jackie Robinson Era." *Ebony* 11 (November 1955): 152–156.
_____. "Jackie Robinson Remembered." *Ebony* 47 (August 1992), 36, and in February 1997, 103, 106, 108, 110–111.
_____. "Negro Writer Hails Jackie." *Sporting News*, 4 August 1962.
Young, A.S. "Doc" as told by Mack Robinson. "My Brother Jackie." *Ebony* (July 1957): 75–82.
Young, Fay. "End of Baseball's Jim Crow Seen with Signing of Jackie Robinson." *Chicago Defender*, 3 November 1945, 9.
Ziegel, Vic. "Champions of Robinson." *NY Daily News*, 16 March 1997.
Zinser, Lynn. "'We Didn't Talk About It.'" *Philadelphia Daily News*, 9 April 1997, 30–31.

Rogan, Wilbur ("Bullet Joe")

"Bullet Rogan." In *Baseball: The Biographical Encyclopedia*. Ed. David Pietrusza, Matthew Silverman, and Michael Gershman. Kingston, New York: Total Sports Publishing, 2000, 962.
Crabtree, Jeremy, and Mike Vaccaro. "Monarchs Star to Be Inducted." *The Kansas City Star*, 4 March 1998, A1, A11.
Dixon, Phil S. *The Monarchs, 1920–1938, Featuring Wilber "Bullet" Rogan, the Greatest Ball Player in Cooperstown*. S.D.: Mariah Press, 2002.
Drewry, Jennifer M. "An Interview with Wilber Rogan, Jr." *Footsteps* (March 2000): 31.
Holway, John B. *Bullet Joe and the Monarchs*. Washington, D.C.: Capital Press, 1984.
_____. "More Negro Leaguers for the Hall." *The National Pastime*, SABR, 1995, 91–95.
_____. "New Light on Bullet Joe Rogan." Baseballguru.com.
_____. "Rogan, Doby Receive Their Due." *Baseball America*, 30 March–12 April 1998.
Johnson, Dan. "Bullet Joe: A Son's Memories." *Kansas City Kansan*, 11 November 1999, 1,6.
Kleinknecht, Merl F., and John Holway. "Rogan, Wilbur 'Bullet Joe.'" In *Biographical Dictionary of American Sports: Baseball*, ed. David L. Porter. Westport, Conn.: Greenwood Press, 2000, 1309–1310.
Lundquist, Carl. "Veterans Weigh Candidates." *USA Today Baseball Weekly*, 25 February 1998, 33.
Mills, Jeff. "'Bullet Joe' Could Do It All." *The Daily Star* (Oneonta, N.Y.), 24 July 1998, 18–19.
"Negro League Pitcher 'Bullet' Joe Rogan Selected for Hall of Fame." *Jet*, 23 March 1998, 48.
Queen, Linwood. "Rogan Strikes Out Eighteen Men and Twenty-fifth Wins from All-Star." *Chicago Defender*, 25 November 1916.
"Rogan Hands Foster's Men 5 to 2 Defeat." *Chicago Defender*, 7 June 1924.
"Rogan Is Beaten, 9 to 0, in Los Angeles Baseball Race." *Chicago Defender*, 20 February 1926.
"Rogan Trims Fosters, 19–5; 15,000 See Giants Lose Game." *Chicago Defender*, 24 June 1922.
"Rogan's Crew Kicks Fosters out of First Place and Go Into the Lead Themselves." *Chicago Defender*, 5 June 1926.
"Rogan's Men Hit the Ball Hard to Win." *Chicago Defender*, 8 May 1926.

"Rogan's Single Ties Up World Series, 3 All." *Chicago Defender*, 18 October 1924, 1.
"Stars of Many Years to Play Here Sunday." *Bismarck Tribune*, 21 July 1938.
Steele, David. "Negro Leaguers Seek Entry Into Hall." *USA Today Baseball Weekly*, 16 August 1991, 17.

Smith, Hilton Lee

Anderson, Dave. "Maz's Plaque Is s Tribute to Dee-fense." *The New York Times*, 7 March 2001.
Baxter, Terry. "Smith, Hilton Lee." In *Biographical Dictionary of American Sports: Baseball*, ed. David L. Porter. Westport, Conn.: Greenwood Press, 2000, 1434–1435.
"Charleston May Start Hilton Smith." *Chicago Defender*, 26 August 1939, 9.
Goodall, Fred. "Maz, Hilton Smith Voted into Hall." *The Record* (Hackensack, N.J.), 7 March 2001, S-4.
"Hilton Smith to Pitch One Game for Monarchs Sunday." *The Bismarck Tribune*, 23 July 1938.
"Hilton Smith Tops East Vs. West Game Voting." *Chicago Defender*, 10 August 1940, 24.
"Hilton to the Hall." *Jet*, 26 March 2001, 50.
Holway, John B. "They Made Me Survive." *The Sporting News*, 18 July 1981.
Letlow, Paul J. "Monroe's Claim to Fame." *The News Star*, 5 August 2001, 1C, 4C.
"Monarchs Hilton Smith Dies at 71." *Kansas City Star*, 20 November 1983.
"Monarchs Star Gets His Due." *Kansas City Star*, 7 March 2001.
"Pitcher Hilton Smith." *Atchison Daily Globe*, 2 August 1948.
Posnanski, Joe. "Hall of Fame Inductee Hilton Smith Often Felt Overshadowed by Paige." *The Kansas City Star*, 4 August 2001.
———. "Hilton Smith Never Should Have Had to Wait So Long." *The Kansas City Star*, 6 March 2001.
Reusse, Patrick. "Fulda Shares a Summer with Future Hall of Famer." *Minneapolis Star Tribune*, 4 August 2001, C1, C8.
Richman, Howard. "Hilton Smith Inducted into Hall of Fame." *The Kansas City Star*, 5 August 2001.
Rock, Steve. "Former Monarchs Pitcher Hilton Smith Elected to Baseball Hall of Fame." *Kansas City Star*, 6 March 2001.

Trash Talking

"1934 Was Satchell's biggest year, belief." *Pittsburgh Courier*, 17 November 1934, sect. 2, p. 4.
Burley, Dan. "Looking Back at the East-West Classic in Chi." *Pittsburgh Courier*. 8 September 1934, sect. 2, p. 4.
Cahn, Leonard. "Satch" Wins 3 in Five Days in Big Denver Tourney." *Pittsburgh Courier*, 18 August 1934, sect. 2, p. 4.
Clay, Gregory. "Robinson Was the Politically Correct Choice to Break Baseball's Color Line." *Knight Ridder/Tribune News Service*, 12 April 1997.
"Cleveland All Excited over Coming of Satchell Paige and the Craws Sunday." *Pittsburgh Courier*, 13 June 1936, sect. 2, p. 4.
Hawkins, Dave. "Satchell to Oppose Jones in Stadium." *Pittsburgh Courier*. 29 September 1934, sect. 2, p. 5.
Hayes, Marcus. "East-West Game Was Jewel of Negro Leagues." *Philadelphia Daily News*, 7 July 1996.
Holway, John B. *Josh and Satch: The Life and Times of Josh Gibson and Satchel Paige*. Westport, Conn.: Meckler, 1999.
Inabinett, Mark. *Grantland Rice and His Heroes: The Sportswriter as Mythmaker in the 1920s*. Knoxville: University of Tennessee Press, 1994.
Lanctot, Neil. *Helping the Race Morally and Financially: Black Professional Baseball and the Philadelphia Stars, 1933–1952*. Unpublished doctoral dissertation, University of Delaware, 2002.
LoConto, David G., and Tori J. Roth. "Mead and the Art of Trash Talking: I Got Your Gesture Right Here." *Sociological Spectrum* 25: 215–230.
Nunn, William G. "'Satch' Stops 'Big Bad Men' of West Team." *Pittsburgh Courier*, 1 September 1934, sect. 2, p. 4.
———. "Satchell Paige Is Magnet at E-W Game; Players of Big League Caliber Perform." *Pittsburgh Courier*, 29 August 1934, sect. 2, p. 6.
Paige, Leroy, and David Lipman. *Maybe I'll Pitch Forever*. Lincoln: University of Nebraska Press, 1993.
"Paige to Aid Craws Pennant Chances." *Pittsburgh Courier*, 25 April 1936, sect. 2, p. 4.
Ribowsky, Mark. *Don't Look Back: Satchel Paige in the Shadows of Baseball*. New York: Da Capo Press, 1994.
"Satchell Must Join Camp or Be Ousted." *Pittsburgh Courier*, 13 April 1934, sect. 2, 5.
Simons, Herbert D. "Race and Penalized Sports

(Trash Talking, continued)
Behaviors." *International Review for the Sociology of Sport* 38, no. 1: 5–22.
Story, Robert. "A Museum of Their Own: Kansas City Preserves the Legacy of Negro Leagues Players." *Pittsburgh Post-Gazette,* 10 July 1997.
Taylor, Paul. "Crackin,' Jackin, Woofin' and Smackin.'" *Sports Illustrated* 77: 82–86.
Washburn, Patrick. "The Black Press: Homefront Clout Hits a Peak in World War II." *American Journalism* 12: 359–366.
Washington, Chester L. "Satchell Has Been 'Babe' to Colored Baseball." *Pittsburgh Courier,* 12 January 1935, sect. 2, 5.
Washington, Chester L. "Satchell's Back in Town." *Pittsburgh Courier,* 9 May 1936, sect. 2, 4.

World Series

Young, Frank A. "Hilldale Leads in World Series." *Chicago Defender,* 11 October 1924, 1.
_____. "Kansas City Wins Championship." *Chicago Defender,* 27 October 1924, 1.
_____. "Kansas City Wins in 12th." *Chicago Defender,* 18 October 1924, 1.

About the Contributors

Terrie Aamodt is a professor of history at Walla Walla College, where she team teaches a course in baseball and American popular culture. A current research project investigates interracial baseball barnstorming in the 1920s and 1930s. It has included a presentation on the House of David participation in the *Denver Post* tournament for SABR33 and a paper on prison ball for SABR36. Her baseball memoir, "The Impossible Dream," was published in *Growing Up with Baseball*, ed. Gary Land (University of Nebraska Press, 2004).

Raymond Doswell has served as curator and education director for the Negro Leagues Baseball Museum since 1995. Doswell is responsible for the care and maintenance of the museum's collections and exhibits and directs all education initiatives and partnerships with universities and school districts for the museum.

He earned his bachelor of arts degree from Monmouth College in Monmouth, Illinois, majoring in history and education. He received his masters of arts degree from the University of California at Riverside in historic resources management in 1995. Doswell is a doctoral candidate in the College of Education at Kansas State University.

Stephanie Fleet-Liscio earned her B.A. from the University of Pittsburgh in history and English writing in 2001 and is working on her M.A. in applied history at Shippensburg University in Shippensburg, Pennsylvania.

An avid Cleveland Indians fan, she hopes to see the Indians actually win another World Series before she dies. Stephanie has visited the home stadiums of nine different major league teams and hopes to eventually visit all thirty.

Originally from Hermitage, Pennsylvania, Stephanie currently resides in Carlisle, Pennsylvania, with her husband John, who, unfortunately, is a New York Yankees fan.

Michael Harkness-Roberto is a graduate of the Kent State University, Stark Campus with a B.A. in history. His research interests include United States sports history, colonial and early American history, and 19th and 20th century

Japan. He is currently studying constitutional law and its effects on modern public policy.

Leslie A. Heaphy is an associate professor of history at Kent State University, Stark Campus, where she also runs the Honors Program. She is the author of *The Negro Leagues, 1869–1960* and editor of *Black Baseball and Chicago* (2006), and *Encyclopedia of Women in Baseball* (2006), all from McFarland. Leslie also edited the souvenir booklets for the eighth and ninth Annual Jerry Malloy Negro League Conference.

Travis Larsen earned bachelor's and master's degrees in history at Fort Hays State University. He has given a number of invited lectures on a variety of American history topics and has presented papers on Curt Flood and semipro baseball in Wichita. He has also served as a judge for the 2006 Kansas History Day competition.

Larry Lester is one of the country's leading authorities on the Negro Leagues. His first book, in collaboration with Dick Clark, was *The Negro Leagues Book* (1994). Lester serves as co-chairman of the Negro Leagues Committee for the Society for American Baseball Research (SABR), in Cleveland, Ohio.

His next four books were part of Arcadia's Black America series and focused on black baseball in Detroit, Chicago, Kansas City and Pittsburgh. In 2002, book number six was published by the University of Nebraska Press: *Black Baseball's National Showcase: The East-West All-Star Game, 1933–1953*. It won *The Sporting News*–SABR Research Award and the Robert Peterson Recognition Award. A few of his other contributions include being a contributor to more than 70 books on baseball history. His writings on African-Americans have appeared in *The National Pastime, Biographical Dictionary of American Sports, American National Biography, The Ball Players, World Book Encyclopedia* and the *Dictionary of American Negro Biography*. Other works include his photographs on General Mill's 75th Anniversary of the Negro Leagues Wheaties box (1996) and an ongoing series of Negro League calendars, "The Forgotten Leagues," by DMD Design (2001–2005), and also the development of the only CD-ROM on the subject, *The Negro Leagues Dream Teams*, by Computerized Educational Resources (1995). Lester has made appearances in the following films: *Behind the White Foul Lines* (1991) by CNN, *Ain't Seen Nothin' Like It Since* (1994) by PBS, *Outside the Lines: A League Second to None* (1994) by ESPN, *No League of Their Own* (1995) by NBC, contributions to HBO's *Journey of the African-American Athlete*, and Ken Burns's *Baseball* documentary, along with hosting numerous player panels.

Nathan Lovato is a senior history and secondary education major at Adams State College in Alamosa, Colorado. Nathan also coaches boys' basketball at the Mountain Valley Middle and High Schools. Nathan plans to start working as an umpire in Colorado.

David Marasco is a regular writer for *The Diamond Angle*, to which he has contributed a wide range of articles on the Negro Leagues and the All American Girls Professional Baseball League. Marasco is a member of the Negro Leagues Committee and has delivered a number of papers on the topic at various conferences.

About the Contributors

Daniel A. Nathan is an associate professor in American studies at Skidmore College. He received his Ph.D. and M.A. degrees in American studies from the University of Iowa. His book *Saying It's So: A Cultural History of the Black Sox Scandal* won the North American Society for Sport History book award in 2003 and the same award for the North American Society for the Sociology of Sport. He wrote an article titled "Bearing Witness to Blackball: Buck O'Neil, the Negro Leagues and the Politics of the Past" for the *Journal of American Studies* in 2001.

Tim Rives is an archivist with the National Archives–Central Plains Region in Kansas City, Missouri. Rives received his master's degree in American history from Emporia State University in 1995. His published work includes articles on the presidency of Ulysses S. Grant, World War I soldier poetry, and prison baseball, and it has appeared in *Prologue, The American Enterprise*, and *New Directions in Folklore*, among other publications. He has presented papers at the Cooperstown Symposium on Baseball and American Culture, the American Folklore Society, and the annual Jerry Malloy Conference.

Patrick Rock has been a member of SABR since 1982. He has been a member or has contributed to the Biographical Committee, the Ballparks Committee, the Minor League Committee, the Negro Leagues Committee, and the Nineteenth Century Committee. Patrick has also been a contributor to the following publications: *Minor League Encyclopedia*, volumes one and two; proofreading and fact checking for *The Negro Leagues Book*; and database programming for rosters and "Researching the Negro Leagues" in *How to Do Baseball Research*. In 2004, Replay Games Co. released a simulation of the 1923 Negro National League season and Patrick supplied complete statistical data and team-by-team write-ups for the game.

W. Bryan Steverson retired in 2005 after 37½ years at ALCOA, Inc. where he worked as the chief metallurgist. Over the years he has met and talked with over 100 former Negro League players. His poetry can be found on the Pitchblack baseball Web site, and Monte Irvin had one of his pieces read at the 2004 Smokey Joe Williams Scholarship Banquet.

Jared Evan Furcolo Wheeler, a Temple University graduate with a B.A. in history, is currently the director of archives and historical data at Mitchell and Ness Nostalgia Company in Philadelphia, Pennsylvania. He is a member of the National History Honor Society, Phi Alpha Theta, and the Philadelphia Athletics Historical Society.

Index

Alexander, Grover Cleveland 58, 59, 67, 68, 104, 126, 128
All Nations 99, 101, 113, 114–15, 225, 237, 246
All Stars 10, 16, 40, 66, 67, 68, 116–17, 133, 158, 175, 200, 204, 208, 209, 210, 211, 213, 215, 230, 234, 242, 249
Allen, Henry J. 145, 146
Allen, Newt 3, 46, 50, 122, 127, 222, 223, 226, 231–32, 245, 247
Altman, George 134, 221
American Negro League 14, 190
Anson, Adrian "Cap" 181, 191
Armeteros, Juan 135, 223, 224, 226
Ashwill, Gary 42
Association Park 118
Atlanta Braves 10–11, 217

Baird, Tom 3, 103, 107, 120–21, 130, 131, 144–154, 160, 249
Baker, Gene 133, 134, 221, 226
Baltimore Afro-American 14, 15, 16, 49
Baltimore Black Sox 3, 9, 13, 14–19
Baltimore Stars 193
Banker, Stephen 22
Bankhead, Sam 49, 50, 67, 226, 230
Banks, Ernie 134, 218, 220, 221, 223, 226
Barnes, Frank 134, 221, 226
Barnhill, Herbert 226
Barnstorming 10, 55, 57, 74, 99, 103, 104, 117, 121–23, 167–68, 172, 175, 190, 198–205, 233
Baro, Bernardo 226
Bartholomay, William 10, 217
Baseball Hall of Fame 2, 4, 11, 13, 21, 26, 135, 144, 161, 174, 205, 217, 219, 233, 235, 236, 246, 250, 254
Baylis, Hank 135, 223, 226
Beckwith, John 43–44
Bell, James "Cool Papa" 9, 37, 45, 56, 66, 67, 68, 124–25, 127, 130, 131, 194, 199, 217, 220, 226, 230
Bell, William 102, 122, 123, 226, 232–33, 245
Benjamin, Jerry 47, 49, 50, 128
Benson, Gene 133
Benswanger, William 195
Bibbs, Rainey 226
Bingo Long 2, 198–205
Birmingham Barons 31
Birmingham Black Barons 8–9, 14, 16, 17, 28, 31, 43, 78, 105, 112, 126, 159, 173, 207, 212, 216
Birth of a Nation 146
Bismarck 60–71, 90, 91, 209, 210, 236, 253
Black, Bill 184–85
Bloomingdale Athletic Club 15
Blues Stadium 136
Blyleven, Bert 44
Bolden, Ed 192
Boston Braves 45
Boston Red Sox 10, 159, 175
Boudreau, Lou 32, 172
Bowe, Randolph 226
Brady, Ed 60, 62
Brashler, William 198–99
Bready, James H. 13
Breda, Bill 151, 226
Bremer, Eugene 226
Brewer, Chet 45, 57, 59, 61, 63, 66, 67, 93, 102, 122, 124, 125, 127, 133, 176, 209, 222, 226, 229, 230, 233–34, 245, 256
Brewer, Sherwood 135, 223, 226, 229
Brison, "Birmingham Sam" 203, 204
Brooklyn Bushwicks 40
Brooklyn Eagles 65
Brown, Barney 60
Brown, Dave 117
Brown, Lahoma 213, 217

295

Brown, Ray 49, 50, 67, 195, 226
Brown, Willard "Homerun" 128, 129, 134, 219, 220, 221, 222, 223, 226, 235, 236, 241, 254
Bruce, Janet 166
Bryant, Allen "Lefty" 138–39, 151, 226
Bugle Coat and Apron Company 15, 16
Bunyan, Paul 1, 169
Burley, Dan 79
Byas, Richard "Subby" 226

Cahn, Leonard 66, 79
Campanella, Roy 168, 244
Campbell, Russell C. 187
Cardwell, Don 27
"Casey at the Bat" 1, 49
Chandler, Happy 132
Charleston, Oscar 9, 100, 210
Chattanooga Black Lookouts 8–9, 25, 170, 207
Chicago American Giants 26, 36, 37, 38, 39, 41, 43, 57, 99, 100, 102, 105, 112, 115, 116, 118, 126, 127, 128, 158, 174, 192, 207, 208, 209, 211, 215, 241
Chicago Defender 38, 39, 42, 49, 56, 78, 86, 234
Chicago White Sox 24, 46, 82, 110, 215, 238, 244
Churchill, Neil 56–57, 60, 61, 62, 65, 66, 82, 90, 92, 93
Cincinnati Clowns 159, 212, 254
Cincinnati Reds 24, 192, 246
Civil Rights 179, 181, 184, 185–86, 187
Clarke, "Eggie" 15
Claxton, Jimmie 192
Clay, Gregory 81
Cleveland Bears 17
Cleveland Buckeyes 139, 233, 235
Cleveland Call and Post 165
Cleveland Indians 9–10, 17, 32, 61, 95, 130, 139, 169, 172, 175, 211, 213
Cleveland Red Sox 39
Cohen, Rob 200, 201, 204
Coimbre, Pancho 40, 213
Coleman, Lulu 7
Collins, Gene 226
Columbus Buckeyes 118
Comiskey Park 9, 38, 40, 79, 112, 158, 168, 213, 215, 242
Cooper, Andy 105, 121, 124, 128, 219, 220, 222, 226, 236, 241, 249, 253
Copeland, Jack 64–65
Cornelius, Willie 38, 39, 40, 128, 208, 209
Costas, Bob 21
Coughlin, Charles 151–52
Courtney, Clint 29, 31
Craig, John 50, 51
Crawford, Sam 101–02, 118, 227, 256
Crosley Field 112, 121, 184, 218
Crutchfield, Jimmie 45, 46
Cuban Stars 15, 102, 126

Currie, Rube 118, 227, 230
Curry, Goose 26

Davis, Charlie 26
Davis, Johnny 129, 213
Davis, Roosevelt 227
Day, Leon 129, 212, 218
Dean, Dizzy 7, 8, 66, 67, 82–83, 127, 175, 209, 212, 242
Debono, Paul 41–42
Denver Post Tournament 3, 56, 57–59, 63, 66, 67, 68, 69, 70, 103, 127, 209, 210, 248
Denver White Elephants 55, 57
Detroit Senators 125
Detroit Stars 100, 118, 128, 207
Detroit Tigers 24, 215
Dexter Park 40
Didrikson, Babe 54
Dihigo, Martin 194
Dismukes, Dizzy 129, 227, 232
Doan, Ray 57, 66, 103
Doby, Larry 129, 139, 161, 168, 172, 173, 176, 218
Donaldson, John 100, 101, 114, 115–16, 225, 227, 237–38, 246, 253
Douglas, Jesse 227
Drake, "Plunk" 114, 115, 118, 227
Dumont, Raymond "Hap" 89–96
Duncan, Frank 11, 40, 47, 105, 121, 127, 129, 158, 160, 162, 210, 213, 218, 227, 230, 238–39, 245, 249, 256
Duncan Cementers 93–94
Dwight, Eddie 230, 236

Eason Oilers 58
East-West Game 38, 74, 79, 81, 82, 87, 107, 167–68, 170–71, 177, 209, 222–23, 232, 233, 234, 242, 244, 253, 255
Easterling, Howard 47, 49, 50, 128
Eastern Colored League (ECL) 102, 192
Ebbets Field 40, 182, 183
Eckersley, Dennis 2
Ethiopian Clowns 176
Expenses 136–37, 170

Feller, Bob (A.S.s) 128, 129, 133, 134, 175, 211–12, 213, 214, 242
Film 198–205
Finley, Charles O. 10, 139–40
Floyd, "Jewbaby" 9, 47–48
Forbes Field 49, 77, 193, 208
Foster, Rube 3, 36, 37, 41, 42, 43, 52, 56, 99, 100, 116, 118, 139, 192, 193
Foster, Willie 57, 126, 127, 128, 207, 209, 210, 220, 227, 238, 253
Fowler, John "Bud" 181
Freedom Fund Drive 185

Gaines, Lefty 61
Gaston, Bob 51

Index

Gaul, J.E. 99, 113
Gehrig, Lou 1, 117, 193
Gibson, Bill 15, 16
Gibson, Bob 44
Gibson, Josh 3, 9, 32, 35, 36, 37, 44–52, 56, 66, 67, 83, 128, 168, 177, 193, 195, 205, 209, 210
Gibson, Kirk 2
Giles, George 126, 127, 139, 210, 227
Gisentaner, Willie 118, 227
Gorbous, Glen 29–30
Grant, Charley 182, 192
Greason, Rev. William 28–29
Greeley Advertisers 57
Greenlee, Gus 9, 39, 56, 60, 66, 126, 167, 171
Griffith, Clark 194–95, 196
Griffith, Robert 67, 68
Grove, Lefty 24–25

Hairston, Sam 46, 230
Halliburton Cementers 64
Hamman, Ed 26, 202, 203
Hardy, Paul 227
Harlem Globetrotters 176
Harris, Greg 24
Harris, Lonnie 26
Harris, Vic 37, 49, 51
Hartman, J.C. 134, 221, 224, 227
Hawkins, Lem 115, 227, 239, 247, 253
Hayes, Marcus 81
Haynes, Sammy 40, 162, 213, 227, 235
Heroes 1, 2
Herrera, Pancho 26, 134, 220, 221, 223, 224, 227
Herzog, Whitey 27–28, 30, 45–46
Hilldale Daisies 15, 102, 218, 232, 246, 248, 251
Hines, Willie 23
Holland, Bill 15
Holway, John 32, 41–42, 84
Homestead Grays 3, 26, 37, 38, 46, 48–49, 51, 75, 105, 112, 126, 128, 129, 159, 166, 167, 171, 190–96, 208, 209, 212, 220
Hornsby, Rogers 67, 68, 132
House of David 57, 58, 59, 60, 61, 65, 66, 78, 103, 104, 126, 127, 210
Howard, Elston 134, 135, 221, 227
Howard, Janet 9, 209, 210, 212
Humble Oilers 58–59
Hunter, Billy 30, 31
Hunter, Spike 58, 59

Images 165, 172
Indianapolis ABCs 41, 99, 100, 115, 237
The Indianapolis ABCs 41
Indianapolis Clowns 32, 176, 177, 202–03, 220
Integration 3, 55, 70–71, 94, 108, 119, 160, 165, 172, 174–75, 176–77, 179, 182–83, 184, 190–91, 194, 195–96
Irvin, Monte 129, 161, 218, 254

Jackson, Reggie 2, 44
Jamestown 57, 60, 62
Jamieson, John "Doc" 132
Jenkins, Fats 13, 16, 210
Jenkins, Harry 150–51
Jenkins Music 100, 225
Jessup, Gentry 229
Jethroe, Sam 159
Johns, Augie 64
Johnson, Byron "Mex" 3, 210, 222, 227, 240–44
Johnson, Connie 128, 129, 134, 138, 221, 223, 227, 243–44
Johnson, James Weldon 120
Johnson, Lou 134
Johnson, Oscar "Heavy" 115, 119, 227
Johnson, Walter 7
Johnson, William A., Jr. 187–88
Johnson, William "Judy" 9, 83–84, 86, 102, 209, 251
Jones, James Earl 200, 201, 202, 204
Jordan, Leon 10
Joseph, Newt 124, 210, 211, 228, 244–45
Josh and Satch 28, 29
Judge, Walter 60, 67
Jumping 101

Kahn, Roger 32
Kansas City Athletics 10, 95, 216, 219
Kansas City Blues 118, 119, 125, 127
Kansas City Call 49, 57, 101, 108, 137, 175, 212
Kansas City Colored Giants 225
Kansas City Giants 225–26
Kansas City Maroons 100
Kansas City Monarchs 2, 3, 4, 9, 18, 22, 26, 31, 40, 45, 46, 47, 48, 49, 51, 56, 57, 58, 59, 63, 65, 66, 78, 81, 99, 101, 102, 103–04, 105, 107, 114, 117, 119, 125, 126, 128–29, 130, 131, 132, 134, 136, 137, 140, 144, 148, 149, 152, 154, 158, 160, 166, 172, 173, 174, 175, 182, 190, 195, 199, 207, 209–212, 216, 218, 226–229, 230, 231–32, 232–33, 233–34, 235, 236–37, 238–39, 240–44, 245, 246–47, 247–50
Kansas City Royal Giants 229–230
Kansas City Royals 133, 141, 176, 219, 230
Kansas City Star 119
Kaplan, Jim 24
Kiner, Ralph 26
King, Martin Luther, Jr. 186, 187
Ku Klux Klan 3, 144, 145–154, 186

Lacy, Sam 194, 195
Lamarque, Lefty 128, 135, 151, 162, 223, 228, 230
Lanctot, Neil 85, 169
Larder, Gary 29
Lawrence Stadium 89, 95
Layton, Clifford 31

Lebovitz, Hal 10, 17, 50
Legends 1, 2, 3, 35, 40, 41, 43, 45, 46, 50, 52
LeGrande, Larry 27
LeJeune, Larry 30–31
Leonard, Buck 37, 47, 49, 50, 84, 128, 193, 195
Lighting 103–04, 110, 111–112, 120–21, 124, 126, 166–67
Lightner, Pete 91–92, 93
Linares, Rogelio 40, 213
Lincoln Giants 15, 16
Lloyd, John Henry "Pop" 87, 118, 220, 228
Locke, Eddie 135
Long, Carl 26
Louden, Louis 40, 213
Louis, Joe 18, 210
Lundy, Dick 17
Luque, Dolf 192
Lyons, Jimmie 100, 117

Malarcher, Dave 43–44
Malcolm X 186–87
Manley, Effa 9, 129
Manning, Max 129
Marcell, Oliver 13, 14, 17
Markham, John 124–25
Maroto, Enrique 135, 228
Martin, Pepper 83
Martinez, Rabbit 40, 213
Maryland Park 15, 16
Mason, Hank 31, 135, 221, 224, 228
Matchett, Jack 46, 51, 128, 162, 228
Mathewson, Christy 7, 79, 246
Mathis, Verdell 230
Matlock, Leroy 67, 69–70, 230
Maybe I'll Pitch Forever 10, 17, 25, 35, 50, 54, 71, 74, 81, 82, 169
Mazeroski, Bill 2
McDaniels, Booker 135, 159, 162, 223, 228, 254
McGraw, John 181–82, 192, 238
McKnight, Ira 224
McNair, Hurley 118, 225, 228, 245–46, 253
Memorabilia 18
Memories 17–18, 19, 35, 52
Memphis Red Sox 25, 26, 91, 112, 212, 220
Mendez, Jose 100, 101, 102, 113, 115, 210, 218, 220, 225, 228, 237, 246–47
Miami Marlins 10, 27, 29, 30, 45, 216
Milton, Henry 222, 223, 228
Mitchell, Robert 228
Mobile Tigers 8
Monarch Boosters 140–41, 158
Monroe Monarchs 63, 91
Montreal Expos 24
Moore, Dobie 115, 228, 239, 247, 253
Morney, Leroy 37
Morris, Barney 61, 62, 63, 90
Morris, "Yellow Horse" 150, 228
Mothell, Dink 102, 127, 228, 247

Muehlebach Field 119
Municipal Stadium 9, 10, 136, 215
Myths 1, 2, 3, 23, 25, 27, 29, 41, 77, 200

NAACP 185, 187
Nashville Elite Giants 9, 45, 126, 207
National Baseball Congress Tournament 3, 94, 95, 96
National Semipro Baseball Congress (NBC) 90, 91, 95
Negro American League (NAL) 105, 128, 130, 139, 165, 176, 221, 232, 244
Negro Leagues 2, 3, 9, 10, 31, 35, 41, 43, 55, 60, 63, 67, 70, 74, 127, 132, 134, 144, 160, 165, 167, 168, 170, 173, 174, 175, 176, 177, 183, 190, 194, 196, 198, 199, 204, 205, 215, 233, 246, 250, 253
Negro Leagues Baseball Museum 31, 46, 148, 154, 204, 219, 243, 250
Negro National League (NNL) 9, 55, 90, 100, 102, 103, 117, 126, 165, 170, 176, 192, 221, 233, 237, 246, 255
Negro Southern League (NSL) 170
New York Age 126
New York Black Yankees 29, 159, 167, 208, 211
New York Cubans 40, 212, 213, 220, 234
New York Mets 27
New York Yankees 24, 80, 101, 105, 117, 175, 176, 214, 215
Newark Eagles 9, 105, 129, 176, 213, 218, 249
Newcombe, Don 161
Newspapers 2, 52, 74, 75, 80, 87, 168, 169, 201, 203–04
Nunn, William G. 78, 79, 80, 81, 87
Nuxhall, Joe 31–32

Ogle, Floyd 121
Oklahoma 122–23
Okmulgee Merchants 122
O'Neil, John "Buck" 3, 18, 46–47, 105–07, 128, 129, 135, 137–38, 218–19, 223, 228, 248–250, 251
Otis, Ed and Amos 24

Page, Ted 16
Paige, John 7, 78
Paige, Satchel 1, 2, 3, 4, 7–12, 14–19, 21–33, 35, 37–52, 54–71, 74–84, 86–87, 89–96, 103, 105, 107, 124, 129, 130, 134, 135, 139, 140, 158, 162, 168, 169–71, 175, 177, 180, 195, 199, 204, 205, 207–17, 220, 221, 223, 224, 228, 230, 233, 238, 243, 253–54
Parnell, Red 67, 70, 230
Parsons, C.L. 59, 66
Partlow, Roy 49
Patterson, Pat 67, 68, 222, 228, 230
Pearson, Lenny 129, 212
Peatros, Maurice 26
Peeples, Nat 135, 228
Pennsylvania Redcaps 15

Perkins, Cy 67, 69
Perkins, George William 17, 56, 127
Peterson, Robert 168, 199
Philadelphia A's 24, 136, 195
Philadelphia Phillies 26, 31, 183
Philadelphia Stars 210, 211, 212, 220
Pitchin' Man 10, 16–17, 50
Pittsburgh Courier 37, 49, 75, 77, 78, 79, 80, 81, 83, 86, 87, 141, 172, 173, 174, 195, 232, 238
Pittsburgh Crawfords 9, 16, 26, 37, 38, 39, 45, 56, 57, 65, 67, 74, 80, 90, 167, 171, 208, 209, 210
Plessy vs. Ferguson 181
Pompez, Alex 126
Porter, Andy 45
Portland Beavers 10, 37, 216
Posey, Cum 128, 190, 192–93, 196
Promotions 95, 139–40, 175
Pryor, Richard 200, 202
Puerto Rican Baseball Hall of Fame 40
Purnell, Benjamin Frank 103

Qualters, Tom 27, 29, 32

Radcliffe, Alex 174
Radcliffe, Ted "Double duty" 61, 65, 92, 93, 158, 162, 228, 240
Raspberry, Ted 107, 136, 137
Ray, Bob 41
Redus, Wilson 228
Renfroe, Chico 228
Republicans 153
Reynolds, Allie 24
Ribowsky, Mark 14, 17, 75, 78, 90
Rice, Grantland 16, 77, 87
Richardson, Gene 135, 151, 223, 228, 250–51
Rickey, Branch 3, 131, 132, 133, 141, 157–58, 160, 162, 174, 182, 183, 196
Rickwood Field 31, 42, 208
Rile, Ed 118
Roberts, Curtis 135
Robinson, Bill "Bojangles" 9, 209, 210
Robinson, Frazier 26, 210, 228
Robinson, Jackie 1, 3, 18, 26, 32, 81, 86, 108, 117, 130, 131–32, 133, 134, 135, 150, 157–62, 168, 172, 173–74, 179, 180, 182–88, 196, 205, 220, 223, 228, 254
Robinson, Rachel (Isum) 161
Rock, Patrick 49
Rodriguez, Hector 40
Rogan, Wilber 101, 102, 104, 115, 118, 128, 210, 218, 219, 220, 222, 225, 229, 238, 241, 247, 251–53
Rossiter, George 13, 16
Rowan, Bill 135
Ruck, Rob 18
Ruppert Field 119
Ruth, Babe 1, 2, 17, 35, 43, 74, 77, 80, 117, 168
Ryan, Nolan 44

St. Louis Browns 10, 24–25, 29, 30, 45, 67, 95, 134
St. Louis Stars 14, 78, 102, 105, 126, 207
Satchel Paige 25
Satchel Paige Memorial Stadium 11, 217
Scales, George 69, 230
Scott, Joe B. 25
Semi-pro 56–57, 60, 62, 70, 89, 94, 96, 99, 113, 127, 166, 169
Serrell, William Bonnie 129, 135, 158, 162, 223, 229, 230
Shades of Glory 25
Sheehan, Jack 150
Slaughter, Enos 184
Slavery 181
Smaulding, Owen 229
Smith, Ford 135, 229
Smith, Hilton 3, 40, 46, 49, 51, 90, 107, 128, 129, 158, 159, 162, 174, 210, 212, 213, 219, 220, 222, 223, 229, 230, 236, 253–54
Smith, Dr. Howard 100
Smith, Theolic 162, 229
Smith, Wendell 141, 171, 172, 174, 176
Souell, Herb 40, 135, 162, 210, 213, 223, 229, 230
Spalding, Albert 179
Spearman, Al 230
Spearman, Clyde 67, 69
Spearman, Henry 212
Spielberg, Stephen 200
Sportsman's Park 112
Stanzal Brothers 93
Starr, Ray 62
Stearnes, Norman "Turkey" 15, 84, 104, 220, 223, 229, 242
Stengel, Casey 115, 116
Stone, Ed 212
Stone, Toni 218, 229
Stovey, George 181, 191
Streeter, Sam 17
Strong, Ted 129, 223, 229
Stubblefield, Mickey 135, 229
Surratt, Alfred "Slick" 229
Suttles, Mule 13, 15, 16, 43, 209, 210
Sweatt, George 229, 231

Taborn, Earl 105, 135, 151, 229
Taylor, Ben 193
Taylor, C.I. 115
Taylor, "Candy Jim" 45
Taylor, Jelly 107
Taylor, Leroy 255
Tebeau, George 118
Terry, Ralph 2
Thomas, David "Showboat" 40, 67, 69, 213, 230
Thomas, Ira 24
Thompson, Hank 129, 135, 158, 162, 221, 229
Thomson, Bobby 2
Thurman, Bob 105, 135, 220, 221, 229

Torriente, Cristobal 41–42, 220, 229
Townsend, Dr. Francis 151–52
Trash-talking 75, 78, 81, 83, 84, 85–87
Travis, Cecil 8
Trent, Ted 37, 38–39, 229
Trimble, William 126
Trouppe, Quincy 61, 90, 94, 127, 158, 210, 221, 229
Trucks, Virgil 24–25, 216
Trujillo, Rafael 9, 56, 67–68
Tucker, John 61–62
Twin City Colored Giants 62–63

Umpires 69, 75, 201
USL 160

Vargas, Tetelo 40, 213
Vaughn, Don 135
Veeck, Bill 9, 10, 45, 139–40, 169, 170, 213
Vietnam 18
Vincent, Fay 28, 176
Vincent, Lefty 60–61

Wagner, Honus 30, 94
Wagner, Leon 201–02
Walker, Fred 133
Walker, Moses "Fleetwood" 157, 181, 191
Waner, Lloyd 127
Waner, Paul 127
Warfield, Frank 14, 15, 17, 118
Washington, Chester 80, 83, 86, 171, 195
Washington Senators 9, 45, 127, 190, 194, 195, 196, 214, 215
Weber, Bill 24
Weirman, Warren 59

Welch, Bob 2
Welch, W.S. 125, 158
Wells, Jim 17
Wells, Willie 127, 132, 210, 220, 230
Welmaker, Roy 46, 51
White, King Solomon 191
Whitworth, Dick 100, 117
Wichita, KS 89
Wilkinson, J.L. 3, 4, 9, 56, 99, 100, 101, 102, 103, 107, 110, 112, 113, 116, 117, 118, 119, 120, 127, 128, 129–30, 131, 137, 140, 141, 144–45, 166, 175, 219, 220, 225, 237, 241, 246, 247, 248
Wilkinson Family 112–13, 114, 125, 130, 131, 132, 211
Williams, Bill Dee 200, 201
Williams, Chester 67, 68
Williams, Harry 37, 56
Williams, Jeff 135
Williams, Jesse 135, 158, 160, 162, 223, 229, 230, 255
Williams, Marvin 159
Williams, Smokey Joe 125, 128, 238, 253
Wilson, Jud 14, 50, 84
Wooten, Hubert, Jr. 32
World Series 9, 10, 43, 46, 47, 49, 52, 70, 102, 105, 107, 117, 128, 129, 139, 161, 167, 175, 215, 218, 221–22, 231, 233, 238–39, 245, 246, 247, 251, 255

Yankee Stadium 16, 35, 70, 76, 140, 168, 209, 210, 212
Yokely, Lamon 14, 15, 17
Young, Ed 241–42
Young, T.J. 122, 229, 256

www.ingramcontent.com/pod-product-compliance
Lightning Source LLC
Chambersburg PA
CBHW051209300426
44116CB00006B/498